SHEFFIELD CITY
POLYTECHNIC LIBRARY
POND STREET
SHEFFIELD S1 1WB

101

KT-150 ~847

SHEFFIELD HALLAM UNIVERSITY
LEARNING CENTRE
WITHDRAWN FROM STOCK

THE PATTERN OF
ENGLISH BUILDING

T0044627

THE PATTERN OF
ENGLISH BUILDING

ALEC CLIFTON-TAYLOR

fourth edition
edited by
JACK SIMMONS

faber and faber
LONDON · BOSTON

First edition 1962
Second edition 1965
Third edition 1972
Fourth, definitive edition 1987
published by Faber and Faber Limited
3 Queen Square, London WC1N 3AU
Printed in Great Britain by
Butler and Tanner Ltd
Frome, Somerset

All rights reserved

© *1962, 1965, 1972, 1987 Estate of Alec Clifton-Taylor*

British Library Cataloguing in Publication Data

Clifton-Taylor, Alec
The pattern of English building.—4th ed.
1. Building materials—England—History
I. Title
691'.0942   TA402.5.G7
ISBN 0-571-14890-5
ISBN 0-571-13988-4 Pbk

SHEFFIELD CITY POLYTECHNIC LIBRARY
691.0942
CL
POND STREET

EDITORIAL NOTE

When Alec Clifton-Taylor died in 1985 he left behind him a carefully corrected copy of the current impression of this book, together with sixteen pages of notes relating to it, in his very small hand, and a substantial quantity of correspondence. A new edition of the book was already then in his own mind and in his publishers', and these were the materials to be considered for incorporation into it.

The notes are, broadly, of four kinds. (1) Some of them correct errors of fact, either observed by himself or pointed out by others. Only a few of these were serious; but to a man so tenacious in getting things right, often in matters of small detail, they all counted as important. (2) Some indicate decisive changes of opinion, or at least acceptance of the opinions of other people. (3) Many list doubtful questions, on which he had not made up his mind. And (4) some of them attempt to record changes that have occurred since the book was last revised, in 1972.

Every one of the alterations in the first and second classes has been made here. The third and fourth groups raise some difficulties.

The purpose of this edition is to present a version of the book as close as possible to the one that the author might be expected to have produced, had he been able to undertake the work himself. It cannot have that finality, for he is no longer able to decide on doubtful points, and it is clearly better to leave what he wrote unchanged than to accept judgments that he had not himself reached. I have introduced no opinions of my own into the text, at any point. As editor, I have performed nothing but a work of carpentry. I have fitted minor changes and corrections into the main text wherever possible. Some that are more substantial will be found printed separately in an Appendix on pages 423–27. They are referred to by asterisks (*) in the margin of the main text.

As for changes that have taken place since 1972, I have amended the text as directed in the notes, but I have also resolved queries on a few matters of fact that were left open there for the author's own further inquiry. I have not succeeded in every investigation, even with the kind help of government officers and authorities on local building and history.

Inevitably, some of the buildings illustrated in the book have now undergone alteration; a few are known to have been destroyed. Two or three of the pictures have been replaced. In certain cases, however, the impossibility of selecting a photograph that would be sure to have satisfied the author has made it seem wise to retain the old one.

I am grateful to a number of Alec Clifton-Taylor's friends of long standing, who have helped me in preparing this edition: particularly to Philip Burkett, to John Brown, Peter Crawley, Denis Moriarty and Roger Wilson. Also to John Dean (Leicester City Planning Officer), Bridget Cherry (*The Buildings of England*), and Olive Smith, who supplied two much-needed photographs.

J. S.

CONTENTS

EDITOR'S FOREWORD

No book could be, more completely than this one, a memorial of the work and the compelling interests of its author's life.

As a record of events, the story of that life is quickly told. He was born on August 2, 1907, the only son of Stanley E. Taylor, corn-merchant, and his wife Ethel, *née* Clifton Hills. He was educated at Bishop's Stortford College and The Queen's College, Oxford, where he read history. He then went for a year to the Sorbonne and after that for a time, under pressure from his father, into insurance-broking. But he found the work so uncongenial that his father reluctantly agreed to his entering the Courtauld Institute, then very recently established. He took a first in the history of art in 1934. In 1934-9 he lectured for the University of London Institute of Education and the Royal College of Art. During the war he served in the Admiralty, mainly at Bath. He then returned to work as a London University extra-mural lecturer until 1957, when he became a free-lance, as he remained for the rest of his life. He also did much work out of the public eye. At the invitation of S. C. Mason, for example, then Director of Education for Leicestershire, he advised the County Council for many years on the purchase of works of art to be placed in its schools. He enjoyed that task and spent a great deal of time in visiting galleries and artists' studios to find what he judged suitable for the purpose. He lived for over fifty years in South Kensington, for the last thirty of them in Clareville Grove, where he created a charming tiny garden. He became President of the Kensington Society in 1979; an Honorary Fellow of the Royal Institute of British Architects; and in 1982 OBE. When he died, unmarried, on April 1, 1985, leaving a substantial estate, the residue of it went to the National Trust.

On the face of it, a very quiet life. Yet it was filled largely with movement, arising from his lecturing engagements throughout Britain and, in his last thirty years, across the world. He became an accomplished lecturer, warmly admired for example on the South Bank in London when he spoke for the National Trust, and in many countries overseas, where he did much good work for the British Council. He lectured, altogether, in thirty-two of the United States. And then, from 1978 onwards, his speech and his knowledge, his habits of looking and moving, became familiar to audiences numbered by millions, week after week, in the television programmes in which he revealed how much was to be seen and understood in eighteen of the smaller English towns.

He had, pre-eminently, two faculties, which are not often combined in one person in the same high degree: he was an observer and a communicator. The union of those faculties was the foundation of his public achievement. He wrote one large book of outstanding merit, *The Pattern of English Building*, and six others, slighter but each very good. *The Cathedrals of England* is the most widely known of them, complemented by *English Parish Churches as Works of Art*. He accompanied each of his three television series with an excellent book on the six towns described in it. And besides these he wrote two works in collaboration: *English Brickwork* with Ronald Brunskill and *English Stone Building* with A. S. Ireson. He left behind him another book, which has now been completed for publication by Denis Moriarty: *Buildings of Delight*.

There are two things here most unusual. All this writing appeared in little more than twenty years, from 1962 to 1986. Here is the case of a man who did not see his first book in print until he was fifty-five, and who then published steadily for the rest of his life. Equally remarkable, the first book of the series—this one—was the largest and the most important of them.

His slowness to begin publishing might have been due to diffidence (though that was not normally among Alec Clifton-Taylor's qualities), to some blockage, to changing direction or losing his way, to indolence or to mere sluggishness. The true explanation was quite different. His life had hitherto been given up mainly to his lecturing, over which he took exemplary pains. And at the same time, often on the travels this work involved, he had devoted himself to an immense task of looking and learning. The results were stored away in his notebooks and diaries, stretching backwards twenty years and more before he put pen to paper; a record of unwearied travelling, some of it into far recesses of the country (stone quarries among them), of questions asked and answers given, of things he noted that other people before him had missed. What he wrote down he indexed, so all that he had seen and learnt over those years lay to his hand.

The Pattern of English Building originated late in 1955, with a request from Messrs Batsford for a book on the English house. This gradually turned itself into a different study, of the history and character of traditional building materials. For a work so long and complicated, it was written with remarkable speed: in two years and a quarter, between November 1958 and March 1961. It was welcomed and established itself immediately, reaching a second edition in 1965 and a third (issued by Messrs Faber and Faber, reset and thoroughly revised) in 1972.

The book demanded a mastery of many disciplines: the science of geology; the crafts and arts of masonry and brickwork; history; architecture, including the fall of landscape and the shape of streets. Other works had been written before on the history and geology of building materials, and good ones. Alec Clifton-Taylor drew on them with gratitude. He was much influenced and stimulated by his friends too. By one perhaps above all: Nikolaus Pevsner, with whom he worked closely and affectionately for forty years and more. When in 1953 Pevsner published the Durham volume of *The Buildings of England* he observed that as far as the building materials used in that county were concerned 'literature is as completely lacking as on those of most other counties'. He came to recognize his friend's peculiar gifts here, and from 1967 onwards most volumes of that series contained a short essay written by Alec Clifton-Taylor on the building materials of their counties. There are eighteen of them in all (including one on Devon that was not yet published when he died), and they are models of lucidity and terseness.

The Pattern is at once a treatise on the qualities of stone, of brick and timber, lead and iron and glass, and on the sources they came from. But it offers also an unceasing aesthetic commentary on the uses to which they have been put.

Unlike many of those who have written about the aesthetics of building, or of other arts, he was always careful to analyse and explain the reasoning that lay behind his preferences, his loves and dislikes. The dislikes were numerous, and pungently expressed. Sometimes a throw-away phrase would do it, a comparison damagingly precise: as when he likened polished Shap granite to potted meat, or characterized the colour of the chippings he specially detested on graves in churchyards as *crème de menthe*. The indictment of malpractices in those churchyards, in his delightful book on English parish churches, is comprehensive. It includes confetti: 'confetti is litter, and not only to throw but to sell it should be a penal offence. My own view is that if people *must* throw something at weddings it should be maize, and that on all such occasions a troop of hens should be included among the guests.' His remarks of this kind are also convincing because he is able to show good reason why these things are wrong. He excelled in a difficult art: the persuasive explanation of aesthetic preference.

In his television performances he was often very dogmatic. If the dogmas were part of the fun, many of them were no more than short cuts. He was invariably hard pressed there for time, though that was well disguised by skilful production. To read his exposition of the preferences he had formed is to come to terms with a patient and reflective man, who arrived at conclusions carefully. And strong as his antipathies might be, they were not mere prejudices. He was seldom, in anything, a doctrinaire. He disliked a great deal of Victorian architecture. He said so and gave his reasons. But he was always ready to go and look at a Victorian building recommended to him; and his eye, when he did that, was candid. Towards the end of his life, for instance, he visited St. George's church in Stockport and came away filled with admiration; as he did at South Dalton in the East Riding wolds, where he never forgot, once he had seen it, the soaring beauty of Pearson's spire.

He was willing to be proved wrong. He kept a careful record of changes to be made in the next printing of his books, and many of them have been incorporated in the text of this edition. 'A bad mistake here,' he observes in his account of Craythorne House, Tenterden, on page 41, for it is 'not brick but timber-framed'. His notes show him reconsidering questions on which he had perhaps been too sure in the past: in timber-framed buildings, for example, the antiquity of the practice of blacking the exposed timbers; the history of tile-hanging and of the introduction of the sash window.

I said he was both an observer and a communicator. He enjoyed communicating, for itself. He wrote and spoke admirably—equally well. Part of the secret of that success is revealed when he says in his foreword to this book that its chief purpose is 'to try to increase the pleasure of those who travel about the country with open eyes'. The wish to give pleasure entered into all his writing, and most conspicuously into his work in television. It sometimes tempered the sharp things he thought of saying. It always gave warmth and infectious enjoyment to his account of anything he himself enjoyed: good thatching and roof-tiles; above all else the properties of limestone. Yet at the same time the wish to please did not stand on its own, for he wrote also to inform, and to inform correctly. He took infinite pains to get things right, to set and keep the record straight.

Though most of what he wrote was about England, he travelled very widely abroad (he was in southern India little over a month before he died), and what he saw and learnt on his journeys all went into the stock of his experience and perception, to enrich his work. He had for instance a special attachment to great islands, and excluding his own island he placed those he had seen throughout the world in a perfectly firm order: 1. Corsica, 2. Sri Lanka, 3. Sicily. After that, he allowed that he found preferences more difficult to establish.

His correspondence gave endless pleasure: to his friends—a letter from him often made the day; to the innumerable strangers across the world who wrote to express their appreciation of what he had written or said, and got punctilious replies. Anybody who put a serious question to him could be sure of a serious answer. It might be terse or copious, as seemed necessary; but if copious it was never long-winded. In this matter he was unsparingly generous with his time and energy. How he wrote all these letters (in his own hand), on top of everything else he did, remained mysterious. But he worked late into the night.

His friends will always remember him as a rich and complex character. Some aspects of his personality have been caught to perfection on television, and are recorded there. The full range of his powers is revealed most completely here, in *The Pattern of English Building*, a masterly and original book.

JACK SIMMONS
24 July 1986

To the Memory
of my Parents
and
of Hazel

You must be so good as to tell me my road, and if
there is anything in my way worth stopping to see
— I mean literally to see: *for I do not love*
guessing whether a bump in the ground is Danish,
British or Saxon . . .

Horace Walpole to the Reverend William Mason,
July 6, 1772

To build, to plant, whatever you intend, . . .
In all, let Nature never be forgot . . .
Consult the Genius of the Place in all.

Alexander Pope, Epistle to Richard Boyle, Earl of
Burlington, Of the Use of Riches.

The subject of Material is clearly the
foundation of architecture.

William Morris, Address to the Art Workers'
Guild, January 1892.

AUTHOR'S FOREWORD
TO THIRD EDITION (1972)

It is nearly nine years since this book first appeared, and over six since there was a second edition. I have now, most unexpectedly, had the chance of revising it again, and as, under the imprint of a new publisher, the type has had to be completely reset, I have been fortunate enough to have had unrestricted freedom of action. I have availed myself of it to the full.

There was a great deal that needed to be done. In a book which endeavours to cover the whole of England, one author can never hope to know it all properly. One is learning more all the time, not only by reading but still more by travelling around England incessantly, looking. Moreover, circumstances change: quarries and brickworks close (and even, occasionally, open or reopen); new technical devices applicable to traditional materials—very fast-moving stone-saws, for instance—are developed; buildings mentioned in the earlier editions are demolished. Errors, too, have had to be corrected: here unknown correspondents have helped, and my debt to several friends has been tremendous. Reference to them is made in the Acknowledgment. As a result of all this, there are very few pages of the second edition—there are in fact fourteen—which do not contain some amendment, while some parts of the book have been extensively rewritten. There are also twenty-six new illustrations and several new line drawings.

The principal purpose of the book remains as defined in the foreword to the first edition: to try to increase the pleasure of those who travel about the country with open eyes. I have also sought to show, as clearly as I can, the close relationship between the geology of our country and the traditional materials which go to the making of the pattern of English building. There are a certain number of books, as indicated in the Bibliography, concerned with aspects of our traditional materials, but as far as I am aware this is the only one in which a comprehensive picture of the whole subject has been attempted. Even so, it has been necessary to work within certain self-imposed limitations.

Except in a brief chapter on marble and alabaster, there is practically nothing in this book about interiors, and much more attention has been devoted to domestic than to ecclesiastical buildings. The reasons for my selectiveness in these respects are explained in the Introduction. All the illustrations have been chosen in relation to secular works. I have also regarded the prodigious technical advances of the present century as outside my subject. These, with their use of materials such as steel, concrete, plastics and so on, have resulted in the erection of buildings of the most dramatic and daring character which nevertheless have little or no specifically national, let alone local, character. My concern is with the products of England's native and traditional building materials: where they can be seen; how they have been used; what are their distinctive physical and aesthetic qualities.

In a sense, therefore, this is a backward-looking book. Yet, since these vernacular buildings still survive in their tens of thousands (I use the word 'buildings' advisedly, as the vast majority never knew an architect), there is another sense in which I trust that I may claim to have focused very firmly upon present and future pleasures. For, despite the constant menace of 'developers', there has never been a time when our old buildings have been so generally appreciated as they are to-day; never has interest in them been so broadly based. If, as is greatly to be hoped, changing views on what constitutes the best education results in far more attention being devoted in the coming years to visual training, our vernacular buildings will come to mean more and more to succeeding generations. It is doubtful whether any other country in the world, except perhaps Italy, has so many buildings upon which, as Hazlitt said, 'the eye may dote, and the heart take its fill'.

AUTHOR'S
ACKNOWLEDGMENT

The debt which I owe to the researches of others is beyond computation. For the books which have helped me most, the reader is referred to the Bibliography. But there have been many more, particularly books of a topographical nature, which it has been impossible to list separately. I should like to record my gratitude to all those writers, living or dead, to whom I have turned for help and on whose researches I have so extensively drawn. In addition, I gladly acknowledge assistance from two unpublished sources. At the Society of Antiquaries I was able to work through the files of material relating to local characteristics in English architecture, assembled by the late T. D. Atkinson and now deposited in the Society's library. And I was also granted access to the typescript of the admirable thesis (1939) on 'Building in Norfolk' by the late John H. Deas, now in the possession of the library of the Royal Institute of British Architects. Among many others who have earned my thanks are those who have replied, sometimes at length, to importunate letters, and the many quarry-managers and foremen-masons who have patiently answered my questions about stone. I should also like to thank my publishers, and Mr. Peter Crawley in particular, for much kindly co-operation, and for the indulgence which has been extended to a somewhat exacting author.

It has been said that acknowledgments, like wine, should be on the dry side; yet I find it impossible to follow this precept when I think of what this book owes to the generosity of friends. This has taken many different forms. Some have driven me about the country in their cars to visit quarries, to inspect Tudor brickwork, to search for pargeting, or galleting, or rare cruck cottages which we might never find; for a long time I have in truth been a dangerous guest, and this continues! Others have made special journeys to seek out, supply me with notes on, and sometimes photograph buildings on my behalf. Here Mr. J. C. M. Blatch deserves a special word of thanks.

I have not felt it necessary, nor indeed proper, to ask friends such as Professor Sir Nikolaus Pevsner, Mr. John H. Harvey and Mr. James Lees-Milne to scrutinize the revised text as they did the original one. But three of those who helped me before have, with great generosity, devoted many hours to correcting and improving the new text: Mr. R. H. Roberts of the Geological Museum, London, on whom I have learned that

I can rely with complete confidence to supply the deficiencies in my own geological equipment; Mr. A. S. Ireson of Stamford who, through his long years of practical working experience of the methods and materials of English building, in addition to a rare feeling for stone, has been able to help fill in another gap in my own equipment for this undertaking; and Mr. N. Monk-Jones, my old sixth-form master at school, who seems as eagle-eyed as ever at spotting a possible ambiguity and in pouncing upon a *gaucherie*. Dr. L. H. A. Pilkington has again been good enough to read and comment on the chapter on glass, and four new names must now be included: Mr. F. W. B. Charles, who, in addition to supplying the pair of fine drawings on pages 310 and 311, criticized the chapter on Wood to such constructive effect that this is the most extensively rewritten of any; Dr. R. W. Brunskill, who also read and commented on this chapter to its great benefit; Mr. G. E. M. Trinick, who gave much help on the difficult subject of stone in west Devon and Cornwall; and Mr. F. G. Dimes, another expert on stone. Mrs. H. A. Feisenberger again read the proofs, and Mrs. N. Forward typed the manuscript. I wish to record my gratitude to one and all.

There are now, I trust, fewer errors in the book than there were, but even in this new version I do not presume to suppose that there are none; corrections from correspondents will therefore be welcomed. Winston Churchill is recorded as having once said that a book which may start as a plaything will presently become a mistress, and then a master, and finally a tyrant. So it is with this one. There is no escaping it now, so I might as well confess it: after the fifteen years that have passed since I first started to write it, this book has become part of my life.

I

INTRODUCTION

About an hour after leaving London, red brick gives place to stone, grey, yellow or golden brown. Whether we have set out from Paddington or Euston, from King's Cross or St. Pancras, whether we have followed the Great North Road, the Bath Road or Watling Street, we do not have to be very observant to notice the change. Sometimes it takes place quite suddenly; at others there is a moment of transition, as at Wheatley in Oxfordshire, where old buildings of grey stone are roofed with mellow red tiles, proclaiming the proximity of both stone and clay. But presently, in all these directions, the change occurs.

The reason, of course, is that we have reached the limestone belt, that long and relatively narrow band which sweeps across England in an ogee curve from Portland Bill to the Humber and terminates in the Cleveland Hills of Yorkshire. On this belt lie the majority of our most famous stone quarries—Portland, Doulting and Bath, Painswick and Taynton, Weldon and Ketton, Barnack, Clipsham and Ancaster, Stonesfield and Collyweston, to mention only some of them. Their names are music to lovers of stone; to those who care for English architecture in all its various phases the legacies of these quarries are subjects for continual thankfulness.

Yet the limestone belt produces only one group of our native building materials. There is, it is true, a dearth of true marble in England; but to the north and west of the oolitic limestone the older geological formations yield plenty of stone of many qualities and colours, from the red, grey, brown and yellow sandstones of the West Midlands, some so tantalizingly friable, to the tough gritstones and carboniferous limestones of the North and the hard granites and slates of the Lake District and parts of Devon and Cornwall. We have every reason to be grateful for the complexity of our geological map; for it is because the changes in the character of the rocks are so numerous, more so indeed than in any other country in Europe of comparable size, that our landscape and our buildings, although not usually spectacular, offer so much variety within so small an area.

Nor are our resources confined to a wide range of stones. Many parts of England have just the right clays to provide the raw materials for bricks and tiles. These may lie directly over strata of excellent stone, which is why even a county so well endowed with good building stone as Northamptonshire struck Horace Walpole (letter of July 23, 1763) as 'a clay pudding stuck full of villages'. There are also, in the South and East, where serviceable stone is not so easy to find, abundant flints, and, especially in Norfolk, reeds which make the best thatch of any. And as if this were not enough, almost every English county grew, until the seventeenth century, quantities of oak, perhaps the best suited of all trees to timber-framed construction. All these different materials imposed architectural forms appropriate to their character and, despite the many visual improprieties of the last century and a quarter, the pattern is still remarkably complete.

It was the great difficulty of transporting heavy materials which led all but the most affluent until the end of the eighteenth century to build with the materials that were most readily available near the site, even when not very durable. Cathedral builders could sometimes afford to bring their stone from afar, although this was not always necessary. For humbler undertakings, whether secular or ecclesiastical, this was seldom practicable; and until Tudor times the need for economy usually favoured the use of wood. If a non-local stone were required, it was sometimes brought laboriously by wagon, but always at high cost; a documented example is furnished by the Hospital of St. John at Sherborne (1438–48), for which, on five rolls of parchment, the building accounts in minute detail have fortunately survived. This beautiful almshouse was mainly constructed of local oolitic limestone, but for the dressings Lias stone from Ham Hill was used. Although this only entailed a journey of twelve miles, the accounts show that the cartage cost more than the stone itself.[1] The first churchwardens' book of Louth notes that the Ancaster limestone used for the famous spire (built 1501–15) was brought as far as possible by water but that the last few miles over the Wolds had to be covered 'in creaking carts by wretched tracks'[2]. In other cases oxen were employed without carts; the stone would be dragged to the loading place on the waterway by teams of oxen, and for the first church at Peterborough (7th century) it is recorded that eight pairs of oxen were needed to draw a single large block of Barnack limestone.

The only comparatively easy way of procuring stone from a distance was to float it.

1 See Joseph Fowler in *Somerset and Dorset Notes and Queries*, vol. XXIX, Part 290 (Sept. 1969). Professor Jope has established that even in the later Saxon period blocks of oolitic limestone were carried as much as seventy miles (in one case at least) by cart; and because the Thames above Wallingford was in the Middle Ages 'an erratic waterway', Taynton stone (from near Burford) was transported in the fourteenth and fifteenth centuries to Windsor, fully sixty miles, by the same means. For short distances sledges were also occasionally used. But all these were exceptions. See 'The Saxon Building-Stone Industry in Southern and Midland England', by E. M. Jope: *Mediaeval Archæology*, vol. 8, 1964 (1965), pp. 91–118.

2 Quoted by Donovan Purcell in *Cambridge Stone* (1967), p. 54.

In much of the East Riding of Yorkshire, for example, there is a shortage of building stone, but for the fine churches of Beverley, Hull, Hedon, Patrington and Bridlington, water transport provided the solution. For Beverley some of the stone was brought in barges from the once well-known Thevesdale quarries near Tadcaster, down the Wharfe, Ouse and Humber and up the river Hull; and until the coming of the railways nearly all our stone continued to be water-borne. For Milton Ernest Hall in Bedfordshire, for example, which William Butterfield built for his brother-in-law in 1856 (it was his only country house), a boat was specially acquired to bring the coarse yellow local limestone along the Ouse (another Ouse) from the quarries near Pavenham, only two miles away. The proximity of the quarries to the sea certainly contributed to the popularity of Purbeck 'marble' in the thirteenth century, and even to-day Portland stone is cheaper in Dublin (where a great deal of it was used for public buildings in the Georgian period) than in Birmingham.

Water transport also made it feasible to obtain building materials from abroad. Bricks from the Netherlands sometimes came as ballast; some, dating from the end of the seventeenth century, can be seen as far away as Topsham on the Exe. Timber, principally oak and, later, pine, was brought from North Germany, Norway and the Baltic countries. Limestone probably quarried near Boulogne was used by the Romans at Richborough in Kent, and again in London in the latter part of the thirteenth century. But the country was so well endowed with stone suitable for building that there was no need to import very much. The only major exception was Caen stone, which was more readily accessible to south-eastern England by sea than the products of almost all our own quarries. This, combined in the early period with reasons of politics, accounts for the widespread use of it in the South-East during the Middle Ages (cf. *191b*); and it is interesting to find that it was still being employed at Canterbury when the rebuilding of the cathedral's northwest tower was undertaken in 1832–34, and by Barry for the refacing of Kingston Lacy, Dorset, in 1835–39.[1]

Fortunately both the varieties of Caen stone look quite at home in England: the chalky limestone that bears a close resemblance to Beer stone, and the light creamy-yellow oolite superficially not unlike Clipsham. It is Clipsham which is now used at Canterbury when repairs to the Caen stone become necessary. But usually no materials look so well as the local ones, which belong organically to their landscape, harmonize with neighbouring buildings and nearly always give the best colours. There are still many old houses scattered

---

1 The first use of Caen stone in England seems to have been at St. Albans, where Paul of Caen was appointed fourteenth Abbot in 1077. It soon became the favourite high quality stone for major buildings in London: e.g. for Old St Paul's and the Tower late in the eleventh century and for Westminster Abbey in the mid-thirteenth.

over our countryside which convey the impression of having grown out of the soil untouched by the hand or mind of Man; and, despite the strictures of Geoffrey Scott, who
devoted a considerable part of his famous book *The Architecture of Humanism* to exposing
the 'Romantic fallacy' underlying the English affection for this kind of building, the fact
remains that such houses nearly always give pleasure. It may be conceded that many of them,
and especially the timber-framed houses, could hardly be described as 'architecture'; that
many of them give the impression of having been 'assembled' rather than designed; and
that with their skylines of irregularly spaced gables and sagging roofs and oddly projecting
chimney-stacks, they do show, as Scott said, 'a deep indifference to ordered form'. But
while one can understand the impatience of the Classicist with this kind of building,
one need not share it. The 'ordered form' of a Georgian house is a choice delight, the full
savouring of which requires a mind and an eye better trained in the study of architecture
than the enjoyment of an essentially scenic house such as, say, Compton Wynyates.
Normally one responds to the Romantic houses first; the appreciation of the Classical
style requires a little more experience in the neglected art of looking. But I do not believe
that a taste for ordered form need, nor should, imply a condemnation of picturesque
disorder, even if Scott's assertion were true, which it is not, that in the Latin countries this
kind of architecture is hardly to be found.

Classical buildings, which in the present context are principally English country houses
from the Restoration to the Regency, do not 'melt' into the landscape in the manner of
their picturesque predecessors; the intentions of their builders were more consciously
architectural. The material was now frequently brick, as often as not a product of the
local clay; and in their different way these gracious, formal houses may also show a strong
feeling for their surroundings. The same is true of towns. An essentially Romantic place,
such as Tewkesbury, will delight us by the variety in the styles and materials of its buildings; but may not a town like Stamford, with its comparative uniformity both of style
and of material, be equally, or indeed even more beautiful? The stone of Stamford is no
less a local product than the variety of materials to be seen at Tewkesbury. In some places
a choice of building materials was readily available; in others one alone is dominant, and
permeates our every memory of them.

The immense development of communications since the beginning of the nineteenth
century, ushered in by the work of Macadam and Telford on roads and canals, has brought
many practical improvements to our houses, but at an appallingly high cost to the visual
appearance of England. This is not the place to inveigh against the solecisms of 'subtopia',
but it is a strangely twisted mentality which can indulge in the erection of a shed roofed
with pink asbestos tiles on the edge of a slate quarry. Yet this is what can be seen to-day

at a place in Cumberland. White asbestos sheets for roofing farm buildings have also done much visual damage in recent years to England's countryside. Acceptable perhaps in flat coastal country, the raw whiteness of these sheets, which remain glaring for a long time, is wholly out of place in landscapes of quiet bronze-greens and weathered stonework. Moreover, this crudity can be avoided at very little cost, through the use of bituminous paints, which are very durable. A single application of a dark colour (e.g. dark bronze green: British Standard Colour 4-051) renders asbestos sheeting quite tolerable; for it is a basic aesthetic truth that a roof which is darker in tone than the supporting walls imparts to a building a feeling of repose, so that it seems to sit more firmly on its site (*108*b, *334*c). The painting of asbestos sheeted roofs in country districts should be, surely, not an option but an obligation.

It is, I am well aware, easy to become sentimental on the subject of local building materials, and to be hypnotized into assertions which have little or no validity. The truth is that their employment matters most where the soil from which they are drawn reveals itself, either, for instance, in rocky outcrops or by the general configuration of the land surface. At the other end of the scale there are districts where the local material is by no means the most agreeable; one would not wish to find pebble-dash in gravelly regions, nor flint and nothing else in the flint areas. Some materials too—thatch is an example—are much more adaptable than others. But now that transport has become simple, the importance of selecting building materials of a colour and texture appropriate to the locality often seems to be overlooked. The Civic Trust has certainly been very well advised to offer awards for 'new buildings in the design of which respect has been paid to the character of neighbouring buildings and natural surroundings'. For nowadays local building traditions are all too liable to be ignored, and with certain honourable exceptions the *genius loci* is a discarded concept. Perhaps the worst offences, and certainly the most common, spring from the intrusion of red brick and tiles into places where visually they can win no possible acceptance. At Bath, for instance, many villas and even bungalows have continued in the present century, and how rightly, to be built of the local yellow stone, but the effect is all but ruined by the roofs, a rash of bright red tiles. At Broadway, just beyond the famous street that is one of the show-pieces of Cotswold stone, somebody had the idea of erecting a group of houses sheathed in white roughcast and roofed with red tiles. Sited elsewhere, these houses would probably evoke no comment, but suddenly to come upon them here is like a smack in the face.

To-day cost is almost always the prime consideration; and although the use of local materials still has the advantage of saving haulage charges, any alien product that is wanted can be quite easily transported. In the past the very uneven distribution of wealth as between one district of England and another certainly had an important influence; but neither this nor other factors, such as the exigencies of climate, or changing social requirements, or the strength of tradition, or the swinging pendulum of fashion, affected the character of our local building activities nearly so radically as the nature of the materials which were available. That is why it has seemed justifiable to devote this book to materials alone.

And since geology is our point of departure, the reader may find it worth while spending a few minutes at the outset with England's geological map (pp. 29–31). The picture, as has been said, is complex, but a few broad generalizations may prove helpful. England's geological pattern runs predominantly from south-south-west to north-north-east; if therefore we wish to review in a single sweep those building stones which are approximately of the same antiquity and character, that is the direction to follow. To travel from the east or south-east westwards or north-westwards is to move not along but across the structure of the country; this is the way for those who wish to see as many varieties of building as possible in fairly rapid succession. And although in some counties the pattern is more straightforward than in others, it is, broadly speaking, true to say that the younger rocks lie to the east and south-east, the older to the west and north-west.

It is unfortunately impossible to include on a single map all the geological information relevant to the theme of this book. The map printed here is concerned with the solid geology of England: that is to say, it shows the distribution of our principal geological formations in historical sequence. Serious students will need constantly to refer also to a lithological map, showing the geographical extent of the predominant rock types when they are at the surface or sufficiently near to it to render quarrying a practical possibility, and also to a drift map, which requires a short explanation. During and since the Pleistocene Ice Age some parts of the country were covered with boulder clay (spread over the surface by ice sheets), sand, gravel and silt (deposited by running water), peat bogs and wind-blown sand. In the earliest days of geology these were widely believed to have been spread by the waters of the Flood. Since 1839, when the term was introduced by Murchison, they have been known to geologists as 'drift'. In some areas they bury the 'solid' rocks to depths which altogether preclude working, but these superficial deposits are sometimes specially relevant to brick-making. Such maps, both for the whole country and for particular areas, can be found in the great *Atlas of Britain* issued in 1963 by the Clarendon Press (pp. 8, 18, and 54–63).

Reference was made in the Foreword to the necessity, in view of the magnitude of the subject, of setting certain limits upon the types of building to be discussed. The concentration upon exteriors rather than interiors seemed to be the natural outcome of my special and declared concern for the visual pleasure of those who move about England.

As for the focus on houses, they are, after all, far and away our commonest buildings, and because the majority of those erected before the Industrial Revolution were the products of moderate means and of local traditions, no other class of building can illustrate so effectively the great variety of our materials and the many ways in which they have been employed.

The parish churches constitute numerically the other major group, and whenever a point is better made by reference to a church than to a secular building, I shall not hesitate to make it. But in addition to the reasons already given, there are several others which have prompted me to devote my attention to houses rather than to churches. First, there is the significant fact that church building virtually ceased for over half a century after 1540, while between the death of Elizabeth I and the Fire of London there was only a very minor harvest; so that during what is the most important period of all for English vernacular building, the churches have very little to offer. Secondly, it must be said that, in the condition in which we find them to-day, the churches can show comparatively little of external interest except in the field of stone; all the other materials can be better studied externally in the domestic sphere. I was also influenced, in the third place, by the fact that T. D. Atkinson's *Local Style in English Architecture*, an interesting and valuable book which appeared in 1947, devotes most of its attention to churches, and on the subject of houses leaves a good deal unsaid.

But what, it may be asked, of the cathedrals? Here are the greatest and finest of all English buildings; should they not claim a place? My answer is that another whole book could be devoted to the fabric of the cathedrals. Yet if the discussion were to be confined as here to exteriors, it would be, except for roofs and for the brickwork at St. Albans and at a few modern cathedrals such as Guildford, a book entirely centred on stone; and, as already suggested, it would have less to say about local stone than a work concerned with more ordinary buildings, for the cathedrals drew some of their materials from afar. For our present purposes these are both limitations. The cathedrals' materials book has still to be written, and, excellent as it would be to have it, one wonders whether it ever will be; the records of building stones are patchy and incomplete, and some important buildings have never been fully examined by a competent expert.

The dearth of documentary material is, however, by no means peculiar to some of the cathedrals. Sir Nikolaus Pevsner, working on his *Buildings of England*, has encountered the same difficulty: 'on the building stones of Durham literature is as completely lacking as on those of most other counties' is a typical observation from one of his introductions. Future writers of guide-books, whether on individual houses or churches or on complete towns or counties, would perform a valuable service if they were to make a point of mentioning the materials of construction whenever they can be ascertained. Absence of documentation is a reason why, particularly in the case of vernacular buildings, the problem of accurate dating is sometimes difficult. Fortunately, in a survey such as this, precise dating is usually of no importance. What matters to me, and I hope to my readers, is the visual aspect of our buildings, and the reason why they look as they do in one place, and perhaps so different only a few miles away. Now and again I shall be tempted to proffer aesthetic estimates, based partly on comparisons. The opportunities are abundant, for, away from the trunk roads, many parts of England are still a wonderful terrain for the lover of buildings. If, as Trollope said, it is a question 'whether many travellers, men who have pitched their tents perhaps under Mount Sinai, are not still ignorant that there are glories in Wiltshire, Dorsetshire and Somersetshire', I could wish for nothing better than to help a little to broaden their field of vision.

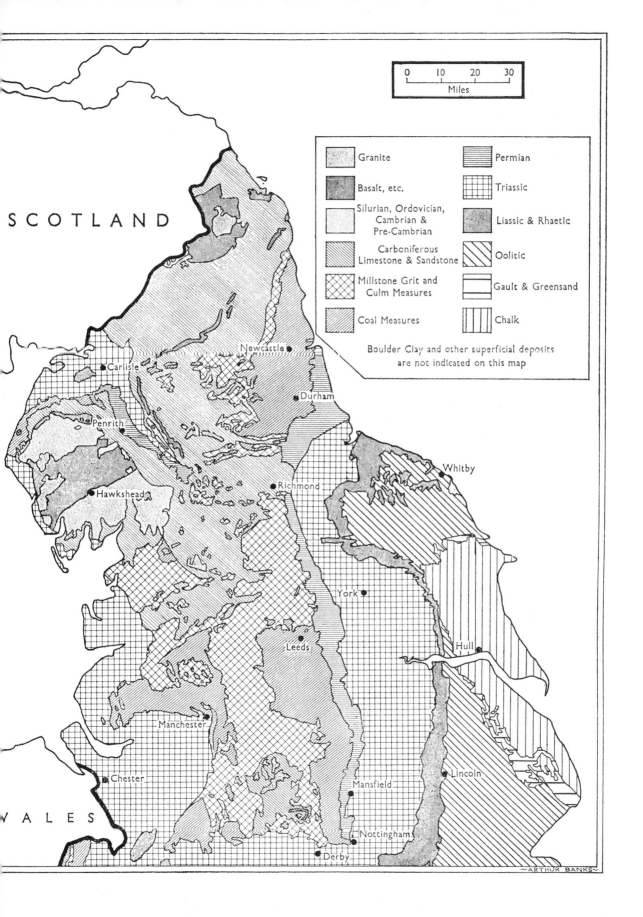

SCOTLAND

	10	20	30

Miles

Granite

Basalt, etc.

Silurian, Ordovician,
Cambrian &
Pre-Cambrian

Carboniferous
Limestone & Sandstone

Millstone Grit and
Culm Measures

Coal Measures

Permian

Triassic

Liassic & Rhaetic

Oolitic

Gault & Greensand

Chalk

Boulder Clay and other superficial deposits
are not indicated on this map

Carlisle

Newcastle

Penrith

Durham

Whitby

Hawkshead

Richmond

York

Leeds

Hull

Manchester

Chester

Mansfield

Lincoln

WALES

Nottingham

Derby

~ARTHUR BANKS~

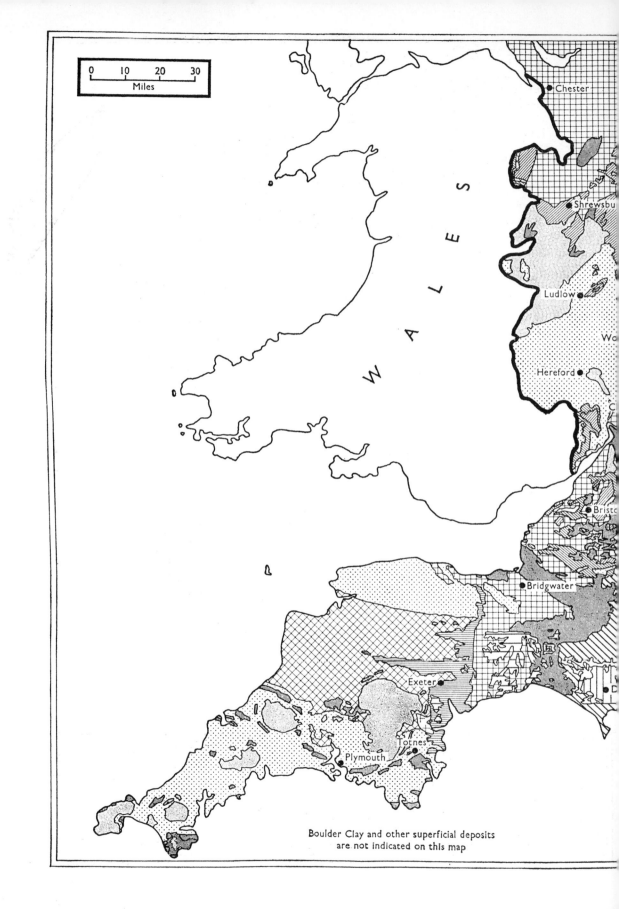

Boulder Clay and other superficial deposits
are not indicated on this map

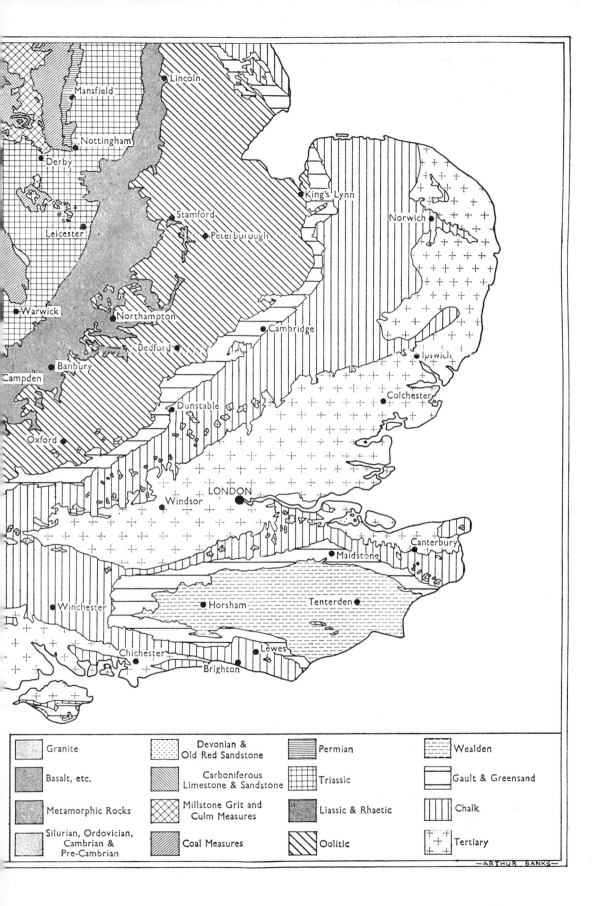

Granite

Basalt, etc.

Metamorphic Rocks

Silurian, Ordovician,
Cambrian &
Pre-Cambrian

Devonian &
Old Red Sandstone

Carboniferous
Limestone & Sandstone

Millstone Grit and
Culm Measures

Coal Measures

Permian

Triassic

Liassic & Rhaetic

Oolitic

Wealden

Gault & Greensand

Chalk

Tertiary

Mansfield · Lincoln ·
· Nottingham
· Derby
Leicester
· Warwick
Campden
· Banbury
· Oxford
Windsor ·
· Winchester
Chichester ·
· Brighton

Stamford
· Peterborough
Northampton
· Bedford
· Dunstable

King's Lynn ·
Norwich ·

Cambridge ·
· Ipswich
· Colchester

LONDON
· Maidstone · Canterbury
· Horsham · Tenterden
· Lewes

—ARTHUR BANKS—

2

STONE: GENERAL

The story of the bridge over the Nene at Wisbech in Cambridgeshire throws an interesting light on the trends of the times as reflected in their building materials. There have in fact been at least six bridges across the river in the centre of Wisbech. Needless to say, the earliest were of wood. One was already there in 1437. A new one was built in 1583 and another in 1637. This was replaced in 1758–60 by a stone bridge which in turn gave way in 1855 to an erection in cast iron. Finally, in 1931, Wisbech acquired a new bridge in concrete. The reader will probably learn with no surprise that a study of old engravings and photographs leaves no doubt that the stone bridge was easily the best as a work of art. It was not only the best from the formal aspect, but the most agreeable in texture, and probably in colour also. For stone is indeed the aristocrat of building materials; and England, as has been said, is specially fortunate in having so many varieties, all within the compass of a few hundred miles. It is only proper, therefore, that nearly half this book should be devoted to it.

Although in many parts of the country stone has always been beyond the means of ordinary folk, it has usually been regarded as highly desirable when the purse would allow it. In our own day the appearance of new materials and new building techniques has altered the situation radically, but hitherto it would seem true to say that only at the most uninhibitedly anti-classical moments in the history of English taste have most men not aspired to dwell within walls of stone. In the Elizabethan age, although a great many timber-framed houses were rebuilt in stone, this process was not invariable. Sir Nikolaus Pevsner observes[1] that, to the well-to-do clothiers of Shrewsbury at the end of the sixteenth century, timber was preferable to stone, 'because it made possible a more ostentatious display and allowed certain fineries of which in stone they would not have been capable'. And in Monmouthshire during those same years, Fox and Raglan found that, although nearly all the new houses were now built of rubblestone, 'the stonework was of secondary interest to the builders'; what the new landowners of rural Monmouthshire really cared for was wood carving, and they 'wanted and were ready to pay for the richest

---

[1] *The Buildings of England: Shropshire* (1958), p. 27.

work the local woodworkers could produce'.[1] In the later Victorian period, which in so many respects resembles the later Elizabethan, stone again lost for a little while some of its habitual preëminence. The original *Little Guides* to the English counties, which were beginning to appear about the turn of the century, throw a revealing light on this subject. For the authors of these books timber-framing is beyond doubt the most cherished material. Although they react in an associational fashion to shapes, so that, for instance, a row of gables is almost automatically 'most attractive', whereas a pediment is as often as not 'incongruous', it is surprising how punctually they also respond to materials. A glossary might run somewhat as follows:

Brick (unless Tudor)	plain
Brick (for a church)	ugly
Colour-wash	homely
Stucco	pretentious
Timber-framing	highly picturesque
Stone	good (e.g. 'a good stone front')

Good indeed. It is no uncommon experience to find that men who spend their lives working stone come to revere it. 'I am a surviving member of the great army who worked in the quarries', wrote one of them to *The Times* in 1969. 'Stone is a miracle of nature. No two quarries are alike and all stones vary within the same quarry. The correct selection taxes the skill of the quarryman. A quarry is like a book written in a strange language: it must be studied to be understood.'[2]

1 Sir Cyril Fox and Lord Raglan, *Monmouthshire Houses, Part II, c. 1550–1610* (1953), Chapter 1.

2 Not all those who love stone may know of the existence of an admirable Society, the Men of the Stones, founded at Stamford in 1947. It is not only a preservation society in the best sense, offering advice regarding the repair of old stone buildings, including choice of the best available materials; it also actively encourages the greater use of stone for building, and the training of masons. This Society gave strong support to the Orton Trust in the acquisition, in 1967, of a charming but disused little Northamptonshire church at Orton near Rothwell, and converting it into a craft centre for training in masonry, stone carving, lettering and all allied skills.

3 + P.E.B.

History

There are, according to the latest computation, 402 churches in England which incorporate fragments at least of Saxon masonry,[1] and in those parts of the country where timber was scarce and stone on or very near the surface plentiful, it is reasonable to suppose that rough stone was used during the Saxon period for the walls—although not for the roofs—of domestic huts. Indeed, stone had been employed in England for such a purpose long before this, as can still be seen, for example, at the Bronze Age settlement of Grimspound on Dartmoor; and at Stonehenge it is evident that stone was crudely dressed long before the arrival of the Romans. Nevertheless it is practically certain that at the Norman Conquest England possessed nothing that could properly be described as a house built of stone, and during the next five hundred years very few humble houses were constructed of this material. A rare survivor (much restored) is the early fourteenth-century fisherman's house at Meare, near Glastonbury. Up to the fifteenth century, stone was primarily used for cathedrals and churches; for houses built in connection with the Church, such as bishops' palaces, rectories and vicarages, and also for the Vicars' Close at Wells; for monastic establishments, including the houses of abbots and priors; for castles; and for bridges. Timber-framed houses needed stone too, but only to provide foundations, a plinth, and occasionally, in the later Middle Ages, a fireplace and a chimney. In some places a particular building might be known simply as 'the stone house', because it was the only one within miles to be constructed of that material. Yet for the better class of house, even before 1400, stone was not quite so rare as has sometimes been suggested.[2]

1 See H. M. and Joan Taylor, *Anglo-Saxon Architecture*, 2 vols. (1965). It is interesting to note that the eight counties with the largest numbers of these churches are all on the East or South coasts: Norfolk, Lincolnshire, Kent, Yorkshire, Sussex, Essex, Hampshire and Northumberland.

2 For our early houses the authority is Miss Margaret E. Wood, whose first researches were published in two issues of the *Archaeological Journal*: (1) 'Norman Domestic Architecture', in vol. 92, pp. 167–242 (1935), and (2) 'Thirteenth Century Domestic Architecture', in a special supplement to vol. 105 (1950). In her book *The English Mediaeval House* (1965), which amplifies but does not supersede these, she writes: 'At present we know of over forty examples of Norman domestic architecture, though many are fragmentary or mutilated. Stone being the chief building material to survive, most occur on the rich limestone belt. . . . Not many have been found in the sandstone country west of it, but the millstone grit of Yorkshire provides examples, and in the chalk and clay lands of the east flint took the place of building-stone. Indeed, it is the south-eastern half of England that preserves most Norman houses. Most date from the second half of the twelfth century. Political unrest discouraged good civil building until the reign of Henry II (1154–1189), and before then stone was not in general use for building, even castles being mainly composed of timber, except for special cases such as London, or in places like Richmond in Yorkshire, where stone was abundant and easily worked. . . . Some hundred surviving thirteenth century houses have been recognized. Of this number perhaps a third are

With the growing prosperity which resulted largely from the wool trade, stone became in the fifteenth century one of the normal materials for the medium-sized as well as for the large houses. Some 'middling' stone houses of very high quality had already been built before the advent of the Tudors. At Great Chalfield near Bradford-on-Avon, for example, Thomas Tropenell, landowner and Member of Parliament, built for himself about 1480 a stone house of the most gracious refinement. The front, with its two finely carved oriel windows and with armoured knights and griffins proudly holding up his coat of arms on the points of the gables (74a and c), still survives unaltered and in almost perfect condition.

The Tudors gave the country strong rule and internal stability; wealth increased, and with it the desire for greater domestic comfort. One way of achieving this was to rebuild one's draughty half-timbered house in a more solid material such as stone or brick; or, if a complete rebuilding was too expensive, at least the old house might be recased in the better material. Various other factors also served to provide an incentive to rebuild. The smoky atmosphere of the mediaeval hall with its often centrally placed hearth was no longer to be tolerated; builders all over the country had at last mastered the art of how to construct an efficient, and sometimes externally very decorative, flue; and everyone began to want fireplaces and chimneys which had to be of brick or stone (261c). Windows also changed greatly during the sixteenth century, for whereas window-glass in 1500 was still expensive and by no means completely transparent, a century later it was of quite good quality and appreciably cheaper. Changing ideas about privacy were another important consideration. The lofty communal hall was no longer required. People wanted smaller rooms, and many more of them. So if a house was not completely rebuilt, a floor would be inserted across the middle of the hall, with bedrooms introduced above. Finally there was the problem of the growing scarcity of timber. This had already made itself felt in some parts of England by the beginning of the seventeenth century, and had brought about a sharp rise in the price of wood; thus to turn to stone might no longer cost so much more.

The urge to rebuild in stone or brick steadily gathered momentum as the sixteenth century advanced. It did not affect the four most northerly counties, which remained comparatively dormant architecturally until after the Restoration. The south-western counties,

very good examples. They are found throughout England, but again chiefly in the south-eastern half, in stone- and flint-working regions. Timber houses in the west have mostly disappeared. . . . Again, the emphasis is on the second half of the century.'

An analysis reveals that with the single exception of Little Wenham Hall near Ipswich (c. 1275), which is mainly brick (see page 211), all these buildings are of stone, and nearly all are of limestone or flint or both.

on the other hand, were undertaking a great deal of distinguished house-building well before the accession of Elizabeth I. One has only to think, in Somerset, of Barrington, Cothay, the hall at Coker Court and the entrance front of Brympton d'Evercy; in Dorset, of Athelhampton, Wolfeton, Parnham, Mapperton and Bingham's Melcombe; in Devon, of Holcombe Court and Weare Giffard; and in Cornwall of Cotehele (*147a*). Not one of these has survived wholly unaltered, and internally some have been rather drastically modernised, but all embody fine stone architecture of the years 1485 to 1558. Also belonging to this early Tudor period are a number of splendid domestic buildings erected by the great ecclesiastics, who were very partial to stone. One thinks of Archbishop Bourchier's tower at Knole (*73d*), the Abbot's Lodgings at Muchelney, parts of Forde Abbey and Thame Park, Lyddington Bede House in Rutland (once a manor house of the Bishops of Lincoln), Saighton Grange in Cheshire and, perhaps most notable of all, the Prior's Lodge at Much Wenlock (*124c*). All these survive to illustrate what had already been achieved in the sphere of domestic architecture, with many kinds of stone, before Queen Elizabeth's accession.

After the Dissolution, an impetus was given to stone-building by the presence of innumerable abbeys and priories for which there was no longer any use; many, like Lacock, were converted into private houses, but many more became available as quarries. Sometimes, perhaps, there was a lingering sense of shame; it used to be said that Whitehall in Shrewsbury, built in 1582, was so called because originally the red sandstone pillaged from the Abbey was whitewashed, to conceal its provenance. This story may well be apocryphal; what is certain is that under Elizabeth I and James I quarries were opened up in many parts of the country. Most of them were small; some supplied the material for no more than a single house and its boundary walls; of many no record survives; practically all of them were long ago abandoned and are no more than overgrown pits, if not already filled up with rubbish. But wherever there is good stone not far below the surface, whether it be limestone in, say Gloucestershire or Northamptonshire, or sandstone in Sussex or Cheshire, or stone of the most various kinds in Devon, an observant eye will not fail to detect these evidences of past activity, sources of the raw material of so much of England's beauty. Many of these old quarries are far from being exhausted; often they remained little worked only because of the formidable difficulties, until the end of the eighteenth century, of removing the stone after it had been dug out. The few English quarries able to send their stone far afield depended in almost every case on the accessibility of water transport.

By the end of the seventeenth century, provided that it could be quarried locally stone had become the accepted building material, even for cottages. On the limestone belt, in particular, whole towns, like Sherborne and Cirencester, Oundle and Stamford, are built of stone, including even the most modest houses. But the proviso is important. For outside the stone areas, the material was still employed for important buildings only, and not for all of those: at Hampton Court, for example, Wren only used stone for the dressings, while Kensington Palace exhibits hardly any stonework. Sometimes a 'skin' of stone might be introduced over the front of a brick-built house, as at Mompesson House, Salisbury, erected in 1700. Outside the stone areas, where recourse was had to stone at all for domestic purposes it was usually only as a facing material; so that in speaking of a stone building we may only mean a stone-faced building. To-day, because of the cost, stone is nearly always used in this way, and aesthetically there can surely be no objection to it.

But why, it may be asked, did anyone trouble to face his house with stone, especially in 1700 when, as will presently be related, bricks of the most excellent quality were becoming widely available? The explanation is a social one. For throughout the whole of the eighteenth century and well into the nineteenth, stone carried with it a social cachet which attached to no other building material. The Georgians, although excelling as   * builders in brick, had a yearning for stone far beyond anything that had been felt in this country hitherto. For monumental public buildings, stone was now considered to be well-nigh essential; for houses, although not essential, it was certainly highly desirable. Within, the most prized materials were marble and alabaster; and if few could aspire to the alabaster magnificence of the halls at Holkham and Kedleston (*182*), many of the grander buildings contained columns faced with scagliola designed to imitate polished stone, while white marble chimney-pieces may quite often be found in houses of the most modest pretensions. For the exterior, a facing of ashlared (i.e. smooth-faced) limestone or sandstone was regarded as a great embellishment, even in a non-stone area; so that when Sir Robert Walpole, for example, set about building Houghton Hall (*114c*), stone had to be brought by sea all the way from Whitby to King's Lynn, and thence at high expense conveyed overland. Although, ironically enough, few of the houses on which Robert Adam worked are of stone or stone-faced, this material continued until well after 1800 to hold pride of place. There is the sad little story[1] of George III driving over from Weymouth about 1794 to visit Morton Pitt at Kingston Maurward. This fine house had been built in 1720 by his grandfather, in red brick. 'The proud owner was expatiating on its beauties, and hoping that it would receive the royal commendation. The King, however, with his well-known iteration, did nothing but utter the words, "Brick, Mr. Pitt, brick." Pitt was so mortified that, at great cost, he thereupon had the whole place encased in Portland stone; and so it remains.' A generation later, a grateful nation presented

[1] Related by Mr. Arthur Oswald in *Country Houses of Dorset* (1935), p. 94.

Apsley House to the Duke of Wellington. As built by Robert Adam in the seventeen-seventies for Lord Bathurst, it was in red brick. This did not satisfy the Duke, which is why the house at Hyde Park Corner was faced with Box Ground Bath stone.[1] A few years after this, as mentioned earlier (p. 23), Kingston Lacy in Dorset was similarly encased. As built by Sir Roger Pratt, this was a red brick house with Chilmark stone employed only for the dressings: Sir Charles Barry was asked to obliterate all traces of the brickwork.

An interesting by-product of the Georgian yearning for stone (whether aesthetic, or merely snobbish, or perhaps a mixture of the two) was the striving to attain 'stone effects' in other materials, such as cement, stucco, plaster, wood and even brick (see p. 227). These of course were not peculiar to the Georgian period; there are plenty of instances in English church architecture of the Middle Ages, the supreme one being the superstructure of the Ely Octagon which, although in wood covered externally with lead, is markedly lithic in character. Here, however, it can at least be said that the use of wood as a substitute for stone greatly simplified the structural problem; a clearer case of the yearning for at least the appearance of stone is provided by some of the East Anglian houses of the sixteenth century. At Giffords Hall, Stoke-by-Nayland, Suffolk, for instance, the lovely brick gatehouse (256a) appears to have stone window-frames and other dressings, but all in fact are of brick, with a thin coating of plaster. At Breccles Hall in Norfolk, the whole of the exterior 'stonework' of a large sixteenth-century house is nothing but plaster. So also on the tower of Sissinghurst Castle (332d), where all the dressings are plaster except the arch over the doorway.

There are also a number of examples of this, mostly dating from the first half of the seventeenth century, in Lancashire. Later, the plastering was so well executed that it is sometimes really difficult to identify it with certainty. Morden College at Blackheath, for example, which was founded in 1695, is constantly described as being of brick with stone dressings, but in fact these are all of plaster. Elsewhere, the substitute material is less successful. On the lower storey of the little brick Market Hall at Amersham, built in 1682, the quoins are of stone; on the upper, cement was employed, and the effect is mean. The cement is not even the right colour, since it lacks the whiteness of the Portland stone.

It is on houses dating from the latter part of the eighteenth century and especially from the first half of the nineteenth that the simulation of stone in other materials is most frequent; and the results are by no means always unpleasing. Now and again the material chosen was wood, in which the cheapest way was to face the house with non-overlapping

1 The Duke's country house had already been treated before he was born. When Stratfield Saye House was made Georgian by Lord Rivers about the middle of the eighteenth century, he had the red brick covered with stucco.

TYPES OF MASONRY
a. *The Manor House, Upper Slaughter, Gloucestershire* (before alteration)
b. *The Haycock, Wansford Bridge, Huntingdonshire*

boards which could be scored vertically at regular intervals, to suggest blocks; this was the method used in Kent over brick at Church House, Brenchley, and also on a number of buildings along the Pantiles at Tunbridge Wells. But the scoring had of necessity to be shallow and the deception therefore not complete. In the better examples each block is separate. An engaging little Regency house in Brighton, 37A Duke Street (40a), is entirely faced with wooden blocks, each $11 \times 5\frac{1}{2}$ ins.; and although successive coats of paint have done something to compromise the effect, the fine divisions between the planks still recall mortar joints. Regency House at Framlingham in Suffolk, facing the east end of the church, is a very curious instance: here a two-storeyed Georgian house was given a third storey in order to accommodate a front composed of wooden blocks imitating stone, brought specially from London. Still more surprising is Craythorne House at Tenterden (40c), for here is a mid-Georgian brick house in the heart of a region justly renowned for the quality of its brickwork; yet its unknown builder thought it worth while to cover the whole house with wooden blocks, all carefully chamfered to suggest rustication. The cutting is extremely precise and the wood here was evidently very well seasoned; but the weakness of using wood in this manner is that in time it is liable to start warping and cracking, and then the stone effect is jeopardized.

On timber-framed buildings the imitation of stone was usually carried out in plaster, stucco or cement. When the jetties remain in evidence, as at the King's School shop in Palace Street, Canterbury (40b) or at Nos. 36 and 37, East Hill, Colchester (40d), the effect is very curious. These little Elizabethan houses were refurbished and refenestrated at the beginning of the nineteenth century, and masonry lines can be seen carefully ruled out on the facing of cement. The house at Canterbury was also given sash-framed windows, which were taken out a few years ago; here again the plaster is moulded to produce a rusticated effect. In both cases the implied suggestion of stonework supported on no more than wooden bressummers is quite irrational. On the front of another and much larger building in Colchester, the Gate House in the High Street, the deeply incised grooves ($1-1\frac{1}{2}$ ins.) on the cement facing (redone a few years ago) which were intended to suggest stones are still more incongruous, as here there is not only a jetty but a quartet of steeply pitched gables!

Even in Stamford there is timber-framing, but by the beginning of the nineteenth century it would seem that owners of such houses hardly dared show their faces, with finely wrought ashlar stonework to be seen on every side. So almost every framed house was stuccoed, and on almost every stucco surface there duly appeared, rather pathetically, the ruled 'joint-lines' of pseudo-stonework. Farther north, few would have been prepared to pay for a deception of this kind; there the only normal covering was limewash. In the

IMITATION OF STONE IN OTHER MATERIALS
a. *37A Duke Street, Brighton, Sussex*   b. *Palace Street, Canterbury, Kent*
c. *Craythorne House, Tenterden, Kent*   d. *East Hill, Colchester, Essex*

south it was otherwise. Cement carried over a whole façade in imitation of stone can be seen at Ayot St. Lawrence, in Hertfordshire. Here the Classical portico of the church, designed by Nicholas Revett in 1768, was intended to be an 'eye-catcher' from Ayot House. (It is so no longer, as big trees have been allowed to intervene.) Because of this the church, which is of red brick, was faced with cement (now falling off) on the side looking towards the house only.

Yet all these are mere drops in the ocean compared with the immense vogue for stucco in this country between 1810 and 1850. Of this there will be more to say in a later chapter. Suffice it to observe here that when the terrace houses of London and Brighton, of Bristol and Cheltenham and Leamington and of many towns besides were originally stuccoed, the material was not left, a smooth overcoat, to be enjoyed for its own sake; it was almost invariably covered with the web of thinly incised lines purporting to represent mortar courses (*382e*), and sometimes even with washes of colour intended to suggest weathering. Later these would-be deceptions were very properly abandoned; but where the incisions were deep they can often be seen even now, after many repaintings, as a reminder that the original reason for the enthusiasm for stucco did not spring from any love of that material for itself but from a craving for stone. London in fact has never at any time in her history had many stone or stone-faced houses, as distinct from monumental public buildings; but because of the extensive use of stucco, well into Victorian times and over whole areas of the capital, the ubiquity of brick is in some boroughs much less obvious than it might be. Nearly half a century later, some men were still thinking of brick as at best a *pis aller*. Here, for example, is William Morris in 1892: 'Stone is definitely the most noble material, and the most satisfactory; wood is the next, while brick is a makeshift.'

It was, however, from about the middle of the nineteenth century that mistakes in the employment of stone began to be made on a large scale. Easy rail transport encouraged the use of the cheaper varieties, regardless of durability prospects and of resistance to air pollution; inferior beds from well-known quarries were no longer discarded; stones got wrongly worked and set; iron cramps were employed to gross excess. Many of the maintenance problems of to-day are directly due to irresponsible commercialism in the handling of stone during the latter part of the Victorian period.

To-day, even in a region with a great stone tradition such as the Cotswolds, new stone-built houses are, alas, no longer usual. In the last few years there have been one or two encouraging signs: the paying of extra subsidies to local authorities who build in stone, and the development since the last war of fast-cutting mechanical saws which, when applied to the less intractable limestones and sandstones, can cut in one minute what with a hand saw would take two men nearly an hour. These may help to render the stone house once again an economic possibility. Good quality stone is still one of the most permanent of all building materials, as it is beyond doubt the most beautiful and, where local material is used, the most congenial to the surrounding landscape.

Masonry

The ideal building stone is one which embodies good weathering properties and agreeable colour and texture, with a consistency fine enough to admit of smooth surfaces and crisply carved details. Such a combination of qualities is not common, and most of the stone employed for English buildings is deficient in one or other of these respects.

There are many ways of cutting, dressing and laying stone, and the methods adopted for these have no less effect upon a building's appearance than the choice of the material itself. The large majority of our old stone buildings are only of rubblestone. constructed, that is to say, of hunks of stone, of varying sizes but mostly rather small, which are sometimes roughly squared but often left quite irregular. These stones may be arranged without any order or direction ('random') or levelled up to form courses about every 12 ins. or 18 ins. ('brought to courses'); or, if roughly squared, they may be laid throughout in courses which are seldom more than 9 ins. high and sometimes as little as 2 ins. ('regular coursed'). Many kinds of stone, especially the very hard kinds, can only be used as rubble, while even in more favourable areas the beds are often thin and yield only small pieces; but whatever the local conditions, this was always the most economical way of building because almost every piece was usable. Thus, when the humbler buildings—farmhouses, cottages, outhouses and barns—are of stone, they are nearly always of coursed or random rubble masonry, obtained with no great difficulty from small local quarries. In some parts of the country, especially to the west of the oolitic limestone belt, from Cornwall to Northumberland and throughout the whole of Wales, there is little freestone, so for all but the most lavish buildings there was no alternative. Churches in these areas would sometimes be covered externally with whitewash or a thin coat of plaster, as always internally (see Chapter 14), until the advent of the Victorian craze for scraping or 'skinning' in the hope of uncovering little early fragments which, even when found, are seldom any asset aesthetically.

In rubble walling, although the joints run as horizontally as the character of the material will allow, many of the stones may be somewhat rounded, so plenty of mortar is essential. Formerly this was always compounded of lime, which set more slowly and was rather less weather-resisting than the Portland cement mortars usually employed to-day. Much of the effect of an unplastered rubblestone wall depends upon the way in which the mortar jointing is carried out, a subject on which there will be more to say later. If the mortar is good, and a very hard stone is employed, a rubblestone wall, whether coursed or random, may prove to be exceptionally durable. In the garden of New College, Oxford, one may inspect a considerable length of the old City Wall built of the local Coral Rag in the eleventh century and still in excellent preservation. Rubble walling has a rough, peasant quality often entirely appropriate in country districts, yet the visual appeal of this type of masonry is artistically somewhat limited. The west front of Rushton Hall in Northamptonshire, mostly faced with excellent Weldon ashlar (cut stone) dating from 1626 onwards, incorporates near its south end a lofty gable from an earlier house built of rubble-faced ironstone. The surface of this portion is not as gracious as the rest. The Cotswold manor house at Upper Slaughter provides another example (39a). Here the body of the Elizabethan building, apart from the excellent dressings (see p. 48), is of rubblestone; that the face of the handsome two-storeyed porch is entirely ashlared much enhances our pleasure.[1] Nevertheless, the high proportion of ashlar masonry which we are apt to take for granted in beautiful stone towns such as Bath (84b), Oxford or Stamford (84a) was a luxury to which comparatively few could attain, and a great deal of rubble masonry is to be found even along the limestone belt (84a: the smaller house). The North Wiltshire towns of Malmesbury and Highworth, for example, are almost wholly stone-built, but except for dressings, ashlar is there quite the exception. Across the Gloucestershire border in the district around Tetbury, the cottages have good stone-slated roofs whilst the walls are only of rubble, with rather mean-looking window-frames of wood. The ironstone villages of west and north Oxfordshire and parts of Northamptonshire (342a) are also mostly rubble-built, as are the villages in the limestone portions of Kesteven. Most of these cottages and small houses date from the seventeenth and eighteenth centuries.

Long before this, masonry of the most urbane kind had been widely used for major buildings such as cathedrals and abbeys; and part of the story of our secular architecture in stone is concerned with the gradual rejection of rubble masonry for public buildings and houses of importance, and even in some places for quite modest houses where the local stone supplies were favourable. It should not be supposed that ashlar was the only alternative. Buildings of more smoothly dressed stone which is none the less not ashlar are not at all unusual; many mediaeval churches fall into this category, known locally in some of the Oxfordshire quarries by the convenient term 'hardstone'. Elsewhere, this type of masonry is usually described as hammer-dressed rubblestone. The larger the blocks the

[1] It is sad to have to record that for some years this house has been unoccupied, with the usual, but, it is to be hoped, only temporary consequences.

DRESSING AND POINTING STONEWORK
a. *Grevel's House, Chipping Campden, Gloucestershire* b. *Bridge Street, Richmond, Yorkshire*
c. *Wilton House, Wiltshire* d. *New Court, St. John's College, Cambridge*

better; the usual practice was to square them, and if they could also be coursed (which did not imply that the height of the courses should be uniform), a more pleasing effect was produced. A good secular example of this type of building is the Haycock Inn beside the fine old bridge at Wansford over which for centuries the Great North Road crossed the Nene from Huntingdonshire into Northamptonshire (39b). The walls, which have a flat but not an absolutely smooth surface, are properly described as being of hammer-dressed hard rubble limestone in random courses; only the dressings are of freestone.[1]

All our most stylish stone buildings are largely or wholly faced in ashlar. The term implies a smooth surface, generally achieved by employing comparatively thin slabs of stone to face rubble or bricks; the blocks, often quite large, are carefully squared and finely jointed in level courses. Ashlar masonry can be achieved with granite (148a), but the usual materials are limestone or sandstone. Not, however, any limestone or sandstone: only high-class freestone is suitable—stone, that is, which is homogeneous enough and of sufficiently fine grain to admit of being cut 'freely', in any direction, either with a saw or with a mallet and chisel. In Scotland and in Wales, partly for economic reasons but still more for geological, ashlar, even for buildings of importance, has always been a relatively unfamiliar luxury. In England ashlar was little used before the latter part of the fourteenth century except for very major buildings, and on the limestone belt itself the majority of churches have never been completely ashlared. By the end of the Tudor period increased prosperity had rendered it widely familiar even in the domestic field. From the time of Inigo Jones until the end of the Regency, if employed at all for a public building, stone would nearly always be ashlared, except when textural variation was a conscious aim.

There are various ways of achieving texture in stone which are, in point of refinement, intermediate between rubble and ashlar. Some of these treatments, such as fluting and grooving by machinery, are recent, and do not concern us here; but rock-facing has a long history, and in this country was particularly in favour in the eighteenth century, in conjunction with what is known as rustication. At this time, in grand houses like Houghton Hall (114c), the principal rooms were no longer on the ground but on the first floor (the *piano nobile*), and the architect's problem was how to prevent the base storey from looking insignificant or even puny. The solution lay in varying the surface texture. If for the base storey the stone, as at Sandbeck Hall (46a), is left rough or, as on the west side of the Horse Guards (46c), given a deliberately rough texture by being punched or tooled, and if in addition the blocks of stone are rusticated (which means that the mortar

[1] Mr. A. S. Ireson tells me that the 'hardstone' of the Oxfordshire area does differ slightly from the hammer-dressed rubblestone of many other districts in two respects: the courses in Oxfordshire are broader, and the surfaces are sometimes rather smoother, i.e. closer to ashlar.

CONTRASTS OF TEXTURE IN STONE
a. *Sandbeck Hall, Yorkshire*
b. *Arnos Court, Bristol* c. *The Horse Guards, London*

courses are carefully recessed so that hollow lines yielding shadows separate them), the effect is to impart to this storey a semblance of strength, and thus to render it apparently better able to support the great superstructure. In fact, of course, it does nothing of the kind, but the visual satisfaction is considerable. On both these buildings the rustication is also carried over the next horizontal division, but in combination now with much smoother stone. Only at the third stage are we confronted with an absolutely smooth finish. For their aesthetic value such contrasts of texture are an essential and most important part of the architect's repertoire. On some buildings only the horizontal joints are emphasized (*124*a): this is known as banded rustication. Other devices were also freely employed by Georgian architects, such as vermiculation (cutting the surface of the stone so as to imitate the winding tracks of worms: illustrated in artificial stone in plate *246*b) and what was known in the eighteenth century as 'frost-work' (cutting the surface to suggest stalactites or icicles as on the frame of the unusual Rococo-Gothick doorway (*c.* 1765) of Arnos Court, Bristol (*46*b)), but they always depend for their effect upon a contrast with the smooth, gentle ashlar. The cost of hand-tooled surfaces such as these would now be prohibitive, nor do they belong in spirit to modern architecture.

The rough shaping has always been done at the quarry, in order to reduce the weight of each block before transportation; but formerly the freemasons, as those men were called whose task it was to cut the freestone, worked largely on the building site. Even ashlar was not the last refinement, for some of the freestone was carefully carved to provide the 'dressings'. In Gothic and Tudor houses, these included door and window mouldings, tracery, dripstones, string-courses, set-offs to buttresses, gable-copings, battlements, crockets, roof-pinnacles, finials and so on. The bay-window of the house of William Grevel, a great wool merchant, at Chipping Campden (*45*a) provides a noble opportunity for the study of some of these. In Classical buildings, there were the architraves for doors and windows, keystones, quoins, capitals, friezes, cornices, balustrades, urns and vases at roof level: the list is still by no means complete. The centre of the Inigo Jones front at Wilton (*45*c) offers a fine illustration of some of these. Houses in both styles, as these two plates also show, might embody sculpture as well, usually in the same stone; carefully placed, this added a further enrichment. Perhaps the supreme achievement in English freestone was the moulded pier, as seen in many of our cathedrals and churches, and to perfection at Wells. It is indeed in the moulded piers, arches and vaults of some of our Gothic cathedrals that, to my mind, English freestones are seen at their loveliest, with the special opportunities which they offer for composition in depth, and contrasts of light and shade. Here stone can communicate a sense of quality which no other material can rival. In domestic architecture it is undoubtedly in the Cotswolds that one has the fullest opportunity of experiencing a comparable sensation, although parts of Somerset, Northamptonshire, Rutland and Lincolnshire may rank as close runners-up.

The partial abandonment of ashlar between the wars, on grounds of cost, was very unfortunate. One of the reasons why the contemplation of a building like the New Bodleian library at Oxford (1939) affords such limited pleasure is that its surface is not ashlar but only hammer-dressed and random-coursed Bladon hardstone, an uncouth country cousin by comparison, which consorts ill with its neighbours and its site. In recent years, however, owing to the invention of the electrically driven saws referred to above, the situation has changed completely. Large slabs of machine-sawn ashlar, not more than 4 ins. thick and sometimes as little as 2 ins., suitable for cladding, now cost less than rubblestone, which cannot normally be used in this way. Where the framework is of steel or ferro-concrete, it is both structurally and economically desirable that the 'skin' of stone should be as thin and as light as possible, with the labour of fixing also reduced as much as possible. Employed over very large areas machine-sawn ashlar can admittedly look monotonous, and often, therefore, architects like to introduce other finishes as well for the sake of variety; but generally speaking the large-scale return of ashlar to urban buildings is a development very much to be welcomed, because no other form of stonework achieves the dignity which, for a large public edifice, must be regarded as an essential requirement. In order to emphasize the non-structural character of stone cladding there is aesthetically much to be said for the use of straight vertical joints, as Londoners can see very well on Waterloo Bridge, an admirable achievement in concrete by Sir Giles Scott which tends to be underrated because of the memory of Rennie's bridge in stone.

Fine stone affords the opportunity for fine masoncraft: but various other factors can contribute to, or detract from, the quality of stone building. The size and scale of the individual pieces of stone are of great importance. In general, the larger the blocks, the greater the effect of monumentality. Among the oolites, Portland stone can be readily obtained in blocks 10 ft. long, 5 ft. wide and 4 ft. 6 ins. high, and now and again blocks of up to 15 ft. can be procured, not only at Portland but also at Guiting in the Cotswolds and elsewhere, although for limestone these sizes are exceptional. Granite can sometimes be quarried in immense blocks, which can have the effect of endowing quite a modest building with an unexpected impressiveness. An example is the church tower of Sennen in Cornwall, the most westerly in England. Perched upon its bleak, wind-swept hillside, it seems entirely right that this modest tower should have been constructed of large lumps of almost indestructible granite. The gritstones and other Northern sandstones tend also to be hewn in larger blocks than farther south, and here again the eye and the mind are satisfied, for the big blocks suggest strength and an ability the better to withstand the rigours of the climate. The sensation of greater size and strength which large blocks convey is, however, not necessarily and invariably an aesthetic advantage. Pugin indeed went so far as to assert that 'large stones destroy proportion';[1] and whereas this dictum cannot in my view be applied with any truth to large buildings designed in a Classical style, Pugin was certainly able to reinforce his point with drawings of masonry surrounding Gothic windows: the smaller stones look much better. I have myself seen a modest farm-building in a sheltered situation in Shropshire, constructed of blocks of Grinshill sandstone over 5 ft. long and 2 ft. high, dimensions that are quite uncomfortably large for such a purpose. The effect is one of monumentality where such a quality is inappropriate.

It is, on the other hand, undeniable that small stones and a profusion of mortar-joints usually lack dignity. One of the incidental reasons why the Blue Lias of Somerset is among the less attractive English limestones is that it can seldom be obtained except in thin pieces. Buildings in this stone accordingly tend to be over-coursed (*90b*).

The happy medium was attained, in this respect as in so many others, in the ashlared buildings of the Cotswolds, where the pieces of stone are small rather than large, yet seldom too small, and laid with a beautiful precision, as can be seen at Medford House, Mickleton (*83b*), by comparing the masonry of the house with that of the garden wall on the left. Absolutely level courses are the rule with ashlar—and one would certainly not wish it otherwise—but this does not mean that every block of stone should be of the same size. In 1870, owing to the decay of the sandstone, the tower of St. James's church at Taunton had to be rebuilt. Although the work was carefully done and, except at the crown, the design of the old tower was reproduced in every particular, the mistake was made of having all the blocks of stone cut to a pattern. As a result, the effect of a tower which is excellent both in design and colour, and entirely satisfying from a little distance, is marred on a close view by a somewhat 'dead' surface quality, the product of parallel mortar courses at absolutely regular intervals. A much more interesting effect is obtained, as the earlier builders were well aware, when the blocks of stone vary in size from course to course, the larger ones normally being laid at the base of the wall (*89*). This is in any case what common sense would dictate, since these were the heaviest blocks to lift. Now and again one finds a specially large stone introduced, stretching up through two courses. This is known as snecking or jumper-work, and is now recognized as a good method of obtaining interesting surface variation; but in the age of Wren and in the Georgian period this practice was not admissible for the most elegant buildings.[2]

1 *The True Principles of Pointed or Christian Architecture* (1841), p. 18.

2 W. J. Arkell, *Oxford Stone* (1947), p. 51. This fascinating book is, *inter alia*, a mine of information on the ways of handling English building stones.

Pointing

The beauty of stonework can also be enhanced, or quite seriously marred, by the choice of mortar; and disastrous mistakes have been made by some restorers in the process of repointing. The basis of mortar is coarse sand, which until about a century ago was mixed with slaked lime, a material which has now been very largely, although not always happily, superseded by Portland cement. The colour is dependent upon the choice of the sand or of the hard crushed stone which can be used as a substitute for it. In the best examples the tone and colour of the mortar are similar to those of the stone or a little lighter. Following the deplorable example of Wyatville, who repointed Windsor Castle with a mortar blackened with ashes, certain Victorian architects became addicted to the use of black mortar; buildings pointed in this funereal fashion were no doubt the appropriate repositories of that black-edged writing-paper to which bereaved Victorians were also so much attached. Black or very dark pointing is always ugly, and is scarcely ever found in England on old buildings.[1] On the other hand, an excessively light mortar can also be an artistic solecism since, as with a very dark mortar, the effect is to over-emphasize the individual stones of a wall at the expense of the whole. It is always a pleasure to find that trouble has been taken, by selecting the right-coloured sand, to match the mortar to the stone; in the South-West, for example, the use of a reddish mortar in conjunction with red sandstone is excellent. Mortar, in fact, should know its manners and not draw attention to itself. It is also necessary chemically that the composition of mortar should vary in accordance with the nature of the stone to which it is being applied.

Over-conspicuous pointing, even if correct in tone and colour, can be very disagreeable. At Madingley near Cambridge, the church has walls constructed of rubblestone harshly repointed to make a kind of vertical crazy-paving. The effect could hardly be more inept or undignified. A particular abomination of the last hundred years is what is known as ribbon-pointing, in which the hard-looking cement-mortar, often given a slight projection, especially at its lower edge (allegedly to help throw off the rain-water), is confined within two brutal trowel-lines. Employed in conjunction with the finer varieties of limestone and sandstone, this method of pointing, which is quite untraditional, can do

---

1 Dr. L. F. Salzman, in his *Building in England down to 1540* (1952), p. 153, quotes two entries from the Westminster accounts of 1532 relating to 'see cole [sea coal] . . . for making of black morter nec(essar)ie for the laying of Flynte', and 'xvj busshilles of Smythys Duste provided for blacke morter to be made of, requisite for the leying of Flynte'. He adds: 'I have come across no other reference to such blackening of mortar; presumably it was required for a special piece of knapped flintwork, where a uniform dark effect was required.' This remarkable book, to which many references will be made in subsequent chapters, is the *sine qua non* for all students of English building in the Middle Ages.

appalling damage to a building's appearance. In the North it may have rather more justi-fication, as a method of imposing a scheme of order upon a wall of rough and chunky rubblestone, as at Richmond (45b); but even here the eye is assailed by a harsh array of seemingly ruled lines which is anything but seductive.

In contrast to rubblestone, which requires a generous mortar-joint, ashlar looks best when the jointing is comparatively thin. It could be held that in Regency architecture, as for example in the Ketton stone facing of the New Court at St. John's College, Cam-bridge (1826–31) (45d), this preference for fine jointing over-reached itself, suggesting sometimes the precision of a machine; but in ashlar masonry mortar should never be allowed to spread over the arrises of the stones, blurring the crispness of their outlines. Unhappily, this is what one sometimes finds after a building has emerged from the attentions of restorers.

The repointing of an old wall must be done with mortar containing little or no cement, for strong cement is injurious to old stone. The Society for the Protection of Ancient Buildings recommends, because it is known to be safe and to set well, a mixture of six or seven parts of coarse clean sand to one part of lime, beaten up with water. To this may be added, if considered necessary, one part, at the most, of ordinary Portland cement.[1] The joints should be flush with the wall surface.

A curious practice which goes back to the Middle Ages is that known as galleting (sometimes galletting, or garreting, or garnetting): the insertion into the mortar courses, while still soft, of tiny pieces of stone or chips of flint, or even clinkers. *Galets* in French, from which the term derives, are little water-worn pebbles such as are found in the beds of streams or in the shingle of the sea-shore. But in England the meaning was extended to embrace the stone-mason's chippings and the flint-knapper's flakes. The purpose of galleting seems originally to have been structural. It was a method of strengthening broad courses of mortar, and making them more resistant to the weather; and where the under-side of a block of stone—or indeed of a course of bricks: early brickwork, at any rate in Essex, was sometimes treated in just the same way—might not be quite flat, the gallets could be used as miniature wedges or simply to reduce the thickness of what otherwise might have been a very wide mortar joint. Gallets were also employed on roofs, as in the Cotswolds; where the edges of adjacent stone slates were not quite parallel, a thin chipping of stone would be worked in underneath the joint, to prevent water seepage. And in Collyweston slating, thin flakes of stone called 'shales' were (and still are) sometimes inserted into lime mortar, to give additional protection, underneath the vertical joints of the slates and over the nail-heads. These do not show on the finished surface of the roof.

1 Another good working mixture is 10 parts of sand to 2 of lime to 1 of cement.

As a rule, however, galleting is purely ornamental, and employed thus, it is an excellent example of a local development. It occurs occasionally elsewhere, for instance in Yorkshire, but there are only two areas in which it is comparatively common: those parts of the counties of Surrey, Sussex and Kent lying between the North and the South Downs, together with a corner of East Hampshire (there is a lot at Selborne); and Norfolk. Both these are regions deficient in freestone. Gallets could never be used in conjunction with ashlar; the jointing of ashlar masonry is in any case too fine, but even were this not so, galleting is too rustic a process to consort with such elegance. Here and there, however, this unexpected practice can add interest and sparkle to a building's appearance, whether applied to the greensand stones of the South-East, as at Witley (*268*), or to the carstone of Norfolk, as at Heacham (*114*b), or carried out in shivers of flint, as on the Guildhall at Norwich. (The gallets at both Witley and Heacham are of the local ironstone.) When used in conjunction with random masonry, the gallets can look like little necklaces, strung over the building's surface.[1]

Several references will be made in later chapters to dry-stone walling: walls, that is, constructed with no mortar at all. Countless miles of boundary walls of this type are to be seen, principally in the North of England, and a fine sight they make. Considerable skill was needed to build in this fashion, and dry-stone walling is to-day virtually a lost craft. Such walls, if properly made, are extraordinarily durable. A party returning to the island of St. Kilda in 1958, twenty-eight years after its evacuation, found that the mortared stone walls of cottages only a hundred years old were already disintegrating rapidly, whereas the dry-stone walling was scarcely affected by the rigours of the climate.

Weathering

In a lecture delivered in Birmingham in the eighteen-eighties, entitled 'The Beauty of Life', William Morris asserted that 'the natural weathering of the surface of a building is beautiful and its loss disastrous'. Nevertheless, it cannot be denied that the condition of the stonework of many of our old buildings is a source of continual anxiety and expense to those responsible for their maintenance. Much has been written in the past about the visual charms of 'pleasing decay', but there comes a point in the life of many buildings when the decay of their stonework is far from pleasing, and may even make them unsafe. Few tasks can have been more difficult, or more tantalizing, than the selection of building

---

1 For interesting information on galleting, see Sir Owen Morshead's *Windsor Castle* (2nd ed., 1957), pp. 24–25.

stone. Even within a single quarry there may be startling variations in quality. Two pieces of stone may have the same visible characteristics and be of identical geological age, yet one will stand up well to centuries of English weather while the other decays. Nor are the hardness or softness of a stone reliable guides to its durability. Its chemical consistency plays a large part too. Quite soft varieties of freestone, in congenial surroundings, may weather remarkably well; whereas there are deposits of hard limestone running into many millions of tons which cannot be considered for building at all because of the certainty that with the first hard frost they would start to disintegrate.

Some varieties of otherwise excellent stone seem to grow 'tired' with age: Ham Hill stone does so after three or four centuries. It then splits and gives much trouble, as has been demonstrated in recent years at Montacute and on the old Grammar School building at Chard, Somerset. Bath stone is liable to show signs of 'fatigue' after as little as two hundred years, despite its other and more convenient property, which it shares with all limestones, of hardening on exposure. The reasons why some stones behave in this way are not completely understood; but although the growth of atmospheric pollution since the Industrial Revolution has placed a severe and sometimes disastrous burden on many kinds of stone, this is not the only cause of decay. In coastal areas seaborne salt can be a serious menace to stonework. The long-term consequences of frost action are another important factor in the weathering of all the sedimentary stones. Since water expands as it freezes and contracts as it thaws, stone which is very porous (such as Bath among the oolites, and many sandstones) is subjected to considerable internal strains during severe weather. It may be able to withstand the resultant damage for a long while; yet each time it is becoming structurally weaker, until ultimately it fails.

In some places, as will be seen in the chapters that follow, the only stone available locally was of defective quality and the certainty of gradual decay must have been realized from the outset. Elsewhere, as in the now notorious instance of the use of Headington and Wheatley freestone at Oxford in the seventeenth and eighteenth centuries, the weakness of the stone was not appreciated at the time, although here the mediaeval builders revealed a much surer judgment. Yet steps could be and often were taken to assist the chances of better preservation. With sandstones and limestones, it is normally most important that every block should be laid in its natural bed: that is to say, as it originally lay in the quarry. Only with Portland stone can this precaution sometimes be safely ignored. Because of the nature of its structure, a block set on its side will generally be far more vulnerable to wind, rain and frost.[1] This was widely but not invariably understood, and

1 A fact which it is no less important for the sculptor to heed than for the architect or builder. Cf. Alec Miller, *Stone and Marble Carving* (Alec Tiranti, 1948), p. 22: 'Any figure or decorative group in the round, if

when one sees a few individual stones badly weathered in what is otherwise a sound piece of walling, this is a likely explanation. In pre-mechanized days, when transport was slow, there was another reason besides the desirability of reducing the weight of the blocks for doing as much shaping as possible of freestones, whether limestones or sandstones, before they left the quarry; they were more easily worked. For when stone is first hewn out and is what the masons call 'green', it still holds its 'quarry sap', highly charged with dissolved mineral matter, and is often comparatively soft. Upon exposure to the atmosphere this evaporates, and only then does the stone become completely petrified.

The great enemy of most of the sedimentary rocks is pollution of the atmosphere. Nothing has been so fatal to the preservation of English stonework as the smoky air of industrialism. Factory fumes bring sulphur compounds into the air. These are converted into oxides of sulphur which, in combination with water, produce sulphuric acid, one of the strongest and most corrosive of the acids, all ready for the particles of soot and dust deposited in the stone to absorb. In time the stone, if of the sedimentary kind, will start to chip, crack, flake or crumble. Deterioration of stone has been very much more rapid in the past 150 years than at any time previously. Wood smoke did no harm at all. Now, for some sandstone and nearly all limestone buildings in towns, the sulphur-laden air means certain destruction, since even rain-water is changed into dilute sulphuric acid. Soot collects in places which are often difficult to reach; the higher parts of a building, usually the least accessible, are also the most vulnerable. All that can be done, before it gains too firm a hold, is to wash it off periodically, and at intervals of no more than twenty years in really smoky places, using only fine sprays of water and bristle brushes; this is not a cure, but it is undoubtedly a help. Great care should be taken to remove only the soot and the grime, and not to mar in any way the patina of age or the naturally weathered surface of the stone which lies under the grime.

In recent years, following an initiative first taken on a large scale in the nineteen-fifties in Paris, many public buildings and monuments have been cleaned in England, notably in London and at Oxford and Cambridge. The cleaning of St. Paul's Cathedral, for the first time in more than two and a half centuries, restored to it the pristine whiteness which Wren intended his great building to have. Only cold water was used: on the west front alone, seven million gallons of it. In some places the incrustations of grime were fully an inch thick, yet such is the endurance of Portland stone that even the carved ornamentation

to be placed in the open air, should be *base bedded*, i.e. the strata of the deposit should be horizontal, or as nearly so as may be. . . . If *face bedded*, i.e. with the strata upright, there is a danger of rain soaking down the softer strata and a frost then flaking the stone. Portland stone has much less clearly marked deposit beds, but even this stone is best used base bedded.'

two hundred feet up on the towers was found to be in surprisingly good condition. Much finely sculptured detail, virtually invisible for several generations, can now be enjoyed again, and despite the initial hesitations of some architectural critics on aesthetic grounds, there can be no doubt that the 'new revelation' of St. Paul's has given great pleasure, not least in the evenings when it is floodlit. The doubts stemmed from the fact, which cannot be disputed, that, as indicated on page 68, the effects of light and shade produced in Portland stone by the juxtaposition of rain-washed and soot-laden surfaces have considerable aesthetic value. But unfortunately grime also settles on places where, so far from being artistically welcome, it is only an eyesore (46c). Nevertheless, it should not now be taken for granted that all stonework, even all limestone, should be cleaned without question. Sometimes a solitary cleaned building can become a very bad neighbour, most glaringly where it is one house in a terrace. For terraces it should be all or none.

Certain sandstones, notably the strong close-grained siliceous sandstones from the Millstone Grit, such as Darley Dale and Bramley Fall, stand up to the smoky atmosphere of industrial cities better than any limestones, even Portland, and so do the granites. But in such conditions these stones soon become jet-black. The grime clings to the slightly rough, compact surface and is very difficult to remove; so the task is seldom attempted. To many eyes there must be something rather forbidding about the black stone buildings of the industrial towns of Lancashire and the West Riding. Yet they have their admirers. One of our best writers on Lancashire[1] describes the thousands of chimneys of the Manchester area with their pall of smoke which hangs suspended in the humid atmosphere, then 'descends again to clothe the buildings with a thick deposit of soot, of the even texture of black cloth. The effect upon stone buildings', he says, 'is one of sombre dignity, far pleasanter to the eye than when it falls on those built of "smoke-resisting" material', and looking 'even more beautiful when outlined by a sprinkling of freshly-fallen snow'.

To most people, nevertheless, stone will look best in a comparatively smoke-free atmosphere, in which its myriad variations of colour and texture can be seen and enjoyed to the full. At first, stone buildings always improve with natural weathering, which helps them to settle into their landscape or townscape. But about the more advanced stages of weathering taste has fortunately changed considerably in the present century. Over and over again, in English water-colours of the eighteenth and nineteenth centuries, old buildings are represented, and with evident relish, in a condition of partial disintegration, martyrs to the over-ardent embraces of ivy and creepers. Nathaniel Hawthorne, visiting the colleges of Oxford in 1856, noted that 'if you strike one of the old walls with a stick,

1 Peter Fleetwood-Hesketh, *Murray's Lancashire Architectural Guide* (1955), p. 159.

a portion of it comes powdering down', and went on to observe that 'the effect of this decay is very picturesque, and is especially striking on edifices of classic architecture, greatly enriching the Grecian columns, which look so cold when the outlines are hard and distinct'.[1] To-day the only possible inference to be drawn from this is that Hawthorne, however estimable in other ways, did not care about architecture. For in classical buildings above all the eye demands 'that neatness in the joints between the stones, and that sharpness in the edges of the mouldings' at which John Wood specifically aimed, in Bath, during the reign of George II. Sometimes this leaves no alternative to a complete refacing, as a number of the Oxford colleges have in the past thirty years come to recognize. Time, it has been said, is a benefactor to stone buildings, because it softens their profiles and mellows their tones. This does not mean that profiles can be allowed to become blurred, nor mellowness to decline into mouldiness.

[1] Quoted by W. J. Arkell in *Oxford Stone*, p. 151.

3

LIMESTONE

It would be no exaggeration to say that at least nine out of every ten stone or stone-faced buildings in England are either of limestone or sandstone, and if flint is left out of the reckoning, the proportion would be more like ninety-nine out of every hundred. In fact, the only other kinds of stone which have been used for building to any appreciable extent are granite and slate, both of which until a century ago were confined to very limited areas. But limestone and sandstone are very general terms, demanding qualification. Both are applied to rocks of many geological ages, differing greatly in character; both are used in pure as well as in very impure forms; it is possible to find both in a single quarry; and in some places it would be extremely difficult by eye alone to distinguish with certainty between them. Moreover, there are varieties of stone which partake of limestone and sandstone characteristics in about equal proportions, and which are accordingly described sometimes as calcareous sandstones, sometimes as sandy limestones. In a book of the present compass there is neither the space nor, it may be felt, the necessity to particularize too much about individual varieties of stone; but it is only proper to state at the outset that some of the generalizations in this and the following chapter would require considerable qualifications in a larger and more detailed work or in one of more specifically geological concern. The problem of how best to present a clear and coherent picture of English limestone and of English sandstone in a chapter apiece is not simple.

They share one characteristic of fundamental importance: both are what are known as sedimentary rocks. That is to say, the matter of which they are composed, whether mineral, chemical or organic, often originated elsewhere and was generally transported and deposited by the action of water; sometimes by wind. The significance of this in relation to building material is that these deposits were accumulated through the ages in layers. Hence sedimentary rocks are usually stratified; and some of their strata are much better for building purposes than others.

Limestones consist basically of calcium carbonate, which may occur in various forms. Some limestones are composed almost entirely of shell fragments or other skeletal remains of fossil animal life. The individual pieces may be large enough to be easily recognized or so small that an electron microscope is needed to identify them. The limy incrustations of primitive algae (seaweeds, etc.) produce other limestones; and in addition to these rocks of organic origin limestone may be formed by the direct chemical precipitation of calcium carbonate, which occurs in certain circumstances on the floors of seas and lakes. When it consists of rounded grains resembling the hard roe of a herring, it is known as oolitic limestone. Great quantities of this kind of limestone were formed during the Jurassic period.

In some rocks, the combined carbonate of lime and magnesium is present; these are known as magnesian limestones or dolomites. Most limestones contain impurities, principally sand grains or mud particles: the amounts vary considerably. Certain varieties consist of hard, compact rock; for example some of the carboniferous limestones, in which the calcium carbonate occurs in crystalline form. On the other hand, chalk, one of the purest forms of limestone, is generally soft.

Travelling backwards through time, our principal building limestones are to be found in four geological systems:

System	Age in million years (approx.)	Principal Stones
Cretaceous	70–140	Chalk (including Clunch) and some Ragstones
Jurassic	140–195	Oolitic and Liassic Limestones
Permian	225–280	Magnesian Limestones (Dolomites)
Carboniferous	280–345	Carboniferous Limestones

Dates in the above table, as elsewhere in this book, are taken from the Geological Society's Phanerozoic Time-Scale, 1964, which differs a little from that propounded by the late Professor Holmes, which previously commanded general acceptance.[1] Limestones older and younger than these, notably the Devonian limestones of the South-West (345–395 million years approx.), have also been employed for building to a limited extent. It is from the youngest to the oldest that we shall now proceed.

1 The ages of rocks are calculated from the known rates of radioactive decay of certain minerals in their composition. The processes are highly complicated, but refinements of technique in recent years have enabled the present time-scale to be propounded. As methods are still further improved, slight modifications are to be expected from time to time.

The Youngest English Limestones

Highest in the geological series come the alluvial and other recent deposits, products of the last million years, of which the most important areas in England are the fen lands to the south of the Wash, around the Humber and the Yorkshire Ouse, and in the Isle of Athelney; Romney Marsh; and the Norfolk Broads. The fens were formerly swamps; the marsh was covered by the sea. These, like the glacial deposits of the Ice Age, include material that is vitally important nowadays for concrete aggregate, but contain no building stone whatsoever.

Next come two regions underlain by rocks of the Tertiary Age (2–70 million years old), known as the London Basin and the Hampshire Basin. The latter covers the southern part of Hampshire with the adjoining parts of Sussex and Dorset, and the northern half of the Isle of Wight. The London Basin is much larger, embracing the whole of the Kennet-Thames valley from Newbury to Southend, part of Thanet, most of Essex, and the eastern parts of Suffolk and Norfolk other than the Broads. These areas mainly consist of clays, sands and gravels. The clays are often admirable for brickmaking, but the London Basin yields very little stone. Scattered here and there are blocks of rugged sarsen, while near the Essex and Suffolk shores are septarian nodules: both these will be referred to later. The only limestone is a hard, rough, slightly purplish-brown material of shelly consistency known as Coralline Crag, which is found in very small quantities close to the Suffolk coast south of Aldeburgh. It is like a frozen sponge. This stone was formerly used at Aldeburgh, Orford and inland as far as Framlingham, and can still be seen at all these places. Good examples are the towers (only) of the churches at Chillesford and Wantisden.

Much more important in our architectural history are the freshwater limestones of the Hampshire Basin, quarried in the Isle of Wight. Known generically as Bembridge limestone, they include two varieties which have been useful to the builder.

Quarr stone has an attractive 'feather-bed' appearance, produced by vast quantities of tiny shell-fragments which were deposited in fresh water. Its colour is usually whitish-grey, and large blocks could be obtained. It was mainly used in the Isle of Wight, the Hampshire Basin and Sussex. Both the Romans and the Normans availed themselves of it for parts of Porchester Castle; the Saxons for the dressings of many small churches; the Normans at Winchester and Chichester Cathedrals, Romsey and Titchfield Abbeys, Christchurch and Lewes Priories and elsewhere. It is also to be seen in the neighbourhood of Canterbury and in the White Tower at the Tower of London.

Binstead stone has a more crushed appearance and no recognizable fragments of fossil shells, but was also available in large blocks. Unlike Quarr stone it embodies a considerable quantity of iron, which on exposure sometimes changes its naturally creamy colour to a rich dark russet. Long ago Binstead stone was also in great demand in Hampshire and West Sussex. It was used in the abbeys of Beaulieu and Netley, and much of Southampton. It can be seen to great advantage at Winchester College, which is largely built of it. Both these stones, but especially Quarr, are in evidence on the front of the Church House in the Close (73a) together with some Caen, and Portland for the nineteenth-century porch. Much of this masonry was taken from older buildings and re-used.

The unexpected feature of both these Isle of Wight Tertiary limestones is their hardness; they weather very well. Although not suitable for mouldings, and still less so for carved ornamentation, they were excellent for plain ashlar. The past tense is necessary because these limestones were more or less worked out before the end of the Middle Ages, Quarr probably as early as the middle of the fourteenth century.[1]

Chalk

To some it may come as a surprise to learn that chalk has been widely used in England as a building stone. In a broken down or pulverised form it is no longer a stone, and this will be referred to in a later chapter. Chalk also yields lime and formerly provided a useful rubble core for walls faced with stronger materials, but only when employed in solid blocks does it qualify as a building stone. In its harder varieties, it is in some areas known also as clunch. This term should properly be restricted to the more compacted type of chalk, mainly found in Cambridgeshire; but it is not rare to find it applied less specifically to any type of chalk used for building.[2]

The Chalk, which extends through much of northern France, Germany and beyond, is a geological formation finding expression in important landscape features in eastern and southern England. The North and South Downs, the downs of Hampshire, Berkshire, Wiltshire and Dorset, the cliffs of Devon at Beer, the Chilterns, the Gogmagogs, the Wolds of Lincolnshire and Yorkshire: all these are chalk. Chalk country is therefore largely

1 For a detailed account of Quarr stone, see F. W. Anderson and R. N. Quirk in *Mediaeval Archaeology*, vol. 8, 1964 (1965), pp. 115–117.

2 On the Nottinghamshire-Derbyshire-South Yorkshire coalfield 'clunch' has quite a different meaning; here it is used to describe certain sandstones and shales (not suitable for building) which occur in the Coal Measures.

upland country; but not entirely so, for the chalk also underlies large parts of Norfolk and Suffolk. Not all these regions have found chalk equally serviceable as an all-weather building material. In Kent, the chalk is mostly too porous to be of much use for this purpose, but it could be worked in certain places at the foot of the North Downs, and occasionally was. In Surrey, although the base of the east face of Guildford Castle is chalkstone and later it provided most of the dressings at Loseley House, it is not often seen externally; inside, it occurs at a number of old churches as the material of the arcades, including some, such as Stoke d'Abernon, Pyrford and Godalming, which are away from the Chalk outcrop. Within the total thickness of the chalk there are some harder, more compact beds. These have been exploited in parts of Dorset and Wiltshire, along the west side of Berkshire, and also in western Norfolk. The counties which have probably made the most use of chalk (as distinct from flints found in the chalk) for external building purposes are Devon and Dorset, Wiltshire, Hampshire and Berkshire, Hertfordshire and Bedfordshire, Cambridgeshire, Norfolk, Lincolnshire and the East Riding of Yorkshire. A little can be found in most of the counties adjacent to these, and notably in the north-western corner of Essex; a good deal can be seen in the fine church at Saffron Walden. The last place in England at which chalk was dug regularly for building was Burwell in Cambridgeshire, where the large church is also of this material; but since 1962 even this pit has been closed.

Chalk was easily quarried, sometimes in blocks of considerable size, which were generally left for two or three years to dry out. It has been described as the whitest of all English stones, and sometimes it is: for unadulterated chalk consists of over 95% calcium carbonate, and is therefore a limestone of exceptional purity. But muddy impurities and the presence of tiny grains of other minerals, such as quartz, glauconite and nodules of iron pyrites often produce tinges of other colours, including cream, yellowish and greenish grey, and even pink. In the neighbourhood of Hunstanton and across the Wash in Lincolnshire there is, below the white, a somewhat older layer, 3–4 ft. thick, of red chalk. In and around Old Hunstanton a cottage wall will here and there exhibit white and red chalk with brown carstone in an unexpected *pot-pourri*.

Chalk is, by comparison with most other stones, usually so soft and compact that it is possible with squared blocks to achieve both an ashlar surface and very fine jointing (73c). This, combined with its comparative lightness, rendered it a useful material in the construction of Gothic vaults, of which Westminster Abbey furnishes an excellent example. It is also a stone which readily lends itself to elaborate carving. Aesthetically, this was one of its drawbacks; it could be worked with such facility that it offered an almost irresistible temptation to the carvers to be over-elaborate and finicky, as can be seen in Bishop Alcock's chapel in Ely Cathedral and even in the much earlier Lady Chapel. The famous wall arcade with which this building was enriched was shockingly smashed by iconoclasts at the time of the Reformation, but much of the foliage carving survives, and it is in truth, with its multitude of small piercings, a little too reminiscent of the parsley bed.

It is significant that all this carving was internal; exposed to the weather, chalk has always, because of its perishability, been prone to give trouble. The quoins at The Vyne, near Basingstoke, (245a) have decayed so badly that some have had to be renewed in a more durable stone. At Legbourne near Louth, the walls of the chalk-built church are so soft that without difficulty one can (although I hasten to add that one should not) pick pieces out. Those who like myself have long cherished the hope, vain as they know it to be, that one day people will start withholding their custom from buildings which are eyesores, be they hotels, restaurants, cafés, shops or merely filling stations, may be interested to learn that at Cambridge there was a time when this actually occurred. Christ's College was originally built, at the beginning of the sixteenth century, of clunch and brick in alternating courses; by the end of the following century, its walls had acquired so repellent an aspect that, according to that excellent authority John Willis Clark, people were deterred from entering their sons at this college.

Christ's was by no means the only Cambridge college to have been partly built of clunch. In fact, according to Mr. Donovan Purcell, nearly all the city's pre-1500 stone buildings were of this material, although most of them had later to be faced with ashlared limestone or brick, or rendered. Two good examples that can still be seen are the south wall of the hall at Peterhouse and the high wall running down to the Cam between King's and Clare Colleges.[1] The closest chalk-pits were to the south-east of the city, at Cherry Hinton. Others were to the south-west, at Eversden, Haslingfield and Barrington, and to the north-east, at Reach as well as Burwell. Isleham, on the edge of the Fens, also had important quarries.

In a smoky atmosphere, chalk would be practically certain to disintegrate within a few decades. Another danger is from frost. Yet, widely scattered over eastern and southern England, buildings in this material survive; a good many may be seen for instance in the country around Salisbury. Although the large majority are only cottages, dozens of churches can still show chalk not only in their internal walls, arcades and capitals, but outside too. It was also used for houses as important as Ashdown in Berkshire (where only the dressings are of harder stone) and Sawston Hall in Cambridgeshire (in conjunction with brown rubble and some oolite). How, it may be asked, have they lasted? The answer would appear to be a compound of good luck, careful building and extra protection on the outer face. It is likely to last better if used in combination with some stronger

1 Both illustrated in *Cambridge Stone* by Donovan Purcell (1967).

material, such as oolitic limestone, flint or brick, which can be brought into service at
the most exposed places; and many examples of such combinations survive. Above all, it
must not be allowed to remain for long periods in a state of dampness. A good base of a
tougher stone is a great asset, as at the little Jacobean school-house at Uffington in Berkshire (73b and c). Generously overhanging eaves are also desirable: on chalk buildings
these will frequently be of thatch. Coatings of limewash and plaster,[1] and especially of
cement and pebble-dash, are artistically less welcome, yet all have had to be used for
protective purposes; and an external facing of brick or stone, later than the original
building, is still by no means rare. If no special precautions are taken, chalk may still
continue in quite good condition, as at Uffington, where much of the village is built of it,
dug from the Downs a mile or two to the south. But here, as in parts of Yorkshire, the
beds are hard; more often the chalk would crumble away after only a few decades.

England's best known chalk, widely used all through the Middle Ages even for buildings as eminent as Windsor Castle and Westminster Abbey, came from Totternhoe, on a
spur of the Chilterns to the west of Dunstable. Totternhoe stone is a hard chalk of gritty
texture, usually greyish or greenish white. Like all the best building chalk, it comes from
the stratum known as the Lower Chalk. As it was the only local stone of any value for
many miles around, it was used for great houses like Woburn Abbey and Ashridge as
well as for smaller houses, the west front of Dunstable Priory Church and many parish
churches in Bedfordshire and Hertfordshire. It can be seen to perfection in the north
arcade of the church at Eaton Bray, the next village to Totternhoe; this exquisite early
thirteenth-century design, stemming straight from Wells, shows us of what this stone is
capable. Yet although it hardens somewhat with exposure, when used externally it generally weathers badly, as is evident at Southill. Here Henry Holland employed it as a facing
material over yellow stock brick; it has given a great deal of trouble and parts of the house
are now faced with cement, while other portions have recently been patched with the
somewhat more durable stone from Burwell. This Cambridgeshire clunch was also used
to replace Totternhoe a few years ago on the lower storey of the west front at Woburn.
With the improvements in transport in the first half of the nineteenth century the Totternhoe quarries, which were partly underground, were abandoned. Chalk-stone almost identical with it occurs in western Norfolk and near Louth on the Lincolnshire Wolds, where
many churches are built of it. Farther up the coast it appears again at Flamborough.

On the other side of the oolitic limestone belt, it is only in the South-West that chalk

---

[1] At Sawston Hall, some at least of the clunch rubble portions were originally plastered over, but much of
this protective coat has since fallen off. Ashdown House has needed protection on the sides facing the prevailing winds.

has been used for building; but at Beer in the eastern corner of Devon there is a hard shelly chalk-stone with many minute shell fragments yielding a gritty texture, which is somewhat younger than Totternhoe, and has probably transcended all these in importance. Here too much of the stone had to be mined, but it was conveniently situated close to the sea, so could be loaded on to ships without excessive difficulty. Especially in the fifteenth and early sixteenth centuries it was used in many of the churches of east Devon and west Dorset. Already in the fourteenth century it had been employed extensively for Exeter Cathedral, where the nearly white walls of Beer stone above the arcades contrast strikingly with the greyish piers of unpolished Purbeck, the yellow bosses and the coarse sandstone infilling of the vaulting. Internally this was, and indeed could still be, a very useful stone, and in the clean country air it can also be quite satisfactory out of doors. In many instances, however, it has not weathered well, especially on south-and west-facing walls and in towns, and since Tudor times has only been used very intermittently; the reopening of one of the Beer quarries a few years ago was unfortunately short-lived.

Kentish Ragstone

Very different from any of the foregoing, but also a product of the Cretaceous system and therefore one of the 'young' limestones, is Kentish Ragstone. Rag or ragstone is a generic term applied to any stone of hard or coarse texture that is not a freestone; and although Kentish rag includes some sandy patches which do not answer to this description, its general character is rough, brittle and difficult to work: even squared blocks can only be obtained with difficulty. It does not readily lend itself to fine dressing and is sometimes used only for the infilling of a wall, with some other and less intractable material introduced for the facing.

Nevertheless, because of the scarcity of good stone in the South-East, Kentish rag, obtained from the Hythe Beds division of the Lower Greensand, is one of the most familiar building materials not only in Kent but in neighbouring counties as well. It was quarried at Hythe and Sandgate, and also at Basted and Offham, south and south-east of Wrotham; but the principal quarries were around Maidstone, whence shipment in barges down the Medway presented no difficulty. It is not therefore rare in south-east Essex, and was carried up the Thames at least as far as Windsor and Eton. Kentish rag has had a very long history, for the Romans availed themselves of it for London's walls; and this stone was more in demand than any other in mediaeval London, not only for churches and for a few secular buildings such as the White Tower of London (which is of rag with Caen stone dressings), but also for engineering works such as river walls.

The usual ragstone masonry, as can be seen at Rochester Castle, Old Soar at Plaxtol, and at many Kent churches, is uncoursed, irregularly bonded and rubbly. Unfortunately, especially in the London area, where it was a favourite building stone for Victorian churches, the uneven surfaces of ragstone buildings are all too liable to harbour dirt, which does not add to their attractiveness; but sometimes it can be a real pleasure, as on the remarkably well preserved West Gate at Canterbury. No better example of Kentish ragstone exists than the great house of Knole. The Jacobean portions show, in the window-frames, string courses, gable copings and finials, that the stone was capable, if carefully chosen, of a good finish; but the quoins are very roughly dressed, the body of the walls is merely rubble, and the covering of the roofs is not stone at all but tiles, while the chimney-stacks are everywhere of brick. The stonework at Knole is not reliable: now and again a few pieces disintegrate, so that there is a good deal of patching. Yet these venerable grey walls with their coarse texture are a source of considerable pleasure; they may lack elegance, but few other buildings in south-eastern England impart such a sense of sturdy independence (73d).

Oolite

Fanning outwards from London beyond the Chiltern hills, which, since they are gently tilted towards the Lower Thames basin, have their escarpments facing away from the capital, we reach a low-lying region composed mainly of heavy clays and soft sands, of which the Vale of Aylesbury is typical. Beyond this zone of lush grassland and heavy tillage we are on the uplands again. As this second line of hills is also tilted towards London, the change from vale to upland may be scarcely perceptible to anyone approaching from this direction. But from Chipping Sodbury, Cheltenham or Broadway, the line of flat-topped hills dominates every eastward-facing view; for to reach any of these places, we shall have had to cross that famous 'limestone belt' to which several references have already been made.

We have now passed from the Cretaceous to the geologically older Jurassic system, which includes thick layers of clay and some limestones quite unsuitable for building. Most of the serviceable stones are contained within two strands, the Oolitic and the Liassic. The former is generally the harder and more resistant, and much the more useful to the builder. The latter, below and outcropping to the west and north-west of it, is more variable and yields a far more broken type of landscape, with many small isolated hills, like Churchdown and Dumbleton, as well as some larger ones like Bredon and Ebrington, which are of Lias capped with Inferior Oolite. But together they run—from

Lyme Bay on the Channel coast to the North Sea between Filey and Redcar. They make a great ogee curve over three hundred miles long, interrupted only at a few points towards its two ends.

In so far as the term 'limestone belt' may suggest a clearly defined band of approximately uniform width, it is an over-simplification. In Dorset, with the southern half of the Isle of Purbeck as a detached outlier, the Jurassic outcrop follows an erratic and serpentine course, but in east Somerset it broadens out and for a while runs due north. In central Somerset the Lower Lias also runs off at a tangent, to reach the shore of Bridgwater Bay. Once across the Bristol Avon into Gloucestershire it expands into the Cotswolds, and south-east of Cheltenham the region of good building stone attains its greatest width. Through the shires of Oxford, Northampton and Huntingdon its direction continues to be north-east, and between Market Harborough and St. Ives the belt is still broader than in the Cotswolds, but contains much that is useless for building. Then for the second time, on reaching Rutland, it turns north, narrowing beyond Lincoln, and still more on the other side of the Humber; across the centre of the East Riding the Lias is no more than a few hundred yards wide, and for a while the Oolite disappears altogether, under the Chalk. Only in the North Riding does it broaden again, and by this time the best Jurassic stone is sandstone rather than limestone. Almost nothing is simple in the geology of England, and the course of the Oolite and the Lias is no exception. But a 'belt' of a kind there certainly is; and the term, so widely accepted, seems far too useful to jettison.

Except in Dorset and Wiltshire, the oolites most suitable for building belong to the two strata of rocks known as the Middle, or Great, and the Lower, or Inferior, Oolite.[1] The tendency, not invariable but in some places strongly marked, is for the Inferior Oolites to have more iron in them; and the proportion of oxide of iron present is the main determinant of the colour of limestone. The oolite colours vary considerably, and include some surprises, such as the quite strong pink of some Ketton stone and considerable patches of blue, as well as some pink, in Weatherbed Ancaster and in Clipsham. But the familiar colours range from silver-grey (which some may think the loveliest) through creamy white to many shades of buff, pale yellow and brown. Limestones cannot rival sandstones in the multitude of small colour variations displayed within limited areas, but their colouring is seldom absolutely uniform. Now and again there will be welcome intrusions, such as the brown flecks that dot the creamy white surface of some

---

1 The terminology here is unfortunately confusing. Used generally, 'oolite' refers to a particular type of limestone, as already defined on p. 59. Employed as a proper noun, the reference is to the rocks from these two strata, not all of which, disobligingly enough, are oolitic. The usage throughout this book is in the former sense, unless qualified by the words 'Great' or 'Inferior'. There is no Upper, or Superior, Oolite.

Hardwhite Ancaster; and more frequently there will be changes wrought by the weather. Interesting textures can be produced, notably in Portland stone, through some of the fossil shells weathering more slowly than the rest of the surface. Particularly striking, too, is the behaviour of Portland in smoky cities; in protected places, and on north and east-facing walls, this stone will tend to collect soot and turn black, but on surfaces exposed to the prevailing winds, constantly washed by rain, it will become bleached to an almost snowy white.

Portland stone is not only the king of the oolites; the middle bed of the Portland stone formation known as Whitbed, with its close grain and unusually even texture, is arguably the finest building stone in England. The finest but not, let it be added, the most beautiful: there are many who find in the close grain and unvarying texture of the Whitbed and of the geologically very similar Basebed a certain dullness, even deadness. For textural interest the coarser and more shelly Roach, from the topmost of the three Portland beds, is actually preferable. Considering the three beds together, however, there can be no doubt that Portland stone is in several respects an uncharacteristic member of the group which we are now considering.

In the first place, like Purbeck-Portland and Chilmark but unlike any other stones of importance in this group, it belongs to the most recent end of the Jurassic formation, at which the ooliths themselves (the rounded granules of carbonate of lime) are often too small to be easily distinguished by the naked eye. Then, unlike most English stones, the oolites included, Portland has not won its great reputation primarily on the strength of its local achievements. This is partly due to the accident of geography. If we think of Bath or the Cotswolds, the Stamford area or Derbyshire, the names of famous local quarries spring at once to mind, quarries to which all of them owe, more perhaps than to any other single factor, their present identity. But the Isle of Portland is a bleak and treeless peninsula, upon which nobody was tempted to build even a monastery. Its stone was known to the Romans and worked intermittently throughout the Middle Ages: in 1303 one barge-load was sent to Exeter, and in the 1340s some was used in London; but local requirements long remained modest. And although the situation of the quarries close to the sea might have been regarded as favourable to export, as was for long the case with Purbeck, there was another reason for the comparative neglect of this stone before the seventeenth century: the difficulty of working it. Portland is obtainable, as already noted (p. 49), in unusually large blocks; but before the time of the Stuarts so hard a stone could only be cut very slowly and laboriously. With the introduction of frame-saws and water power, and later steam power, large-scale cutting at last became a practical possibility. It was not therefore until the reign of Charles II that Portland stone really came into its own, and its fame was then made not in Dorset but in London. Wren, who was particularly attracted to this stone because of the size of the blocks available, used over a million tons of it for St. Paul's and for parts of many of his City churches. Since Wren's day it has been employed, generally as a facing material, in most of our cities and large towns.[1]

The third reason why Portland is an uncharacteristic member of the limestone group is that, despite its splendid properties, it is not a stone which looks well everywhere on the Jurassic belt. Although one can make a few reservations, it is broadly speaking true to say that, whereas 'foreign' stones such as granites or gritstones always look out of place if introduced into the limestone areas (which never occurred until the last century), the products of the oolitic quarries can be moved through the limestone region with complete aesthetic propriety. Clipsham stone for example looks quite in keeping eighty miles away at Oxford, where in fact it is now being used far more than any other. From this dictum, however, Portland must be firmly excepted. The reason for this is its whiteness. Creamy white or buff when quarried, most Portland stone becomes still whiter when washed by rain, which in England means in any exposed situation facing south or west. Portland, in fact, unlike any other limestone, achieves its most striking effects not by 'melting into the landscape' nor 'growing out of the soil' but by contrast. Hence, while in other limestone regions it would often be out of place, its transportation into alien districts is not only acceptable but often very welcome. With the exception of the Provost's House at Trinity College, all the principal Georgian buildings in Dublin are faced partly or entirely with Portland stone, and the manner in which these are contrasted with what is otherwise a city of brick is immensely effective. London, when Canaletto painted her in 1746 from the river terrace of Richmond House, must have been one of the most beautiful cities in Europe, and remarkable above all for her skyline. Grouped around the great dome of St. Paul's, the artist depicted no fewer than thirty-six steeples, and these were not all. Some were of wood, sheathed in silver-grey lead, but many, including all the finest, were entirely of Portland stone; and although London has long been predominantly a city of brick, it is to this stone, far more than to any other material, that she owes her particular character.

Portland stone can certainly look extremely well when used for the dressings of a red brick building, above all when the building is a large one, as can be seen to striking effect in Wren's part of Hampton Court, where each material seems to enhance the brilliance of the other (239c). It can also occasionally be found in combination with warmer-

---

1 Portland stone was also used throughout the Colonial period in Virginia for such features as flights of steps, doorways, sills, keystones, parapets and chimney-stack caps, while a little farther north it provided some at least of the marker stones of the Mason-Dixon line.

5 + P.E.B.

tinted limestones: Oxford now has two examples. At C. R. Cockerell's Ashmolean Museum (1841–48) the contrast between the rather yellow Box Ground Bath stone and the white Portland dressings may be felt to be somewhat excessive, but Christ Church library, since the refacing of 1962–63, is a delight. Designed in 1716 by the amateur architect Dr. George Clarke, this library was built mainly of Headington stone but with Taynton for the ornamental parts: capitals, cornice modillions and the like. The colour contrast had practically disappeared under very bad decay. Now Clipsham stone replaces the Taynton and Portland the Headington, and Oxford has recovered a building of massive authority and distinction, avowedly inspired by Michelangelo's Capitoline Palace in Rome. On the principal front at Petworth, again, the Portland stone centrepiece and dressings effectively enhance, by contrast, the principal walling stone, which is a local greensand.[1] But because it is so conspicuous, Portland stone should only be introduced, whether for dressings or, still more emphatically, as a complete facing material, on buildings with some claim to distinction. Moreover, a single small building in a street, if fronted with this stone, tends to 'jump' uncomfortably. In short, admirable as it is, and particularly suitable for buildings of imposing scale and proportions because of the size of its blocks, it is at least arguable that from the artistic standpoint Portland stone has been used to excess, especially within the present century. The reason no doubt is mainly practical: no other English limestone stands up nearly so successfully to the polluted atmosphere of industrial towns as Portland, if carefully selected, and no other English stone of any kind lends itself better, if indeed as well, to the achievement of smooth-sawn ashlar, crisp arrises and finely finished dressings. Needless to say its use to-day is only as a facing material. A typical block, sawn and rubbed, will be 30 ins. high and 4 ins. thick. Several quarries are active. For economic reasons the overburden, which may be as much as thirty-five feet, cannot now be discarded. This is crushed for lime (used in aggregates) or road-metal.

To most people Purbeck stone means the so-called 'marble', which enjoyed immense

1 The most illustrious example of the use of warm-tinted stone as a foil to the cool brilliance of Portland was the Banqueting House in Whitehall (1619–22). Inigo Jones employed 'Oxfordshire stone cutt into Rustique' for the facing (over brick) of the base storey and 'Northtonshire (sic) stone cutt in rustique' for the upper ranges, 55 ft. high. The former was Headington, the latter Duston from Northamptonshire (see p. 121). All the 'ornaments'—columns and pilasters, entablature (with rich frieze) and roof balustrade—were of Portland, as they still are: so far as is known the first use of this stone in London. The accounts (1633: Public Record Office, E 351/3391) include a big item, £712 19s. 2d., for the building of a 'new Peere in the Isle of Portland', and more for 'making a new cartwaye at Portland Quarry for the more easy conveyance of stone to the Peere for the use of the said building'. It is a great pity that, on grounds of superior durability, this tone and colour contrast were later lost by refacing the whole of the west and east elevations with Portland stone. The base storey was so treated in 1773; the rest by Soane in 1829.

fame in the thirteenth century and can still be worked when required. This will be considered in Chapter 7. But there are many other seams of Purbeck, falling geologically into two main groups. The deeper, only accessible at St. Aldhelm's Head and along the southern coastline, is of the same age as the Portland limestone. It is a fine-textured oolite with few shells, very similar to Portland Whitbed but not so white and less tractable. This is known as Purbeck-Portland stone and is said to stand up to the weather even better than Portland itself; but since it costs a lot more to quarry it is no longer worked, although supplies are unlimited. At Winspit, a little to the east of St. Aldhelm's Head, it was mined; the shafts inclined downwards towards the sea.

The quarries of Purbeck stone proper (seven of which were still working on a small scale in 1969) are all in the hilly district to the south of Corfe Castle and to the west of Swanage. The very shelly Langton freestone can provide a good hard ashlar, and so could the seam known as Bottom Bed Burr, no longer obtainable. Spangle-bed Purbeck is a lovely pearl-grey, fossiliferous stone which will take a polish and is in demand for memorial tablets and the like. The Purbeck quarries have also produced admirable roofing slates (see pp. 105–106) and fine paving stones: a notably good example of the latter, for which a new quarry was specially opened, is provided by the floor of the choir and sanctuary of Guildford Cathedral.

Most of these varieties show quite a warm colour (cream to pale gold) at the quarry, but they quickly turn to grey on weathering. Between Swanage and Dorchester there is a charming group of gentle grey houses that do honour to this noble stone. Portesham stone from near Abbotsbury, another Dorset oolite, employed for Athelhampton Hall, has long ceased to be quarried. So has the Inferior Oolite known as Sherborne Building Stone, the principal material of that attractive town.

Thirty-two miles due north of the Isle of Purbeck, and in Wiltshire, are the once famous quarries of Chilmark (now reopened) and its neighbour Tisbury. They yielded oolites with a fine-grained sandy texture; creamy-white when first dug out, the presence of specks of glauconite (see p. 120) may give them a greenish tinge when exposed to the weather. That is why Tisbury stone, when obtainable, is used to-day as a substitute for another Isle of Wight stone, Green Ventnor, at Winchester College. The Chilmark quarries, in operation until about 1937, are now closed and overgrown, but they have a most distinguished record; from here came stone seen at Salisbury Cathedral, Romsey Abbey, Longford Castle, Wilton House, and many other buildings besides. The fine quality of the stonework on the south front at Wilton can be seen in plate 45c.[1]

1 But because it was closer at hand, the sixteenth century house was built of a very different, and markedly softer, stone: a greyish green sandstone from the Upper Greensand, which was cut into rather square blocks, as can still be seen on the east front.

In Somerset the principal Jurassic stones south of Bath are Ham Hill, to be considered later (see p. 88), and Doulting, quarried near Shepton Mallet on the limestone belt. Doulting, first worked about 1175, is a stone with a distinctive granular structure, not always wholly resistant to frost; its colour when freshly dug varies from light brown or buff to cream, but it too becomes greyer after prolonged exposure. Its somewhat coarse grain makes for an interesting texture. Wells Cathedral and the remains of Glastonbury Abbey bear witness to the quality of this historic stone, but the old quarry is now so overgrown as to be hardly recognizable. The new one, operated on a smaller scale, provided stone for the internal dressings of the cathedral at Guildford. Farther north, across the Mendips (and, for once, to the west of the belt), there is the isolated hill of Dundry, with stone worked from early Norman times which later made an important contribution to the architecture of Bristol. The church of St. Mary Redcliffe in that city was wholly built of it; but by 1960 the condition even of the Dundry stone used in the restoration of 1840 showed that, like so many of the oolites, it has not the structural strength to resist the smoke and fumes of an industrial city.

'Bath stone' is a name that is used generically to denote the products of many Great Oolite quarries, of which the best known are the following: Corsham Down, Hartham Park and Monk's Park, all near Corsham; Box Ground (also known as St. Aldhelm) and Hazelbury, both near Box; Farleigh Down at Monkton Farleigh; Stoke Ground at Limpley Stoke; Combe Down, Odd Down and Hampton Down on the hills above Bath. Other quarries were at Westwood and at Bradford-on-Avon. Of all these, only Combe Down, Odd Down and Hampton Down are in Somerset; the rest are in Wiltshire. Several of these quarries are no longer worked: Hampton Down had yielded all its high-class stone by about 1810. Since the closure of Hartham Park quarry in 1961, all Bath stone now comes from Monk's Park or Box Ground. It is the most important example of an English stone which has always been largely mined, not quarried. This depends, of course, on the depth at which the good stone occurs. In the present Monk's Park quarry, which was first worked in 1872 and now covers an enormous area (38 acres), the freestone is about 95 ft. below the surface. Wherever stone is mined, it is because the cost of removing the overburden renders open quarrying uneconomic.[1]

1 Other English stones which were wholly or partly mined include Totternhoe (p. 64) and Beer (p. 65); Purbeck (p. 71); Windrush, a near neighbour of Taynton (p. 77) and Quarry Hill, between Barnsley and Bibury, which provided stone for Barnsley Park and for Cirencester church; Weldon (p. 80: in the nineteenth century only) and Edithweston (p. 81); all the Reigate group (p. 116); Stonesfield (p. 103), Collyweston (p. 104), Purbeck (p. 105) and Duston (p. 141) slates; some York paving stones (p. 134) and some Derbyshire alabaster (p. 190). Some of these stones were worked by adits—galleries driven more or less horizontally into a hillside. These were much more convenient, and less expensive to operate than normal mines.

TERTIARY AND CRETACEOUS LIMESTONES
a. *The Close, Winchester, Hampshire*
b. and c. *The Old School House, Uffington, Berkshire*
d. *Archbishop Bourchier's Tower, Knole, Kent*

Bath was one of the few English building stones (the principal others were Barnack, Taynton-Burford and Quarr)[1] to have been used outside its own locality before the Norman Conquest. Admittedly, when stone travelled far afield in these early days, it was only for details such as long-and-short quoins, pilaster-strips, cross-shafts and tomb-slabs, and never for whole buildings; but as early as the ninth century blocks of Bath oolite were going to places in the Salisbury neighbourhood (Amesbury, Britford, Codford St. Peter) and even to London. This stone was quarried by the Romans, and from the beginning of the eighth century by the Saxons for St. Lawrence's church at Bradford-on-Avon, where some of the later blocks weigh as much as a ton. It was employed from the thirteenth century onwards at Lacock Abbey, whose monks had been given the original quarry at Hazelbury, and in the mid-sixteenth century at Longleat, to which it was brought up the river Frome from Limpley Stoke; but until the second quarter of the eighteenth century it was not much used beyond the valleys of the Avon and its tributaries, with one notable exception: substantial quantities of St. Aldhelm stone were sent to Winchester about 1400 when William of Wykeham was reconstructing the nave of the Cathedral. Under George II Ralph Allen developed the quarries on a much larger scale, especially those on Combe Down, the closest to Bath. The city that we know to-day, which many would regard as the most beautiful in England for its architecture (although one would not place the stone quite on that pinnacle), is largely built of the products of this quarry and of its neighbour on Bathampton Down. In the later eighteenth century and still more in the nineteenth, thanks largely to the construction of the Kennet and Avon Canal, Bath stone was one of the best known and most extensively used in the kingdom. It was patronized in the most exalted circles: it went to Windsor Castle and also to Buckingham Palace, where Nash decided to employ Combe Down stone in preference to Portland, not only because it was one-third cheaper but also because in his view it would wear better.

Nash was mistaken, and later generations have paid dearly for his error. Bath stone has many virtues: it lends itself, for example, to ornamental work, such as fluted pilasters, balustrades, balls, urns and vases, obelisks, garlands and swags of fruit, piers and pedestals. This can be seen at St. Catherine's Court (74d) and still more strikingly on the front of General Wade's House (c. 1720) in the Abbey churchyard of Bath itself (84b). It looks singularly well in its own locality, and to-day the city of Bath is again its principal user. But it is highly porous, so that driving rain may sometimes penetrate to a depth of several inches.[2] Nor will it stand up with any reliability to a smoke-laden atmosphere. Some of the

1 See the article by Professor E. M. Jope cited on p. 22.
2 The porosity of Bath stone can be largely rebutted by the application of a silicone water repellent. The reduction in moisture produces a different lichen, which also helps.

OOLITIC LIMESTONES
a. and c. *Great Chalfield Manor, Wiltshire*   b. *Kirby Hall, Northamptonshire*
d. *St. Catherine's Court, near Bath, Somerset*

Bath stones are better able than others to resist weather and decay, and they are not all equally agreeable. When it is a delicate honey-colour turning to gold in the sun, Bath stone can give exquisite pleasure. But it may assume a rather aggressive yellow, as can be seen all too often outside old churches which had their traceried windows copied in this stone during a Victorian restoration. And sometimes it turns black with soot and, unable to provide the contrast with rain-washed white surfaces which can be so effective in the case of Portland, it loses all interest.

One knows of people who find the architecture of the Cotswolds too obvious. Others there are who call it smug. But if Cotswold people are pleased with themselves, they have every reason to be, for theirs are the village show-pieces of England. Broadway has been persistently reproved for self-consciousness; but should it not rather be termed *bien soigné*? It is only when a thousand others come to look that one's own pleasure vanishes. The right time to see Broadway is on a sunny mid-week morning in early spring, without a visiting motor vehicle in sight. It is easy enough to dub it 'a refined Cotteswolde village', with something of a sneer, but what in fact one finds there, as all over the Cotswolds, are gentle variations of design and style, bound together into a harmonious unity by the use of the same lovely stone throughout. Bourton-on-the-Water is another village by no means unaware of its attractions for tourists, and not unwilling to reap the rewards which they bring. The same might perhaps be said of Bibury and Castle Combe, charming though they are. But for those who prefer rather more reticence, there are many others: Ilmington, Stanton, Snowshill, Bourton-on-the-Hill, Longborough, Lower Slaughter, Bledington, Little Barrington, Barnsley and Sherston are but a few of them. Excellent small towns also survive almost unspoiled: Cirencester, Painswick, Minchinhampton, Tetbury and Lechlade are all places of distinction, while Chipping Campden and Burford have substantial claims to be regarded as the two most enchanting little towns in England. The inhabitants of this region were indeed fortunate; in the vital period, from the middle of the fifteenth to the middle of the eighteenth centuries, they had the money (from the fleeces of their innumerable sheep), they had the masons and, most important of all, they had the stone.

The north-western edge of the Cotswolds, rising abruptly several hundred feet, is easily seen, but in other direction the limits of the area are not so sharply defined. It embraces a considerable part of Gloucestershire, a sizeable corner of Wiltshire, a small one of Worcestershire and the western fringe of Oxfordshire. Cotswold stone varies considerably from place to place. The best came from the Great Oolite series, mostly to be found along an arc running from north of Bath through Badminton, Minchinhampton and Northleach to just north of Burford. But although in the clean air of its native region the better kinds weather well, even the best lack the strength and durability of Portland, and none of it is suitable for external use in smoky towns. What is particularly striking is its abundance. Stone, usually of a creamy or pale golden tone, very responsive to light, was used not only for stately Perpendicular churches and prosperous clothiers' houses, but also for more modest dwellings like the one at Snowshill which still has its projecting bread oven (*83a*); not only for churches and houses but for farm buildings too, field-walls, stiles, even staddle (or steddle)-stones.[1] A special beauty of Cotswold architecture springs from the widespread use of stone for roofs as well as for walls: these will be discussed presently. Quarries were everywhere; almost every village had one. Most of them were quite small; nearly all lie abandoned and overgrown. Only at Temple Guiting (the large quarry formerly known as Coscombe) and Cirencester (a small modern quarry which does not provide ashlar) is Cotswold stone still worked for building purposes, although other   * quarries, such as Farmington (near Northleach) and Painswick, will sometimes work to order. Westington quarry (Chipping Campden) was bought in 1975 by Mucklow & Co. of Halesowen to make reconstituted stone. Painswick stone, employed long ago for Gloucester Cathedral, was used again in London after the Second World War for the internal restoration of St. George's (Roman Catholic) Cathedral, Southwark, as was Farmington for the Temple Church. Painswick, Guiting and Campden, together with Leckhampton, Nailsworth, Minchinhampton and Taynton, are perhaps the best known of the Cotswold building stones: all these have made memorable contributions to the local architectural scene. Taynton, the oldest of this group of quarries, was worked by the Saxons, and is recorded in Domesday. It supplied some of the stone for Blenheim.[2]

The stone was not only readily available; it was also quite easy to work, as it was comparatively soft when first prised from the quarry. This rendered possible the many and beautiful refinements which are associated with the Cotswold style of building. The late retention of well-moulded mullioned windows; the elaborate labels or dripstones, dropped down a few inches at each end of a window, and then neatly returned, as can be seen on the gables of St. Catherine's Court near Bath (*74d*); the gracefully finished gable

1 These were employed, in combination with wooden planks, to lift the bottoms of ricks off the ground. They were usually shaped like mushrooms, and many survive to-day as ornamental features in English gardens. In some places they are known, delightfully, as dottles.

2 Although the most important, Taynton was but one of at least twenty local quarries from which great blocks of stone, loaded on to carts dragged by teams of horses (six to a team), were brought to Blenheim. The Duchess of Marlborough's insistence on economy finally induced Vanbrugh to agree, against his better judgment, to bring stone from Glympton, just to the north of the park, and from Heythrop. These rather indifferent materials, which were used in the Kitchen Court, are now in decay.

copings; the frequent appearance in gables of dated stones, oval or circular, with initials elegantly lettered; the abundance of ornamental finials, sometimes carrying balls, sometimes more fanciful forms, as for instance those which suggest flames; the lofty, well-designed chimney stacks crowned with generous cornices: these are all characteristic of the Cotswolds. The most striking feature of the domestic style of this part of England is, however, the great place occupied by the gable. Where other regions used dormer windows, either standing on the wall or set back on the roof, the Cotswold builders carried up the main wall to form a gable, often all but touching its neighbours on either side, and with a ridge as high, or nearly as high, as the main ridge of the roof (39a, 90a). And below the gables, especially in moderately-sized or small houses, run those long ranges of rather low windows which are another attractive feature of Cotswold buildings.

The formula for a Cotswold house may appear to be rather simple. Indeed, say Fox and Raglan,[1] 'the formal and parallel verticalities of the Cotswold tradition seem, after a time, dull, because they are so obvious'. 'But', they are careful to add, 'when they are flouted or ignored, . . . the result is disastrous.' The Cotswold builders knew this, perhaps for the most part instinctively. The style in fact avoids monotony, partly because it was possible, even with no structural features other than gables, chimney-stacks and windows, to play a large number of variations on the theme, and partly because the quality of the stone enabled the builders to indulge, every now and again, in a feature of greater extravagance which furnished a note of variety, and perhaps a new focal point. It might be just the curving of a gable to support a vase-shaped finial (83b) or to give space for a modest coat of arms; on the other hand, it might be a sumptuous entrance-doorway, or a rich bay-window (45a), or something still more spectacular, such as the wonderful, cinquefoil bow-window at Thornbury Castle which, although not quite in the Cotswolds, may well have been an achievement of Cotswold masons.

The key-note of these Cotswold buildings is an elegant refinement, deriving not a little from the frequent use of ashlar, at least for the front walls, even of cottages. Nowhere else can so much ashlar masonry be found, nor such a high quality of finish in the dressings. There are some parts of England, particularly the North, where such richness, such grace, such urbanity would be out of place. In the Cotswolds these elegances not only suit the stone: they suit the country too. Nothing is more striking about Cotswold buildings than the visual accord which they achieve with the landscape in which they are placed. But whereas our vernacular buildings are usually mere incidents in their landscape settings, albeit often agreeable ones, in the Cotswolds the buildings themselves, even the barns, are of such high quality that at every turn it is they that we notice first. The landscape here

1 *Monmouthshire Houses, Part III* (1954), p. 30.

plays second fiddle: it is the background, the *mise-en-scène*, the frame. That is why, for those who cherish our building heritage, the Cotswolds occupy a special place, and why any development proposals affecting this region cannot be too carefully scrutinized.

The other great area for English oolite comprises the northern part of Northamptonshire, the Soke of Peterborough, Rutland and Kesteven (south-west Lincolnshire). If the Cotswolds contain more fine domestic buildings, great and small, to the square mile than any other part of England, the region of which Stamford is the centre certainly ranks next. Within twenty-five miles of this lovely town quarries abounded. At least two of them, Barnack and Ancaster (both within a mile or two of Ermine Street), were worked by the Romans and by the Saxons; and one, Clipsham, is among the most important in the country to-day. This part of England has yielded unceasingly through hundreds of years a magnificent bounty of stone which, thanks principally to the availability of water transport, has travelled far beyond the confines of the district.

These stones are usually described as belonging to the Lincolnshire Limestone formation, although most of them do not actually come from that county. They are tougher than the oolites of the Cotswolds and more durable also than Bath stone. They are not the equal in strength of Portland, and some display better weather-resisting qualities than others; but all have the usual limestone property of hardening on exposure to the atmosphere, and the best varieties respond admirably to cleaning. When Wren's Library at Trinity College, Cambridge, was cleaned some years ago, its Ketton stonework was found to be in remarkably good condition.

Of the many quarries which once belonged to this part of the limestone belt, attention must be mainly focused on the six most famous: Weldon, Ketton, Barnack, Clipsham, Ancaster and Collyweston. The last produced roofing slates, which are treated at the end of the chapter. All were well known in the Middle Ages and all except Barnack are still worked. The colours of their products embrace the gentlest of greys, creamy whites, and many tones of buff, brown and yellow, and at Clipsham the warmer tints may sometimes embody areas of blue-grey, known locally as 'Blue Bed'. This is stone of excellent quality, often preferred for restorations because its cooler colour looks better in walls that have already weathered to grey; the blueness generally goes after a few years of exposure. Ancaster also yields patches of blue here and there, and is sometimes flecked or mottled. Lastly, and most surprisingly, there is an attractive pink variety, a rarity at Clipsham and not frequent at Ancaster, but at Ketton something of a speciality.

Barnack, in what was the Soke of Peterborough, three miles south-east of Stamford, yielded the most durable of all these limestones (with the possible exception, which only time can prove, of the best Clipsham). There were in fact three distinct kinds of Barnack stone: one, a hard walling stone; another, a limited deposit of a fine-textured oolite; and the much more famous ragstone. In the Middle Ages the ragstone quarries were among the largest in England, and an important source of wealth to the monks of Peterborough who owned them. When sewers were laid here in 1961, it was proved (as had long been suspected) that almost the whole village—cottages, roads, lanes, orchards, gardens—rests on land from which the stone has been quarried. Many abbeys, Ramsey,[1] Crowland, Thorney and Bury St. Edmunds among them, were at different times granted quarrying rights at Barnack, and great quantities of the hard, shelly, coarse-grained ragstone were carried off in flat-bottomed boats. For this the quarries were well placed, being barely a mile from the Welland, only four from the Nene, and less than three from the old Roman canal known as Car Dyke; before the fens were drained it is believed that navigation was possible across the deeper fenland meres into the Ouse, and thence past Thetford into the river system of Broadland. Barnack rag, which could be worked to an ashlar, was the principal stone used for Ely Cathedral as well as for Peterborough, and some also went to Rochester and later to Norwich. It provided the facing material for the great Norman keep at Castle Hedingham in Essex, and can be seen at several of the older Cambridge churches and colleges, notably Corpus Christi. But before the advent of the Tudors the ragstone quarries were already almost exhausted, and most of the stone for Burghley House seems to have come from a freestone quarry to the north-west of the village. The other variety of Barnack stone was more humdrum: a hard stone obtainable only in rather thin beds (up to about $4\frac{1}{2}$ ins.) but very useful for hammer-dressed rubblestone walling, both dry and mortared. This stone, which is similar to many others throughout Northamptonshire and the whole Cotswold area, continued to be quarried until the early years of the present century.

In 1965 Barnack was transferred to the new county of Huntingdon and Peterborough. So Weldon is now the most illustrious of the Northamptonshire stones. Happily the quarry, which lies a little to the east of the modern steel town of Corby, is now working again, after a period of enforced closure. It can look back upon an august past. From Weldon came most of the stone for the original buildings of Jesus College, Cambridge, as well as for the upper (and later) part of King's College Chapel; in Northamptonshire it is splendidly seen at Kirby Hall (74b), only three miles away, Castle Ashby, Rushton Hall and Boughton House. The two surviving Eleanor crosses in this county, which were

1 As rent for their stone, the monks of Ramsey in the reign of Edward the Confessor undertook to provide their brethren at Peterborough with four thousand eels annually during Lent. Ramsey, on the edge of the Fens, was well placed for titillating the palates of monastic gastronomes.

erected about 1295 at Geddington and at Hardingstone (just south of Northampton) and which are still in first-class order and practically unrestored, also bear witness to its quality. Weldon stone is distinguished by its fine, even texture, and at the quarry it can be sawn out like cheese, sometimes in blocks of considerable size. The usual colours are pale or warm buff. Among the oolites it is notably resistant to frost. Above this famous freestone lies another, of more open grain with large ooliths and some shell fragments; and between them there is a coarse, fossiliferous ragstone, strong and durable, and, like the third variety of Barnack stone mentioned above, excellent for walling, for which it is still used. This stone will take a high polish (cf. p. 186).

Very similar to the well-known kind of Weldon stone in colour and texture, and hardly less admirable for elaborate carved decoration, is the oolite formerly quarried at King's Cliffe at the north-east end of Rockingham Forest, about half-way between Weldon and Barnack. In the years 1525 to 1538 this stone travelled as far as Hengrave Hall near Bury St. Edmunds in Suffolk, where it was used for the spectacular tri-lobed oriel window and accompanying sculpture above the main entrance (84d). As the builder, Sir Thomas Kytson, was the richest cloth merchant in England, the cost of transporting the stone presented no problem.

The Welland approaches Stamford between low limestone hills that are pitted with quarries, many overgrown, a few still working. There are those of the two Westons: Collyweston on the Northamptonshire side and Edithweston in Rutland (abandoned half a century ago), and between them, also on the Rutland bank, there is Ketton. One does not need a microscope to appreciate the texture of Ketton stone, which is one of the purest oolitic limestones in existence. This beautiful stone appears to be entirely composed of tiny spherical fragments clinging firmly together, and provides the finest of all examples of the 'herring's roe' effect referred to earlier. To some extent this becomes blurred when the stone is exposed to the weather, but there would normally be little difficulty in distinguishing Ketton from a markedly shelly oolite such as Weldon.

Ketton stone, although worked in the Middle Ages, did not come into wide favour until the sixteenth century, after no more of the famous ragstone was available from Barnack.[1] It then entered upon four centuries of glorious life. Besides satisfying local demands, it travelled, for instance, to Audley End under James I and to Belton House near Grantham (often wrongly thought to be Ancaster), while beyond all others this is the stone of Cambridge. With no stone except clunch close at hand, Cambridge was compelled either to build in brick (which she did, much more often than Oxford) or to import stone

1 Even the church at Ketton is built of Barnack rag.

from a distance. From the time of Wren onwards for two hundred years, this was what usually occurred, and happily for Cambridge Ketton stone was about the most easily accessible. Few now are the colleges which cannot show Ketton ashlar on at least one of their buildings. The New Court at St. John's College (45d) was referred to on p. 52, where it was suggested that for lovers of stone the cutting and jointing here might seem almost too perfect. This was not, however, the view of W. J. Arkell, who wrote that 'the undeniable success of this building is to a great extent due to its superb stone masonry: it contains some of the largest and soundest blocks of ashlar in Cambridge'.[1] Ketton's even, regular texture renders it particularly suitable for buildings designed in a precise, Classical style.[2]

The supply of Ketton stone is now incidental to the work of the Portland cement company which owns the whole quarry area. The good freestone seams are exposed in the course of excavating the hard limestone underlying them which goes to make the cement. Ample quantities are at present available; even the pink variety is obtainable. Blocks measuring 6 × 6 × 5 ft. are not unusual, and, except in a polluted atmosphere, this stone usually weathers admirably. Something like ninety per cent of all the Ketton building stone now quarried finds its way to Cambridge.

Clipsham and Ancaster are a little farther north. Clipsham is on the Rutland-Lincolnshire border; Ancaster is almost exactly in the centre of Kesteven, half-way between Grantham and Sleaford. Many Lincolnshire churches are built of oolite from the quarries at Ancaster. It also travelled, notably to Norwich, where it is said to have been used in all the principal churches, including St. Peter Mancroft, in the fifteenth century,[3] and also into Nottinghamshire, where it provided the material for the church and the castle at Newark, for the extraordinary display of carving in the chancel at Hawton, and under Elizabeth I for Wollaton Hall. Nearly three centuries later a still more ostentatious house, Harlaxton Manor, owed not a little of its undeniable effectiveness to its very fine smooth-faced Ancaster stonework. It was also the principal stone employed for Belvoir Castle. The three varieties of this stone can be seen at the quarry one below the other, in very level strata. The Weatherbed, the uppermost, is also the hardest: this is a very shelly stone and will take a polish.[4] Below this comes the Hardwhite, the finest grained of the Ancaster stones; and then the Freebed. Even this, the softest, will last for centuries in most situations

1 Article on 'Rutland Stone' in the December 1948 issue of the now defunct *Leicestershire and Rutland Magazine*. At least one authority states that the facing stone of this building is Ancaster, but this is not so. Another widely read book on Cambridge describes it as stucco!

2 Most Georgian headstones in East Anglia were also of Ketton stone, shaped at the quarry and often carved there too: information from Mr. A. S. Ireson.

3 See Donovan Purcell, *Cambridge Stone* (1967), p. 54.

4 See p. 186.

OOLITE IN THE COTSWOLDS
a. *Snowshill, Gloucestershire*
b. *Medford House, Mickleton, Gloucestershire*

and for most purposes, provided that no water is allowed to seep into it. More than the others in the 'Stamford group' this stone shows considerable variations in colour as well as in grain. Mention has already been made of the patches of blue and pink and of the flecking and mottling which it embodies. The normal colour of the Hardwhite and Freebed Ancaster is pale honey, and of the Weatherbed warm brownish yellow, due to oxide of iron staining. Internally the yellowness persists, in some places to excess, but externally this stone has often weathered beautifully. The two quarries, while now only giving regular employment to about half a dozen men, are still able to satisfy a constant demand.

    *

Known in the Middle Ages and used not only for local churches but as far away as Windsor Castle in the thirteen-sixties, Clipsham stone nevertheless had to wait much longer than the others before its merits came to be widely recognized. The reason, almost certainly, was the same as with Portland: the difficulty of cutting it with the only saws available in mediaeval times. For Clipsham is easily the hardest of the so-called Lincoln-shire limestones. Now it rivals Portland as the most popular of all English building lime-stones. Like Barnack, Weldon and Weatherbed Ancaster but unlike Ketton, it is a stone which embodies a large number of shell fragments in its composition and which can be rubbed down to produce, if required, an unusually smooth surface for a limestone. It will also take a good arris. A coarser stone than Ketton, it is also more robust, although in this respect it is certainly not the equal of Portland. There is indeed nothing to suggest that Clipsham stone, for all its fine qualities, will withstand the depredations of a smoke-laden atmosphere so well as Portland. Yet it is sometimes preferred, as for example in the re-building of the House of Commons after the last war. Portland stone, because of its white-ness, is not a good harmonizer. Clipsham, on the other hand, which is usually pale cream, light brown or buff-coloured, and cool yet not too cool, is in this respect excellent. Hence its employment for the restoration of cathedrals as far apart as Canterbury and York, Ripon and Salisbury, as well as at Peterborough, Ely and Norwich. Hence, too, the great liking for this stone at Oxford since its first introduction into that city in 1876; over ninety per cent of the stone now used at Oxford is from Clipsham.

In the architecture of Stamford Ketton stone, less than four miles distant, has natur-ally played a part. But this fortunate town has another quarry still nearer, barely a mile to the north-west on the road to Little Casterton; and it is of this material that it is mostly built. Stamford stone, or Casterton stone as it is sometimes called,[1] is closer in composition

---

1 The quarries, which occupy an area more than a mile long by half a mile broad, are partly in the borough of Stamford in Lincolnshire and partly in the parish of Great Casterton in Rutland.

OOLITE AND LIAS
a. *3 All Saints' Place, Stamford, Lincolnshire*   b. *14 Abbey Churchyard, Bath, Somerset*
c. *The Triangular Lodge, Rushton Hall, Northamptonshire*   d. *Hengrave Hall, Suffolk*

to Ketton than to any other, but does contain some small shell fragments (although finer than in Weldon or Clipsham). In this stone the forms of the ooliths are not quite so regular as in Ketton, and the colour is a little browner: Stamford stone is a pale brownish-cream. Nor is it as hard as Ketton. Yet it has usually weathered well, as is evident in the typical Stamford house here illustrated (84a).[1] Between the fifteenth century and the early years of the twentieth, Stamford stone was not only used on a considerable scale locally but shipped in substantial quantities into Fenland and East Anglia, including Cambridge, where it is sometimes mistaken for Ketton. The reopening of the quarry, with modern methods of mechanical cutting, in 1960, after a closure of about fifty years, was a highly satisfactory development. A new building at Downing College, Cambridge, completed at the end of 1969, is faced throughout with this stone.

The stone for the cathedral at Lincoln—probably the finest of all our cathedrals—came originally from quarries close by on Lincoln Edge, long ago worked out and built over. The 'Dean and Chapter' quarry, on the northern outskirts of the city, is still occasionally worked when stone is required for restoration. After this, still moving northwards, the quality of the oolites is generally not as good, and ashlared stonework becomes rarer, but the East Riding had three good mediaeval quarries at Brough, Brantingham and Newbald. In the thirteenth century, the last of these produced some of the stone for Beverley Minster. In the North Riding there is one excellent oolite at Hovingham. Its top stratum yields a hard rubblestone now often specified for buildings in the nearby National Park; the grey-white freestone lies below. This is another example of a stone which has a grey-blue 'heart', amounting to something like twenty per cent of the whole.

The oolitic limestones, with the exception of Portland, are not by any means the best that England can produce to withstand the smoky air of a large industrial town; but that is not where nature intended them to be and not where one likes to think of them. Nor do these stones belong to the wild places. Oolite is the stone of the gracious country, of the counties still free from industrialization, yet generously strewn with market towns, villages, country houses and farms. In such a setting it is beyond doubt the perfect building material.

No more than the briefest mention can be made of those coarser Jurassic limestones which abound mainly in the South Midlands. Among them are the stones of Heading-

---

1 This house, No. 3 All Saints' Place, is marred only by three later additions: the ugly Victorian chimney-pots, the poor dormers introduced in place of the original ones during the nineteen-thirties, and the wooden sunblind frames. An attractive feature which still survives is the small wrought iron gate facing the front door: this gives on to a projecting ledge of stone which long served as a mounting block.

ton and Wheatley, Coral Rag, Cornbrash, and the so-called Forest Marbles. Coral Rag, the most durable of them, mainly composed of the fossilized remains of corals and other shells, is not amenable to sawing and therefore only normally used in rubble lumps.[1] There is, however, a great deal of this stone around Oxford (the low hills to east and west of the city are all formed from it), and it continues throughout the length of north Berkshire from Cumnor to Coleshill and beyond into Wiltshire. It can still be seen not only in some of the earliest buildings in Oxford itself, such as St. Michael's North Gate with its early eleventh-century tower, and the city walls partly of the same date, but also in many villages and small towns in the direction indicated: among them Faringdon, Highworth, Wootton Bassett and Calne. Somerset has no Corallian oolite, but it reappears in Dorset to the west of Shaftesbury, where the quarries at Marnhull and Todber yielded a freestone to be seen in the mediaeval churches of this locality. The lumps of coral rag rubble   *
stone are always laid random with plenty of mortar in between; but this primitive-looking stone is virtually unaffected by the weather and its rugged masonry often gives an impression of great endurance. Headington, from about 1400, and Wheatley from somewhat earlier, provided not only coral rag but hardstone and freestone as well. For a detailed account of the calamitous results of the widespread employment of Headington freestone at Oxford in the seventeenth and eighteenth centuries, the reader is referred to W. J. Arkell's *Oxford Stone*, which on this subject is unlikely ever to be superseded.

Cornbrash limestone and the Great Oolite formations immediately below it are mostly indifferent building stones, coarse, crumbly and irregular, and are nowadays only quarried for road-making, lime-burning and occasionally dry walling. Yet they were once employed extensively, for want of anything better near at hand, from Cirencester through central Oxfordshire, the northern part of Buckinghamshire and the whole length of Northamptonshire on the Bedfordshire-Huntingdonshire border. Inferior though these stones generally are, and not oolitic despite their name, whole villages were built of them; they can be seen at many churches in the neighbourhood of Buckingham and also at Claydon House, where the tendency of the stone to spall and crumble is all too evident. Bladon stone, the stone of this type to be worked for building, was a light-toned Forest Marble, coarse but very serviceable, although it could not be ashlared. Quarried just to the south of Blenheim Park, it was employed extensively at Oxford between the wars as a cheaper alternative to Clipsham, to which, however, for urban use it is aesthetically much inferior. Bladon quarry is now closed.

[1] Coral rag is a product of Corallian limestone (pronounced to rhyme with 'stallion'). In practice the two terms are synonymous.

Lias

The Lias, as has been said, follows the oolitic belt throughout its whole length, outcropping immediately to the west or north-west of it. Only at the Mendips, a range which, for once, runs across the general stratification of the country, is there a short break in the Lias, although not in the Oolite. The easiest way to tell where the Oolite ends and the Lias begins is to look at the hill-tops. The Oolite country is comparatively flat-topped and featureless between the frequent valleys, in which lie most of the villages and most of the pleasures. In the liassic belt, on the contrary, it is the hills, quirky, tumbled, often abrupt, which provide the special delights. When we reach the Lower Lias we are already down on the plain that includes the Vales of Gloucester and Evesham. This is floored by heavy clay with thin bands of limestone in its lower part, which yields an excellent hydraulic lime, much used for mortar, but is no longer worked for building. Elsewhere the Lias beds may be decidedly sandy, and only suitable for rubblestone. Liassic limestone, in fact, is usually an untrustworthy material for building: often it weathers badly, and although much used in the past in the Midlands, Somerset and Dorset, it is nowhere quarried for building to-day, except to a very small extent on Hamdon Hill in Somerset and on Edge Hill, where Oxfordshire drops into Warwickshire. With Oolite never far away, improved transport was bound to render the inferior material redundant.

Ham Hill stone (as the product of Hamdon Hill is always called) used to be classified with the Inferior Oolites which it closely resembles, and is still understandably described as an Oolite by some writers; but with its shelly structure and a good deal of crystalline calcite, it is only very slightly oolitic, and modern geology places Ham Hill, which is also strongly impregnated with iron, at the top of the Upper Lias.[1] It is not one of the most durable of our limestones, yet it was quarried in Roman and in Saxon times, and from the fourteenth century, if not earlier, its employment for building was until a few years ago continuous. It was used extensively in the nineteenth century and can be seen all over southern Somerset and in the adjacent parts of Dorset as well. Most of this stone is now worked out, but one quarry was re-opened in a small way in 1968, and at the present time blocks are again available. It is one of England's most seductive stones, and places such as Crewkerne, Ilminster, Martock and Montacute (*89*) owe it an unending debt. It is attractive to lichens, which can give it a mottled appearance, but, far from being a dis-

[1] Cf. W. J. Arkell, *The Jurassic System in Great Britain* (1933), p. 169; *R.C.H.M. West Dorset* (1952), p. xxv; *Geological Survey of Great Britain*, sheet 312 (1958); etc. This stone comes in fact from the Yeovil Sands, which are sometimes regarded as intermediate between the Lower Oolite and the Upper Lias.

HAM HILL LIAS
Garden Pavilion, Montacute, Somerset

figurement, this is usually an asset. Like all iron-tinted stones, it may seem rather to soak up the sunshine than to reflect it back, but in the contemplation of these rich, golden brown surfaces spotted with lichens, usually of freestone and here and there sumptuously dressed, the eye may find insatiable pleasure.

Ham Hill apart, all the most beautiful liassic building stones come from the Middle Lias formation. The several varieties of Marlstone, as the Middle Lias rocks are often called, occur in western Dorset, Somerset and a number of Midland counties, and are distinguished by a warmth of colour induced by the presence of oxide of iron. This, as we have already seen, has determined the colour of several of the oolites. Its effect upon some of the liassic rocks has been still more marked. These marlstones are frequently, and quite properly, described as 'ironstones'; but it should be understood that this term conveys no indication of geological age. It is applied to any stone that has become impregnated with iron, including many sandstones which have no connection with either Oolite or Lias. All ironstones darken on exposure to the weather, since the particles of iron are soon oxidized to produce rust; this often yields richly satisfying hues.

The Marlstone region of the Midlands extends from the north of Oxfordshire through western Northamptonshire, eastern Leicestershire and western Rutland, to Kesteven. Bloxham, Adderbury and King's Sutton, with their stately churches, Broughton Castle, Wroxton Abbey, the enchanting village of Rockingham from which a typical cottage is illustrated (342a), Great Easton across the Welland: these are but a few of the delights which the Midlands owe to the iron-tinted Lias stone. The colours vary from the tawny yellow Helmdon stone, which Hawksmoor employed to fine effect at Easton Neston, through orange and golden brown to a nutty dark brown and sometimes even dark red. Here and there these warm colours are combined on a single building with the cool grey of an oolite. Examples include the church tower at Melton Mowbray and in Northamptonshire Whiston church, the village street at Moreton Pinkney near Towcester, and that strange product of religious obsession, Sir Thomas Tresham's Triangular Lodge in the far corner of Rushton Park (84c). Effective, in isolated instances, as this polychromy is, one can be grateful that the taste for horizontal stripes of variegated stonework never aroused more than limited enthusiasm in this country until the time of the Victorians.

Marlstone was used on a considerable scale all through the Middle Ages and for a hundred years after. From the middle of the seventeenth century it declined somewhat in popularity, partly no doubt because of its inferiority to oolite when exposed to the weather. It did not often yield a reliable freestone, and in the Midlands it is not rare to find a Marlstone building with dressings of oolite, or sometimes of sandstone.

The best of all the Liassic ironstones of the Midlands is Hornton, from the north-west

OOLITE AND LIAS: A CONTRAST IN ALMSHOUSES
  a. *Chipping Campden, Gloucestershire*
    b. *Somerton, Somerset*

corner of Oxfordshire. It can be well seen at Farnborough Hall, just over the boundary with Warwickshire. This beautiful stone, understandably beloved of sculptors as well as formerly for building, is unusual, inasmuch as deep brown, tawny yellow, greenish and greyish-blue tints can be combined within a single block. The original quarries just north of the village have long been abandoned, but, as mentioned above, a closely similar stone is still dug for building at Edge Hill just across the Warwickshire border. This is a close-grained material of proven durability. Where stone of a greenish hue is required, Hornton is invaluable. In 1955 it was used for the window-frames of the rebuilt hall at Compton Castle in Devon, to replace the original green schist, no longer obtainable. Only six or seven miles away from Hornton is Broughton Castle, one of the most lovable country houses in England, and almost without peer for the subtle beauty of its colour. The gabled walls are a mixture of grey and gold, grey-green and golden-green, and almost everything in between! Lichens add, here and there, a gently mottled texture which is quite inimitable.

The Middle and Lower Lias limestones are separated by a broad band of clay. It is the lower stratum which yields the so-called Blue Lias, a material of totally different effect from the ironstone just described. This stone is not much closer to blueness than the guelder rose to roses. It is about the same colour as a slate-pencil, or somewhat whiter. The individual pieces are usually small, acquiring no patina with age (90b). Nor could they be ashlared.

Blue Lias was quarried on the Dorset-Devon border, and is much in evidence at Lyme Regis; but to see it used really extensively we must go to Somerset. From the Polden Hills south-east to Somerton and south-west all the way to Staple Fitzpaine on the slopes of the Blackdowns, dozens of churches were built of it; whole villages too, and even little towns, like Langport or Somerton itself (90b). At High Ham and at Weston Zoyland, where the stone is greyer, the effect, although not radiant, is better, but in order to take the measure of this stone's aesthetic inferiority, one should go to Ile Abbots. Here the church tower, not a large one but of exquisite design, is on its principal (west) side entirely faced with Ham Hill Lias, but on its other three sides the facing stone is Blue Lias, presumably employed to reduce the cost. The dichotomy is anything but welcome.[1] Elsewhere, since the Blue Lias was too coarse to be suitable for dressings, it was employed in combination with some other stone, as can be seen on two of the most magnificent village church towers in Somerset (which is to say, in England): Huish Episcopi and North

---

1 At least, however, these are both local stones. Within 3 yds. of the base of this very beautiful tower are a grave consisting of a pink granite surround and a covering of pink chips, dated 1950; another of whitish synthetic stone, with white chips and a centre-piece of screaming white marble, dated 1951; and a third of whitish granite, with more chips, only 4 ft. from the tower. One can hardly wait now for another of black polished marble and gilt lettering, with crème de menthe chips, to complete the set. That such things should still be tolerated defies all understanding. It is proper to add that in some dioceses this is so no longer.

Petherton. At Huish Blue Lias is the main material, both of the tower and of the diminutive church to which it is attached, but the dressings are of Ham Hill stone throughout. Thereby were obtained contrasts of tone (the Ham Hill being much the darker), of colour (the Ham Hill brown, the Blue Lias whitish-grey), and also of texture, as the Ham Hill stone is all beautifully ashlared, with a profusion of rich carving, whereas the Blue Lias consists simply of small pieces of squared rubblestone, carefully coursed but altogether rougher. These contrasts are undeniably effective, yet to some eyes they may well seem excessive. To those who find them too shrill, North Petherton will afford greater pleasure, for here the Blue Lias is confined to the lower portions of the tower: the sumptuous belfry stage and its coronal are of the much finer quality brown stone throughout. Moreover, the somewhat harsh effect of the Blue Lias has been mollified, on the face adjoining the church entrance, by an abundant growth of lichen.[1]

Blue Lias appears again as a building stone at many places farther north, to the west of the limestone belt. One finds it in Gloucestershire at Deerhurst, Ashleworth and elsewhere in the Vale of Severn, in Worcestershire around Pershore, in south-central Warwickshire, and on the borders of Lincolnshire and Nottinghamshire. At Lincoln itself it was the stone used for the infilling of the vault of the Angel Choir: the small pieces were laid carefully on end. In some of these Midland counties it is more acceptable than in Somerset; at Kineton in Warwickshire the grey Lias makes a really attractive contrast with the rich toffee-brown ironstone. Seldom, however, does it stand up very well to the weather.

Transitional between the Jurassic and Triassic series, and of little importance in the pattern of English building, lie the Rhaetic rocks, which vary considerably in composition. The best known of them, Quarella stone obtained from Bridgend in Glamorganshire and to be found in the parts of the cathedral of Llandaff restored in 1869, is an uncharacteristic member of the group in that it is classified as a sandstone. The Rhaetic stone of England, with the exception of Cotham marble (see p. 186), is generally known as White Lias. Since the beds are seldom more than 20 ft. thick, the outcrops are narrow. The employment of Rhaetic stone for building is virtually confined to two restricted areas: north Somerset, where it can be well seen at Radstock, and Warwickshire between Stratford-on-Avon and Shipston-on-Stour. Although close-grained and comparatively hard, it is no more attractive to look at than Blue Lias. It may still be worked on a small scale at Whitchurch, south of Bristol.

1 Although too coarse to be chiselled, Blue Lias could, by dint of much labour, be polished. Its use in Somerset churches, and especially at Wells, as a (much more accessible) substitute for Purbeck marble is referred to in Chapter 7 (pp. 183–184).

Magnesian Limestone

In the limestones of the Permian system chemical action, some two hundred million years ago, led to carbonate of magnesium taking the place of carbonate of calcium. The latter is still the predominating constituent, but the former is the distinctive one: hence the name, magnesian limestone, by which this stone is usually known. It is equally correct to describe it as dolomitic limestone.

Magnesian limestone is essentially a stone of north-eastern England and particularly Yorkshire. There are a few pockets of it in Cumberland, but nearly all our magnesian limestone is to be found along a comparatively narrow strip which starts just north of Nottingham and runs along the Nottinghamshire-Derbyshire border between Mansfield, Bolsover and Worksop. It then enters Yorkshire and passes north-north-west through the whole of that county, marking the western edge of the Vale of York, and into County Durham close to Darlington. Here for a while it swings north-east, to run finally into the sea between Hartlepool and South Shields. Along this strip there were at one time many quarries, the most famous of which were all between the Trent and the Yorkshire Ouse. Mansfield Woodhouse, Bolsover Moor, Church Anston, Roche Abbey, Park Nook, Huddleston, Bramham Moor, Thevesdale (Tadcaster): these are the principal quarry names in the story of our magnesian limestone buildings. The last was certainly known to the Romans, who dug it to provide material for buildings at Calcaria (Tadcaster: the Roman name is significant) and at Eboracum (York). In the Middle Ages, all of them yielded stone for the great churches of the north-east, such as York, Ripon and Beverley Minsters, Selby Abbey and the collegiate church at Howden. In the seventeenth century, Sir Christopher Wren is said to have believed that Roche Abbey was the best building stone in England after Portland. It can be seen at Sandbeck Hall (46a), a couple of miles from Roche, and also (sparingly) at Serlby Hall, a few miles farther east: both these are large mid-Georgian houses by James Paine.

The usual magnesian limestone of the North-East has a fine-grained texture, which sparkles when freshly hewn, especially in sunshine after a shower of rain. It shares with other limestones the characteristic of being comparatively soft at the quarry and of hardening on exposure. Thus it lends itself to the attainment of clean arrises and crisply cut detail. Its colour can also be attractive, especially when it is creamy-white. It is seen at its best, needless to say, in places where the air is still comparatively unpolluted, as in the South Yorkshire villages of Arksey, Campsall and Darrington.

Unfortunately, the magnesian limestones—especially Roche Abbey stone—tend both to change to a drab dark grey and, for chemical reasons, to produce a few excessively white patches when exposed to the weather (46a). More serious, despite the fact that some veins surpass Portland in their hardness, is the general failure of magnesian limestone to withstand the chemicals contained in coal smoke, which eat into the stone below its surface and render some portions spongy or, still worse, convert them into flaky dust. This has been the cause of immense trouble and expense, as at York Minster. Chemically, moreover, this stone is a poor mixer. Like many limestones, it should not be employed in juxtaposition with sandstones, because chemical reactions between the materials lead to rapid decay. Owing to the absorption of magnesium sulphate, magnesian limestone cannot even be used with safety in conjunction with other limestones.

Although principally to be seen in parts of Yorkshire, Nottinghamshire, Derbyshire and Durham, magnesian limestone made contributions to the fabrics of a number of important buildings in south-eastern England from the fourteenth century onwards. Among them may be mentioned Westminster Hall and St. Stephen's Chapel, Rochester and Windsor Castles, Eton and King's College, Cambridge, and, in 1699, Greenwich Hospital. In 1839, after a prolonged enquiry by a Royal Commission, Bolsover Moor was the stone chosen for the new Houses of Parliament, but the supply of blocks of the size required soon ran out, and Mansfield Woodhouse, the Commission's next choice, also proved inadequate in this respect. This is how recourse was had to the quarries at Anston a few miles farther north. Much of this Anston stone has worn well, even in the smoky air of London, but unfortunately the hard beds were interspersed with a few that were not so hard, the stone from which should have been rejected out of hand. Instead, owing to parsimony and the absence of expert supervision at the quarry, all were used, with the result that signs of decay began to appear almost as soon as the building was finished. To-day, with one exception, our magnesian limestones are scarcely worked except for industrial purposes; for buildings, even in Yorkshire, if limestone is employed at all an oolite is preferred. But recently, it is good to record, Huddleston quarry (near Sherburn-in-Elmet) has been reopened in order to obtain blocks for the restoration of York Minster, in addition to the Clipsham which has been extensively used there for replacements of what was once all Tadcaster. In the North-East this stone has left us a noble inheritance; although there are many other building stones in Yorkshire, 'the white magnesian limestone is the aristocrat among them all'.[1]

---

[1] Arthur Oswald, 'The White Stone of Yorkshire', in *Country Life Annual, 1959*: a most interesting and informative article.

Carboniferous and Pre-Carboniferous Limestones

In every kind of English limestone which has been discussed, the buildings have achieved a harmony with nature which is at once complete and deeply satisfying. If we now move back into what geologists term the Carboniferous period, the character of the buildings will be found to be different, but it will soon be apparent that the landscape has changed too, so that the all-important congruity with nature remains as strong as ever.

The great Carboniferous system embraces three principal formations: the Coal Measures, the Millstone Grit and the Carboniferous Limestone. Where the two former are the chief rocks, the building stones will normally be sandstones, which will be considered in the chapter that follows; here we are only concerned with the last, which is also the oldest. The Carboniferous Limestone regions are scenically some of the loveliest in England, with their scars and tors, caves and waterfalls, steep grey cliffs and precipitous gorges, and treeless moorlands cut by rich green dales. The chief areas are the Pennine hills north of the Craven Gap,[1] with wide stretches to either side of them, including substantial parts of the four northern counties; the Peak district of Derbyshire with the adjacent portions of Cheshire and Staffordshire; several 'pockets' in Gloucestershire and Monmouthshire, including parts of the Forest of Dean, the lower Wye valley and the heights around Bristol; and the Mendips. Almost all this country is sparsely populated, so that our Carboniferous Limestone buildings are, as often as not, lonely farmhouses. This stone, for which an alternative name is mountain limestone, was also used with unforgettable effect in the regions mentioned for mile upon mile of dry-stone walls.

Chemically parts of the Carboniferous Limestone, like the Chalk, are exceptionally pure; but whereas chalk tends to be soft, this stone, rich in fossils and sometimes highly crystalline, is hard and intractable: so hard in fact that it will frequently take a high polish, and some of England's so-called marbles, as we shall see later, are really mountain limestone. Seldom, however, can the attainment of a high polish be regarded as the most sensitive or the most agreeable way of using this stone, the essential character of which resides, on the contrary, in its rough-textured sturdiness and strength.

By comparison with the oolites it cannot be denied that, as a building stone, the mountain limestone has less urbanity and less charm. Nor does it readily lend itself to ornamentation, for in a stone so resistant to the chisel, undercutting is difficult and detailed carving out of character. In Somerset, therefore, where plenty of more accommo-

---

1 The Craven Gap is a break in the Pennines, very important for communications, between Clitheroe in Lancashire and Skipton and Keighley in Yorkshire.

dating stone was available, it is not surprising to find that the hard grey stone of the Mendips was seldom employed for a building of importance, and even village churches in this material are the exception. But there are a good many English people, especially in the North, to whom charm, and indeed all smoothness, is slightly suspect, and some of these will be found to prefer the Carboniferous Limestones to the Oolites as having, they feel, more 'character'. To such eyes the rough finish of the mountain stone is a perpetual delight, and the very sobriety and lack of adornment of its buildings are themselves a recommendation. That the limestone buildings of the North are considerably ruder and less carefully constructed than those of the South is not in question; compared with a gabled farmhouse in the Cotswolds, one on the Pennines, almost always with only a straight roof-ridge parallel to the front wall and little or no eaves projection, seems to belong to a more primeval order of society. Yet the latter can be seen to possess a vitality and a forcefulness that are entirely right for the harsher climate with which it has to contend, and if ashlar is exceptional in the North for all but the most important buildings (and not always even for these), it can at least be argued that perhaps it hardly matters, since the rougher textures are completely in tune with those rocky escarpments which so frequently add character to the landscape. This can be appreciated at Castleton in the Peak district (130a).

Although the walls embody a good deal of the local Lees Manor gritstone, quarried on the estate, one could find few more memorable examples of the use of Carboniferous Limestone for building than at Haddon Hall in Derbyshire (108a). In the garden the terrace walls are built of dry-stone; blocks of gritstone, bigger and smoother, are used for the quoins, the copings and the steps. On the house itself the bulk of the walling is rubble, much of it roughly coursed but some only random; the high proportion of small pieces (these are the limestone) has demanded plenty of mortaring. For the dressings—window and door frames, quoins, roof-cornices, battlements, chimney shafts—the less intractable gritstone, which could be shaped into much larger blocks and ashlared, was understandably preferred. This is not only softer but distinctly yellow, in contrast to the predominant grey. Mortham Tower, close to Greta Bridge in the far north of Yorkshire (108b), presents a similar combination, except that here the gritstone is more in evidence. As at Haddon, both kinds of stone were readily obtainable locally.

Grey is the usual colour of this limestone, and sometimes a cold, rather dense grey, which induces a mood of melancholy. In the northern dales the grey stone is sometimes whitewashed, a practice that is welcome and appropriate. Elsewhere, however, as in the Peak District, it weathers to quite a pale grey, which lightens the whole landscape, while in the North-West around the shores of Morecambe Bay and over much of the north-eastern part of Westmorland, the mountain limestone has a natural whiteness which is anything but dour. Amid the rich greens of the rain-soaked northern valleys the light-toned stonework of the buildings will sometimes stand out with quite unexpected brilliance. Here, architecturally, the mountain limestone is seen at its best.

In parts of Cumberland the Carboniferous rocks assume warmer tints. Between Cockermouth and Egremont the presence of haematite ore has stained the limestone red, while in the district north and east of the lower end of Ullswater ferric oxide from the formations that once lay above the present rocks has changed them to a delicious grey-pink. At Dalemain Hall near Dacre the stone is among the most beautiful in the north of England.

Carboniferous limestone has been used for many centuries, and almost until the present day, in some parts of England in which it can be obtained locally. In a smoke-free atmosphere it is often exceedingly durable, appearing after several centuries of exposure to wind and weather just as fresh as when it was first set up. But to-day, unhappily, whilst millions of tons are quarried annually for lime, cement, the chemical industries and for roadstone, it is rarely employed for building. In central Derbyshire, once an important source, even Derbydene and Hadene have been out of production for a number of years, and the well-known creamy grey Hopton Wood stone for much longer. There are, however, a number of quarries at which this stone is still worked, if only in some cases intermittently. The chief are Frosterley, in County Durham, where it is dark grey; Orton Scar, in central Westmorland, where most of it is light fawn; Deepdale near Dent and Barton near Richmond, both in Yorkshire, both grey-brown and both full of fossils. All these rocks can be polished, and often are, and several have a lower stratum that is closer to marble, to which reference will be made in Chapter 7. But the principal uses for all of them to-day are internal.

There are still older limestones than the Carboniferous. First come the Devonian rocks, which include as well as limestones hard sandstones and plenty of slate. The Devonian limestones of the South-West are also hard and capable of taking a polish if required, thus qualifying as semi-marbles (see p. 187). The colour is sometimes pink but more often grey, of every shade from the very dark to the nearly white. All round the southern fringe of Dartmoor, from Chudleigh to Plymouth, and southwards to the coast, for instance at Torquay, this sturdy-looking stone was at one time used extensively. After the second world war unpolished Devonian limestone was employed to excellent effect as a paving stone in the rebuilding of Plymouth.

Yet more ancient (at least 395 million years old) are the Silurian rocks, which include some limestone. They occur extensively in Scotland, Ireland and Wales, but in England they are to be found in north-west Herefordshire and in two small areas of that county west of the Malverns. In Shropshire it is to be seen round Wenlock Edge, at Stokesay Castle (a memorable and much-loved building) and in Ludlow and the region to the west of it. Some of these compact, fossiliferous rocks are intensely hard and splintery, but more rubbly beds, which can be broken up into rough blocks, also occur. They have never been of much importance for building.

Tufaceous Limestones

There are certain places in which new rocks have been formed by spring water bubbling forth from existing limestones laden with calcium carbonate, which is deposited upon exposure to the air in the form of a precipitate, and gradually accumulates and hardens. The age and character of the 'parent' rock may vary considerably, but these tufas are geologically of recent formation. For some time they retain their moisture, and are too soft and crumbly for building. By degrees, however, they dry out and harden, assuming their characteristic pitted appearance, like a petrified sponge. Later, if lime-laden water percolates through the holes, these may become filled up with further deposits of calcium carbonate, thus yielding a stronger and more compact, but also heavier, stone.

These limestones were employed for building purposes by the Romans and in the Middle Ages from Saxon times until the fourteenth century, but not apparently after 1400, and never extensively. Yet examples of their use can be found at widely separated places. They can be seen in association with Kentish ragstone at several churches near Maidstone (West Farleigh, East Malling, Leeds), with the Chalk at Totland Bay in the Isle of Wight, and with Carboniferous limestone at Matlock. A Saxon example is the upper part of the tower stair turret at Brixworth in Northamptonshire, added probably in the tenth century. There is also a much restored Norman church at Moccas in Herefordshire that is largely built of calcareous tufa, a material, incidentally, which contrasts ill from the aesthetic standpoint with the surrounding old red sandstone. Principally, however, it is to be seen in association with the limestone of the Purbeck beds in Dorset, the limestones of Gloucestershire and a thin bed of Devonian limestone which occurs in the Old Red sandstone rocks of north-west Worcestershire. The tufa deposits here are on the right bank of the Teme, between Tenbury and Shelsley Walsh; the churches at Shelsley Walsh and Clifton-on-Teme (tower) are specially good examples. Plenty of tufa is also to be seen at Dursley church in Gloucestershire, at the foot of the Cotswold escarpment, where the ground is full of springs; and only half a dozen miles away stands the most considerable building in England to have been constructed largely of tufa: Berkeley Castle.

At Dursley the walls are grey; at Berkeley, owing to the percolation of iron, they are an
enchanting blend of pink and red, grey and buff and brown.

For the builder, the particular virtue of tufa is its lightness: few kinds of stone weigh
less. For this reason it was specially well suited to fill the webs of high ribbed vaults.
Thus was it employed at Canterbury in the rebuilding of the choir after the fire of 1174,
at Worcester in the two western bays of the nave at about the same date and in the choir
and retro-choir during the thirteenth century, and in the next century for the choir vaults
of the abbeys, now cathedrals, of Bristol and Gloucester.

Limestone Roofs

No survey of the employment of English limestone for building would be complete without a short section devoted to roofs. For, in the right context, limestone can yield a roof-
covering of incomparable dignity and beauty. When the building is itself constructed of
local limestone, a roof of stone slates adds the crowning touch of harmony, in colour and
in texture, with the surrounding landscape.

The term 'stone slates' is unfortunate, for geologically, of course, they have nothing
whatever to do with slate. In some parts of England, notably in the Cotswolds, the usual
term is 'stone tiles',[1] but this is not satisfactory either, for a tile is a manufactured article,
whereas the stone was always quarried. After several centuries it is clearly too late now to
try to introduce a different name. So in this book the term 'stone slates' is employed
throughout, despite the fact that this does not everywhere comply with local usage.

To be suitable for slates, the stone must be naturally fissile: that is to say, it must be
possible to split it into comparatively thin pieces. The beds of stone of any variety which
lend themselves to this are not very numerous. On the other hand the slates, once prepared,
are much easier to handle than blocks of stone; so oolitic slates, in particular, because
they could be produced in smaller sizes and lighter weights than sandstone slates, sometimes travelled considerable distances. Stone slates, not always rectangular, were used by
the Romans (for the villa at Chedworth, for instance, which was really a fair-sized country
house), but Saxon buildings would usually have been too flimsy to support their weight,
and they were still a rarity in the thirteenth century, even in the Cotswolds.[2] From the

1 An Estate map of 1626 marks a 'Tyle Pitt Feylde' close to Hazelbury Manor, Box.
2 Cf. H. P. R. Finberg, *Gloucestershire* (1955), p. 64: 'A little before 1221, the prior of Winchcombe built
two houses in the borough and roofed them with stone tiles. The terms in which this is recorded imply that
it was an unusual and costly proceeding.'

fourteenth century, primarily in order to reduce the risk of fire, stone began to be used for the roofs of private houses as well as of churches and other public buildings where it was available and where the clients could afford it.[1] From Tudor times until the first quarter of the nineteenth century, stone (as distinct from slate) became the favourite roofing material over wide areas of England, which included parts of Sussex and Surrey, Dorset and Somerset; the whole of the Cotswolds, western and northern Oxfordshire, Northamptonshire and Rutland; all the counties along the Welsh border; and large parts of all the northern counties from Derbyshire to Northumberland. Some of these stone slates were sandstones, to be discussed later. Here our principal concern is with the Oolites, which also tend to be sandy when suitable for roofs. They are seen to their greatest advantage in the Cotswolds and in Northamptonshire.

For the splitting of the laminated stone, what was needed was a good hard frost. The time-old practice, still followed in one or two places, was to quarry the stone in the autumn, and then to enlist the help of nature. The force of even a single sudden thaw following a hard frost could achieve in a few hours what would take the hand of man many weeks, cracking the stone into more or less flat layers of varying thickness. To assist the process it was usual, after the slabs of stone had been dug out and laid upon the ground, to water them every evening from December, if necessary until March, for it was essential that the stone should remain 'green'. If the quarry sap once dried out of it, the stone could only be used for dry walling or road metal, or be burnt for quicklime.

If the frosts obliged, a skilled man could quite easily cleave the stone along the fissures and trim each piece with a hammer. In order to reduce the weight of the roof, the larger slates were sometimes tapered or rounded towards the head: that is, in the part not exposed to view. Then, battens having been nailed across the rafters, every slate had, with a slater's hammer, to be holed near its head. (To-day power drills have replaced this laborious process.) Fixing was done either with oak pegs,[2] iron nails, or, not infrequently in the North until Tudor times, with the small leg-bones of sheep. At Walworth Castle in Co. Durham the breast-bones of chickens were used. To-day copper nails are considered the best; they are cheaper than oak pegs, more easily obtainable, and no less durable. Iron nails, unless galvanised, are avoided on account of rust. The slates were always hung over the battens, not nailed to them. In the Cotswolds no attempt was made, as a rule, to produce slates of uniform size or thickness; indeed, it has been said that in this part of England no two roofing slates are ever exactly identical.

[1] A vital consideration. To roof the church at Potterne, for example, required 10,000 slates. See J. E. Manners, 'Repairing a Church Roof' in *Country Life*, April 24, 1969.

[2] Collywestons were always fitted with oak pegs: information from Mr. A. S. Ireson.

After trimming, they were sorted according to their approximate sizes, all of which had their traditional names—lovely Lewis Carroll-sounding names like muffities and wivetts and tants and cussems (or cussomes). The various sizes were used in combination, as can be well seen at Westwood Manor (*363*a) and at Snowshill (*83*a). The largest slates, which averaged about 16 × 24 × 1¼ ins. but which might occasionally be as much as 30 ins. long and 50 ins. wide, or even more, were placed at the bottom, along the eaves, which always look best when they are of generous depth. The succeeding courses were graduated, until finally the slater reached the last course below the ridge. These slates, which might be no more than 4 to 6 ins. wide and only ½ in. thick, were sometimes known as cocks or tants, and sometimes as farewells since with them the task of slate-laying was complete. At Collyweston they were called 'outrules' because they were smaller than the shortest size marked on the slater's rule. In the Cotswolds the ridge, too, was always of freestone, a special V-shaped slate being sawn out of the block for this purpose (*83*a). Cement mortar, sometimes employed at the ridge in the present century for reasons of economy, is a miserable substitute. Ceramic ridge tiles of suitable shape and colour, which have now been in general use for some time, are more acceptable. At the apex of a gable marking the end of the roof ridge, there will often be a stone finial, the ball being a favourite and always delightful form (*74*d, *83*b); similar finials may adorn the two kneelers (flat-topped stones) at the base of the gable.

It is hardly necessary to point out how much skill and artistry were (and indeed still are) required in laying a Cotswold roof. Each slate had to be chosen for its suitability to a given position. Since there was continual variation not only in size but in thickness, the choice of two good neighbours for every stone could present considerable difficulties. Particular ingenuity was shown at points of junction between two inclined planes, such as where a projecting wing meets the main roof or where a dormer breaks forward. For such places were evolved the 'swept valley' and the 'laced valley'. Where normally lead would be used to cover the angles, with a swept valley our eyes are carried gently round (*363*a) over specially cut, wedge-shaped, and even triangular, slates. With a laced valley, a speciality of the Collyweston slaters (see p. 104), each pair of horizontal courses turns upwards as it approaches the point of junction, to meet in a specially cut slate of diamond form. Swept and laced valleys are equally beautiful.

The weight of a Cotswold roof is formidable: every 100 sq. ft. weights nearly a ton, and the big slates at the eaves may weigh 50 lbs. or even more. Thus a good stout wooden framework was essential. Wherever possible, the timber was also a local product. Since the slates were not absolutely flat, a moderately steep pitch was also important, in order to reduce the possibility of the rain driving in. So the pitch of a Cotswold roof is never less than 45°, averages between 50° and 55°, and may reach 60° or even 65°: a very fortunate circumstance aesthetically. Roof timbers, if neglected, may ultimately cave in under the weight of the slates. But often a slightly sagging ridge-line adds charm to an old house (*39a*, *107c*), and may also have the practical advantage of helping the slates to fit more tightly together.

So long as the stone is carefully selected, good oolite slates, exposed though they are to all the vagaries of the weather, should last at least two hundred years, and many will endure for much longer. When the roof of the Sir Baptist Hicks almshouses at Chipping Campden, a classic of Jacobean building (*90a*), was stripped for repairs some years ago, it was found that about half the slates, which were laid in 1612, were still perfectly sound. ∗ The first part of a stone-slated roof to require attention is nearly always not the stone but the wooden battens and pegs which support it: these may need renewal as much as once every century.

Oolitic slates provide what is probably the most beautiful of all roofing materials, but they are expensive to dig and prepare, and costly to erect because of the need for this strong supporting framework. Furthermore, there are not many men now with sufficient skill to lay a stone roof as it should be laid. Where at one time in the favoured areas every cottage, every barn, every pig-sty even, was accorded the dignity of a stone roof, to-day the reverse process is more probable. An old roof needs repair; a tempting offer is received for the slates, which are thereupon stripped off and sold. The replacement, with tiles, often much too red, asbestos or corrugated iron, can be a real misfortune for a stone village.

In the Cotswolds, the most celebrated slates formerly came from Stonesfield in Oxfordshire, four miles west of Woodstock (and therefore only on the fringe of the Cotswold area). Stonesfield slates, which belong to the lowest level of the Great Oolite, have the usual characteristic of oolitic slate of occurring in only a very thin seam (varying from about 30 ins. to 6 ft.); but here a further difficulty was that they had to be mined from a depth of 60–70 ft. Nevertheless their fine quality ensured a steady demand, and many buildings in western Oxfordshire and in the adjoining counties were roofed with them in the seventeenth, eighteenth and nineteenth centuries. The Old Swan inn at Minster Lovell is a characteristic example (*107a*). As Stonesfield is only twelve miles from Oxford itself, these sandy slates were much used by the colleges, beginning with Wadham in 1612. The last quarry was finally closed in 1909, and even the sites are now difficult to identify.

Farther west, Gloucestershire produced stone slates of almost identical character and from the same geological stratum. These quarries were all between three and twelve miles west and west-south-west of Stow-on-the-Wold. Eyford was well known, and

Slaughter supplied slates for New College, Oxford, as early as 1452. But the largest of them was Naunton, where in their heyday the pits are said to have produced about thirty thousand slates a week, and where only sixty years ago one pit alone was still able to employ a hundred men. A little farther off, to the north and east of Stroud, the slates from other quarries were no less good: many of those at Daneway House, Sapperton (*107*b), date from about 1620. The supplies of Cotswold stone suitable for slates are still almost inexhaustible, but nowhere are they now worked; it is the conditions of our time which prevent their exploitation.

The only oolitic slates which vie in fame and importance with those of the Cotswolds are the products of Collyweston, in the north-eastern corner of Northamptonshire, close to Stamford. They were also used by the Romans,[1] and again in the later Middle Ages; Dr. Salzman records[2] that 14000 went to Rockingham Castle in 1375 and 1390 and 5000 to Oakham Castle in 1383.

After the discovery of the frosting process, probably during the sixteenth century, the demand for stone slates from Collyweston and the adjacent village of Easton-on-the-Hill spread all over Northamptonshire and into Rutland, Leicestershire and Kesteven, Huntingdonshire, Bedfordshire and Cambridgeshire. Plate *84*a illustrates a roof of Collywestons at Stamford. They were as much in demand at Cambridge as were Stonesfield slates at Oxford. Collyweston slates, which come from the base of the Inferior Oolite, and also have to be mined (but not from more than 40 ft. below ground), are aesthetically inferior to the Cotswold products. They have less richness of texture and show less variation in their colour: the wonderful golden browns and honey yellows characteristic of the Cotswold roofs are here replaced by more sober tints, for Collywestons, fawn and light grey when freshly dug, assume a darker hue on weathering. From the practical standpoint, however, they possess several advantages over their rivals. Collyweston slates are also produced in various sizes, but the average is larger: slabs measuring 24 × 36 ins. are not rare. Because they are appreciably thinner than the Cotswold slates, a roof of Collywestons may weigh no more than half as much. Because the surfaces are smoother and the shapes more regular, these slates are not quite so difficult to lay, although they too require a roof-pitch of at least 45° and preferably more. A building such as the Haycock at Wansford bridge (*39*b) gains much dignity from the prominence of its Collyweston slate roof, with laced valleys at the angles. Thus, although on a very much smaller scale than formerly, modest produc-

1 Collyweston slates found during excavations on Roman sites at Great Casterton and at Godmanchester were shaped roughly into diamond or lozenge forms, with a single peg-hole near the top.

2 *Op. cit.*, p. 232

tion still continues at Collyweston in hard weather. Since 1945 these slates have been used on the Guildhall, London, for Nuffield College at Oxford and for the Master's Lodge at Trinity College, Cambridge. In 1968 they were used vertically (like slate-hanging) for perhaps the first time, on a new building in the High Street at Stamford, to excellent effect.

These are the choicest of the English limestone roofs. But there were many other quarries on the limestone belt, from Dorset to Yorkshire, which could produce laminated stone suitable for roofing. Until the end of the nineteenth century large quantities of excellent slates, mostly coarser than Stonesfield but including some of a most convenient thinness which needed no frosts to split them, were obtained from the so-called Forest Marble, both in the Forest of Wychwood (whence the name of the stone) in west Oxfordshire and especially at a number of places to the south of the road from Burford to Cirencester. There are plenty more of these slates, and the quarries, Poulton especially, could * easily be reopened if the demand arose. Fortunately limestone slates can still be seen on countless Cotswold roofs and on many others besides. At Sulgrave Manor, for instance, at the south-western end of the long county of Northamptonshire, the perfect stone slates, easily the best feature of the house, probably came from the nearby quarry of Helmdon. At West Coker Manor, an enchanting little Somerset house, the roof covering, like the walls, came from Ham Hill. For the Hospital of St. John, Sherborne, the likely source was a Forest Marble quarry at Long Burton, a couple of miles to the south. Between Dorchester * and Swanage many old houses are still roofed with slates of Purbeck stone.

Of the many kinds of stone slates obtained from the rocks of the Jurassic formation, those from the Isle of Purbeck are the most durable of any, and the heaviest. A Purbeck slate roof weighs no less than $1\frac{1}{4}$ tons to every 100 sq. ft. Such roofs can look splendid, but they impose structural problems. In the first place, they require an exceedingly robust supporting framework; and indeed a possible explanation of the rather odd change-over halfway up the roof of the Old House (c. 1660) at Blandford (255c) from Purbeck slates to tiles is that the former were found to be dangerously heavy. Needless to say, it is the weight of these stones which has produced the sagging so characteristic of Purbeck roofs (107c). And to this is due another very common feature of these roofs: the excessive use of mortar. If because of the shifting of the stones it is necessary to introduce additional mortar, this should be kept well back and unseen, for the little shadow under the lower edge of every stone is of importance aesthetically (74c). In the village of Corfe Castle, delightful though it is, there are few roofs which have not been so excessively flushed up with mortar that the mesh of shadows has been lost.

Purbeck slates were also among those that, owing to their natural lamination, could be split quite easily without the help of frost; but they too had mostly to be mined, and it is the cost of explosives and the reluctance to work in mines which have rendered them practically unobtainable since 1939. The great age for these slates was from 1700 to 1900, but they were already in considerable demand before the end of the fifteenth century. At that time, in order to gain more warmth, they were frequently laid upon a bed of moss. Later, as the slaters became more skilled, this practice was abandoned, and in Dorset as elsewhere the heads of the slates were bedded in hair and lime mortar. They were also torched from underneath with the same mix and by the same men; this was work reserved for wet days. The moss stayed outside, and in moderation we may be glad it did. For an old stone house can have no more endearing possession than a stone-slated roof, spotted with bright green moss and dusted with silvery lichens.

LIMESTONE ROOFS
a. *The Swan, Minster Lovell, Oxfordshire*   b. *Daneway House, Sapperton, Gloucestershire*
c. *Knitson Cottage, Corfe Castle, Dorset*

4

SANDSTONE

Sandstones are principally composed of particles of quartz, with the addition in some cases of other minerals such as mica and felspar, which have been eroded from older geological formations and are bound together by a cementing material. Fragments of shells and other organic remains may also be present. The character of the cement varies considerably. It may be silica, calcite (calcium carbonate), dolomite (calcium-magnesium carbonate), oxide of iron, or perhaps just clay; hence sandstones are spoken of as being siliceous, calcareous, ferruginous or argillaceous, or they can be a mixture of any of these. This cementing material, often referred to as the 'matrix' of the stone, could have been laid down with the rock particles at the time of their deposition, but usually as with limestones it has been due to the later action of water. The quartz or other grains of a sandstone are very hard and virtually indestructible; the vulnerable part is always the matrix. The shape of the grains varies a good deal, some being angular and others rounded, and to some extent the strength of a sandstone is determined by the degree of uniformity or compactness of these particles; but the character of the matrix is the vital factor.

Sandstones vary even more than limestones in their durability. In the harder and more useful kinds, the matrix is always siliceous, and among the Carboniferous sandstones are some which have a greater physical strength than any limestones. Many sandstones on the other hand are notably friable, porous, and lacking in adequate cohesion. The calcareous sandstones almost always deteriorate before long if employed out-of-doors; some of the sandstones quarried from the Greensand deposits of the Cretaceous system can be very treacherous. When the matrix of the sand grains is simply clay and the consolidation is only by pressure, the stone is quite unsuitable for external use. Often the physical weakness of a sandstone is due to the lack of uniformity in its composition; within a single piece the graining may vary substantially. The presence of soft areas within blocks that appear to be tough and hard can be a source of great trouble and expense.

Pure siliceous sandstones have the great advantage over pure limestones of being chemically inert. This enables them to withstand the rigours of a smoke-laden atmosphere as no limestone can, a great boon to builders in the cities of the industrial North; but it cannot be said that in the funereal aspect of these grimy Northern buildings, to which

CARBONIFEROUS LIMESTONE AND MILLSTONE GRIT
a. *Haddon Hall, Derbyshire*
b. *Mortham Tower, Rokeby, Yorkshire*

reference was made in Chapter 2, sandstone is seen at its most attractive. Aesthetically the principal charm of these stones resides in the beauty, variety, and sometimes the complete unexpectedness of their colours. Step on a sunny morning into the choir of the Priory church at Great Malvern, and you will see exquisite stone colours, pastel pinks, pale under-water greens, delicate warm greys, all most subtly blended. Much of this stonework has had to be renewed, but the task has been admirably performed and it would seem that nothing has been lost. At Fountains Abbey, grey, brown, fawn, pink and lavender tints are all juxtaposed. Some sandstone buildings vary a little in colour almost from stone to stone, which is not always an artistic advantage, but in the Romantic context can be most attractive. Examples of such minglings could be multiplied, and there will be many references to colours in this chapter. To describe accurately the colours of a sandstone building is not always easy, for the variety of mineral substances which may contribute to this stone's composition is such that there are quarries where the colour appears to change slightly every few feet. The range of hues is indeed remarkable. There are pure grey, blue-grey, yellow-grey and grey with a blush of pink; every shade of yellow and buff from the deepest ochre to the lightest honey; the warm browns of chocolate and cinnamon and all the reds and pinks from the lightest and brightest to a dark smouldering crimson. There are pale lavender and mottled purple, deep green, pale green and brownish green. Many of these colours change considerably on exposure to the air, often but not always for the better. It is perhaps worth adding that sandstones belonging to the Old Red and New Red formations are by no means always red, nor, generally, are those from the Greensands even slightly green.

The purest sandstones, chemically, are the whitest. The colours are all due to the presence of other minerals either in the grains or in the matrix. As with limestone, the most important colouring agency is iron; all the various shades of red, brown, buff and yellow are due to the presence of ferric oxides in one form or another. Greyish tints may indicate the presence of clay. Greens sometimes derive from ferrous iron, but also from glauconite, an interesting mineral of which there will be something more to say presently.

Some sandstone buildings are rich not only in colour but also in texture. Here, however, they are usually at a disadvantage when compared with many limestones. For a rich texture often indicates coarse grains in the stone's composition, and not seldom a tendency to fracture or crumble. In such a material the crisply cut details and delicate refinements which characterize the best oolites were no longer a practical possibility. Where they were attempted, as on the towers of Worcester and Chester Cathedrals and on the church at Nantwich (to cite only three examples), it was not long before the original details were blurred and defaced almost beyond recognition. Restoration of these sandstone churches has been necessary not once but many times: Worcester Cathedral, in many ways so admirable in its architecture, would make far more appeal to us than it does, were it not that the stonework has had to be incessantly renewed and all the external details recut. Usually therefore a plainer style of architecture, with the elegances omitted, is more appropriate to the softer kinds of this stone. With the harder varieties a similar reticence is common, for quite a different reason: although the best of them (those with the finest grain) will take a sharp arris and the most intricate ornamentation, these sandstones are difficult to work and thus there was always a temptation to refrain from that undercutting which, in a good oolite, can add so much depth and generosity to a work of architecture.

As with the limestones, the English sandstones suitable for building will now be surveyed in geological sequence. There are a great many of them: although I shall do my best to simplify, you are likely to find this the most complicated chapter in the book. The large majority of our building sandstones fall into one of three groups: Cretaceous, Triassic or Carboniferous. But every geological system between the Tertiary and the Ordovician has made its contribution. The sequence, again according to the Geological Society's Phanerozoic Time-Scale, 1964, runs as follows:

System	Age in million years (approx.)	Principal Stones
Tertiary	2–70	Sarsens
Cretaceous	70–140	Upper and Lower Greensand stones and Wealden
Jurassic	140–195	Sandstones replacing the Oolite (mainly in Yorkshire)
Triassic	195–225	New Red Sandstones
Permian	225–280	
Carboniferous	280–345	Coal Measures Sandstones, Millstone Grit, Culm Measures and Lower Carboniferous Sandstones
Devonian	345–395	Old Red Sandstones and (in the South-West) Devonian
Silurian	395–440	(S. part of the Lake District)
Ordovician	440–500	(Chiefly Lake District and Shropshire)

Sarsens

The youngest English sandstone used for building (under seventy million years) is also the most eccentric. Sarsens are sandstone boulders of indeterminate size and shape found on or just below the surface of the downs and heaths of southern England, particularly the Marlborough Downs to the east of Avebury. They are firmly cemented remnants of what were once much more continuous layers of Tertiary sand, now largely destroyed by erosion. Their very name is an indication of their strangeness, for 'sarsen' is a variant of 'saracen', and Saracen was once a convenient soubriquet for any foreigner. The sarsen-stones were also frequently known as grey wethers, apparently because there were places where they lay upon the ground like flocks of sheep in repose. There are still such places, notably on the downs of Wiltshire. For H. J. Massingham there was 'no building stone in England, unless it be Cotswold stone, to equal the primeval sarsen, and it is the noblest material of all for the cool and subtle harmonies . . . of the downland scene'.[1]

Sarsens, picked up off the land, were used by the primitive inhabitants of this island in the construction of the tomb chambers known as long barrows. Dolmens and stone circles, notably at Avebury, and all the eighty larger stones at Stonehenge are also sarsens. Thus isolated, their attractive colours can be well appreciated: at Stonehenge, a few of the sarsens are brown but the majority are a delightful grey touched with pink, enriched with moss and plenty of lichens of various colours. Elsewhere bluish-greys predominate.

In mediaeval times sarsens, greywether sandstone or heathstone (all these names are current) made intermittent appearances as a building material, if never a very important one. Several references were made in the previous chapter to supplies of stone for Wind-sor Castle, but none of those mentioned was employed nearly so widely as the sarsens dug from the sand of Bagshot Heath, ten miles to the south. The twelfth-century castle was principally constructed of blocks of chalk quarried on the site. These were faced throughout with the grey, siliceous heathstone which has survived to this day wherever it has been permitted to do so. In the nineteenth century this stone was used again, brought now from the neighbourhood of High Wycombe in the Chilterns.[2] Sarsens can also be found here and there in the fabric of churches, as at Chobham, Pirbright and Worples-don in Surrey, at Compton near Winchester, and at Bramford near Ipswich. But generally, it would seem, only very limited supplies of this stone were available. The one small region

1 *English Downland* (3rd ed., 1949), p. 92.
2 See Sir Owen Morshead, *Windsor Castle* (1957), pp. 15, 24–25.

WEALDEN SANDSTONE
Bodiam Castle, Sussex

in which they were used extensively was in the Downland villages on the border of Wiltshire and Berkshire, south of White Horse Vale. Lambourn has several good grey sarsen houses, and so have Ashbury and the nearby hamlet of Idstone. Sarsens were even more readily available in some of these villages than the alternative materials, which were chalk and flint. Many can be seen at Avebury, which Massingham rightly called 'the classic example of a sarsen village'. The illustration (114a) shows the end-wall of the former stables of the manor house, now a museum belonging to the National Trust. The village of Aldbourne is full of them.

Being a siliceous stone, it was no easy task in the Middle Ages to cut it; and when sarsens were employed merely to provide strong foundations they might not be shaped at all, as at Bramford, where a buttress of the tower reposes gratefully upon a great sand-stone boulder. When required as masonry in mediaeval times, only the roughest coursing was attempted. For the grey, fifteenth-century church tower at Chobham (and only the tower here is of sarsens: the rest of the building is of a disagreeable, dark-brown pudding-stone), although each block was roughly squared, the stones could only be laid in an irregular patchwork. It is believed that the splitting of the boulders was sometimes achieved by the application of heat. Despite these difficulties, the use of sarsens here and there continued. At Uffington in Berkshire, for instance, where, as already noted, the older buildings are mostly constructed of chalk, the plinth of the Jacobean school-house is of sarsen-stone (73b and c). In Georgian times, when the stables were built at Avebury, an approach to regular coursing was achieved (114a). By the nineteenth century it was possible to trim the sarsens, as Sir Owen Morshead observes, 'to a prim and depressing exactitude', which the tasteless black mortar-joints at Windsor serve to underline. Perhaps the last occasion on which sarsens were used in any quantity as a building stone was for the bridges on the railway, now no more, which linked Marlborough with Andover.

Cretaceous Sandstones

The fabric of Shere church in Surrey is described in the booklet on sale in the building as being 'a mixture of Bargate stone and rubble, ironstone, flints, Caen stone, re-used Roman tiles, clunch from the chalk pits of the North Downs, Horsham slab on part of the roof, Purbeck and Petworth marble, English oak, and Tudor brick'. Here is a good indi-cation of the scarcity of materials available locally in this part of the country in the medi-aeval period, and the resourcefulness which was required of the builders. Yet south-eastern England was by no means so short of building stones as has often been stated. There

SARSENS AND CARSTONE
a. *The Museum, Avebury, Wiltshire* b. *Heacham, Norfolk*

JURASSIC SANDSTONE
c. *Houghton Hall, Norfolk*

were chalk and Kentish ragstone, flints in abundance, and extensive deposits also of sandstone. Nor is it even true that all this sandstone was of inferior quality.

The stones with which we are now concerned were mostly quarried where the Greensands of the Cretaceous system come to the surface through the denudation of the chalk which normally lies above them. The Upper and Lower Greensands, two distinct formations, both yield building stones. Their age is from about a hundred to a hundred and twelve million years. For sandstones the principal areas are to the south of the North Downs, in a long line running from Ightham in Kent, east of Sevenoaks, to Selborne in Hampshire; another long line running north-eastwards from Leighton Buzzard across Bedfordshire (accounting for the place-name, Woburn Sands) and central Cambridgeshire, almost to Ely; a shorter line in north-west Norfolk from Downham Market to Hunstanton; and the southern rim of the Lincolnshire Wolds. The outcrops of greensand are nowhere more than a few miles wide, and often less. With these sandstones may also be considered one or two others dug from the Wealden formation, which comes to the surface in parts of the three south-eastern counties where again the greensand has been worn away. Of these the best known is Horsham stone, much used for roofing, as will be described later.

In former days the greensand stone quarries, although mostly very small, were innumerable. To-day scarcely half a dozen remain open, and none, I believe, is any longer regularly working for building material. In the nineteen-thirties one, at Dunscombe in east Devon, provided stone for a new church at Woolbrook, Sidmouth.

The colours of these stones are characteristically variable. Whereas some are greenish yellow or a pale greenish-grey, the majority, stained by iron oxide, have lost their green tinge entirely. The usual colours are browns, including purple-brown and a dark chocolate, reds, and yellows of every shade from the lightest buff to the deepest gold. Thus many of these sandstones are described loosely as ironstones. Other terms applied to some of them are Malmstone (malm is a soft, friable sandstone from the Upper Greensand, the grains of which are held together by lime), Firestone (the same: employed principally in Surrey) and Carstone (applied to stones from the Lower Greensand in a number of counties, particularly Norfolk).

Historically, the most important stone in this group came from under the North Downs, at Reigate and at several places to the east and west of it: Gatton, Merstham, Bletchingley and Godstone; Betchworth and Brockham. Most of it was not quarried but mined, usually by adits running into the hillside at gentle gradients. At Godstone the last mine was closed only in 1946. Chemically, this is one of the 'border-line' stones referred to in the previous chapter: a sandstone so calcareous that it could with almost equal accuracy be described as a limestone. From the eleventh century to the sixteenth, large quantities were dragged by ox-cart across the Home Counties. It was in demand across the river for some of the churches of Essex and Middlesex, but above all it was needed for London. It provided the stone for old London Bridge in 1176 and for the non-flint portions of the priory church, now the cathedral, of Southwark a generation later; and Reigate was beyond all others the stone of the royal works from the time of Edward the Confessor's Westminster Abbey onwards. The present Abbey and the former Palace of Westminster were built partly of this material, which was also used at Windsor, and in 1538 at Nonsuch. Although by no means as tough as Kentish rag it was, unlike the Kentish stone, a freestone (of sorts), and herein lay the great attraction: it could be moulded and carved. Indeed, for internal dressings, and in default of anything better, Reigate stone long proved a boon. Externally, however, the story was very different. Wren in his middle sixties was appointed Surveyor to Westminster Abbey, and in 1713, in his eighty-first year, wrote a long report (his 'Memorial') on his experiences in this post, a most fascinating and valuable document. Here is what he says about the stonework:

> 'That which is most to be lamented, is the unhappy Choice of the Materials, the Stone is decayed four Inches deep, and falls off perpetually in great scales. I find, after the Conquest, all our Artists were fetched from Normandy; they loved to work in their own Caen-stone, which is more beautiful than durable. This was found expensive to bring hither, so they brought Rygate-stone in Surrey, the nearest like their own, being a Stone that would saw and work like Wood, but not durable, as is manifest; and they used this for the Ashlar of the whole Fabrick, which is now disfigur'd in the highest Degree: this Stone takes in Water, which, being frozen, scales off, whereas good stone gathers a Crust, and defends itself, as many of our English Free-stones do.'

At the time Wren was writing, much of this crumbling Reigate stone had been replaced by Taynton oolite from Oxfordshire, brought by river from Burford; but Henry VII's chapel, 'a nice embroider'd Work' also constructed of Reigate stone, had not yet been touched, and of this, in an engaging phrase, Wren says that 'it is so eaten up by our Weather, that it begs for some Compassion'. It is no wonder that every mullion of the unlucky Abbey, every moulding, every pinnacle exposed to the weather has had to be carved anew, and that we look in vain here for that patina which is one of the charms of a mediaeval building.

The Malmstone also occurs abundantly in the Farnham neighbourhood, and across the Hampshire border, around Selborne, whence it was taken to Winchester for the Castle. It was worked in many small pits. Sometimes it is grey; at others almost as white as chalk.

But Surrey has more durable stones than this: the products of the Lower Greensand, which farther east yields the ragstone of Kent. Unlike Reigate they are not freestones, and, as can be seen at Witley (*268*), where the large blocks come from what are known as the Hythe Beds, they are a good deal coarser in texture. Their warm brown, yellow and occasionally greenish tints are, however, perfectly in tune with a landscape of exceptional charm. The best known of this group is the calcareous sandstone, lightly tinged with iron oxide, known as Bargate, which was formerly quarried at a number of places in the Guildford-Godalming neighbourhood.[1] As early as the twelfth century, most of the walls of Guildford Castle were faced with it; over seven hundred years later it was still being used by Lutyens for several of his country houses around Godalming. Charterhouse School is largely built of it. It is a hard, intractable stone which with an effort admits of regular coursing but cannot be ashlared, and often, as in the garden wall in the foreground of plate *268*, it has been used only as rubblestone. Variants occur a few miles south and west of Haslemere, on Henley Hill in Sussex and on the edge of Woolmer Forest in Hampshire.

Of the Cretaceous sandstones of Sussex suitable for building, the most important was the so-called Wealden stone, quarried from what are known to geologists as the Hastings Beds (of sands and clays) in various places in central and eastern Sussex, especially to the south and south-west of East Grinstead, and also along the south-western fringe of Kent. Two quarries at West Hoathly are still working. The variegated brown Calverley sandstone, quarried at Tunbridge Wells and much in evidence there, belongs to this group. Wealden stone, the oldest of the Cretaceous group, is in my opinion the loveliest building material in south-eastern England, and one of the most reliable. At Wakehurst Place, Ardingly, the best Elizabethan house in Sussex, a virtual rebuilding had to be undertaken in 1936–38 owing to the ravages of the death-watch beetle in the woodwork and to the decayed state of the mortar. But the condition of the stonework itself, a subtle blend of dark grey and pale fawn, with an efflorescence of finials and climbing scrolls on the gables, was still excellent. Wealden stone is a freestone of fine grain which will yield a good ashlar. It can sometimes be obtained in massive blocks, as can be well seen at Bodiam Castle (*113*); here, on the east side especially, pale greenish-grey lichens add still further colour enrichment to the stone's mingled greys and fawns.

By comparison with the best products of Sussex and Surrey, Hampshire sandstone is

[1] It is an odd fact that there is no such place as Bargate in Surrey. Mr. John Harvey has pointed out to me that in older books this stone is sometimes called 'Burgate', which, he suggests, may imply an origin close to Burgate House, Hambledon, 3½ miles south-south-east of Godalming. It is also termed 'Burgate' in the first edition (1962) of Nairn and Pevsner's *Surrey*, but not in the second (1971). It must be added that the nearest deposits of this stone are over a mile away from Burgate House.

inferior. The best is to be found not on the mainland but on the belt of greensand along the southern side of the Isle of Wight, especially between Bonchurch and St. Catherine's Point. This Malmstone, usually known as Green Ventnor, is a greenish-grey freestone which was once widely used in the island, and at different times was deemed good enough to carry as far as Chichester (for the detached bell-tower) and Winchester cathedrals. It is well seen at Appuldurcombe, the grandest house on the Isle of Wight, now unhappily a ruin but carefully preserved by what was long known as the Ministry of Works. Some years ago it was used for repairs at Herstmonceux Castle, but it is no longer obtainable. Nor is it usually very successful, especially in towns, in meeting the challenge of the weather.

Wiltshire, Dorset, Somerset and Devon all possess greensand stone which has been used for building, as, for example, for the original Wilton House (cf. p. 71, footnote); it is also the principal material at Shaftesbury, and is to be seen at most of the north Dorset churches between there and Blandford. Vanbrugh's Eastbury was of greensand; only one wing of the great house escaped demolition after its builder's death, but the stone was re-used by Wyatt in 1788 eight miles away, at Bryanston. Here too only outbuildings survive, the main block having been replaced in 1890 by Norman Shaw's mansion in bright red brick and Portland stone. These greensand stones have charm, but all these counties are well endowed with others that weather better, and in east Devon, for instance, even a limestone of only moderate quality like Beer stone was nearly always preferred to the nearby greensand of Salcombe Regis.

The term Carstone, or Car-stone, current in Surrey to describe veins of very hard rubbly stone occurring in the Lower Greensand (Folkestone Sands), and occasionally in Hampshire and the Isle of Wight, is otherwise hardly heard south of the Thames, but it is frequently applied to the greensand stones used for building farther north, in Bedfordshire, Cambridgeshire and especially Norfolk. The word indicates a stone of coarse, pebbly or gritty consistency, strongly impregnated with iron oxide, and therefore always some shade of brown, ranging from *café-au-lait* to deep chocolate. Norfolk people often call it 'gingerbread stone' on account of its colour. It becomes somewhat harder on exposure but nowhere can it be said to weather well, nor is it of good enough quality to invite fine workmanship. Yet it is, apart from flint, the only building stone in Norfolk; the principal quarries were at Snettisham. One of them is still worked intermittently, but no longer for building.

Snettisham Carstone can be seen at its best some eight miles away at Houghton Hall, where it was used about 1730 for the stables (40 horses!). Although weather-worn, these are charming, and present an effective contrast in colour and tone with the light-grey Jurassic sandstone, tinted here and there with buff, of the house, to be referred to shortly.

Very properly, the yellow-brown stables are the more subdued. Here the Carstone is carefully coursed, as it is in the house at Heacham (*114*b); but elsewhere it was often used random, which meant plenty of mortaring. Modest-sized blocks are occasionally obtainable, but most of this stone is heavily fractured. Many houses at Downham Market and in such west Norfolk villages as Stow Bardolph, Setchey and North Runcton, as well as on the Sandringham estate, are built of tiny pieces, no more than 1–2 ins. thick. The effect, although less regular, resembles that of very small bricks, and is decidedly pretty. Here and there the Carstone is chequered with brick, as at Wallington Hall (*222*c: cf. p. *253*), with flint or, as at Hunstanton Old Hall, chalkstone. This is excellent. Sometimes it is galleted (*114*b).

In Bedfordshire the yellowish-brown Carstone, principally quarried at Silsoe near Ampthill, was sometimes used in combination with white Totternhoe chalk, as in the church at Northill, whilst for greensand stone the most interesting building in Bedfordshire is the church of Husborne Crawley on the north side of Woburn Park. Some of the walls here are of the normal brown Carstone, but those of the chancel, the north aisle of the nave, and the tower contain a generous admixture of a strongly contrasted glauconitic sandstone. Glauconite is present to some extent in a number of the greensand stones, Reigate, for instance, and Ightham, and has already been mentioned as the cause of some stones having a greenish tinge. Nowhere else in England, however, can it be seen as at Husborne Crawley, where it makes a most attractive contribution to the masonry. Partly yellow-green, partly blue-green, and here and there decidedly glassy, this stone is of variable hardness. In the aisle and chancel walls, which were rebuilt in 1911, it is used in roughly dressed, rectangular blocks; in the tower, which was not rebuilt, it is still in large amorphous lumps. The builders must have chanced upon a freak deposit in the local greensand.

Glauconite also occurs in the Spilsby sandstone of eastern Lincolnshire, one of the favourite greensand stones of Lindsey. These are basically very similar to the Norfolk Carstone but more agreeable in colour: at churches such as Burgh-le-Marsh and Halton Holgate the brown stone is seen to have a distinctly greenish tint. If they had more strength these Lincolnshire churches would be among the most beguiling of all the English greensand buildings; but their condition, weather-beaten, crumbling, and patched often with quite incongruous materials such as red brick, imbues the spectator with feelings of inescapable melancholy. Yet both on the fringes of the Wolds and in the adjacent coastal regions known as the Marsh, from the fifteenth century until brick-building began to become general in Lincolnshire, towards the end of the seventeenth, the stone from the greensand was extensively quarried.

Jurassic Sandstones

The Jura Mountains, whence the Jurassic system of sedimentary rocks derives its name, are chiefly composed of oolitic limestones; and in England, too, 'the Jurassic age' at once evokes pictures of these, our finest building stones. This system also includes certain sandstones, but the distinction between sandy limestones and calcareous sandstones is somewhat arbitrary, and a non-geologist will not fail to observe that the experts do not always agree about terminology. Reference has already been made to the differing assessments of Ham Hill stone, some classing it as Oolite and others as Lias; on this subject it now only remains to add that no less an authority than the most recent Geological Survey of Great Britain (Sheet 312:1958) terms it a shelly sandstone. From the aspect of building material, it does not really matter very much; this is one of those stones which embody limestone and sandstone characteristics in almost equal proportions.

Among the Jurassic regions of England, there are perhaps only two where some of the calcareous stone is sufficiently siliceous to rank as a sandstone and of fine enough texture to be worked as a freestone. One is in the neighbourhood of Northampton and the other in the north-eastern moors of Yorkshire. From the Northampton Sand, at the base of the Oolite beds, comes a sandstone of variable quality which has never enjoyed more than a local reputation, but which can be seen in Northampton itself and in some of the surrounding villages: the colours range from pale fawn through yellow-brown to deep red, induced by the presence of iron. The best-known quarries were at Duston, two miles north-west of the county town; one is still working.[1] So is another near the neighbouring village of Harlestone.

The Yorkshire stone is decidedly more important. That beautiful region embracing the Cleveland and Hambleton Hills and the moors and dales behind Pickering, Scarborough and Whitby contains a certain amount of Jurassic limestone suitable for building, such as the brownish stone from Wass used at the nearby Abbey of Byland, but most of the quarries of this part of Yorkshire yielded sandstones. The best of all came from Aislaby near Whitby: a fine-textured, light brown stone which had a considerable reputation in the Middle Ages. This was one of the materials used at Whitby Abbey and at Guisborough Priory; and stone of closely similar character was taken from Ingleby Moor for Mount Grace Priory and from Bilsdale and Hollin Hill (opposite Duncombe Park) for what

1 See J. M. Steane: 'Building Materials Used in Northamptonshire and the Area Around', in *Northamptonshire Past and Present* (Journal of the Northamptonshire Record Society), vol. IV, no. 2 (1967). He cites Manor Farm (formerly New Hall), Naseby, as a notable example of the use of Duston stone. A far more eminent example of its use was by Inigo Jones for the Banqueting House in Whitehall.

is to-day probably the loveliest of all England's ruins, the Abbey of Rievaulx. Centuries later, this North Riding sandstone was still making great contributions to English architecture: most of Castle Howard is built of it, supplies here coming from a quarry in the park, and this was also the stone, mentioned three pages back, which was used to face Walpole's great house at Houghton (*114c*). From Aislaby itself large quantities of stone were still being shipped down the coast as far as London until the end of the last century.

New Red Sandstone

Some geologists avoid the term New Red Sandstone, because it is not the name of a period nor of a system; but for those concerned with building stones its comprehensiveness is convenient. It is applied to sandstones from the Triassic and the somewhat older Permian series, rocks, that is to say, which were formed between about 195 and 280 million years ago. The texture and the characteristic colours of the two groups are so similar as to be indistinguishable, and the border-line between them is uncertain. New Red Sandstone is the principal building-stone of the western Midlands, and a material of importance in all the western counties from Devon to Cumberland.

In much of the country in which it holds sway it lies, sometimes at a considerable depth, under beds of clay and marls. Here in the west Midlands are some of our richest arable lands and some of our finest pastures; timber is plentiful and there are many beautiful parks. Into this agriculturally prosperous and often lush landscape, the colours of the sandstone buildings (which are sometimes charming and, despite the geological name, often anything but red) add a note of richness which is in harmony both with the soil wherever it is ploughed and with every sign of building activity down to the humblest boundary wall. There lies the great value of using local stone. So long as this is done, it is practically certain that the building will not be out of tone, and this is a very important aspect of the *genius loci*. However good the design, if a stone is employed which is too light in tone—too white, that is—or too dark, the building will never look right in that particular locality.

Unluckily there is a fly in this seemingly delectable ointment. Much of this sandstone, exposed as it is to the vagaries of the English weather, blisters and spalls, flakes and crumbles. In that interesting book *Goths and Vandals*, Mr. Martin Briggs gives a number of quotations from the cathedral reports included in Sir George Gilbert Scott's *Recollections*. Thus at Chester in 1868, he found that 'the external stonework was so horribly and lamentably decayed as to reduce it to a mere wreck, like a mouldering sandstone cliff.

NEW RED SANDSTONES
a. *Wootton Lodge, Staffordshire*
b. *Scraptoft Hall, Leicestershire*

The most ordinary details could often only be found in corners more protected, through accidental circumstances, than the rest. . . . The frightful extent of the decay forced upon me, most unwillingly, very considerable renewal of the stonework.' In the case of the Lady Chapel, 'the exterior had been so cut to pieces that it was only by study, spread over several years, that its beautiful design was at all recovered'. At Worcester a very extensive restoration was undertaken between 1857 and 1874, yet a report made public in 1949 stated that 'although little can be seen from the ground, nearly all the decoration of the tower has been weathered out of recognition, and will have to be replaced. Figures of saints, heads, flowers, leaves and tracery work have been worn away. Small pinnacles are missing, and parts of the plain stonework have been eaten away like the face of a sandstone cliff.' The restoration again took several years. The other two mediaeval cathedrals built of Triassic sandstone, Lichfield and Carlisle, have fared no better. (For the latter, cf. *381*b.) Up and down the western counties, the story is the same. At Taunton, to cite just one more example, both the principal church towers had to be rebuilt from the ground about a hundred years ago, because the condition of their stonework had become so perilous.

There are nevertheless a few excellent Triassic sandstones, principally towards the North-West. The New Red Sandstone covers most of the counties of Worcestershire, Warwickshire, Staffordshire and Cheshire, with almost all Shropshire north and east of the Severn, south Derbyshire, and the western half of Leicestershire. From this central area, roughly triangular in shape, the same rock formation is continued in three long arms, reaching out to the north-west, the north-east and the south-west. The north-western arm stretches across coastal Lancashire including the tip of the Furness peninsula, and along much of the coast of Cumberland until finally, at Carlisle, it turns back up the valley of the Eden. The north-eastern arm takes in most of Nottinghamshire, a broad strip through central Yorkshire, and the south-eastern corner of Durham. The south-western arm points down the Severn valley across Gloucestershire, suffers interruptions in central Somerset, then continues again to the coast of Devon at Sidmouth. All these are regions of rich farm land, mostly low-lying. From the apple orchards of east Devon to the diary pastures of Cheshire, from the Vale of Eden to the Vale of Evesham, nature and man have together prepared a most beautiful setting for these warm-tinted buildings.

The sandstones from the Permian series are much less abundant in England than those of the Trias. The only counties in which they have been of any importance for building are Devon, Warwickshire, Nottinghamshire and Cumberland.

It is an ironic circumstance that two of our most weather-worn and patched cathedral churches, Carlisle and Lichfield, should be situated in the two counties which possess the best New Red sandstones in England. If Carlisle had been built of stone from St. Bees, or

SANDSTONE CONTRASTS
a. *Attingham Park, Shropshire*   b. *Arbury Hall, Warwickshire*
c. *The Prior's Lodge, Much Wenlock, Shropshire*

from Aspatricke (now Aspatria: only twenty miles away), instead of (probably) the inferior Wetheral stone from the Eden valley, preferred because it entailed no more than a five-mile river journey, the cathedral authorities might not have had to appeal, as they did in 1956, for a hundred thousand pounds to save the walls from becoming 'a shapeless mass of crumbling stone'. St. Bees Head sandstone is the strongest of all the New Red group, and one of the most uniformly reliable. Like nearly all the sandstones of Cumberland it is red or pink. Bransty Blue, which has a delightful, pale lavender tint, and the grey, or mottled grey, stone quarried at Whitehaven are the only exceptions. St. Bees Head sandstone can be seen to great advantage at Furness Abbey where, amid lawns and trees, it looks salmon-coloured in some places, deep peach-pink in others; after eight centuries it has of course weathered considerably, but in contrast to many sandstones, its texture is so compact and its grain so fine that it does not harbour the dirt. St. Bees Head quarry is now closed but Bank End nearby is working. Aspatria, another freestone, is a deep cocoa-powder-brown. The long abandoned quarries are now filled with elder bushes. Penrith stone, which belongs to the Permian series and of which all the older part of that ancient market town is constructed, is similarly coloured, and, it must be admitted, seems a little sombre despite its 'warmth'. This stone is also less durable: the old sandstone church, for example, had to be entirely rebuilt, except for the tower, in the reign of George I. It lasts better where there is no carved nor moulded detail at all, as at a number of neighbouring farmhouses. Two quarries near Penrith are still working.

From Hollington near Uttoxeter in Staffordshire comes a well-known and much used group. A 'white' quarry on the hill close to the village yields a stone which is actually light grey, with here a greenish, there a pinkish, tinge; the 'red' quarry is at Great Gate, across the valley to the north. It was the stone from this quarry which, after careful consideration and analysis by the University of Birmingham Department of Geology, was finally selected by Sir Basil Spence as the best for the cathedral at Coventry. Predominantly pinkish, it owes much to the slight sparkle which sandstones sometimes have, produced by the fragments of quartz of which its sand grains are largely composed. Hollington stone can also be seen on the walls of at least two other cathedrals: Hereford and Birmingham. The story of Birmingham's sandstone is all too characteristic. The cathedral, then the parish church of St. Philip, was not completed until 1725, but it was built of Rowington stone from Warwickshire, which proved disastrously soft. The whole building had to be refaced, and Hollington stone was selected for the main body of the church as long ago as the eighteen-eighties. The refacing of the tower, again in Hollington, took place some years ago. This stone has also been employed for the restoration of the fine church at Ludlow in Shropshire, and for many other refacings as well as for new buildings in the western Midlands and elsewhere. In its 'green' state Hollington stone is extraordinarily soft; large blocks, weighing up to six tons each, can be cut out like cheese. Fortunately it becomes much harder on exposure to the air, and as it possesses a very even texture it lends itself to carved detail better than most sandstones.

Formerly Staffordshire had many other sandstone quarries, some yielding durable stone, others not. After Hollington, the best was at Stanton, not many miles distant and quite close to Dovedale. It was this quarry which probably provided the stone for Wootton Lodge (*123a*), the most dramatically sited of all Jacobean houses. This fascinating building, with its flanking lodges, owes much to the beauty of its stone, grey-fawn with here and there a blush of pink.

*

Until the Industrial Revolution, Cheshire and South Lancashire preserved extensive areas of woodland, and stone was confined as a rule to the more important buildings; but when it was used at all, either for a church or a house, it would nearly always be a red, pink or buff sandstone. Much of this stone had proved friable and treacherous, but both counties had important quarries close to the Mersey. Cheshire had Storeton in the Wirral, a pinkish stone not unlike Hollington, and, where the estuary narrows again, Weston and Runcorn. The Runcorn quarries yielded an excellent freestone, the best in the county. On the Lancashire side of the Mersey there are two sandstones, Woolton and Rainhill, sufficiently reliable to have been chosen for the Anglican cathedral at Liverpool. These are dull red stones, very conveniently placed: the Woolton quarry is only five miles away, and actually within the city boundary. Rainhill, to the east of Liverpool, produces a slightly softer stone which is used in the interior.

The great building stone of Shropshire came from Grinshill, eight miles north of Shrewsbury. A visit to these quarries to-day is a fascinating if also somewhat doleful experience. Behind the village rises an isolated hill no more than a mile and a half in length, upon which in the course of a few minutes it is possible to gather stone fragments ranging from purplish pink through brownish red to pale greenish grey; in gastronomic parlance from mushroom to chocolate and celery. The 'red' quarry at the base of the hill just behind the village was abandoned many years ago. The 'white' quarry on the hill-top farther east is much more striking: a vast pit nearly two hundred feet deep. From both, as from Hollington, the stone could be taken in very large blocks leaving smooth, clean cuts, for the grain is close and even. Grinshill stone was employed by the Romans in the building of Uriconium (Wroxeter), then the principal town of the district. It was used extensively in the centuries before the Industrial Revolution, as some of the mellow villages in the northern half of Shropshire still testify. Both varieties are in evidence in Shrewsbury. The virtues of the latter in the achievement of finely-jointed ashlar can be well seen at

Attingham Park, built in the seventeen-eighties; and not only on the mansion itself but
on the outbuildings too, notably the charming entrance to the office court (*124a*). On
a very modest scale, white Grinshill is still worked.

Shropshire has other sandstones sufficiently compacted to be suitable for ashlar,
among them Highley and Alveley, facing each other across the Severn below Bridgnorth.
Highley was worked as early as the eleven-seventies for the two westernmost bays of
Worcester Cathedral, where it can still be seen internally, a grey and fawn stone with just
a hint of green in it. Some beds have yielded hard, gritty material which has been of service in the construction of a number of the Severn bridges, notably the fine one which
Telford completed in 1801 at Bewdley in Worcestershire, a few miles downstream from
the quarry. But much of this stone has proved embarrassingly friable, as can be seen at the
Prior's Lodge (now known as the Abbey), Much Wenlock (*124c*), where, in marked
contrast with the wonderful roof, the walls of red, pink, fawn and grey Alveley stone are
now in a very poor state.

The surface of Nottinghamshire is mainly Triassic sand in the western half, with red
marls covering the sandstone in the eastern half. Near Tuxford there are quarries in the
Trias, long ago abandoned, which once had considerable local importance. But the principal quarries of this county are at Mansfield, where the Permian rocks emerge from below
the Trias. Mansfield Woodhouse, a magnesian limestone, has been mentioned in the
previous chapter; other Mansfield stones, 'white' (which is in fact pale yellow) from the
Gregory (formerly Lindley) quarry and 'red' (pinkish-brown) from the Sills quarry (no
longer worked), are dolomitic sandstones, although the distinction between them is not
insistent: the limestones are sandy and the sandstones contain a good deal of lime. The
Mansfield sandstones exhibit many of the characteristics of the limestones of similar age:
they are freestones of considerable charm, of fine enough grain to cut very smoothly,
but soft enough to weather, sometimes none too well. The most important building in
White Mansfield is Southwell Minster, where the stone is still used for all repairs to the
fabric. Another prominent example is the front of the Palladian Town Hall at Newark by
Carr of York, erected in 1773. This is well-proportioned and dignified, but not improved
by an array of unsightly but necessary patches where the stone has decayed. A hundred and
thirteen years later, when Bodley built that sumptuous church in Clumber Park which
now stands in romantic isolation by the lake (the house having been demolished), he
preferred to bring sandstone all the way from Runcorn rather than use Mansfield. Yet in
unexposed places this remains a desirable stone, and the white variety is still available.

Little more need be said about the north-eastern arm of New Red Sandstone, for it has
not played a leading part in the buildings of Yorkshire, except to some extent in the North

THE CARBONIFEROUS SANDSTONES
a. *The Banquet House, Weston Hall, Yorkshire*   b. *The Gatehouse, Kirklees Priory, Yorkshire*
c. *Wallington, Northumberland*

Riding; the striking church at Thirsk, buff-coloured and much weathered, is a good example.

The sandstones of the Midland counties, Leicestershire, Warwickshire and Worcestershire, can look very picturesque on account both of their colours and of their frequently coarse, rough textures, of which Scraptoft Hall near Leicester (*123*b) is an excellent example. Nonetheless, most of them make poor building stones. Arbury Hall near Nuneaton, our most perfect Gothick house, dates in its present form only from the second half of the eighteenth century, but the patched condition of its garden front is as characteristic as it is inevitable (*124*b). Inferior stone and the presence of ample and excellent clays favoured the great development of brick building in these counties from the end of the seventeenth century onwards.

Only one other region is of importance for its buildings in New Red Sandstone: western Somerset with the adjacent (eastern) part of Devon. There is a good deal of pink sandstone in evidence in the Clevedon-Portishead district, but one really enters 'the red country' soon after leaving Taunton, and the effect upon the eye as one approaches Exeter is unforgettable: the whole countryside seems to be bathed in a warm red glow. In west Somerset the hills (the Quantocks, the Brendons, Exmoor) all belong to the Devonian formations, but down in the valleys between them, where the villages cluster, the soil is red marl over New Red Sandstone. Specially delightful are some of the church towers under the lee of the Quantocks. Kingston St. Mary is very grand. Its walls are not ashlared and their roughness certainly means a loss of urbanity and 'finish', but the design is magnificent, and the masonry accords it the vigour and strength of a good sturdy countryman. This is a blend of several colours, red, grey and green; but at Bishop's Lydeard the tower is almost a wine red, a very rich shade which adds not a little to its attraction. Entering Devon, the pageant of rich red churches continues, from Cullompton to Paignton. Sometimes, as at Kenton, a very red building, the dressings are of white limestone, brought without much difficulty across the water from Beer; the colour and tone contrasts are lively but excessive. At Cullompton the effect is better because they are more muted.

Despite its possession of several other kinds of stone which were of importance for building, Devon might well be regarded as the sandstone county *par excellence*. For here are both the New Red and the much older sandstone of the Devonian system; and within the New Red series, both the Triassic and the Permian rocks are strongly represented. The former belongs to the eastern side of the county, from Culmstock to Ottery St. Mary and Sidmouth. The latter gives us the famous and much loved red cliffs of Dawlish and Teignmouth, and also extends a long, thin tongue westwards, through the Vale of Crediton, nearly to Hatherleigh. Many small quarries were once worked for this stone

SANDSTONE ROOFS
a. *Castleton, Derbyshire*   b. *30 The Causeway, Horsham, Sussex*
c. *Brick House, Pembridge, Herefordshire (this roof replaced in 1972)*

from the end of the fourteenth century onwards, and a few larger ones around Exeter itself.

The Carboniferous Sandstones

The sandstones of the Carboniferous series are not the most beautiful of the English varieties, but for strength and durability they are the best. In the south-western counties, Gloucestershire, Somerset, Devon and Cornwall, they have always had to compete with other and more attractive materials; but in the North there is no other building stone of comparable importance. To see the best of all Britain's Carboniferous sandstones, it is generally considered necessary to go to Edinburgh; the Scottish capital is largely built of Craigleith stone, now no longer worked, and it has been said that 'Craigleith is to Edinburgh what Portland stone is to London, Pentelic marble to Athens, and Pietra Serena to Florence'.[1] Craigleith stone with its fine even texture weathers splendidly, certainly a very necessary attribute in Edinburgh; but those familiar with the Scottish capital, and particularly with the New Town area to the north of Princes Street laid out during the last third of the eighteenth century and the first third of the nineteenth and built almost entirely of Craigleith, will also know that this stone makes a much less favourable impression than Portland because, dun-coloured when clean, much of it is now dark. Thus, for all the dignity of the buildings and fascination of their siting, the impression which one carries away is of a city in which the stone is not one of the principal attractions.

There are, as was noted on p. 96, three formations which go to make up the Carboniferous series: the Coal Measures, the Millstone Grit, and the Carboniferous Limestone, which also includes certain sandstones (of which Craigleith is an example). These rocks were formed between about 280 and 345 million years ago, and the Pennines are almost entirely composed of them. Where the surface rock is Millstone Grit, as is largely the case from the Craven Gap[2] southwards nearly to the Peak, the characteristic landscape is wild, sweeping moorland, frequently covered with peat: in certain areas the gritstone formation reaches a thickness of 5000 ft. or even more. The Coal Measures form somewhat lower ground to either side of the main range of the Pennines: that is to say, in Lancashire; in Yorkshire, east Derbyshire and a corner of Nottinghamshire; and in Durham and Northumberland. These, now three of the most heavily industrialized regions in

1 *The Architectural Use of Building Materials: A Study by a Committee convened by the Royal Institute of British Architects* (H.M.S.O., 1946), para. 124. This publication, which was reissued in 1954 but is unfortunately now out of print, is full of helpful information and wise criticism, mainly from an aesthetic standpoint.

2 See p. 96.

the world, were scenically beautiful until about 1800: they still possess many valuable and important sandstones. The sandstones of the Carboniferous Limestone formations, known as the Lower Carboniferous Sandstones, are to be found in some of the dales and moors of north Yorkshire and especially in Northumberland.

Structurally these rocks have much in common. The sand grains of which all of them are composed are principally quartz, with some felspar, and the matrix which cements the grains together is mainly silica. So high indeed is the silica content in some of them that the trade unions are liable to ban their use owing to the danger of silicosis: this happened after the last war when it was proposed to use Stancliffe sandstone from Darley Dale for the rebuilding of the House of Commons. Since men's lungs will be bound to suffer if they inhale dust containing grains of glassy silica, the fullest protective measures are clearly essential; accordingly, wherever possible these stones are now only worked by wet methods. The great value of a silica matrix, remembering that with sandstone it is not the sand grains but the substance binding them together which is always the potential source of weakness, is its strength and durability. Whether the grain be fine or coarse, it is possible with a siliceous matrix to achieve a homogeneity of structure which stands up to the rigours of the weather, and in particular to a smoke-polluted atmosphere, better than any limestone.

A characteristic of these Carboniferous sandstones, continually in evidence as one travels round the Northern counties, is the size of the blocks which can be quarried (cf. p. 49). Sometimes, as has been observed,[1] the massiveness of the masonry, especially when it is the dark millstone grit, seems to endow the buildings with a positively Cyclopean character, which has no parallel in English limestone. This helps to produce the impression of a rugged and purposeful architecture, not much concerned with the graces of ornamental enrichment, to which indeed the material is not well suited (*129b*). But what contributes still more to the pervasive air of sobriety is the colour. Among the Carboniferous sandstones it is exceptional to meet the delightful colour ranges of the greensand stones and of the Red sandstones, both New and Old. Even when these northern stones are not blackened by smoke, the usual colours are unexciting; browns, buffs and greys are the rule, sometimes speckled or mottled with darker spots. Such reticence is, however, in complete harmony with the landscape settings of these northern buildings.

The sandstones and shales of the Coal Measures, unlike the Triassic sandstones, do not usually offer a fertile subsoil. The riches lie embedded in the rocks themselves: principally, of course, in the coal, but also in the fire-clay and in the sandstone, which was formerly taken from innumerable quarries in these areas. Many were small and of purely

---

1 By Peter Fleetwood-Hesketh, *Murray's Lancashire Architectural Guide* (1955), p. ix.

local importance, like that on the estate which supplied most of the stone for Hardwick Hall (*400*), a quarry that was reopened a few years ago after a long period of disuse, to provide stone for extensive external repairs to the house. An abundance of this stone can be seen in such Lancashire towns as Oldham, Rochdale and Colne, and farther west too, at Wigan, which was supplied from an excellent quarry of light grey sandstone at Appley Bridge, a few miles to the north-west. But for sandstone from the Coal Measures far and away the most important county was, and still is, the West Riding of Yorkshire. From quarries scattered over a wide terrain to the south of Leeds and Bradford and around Halifax comes the famous material, light brown and of fine, even grain, widely known under the generic name of York stone. Park Spring stone from Farnley, and Howley Park stone from near Morley, both south-west of Leeds, may be cited as typical: many buildings in Leeds owe their appearance to Park Spring. Other well-known quarries, all working, include Bolton Wood, Hipperholme, Elland Edge, Crosland Hill, Greenmore, Hillhouse Edge and Woodkirk. Huge blocks, with a fine arris, are normal. Some quarries now offer blocks measuring as much as 10 × 6 × 4 ft. 6 ins. and weighing up to twenty tons each. Even in the eighteenth century the sizes used are remarkable. At Kedleston two of the steps leading up to the main portico were cut out of a single block of stone. Three of the six columns of the portico are monoliths weighing $7\frac{1}{2}$ tons each, and were brought, very laboriously, from Horsley Castle, some seven miles away, on a special six-wheeled dray.

Some York stone is highly laminated, which means that it can be split into quite thin slabs, sometimes no more than an inch thick. This useful property does not render it suitable for roofing because it holds so much moisture; but for such purposes as paving, coping, sills and steps York stone, hard and durable without being brittle, is ideal. Thus, in addition to being very widely employed locally, this stone, especially in its laminated form, has travelled far afield. Many London buildings have floors and sills, many streets (though, alas, not so many as formerly) have pavements of York stone. Where strength and durability combined with the need to resist the blackest chimney-smoke are what is required, it still proves invaluable.

Millstone Grit, or gritstone as the building stone from this formation is usually called, was quarried by the Romans and was also in use again in parts of Yorkshire before the Norman Conquest. Its very name is rooted in history, for when water-power operated the little corn-mills of the Pennine villages it was from this tough, gritty sandstone that they fashioned the millstones. I have referred to it as the principal stone of the Southern Pennines, but they are only the heart of the gritstone region. Narrower outcrops run down through Derbyshire on either side of the Peak, the western one extending into the adjacent parts of Cheshire and Staffordshire. The eastern arm includes Beeley Moor quarry on the Chatsworth estate, whence came most of the stone for the great house. Gritstone comes to the surface over considerable areas of Lancashire between Blackburn and Morecambe Bay; and in Yorkshire it extends northwards beyond the Craven Gap almost to Richmond, and thence in a less continuous outcrop south, west and finally north of the Durham-Northumberland coalfield, to reach the sea at Warkworth.

Everywhere over this wide area it has been used for building, the distinguishing feature being the angularity, and often also the large size, of its quartz grains. Some quarries yield a stone of such strength that it is in demand for dams and other engineering works as well as for buildings. As with other geological formations, there are variations. In Staffordshire the gritstone is not outstandingly durable; yet just over the border in Cheshire, one is struck by the contrast betweeen the large number of new red sandstone churches, all without exception badly weathered or glaringly restored, and the lovely late fifteenth century church at Astbury, a rare example of gritstone in that county, with outside details, after nearly five hundred years, still crisp and sharp. Here the gritstone, a mixture of grey and pale buff, is pleasing in both colour and texture. (Inside the building some of the stone, including the whole of the north arcade, is pink.)

The two classic Millstone Grit sandstones are Darley Dale and Bramley Fall. The former comes from a number of quarries in the centre of Derbyshire, mostly between Matlock, Winster and Bakewell. Stancliffe, Peasenhurst, Stanton Park, Stanton Moor, Hall Dale, Endcliffe, Birchover, Pillough, Lumshill, Wattscliffe, Whatstandwell: all these are Darley Dale stones or closely associated with them, and several of their quarries are still flourishing. All are highly siliceous, even-grained stones, suitable for ashlar and absolutely dependable. Stancliffe, exceedingly hard, is also excellent for paving. Stoke, quarried a few miles farther north at Grindleford, is a micaceous gritstone of equal virtue. But although agreeably light-coloured at the quarry-face (most are yellow-brown, sometimes speckled, and some have pinkish tints), all these stones tend to become darker as they weather; moreover, if exposed to smoke, as they often are, they become absolutely black, and as mentioned earlier, the soot is practically impossible to remove.

The Bramley Fall stones are also in steady demand, largely for engineering enterprises, on account of their great strength. This is the material which was used in the construction of some of the London docks, and also for the Euston Arch, regrettably demolished in 1961–62. The quarries are to the north-west of Leeds, in the direction of Otley. This pale yellow-brown stone, much weathered yet strong, can still be seen after eight centuries, under a layer of grime, in the extensive ruins of Kirkstall Abbey. The original Bramley Fall quarry was worked out more than a hundred years ago, but several others have since taken its place. One at least, Pool Bank, has yielded a stone of fine grain; but most of the

Bramley Fall group are decidedly coarser than the Darley Dale stones and therefore more sought after by engineers than by architects.

Other Yorkshire gritstones of fine even texture come from the Wellfield quarries near Huddersfield and from the Ringby quarries on Swales Moor, near Halifax. Large sawn slabs of the latter have been used for renovation at several historic houses, notably Gawthorpe Hall in Lancashire. Excellent ashlared gritstone, with typically massive blocks, also characterizes the three-storeyed Elizabethan Banquet House in the garden of Weston Hall near Otley in Wharfedale, a rare survivor among buildings of this type (*129*a). But many of Yorkshire's gritstones are too coarse in texture to permit of a fine finish, and so hard that detailed working is out of the question. Hence the blocks of stone, although often coursed, are seldom ashlared, and in the far north gritstone is frequently plastered over and whitened. This is an excellent practice, for the dark tones of these stones after weathering can be lugubrious. Few pre-Industrial Revolution buildings are indeed more depressing than some of the dark brown weavers' cottages scattered along the eastern slopes of the Pennines above Huddersfield, Holmfirth and Penistone. These cottages are nevertheless interesting on account of the mullioned windows of their upper storeys arranged in long, continuous rows, a specialized development[1] designed to give the weavers as much light as possible. One of the best features of the gritstone houses is that many of them still have stone upon their roofs (see p. 143).

There are some excellent gritstones in Co. Durham: Dunhouse, for example. This quarry, which is near the Tees at Winston, east of Barnard Castle, has for the past forty years supplied all the stone needed for restorations at Durham Cathedral and Castle. In Northumberland Kenton gritstone was formerly used a good deal in Newcastle, but some years ago the quarry was filled in and grassed over.

There are Carboniferous sandstones which are older than those of the Coal Measures, older also than those of the Millstone Grit. These rocks, which are of the same age as the Carboniferous limestones discussed in the last chapter, are only distinguished from the others described in this section by the fact that their matrix contains a certain proportion of calcium carbonate as well as a preponderance of silica. In the moorland country of north-west Yorkshire there are somewhat impure sandstones among the limestones. On Gatherley Moor, about four miles north of Richmond, a warm-hued Carboniferous sandstone was quarried over a very long period; it was used for Aske Hall and for a number

1 Weavers' houses dating from the early years of the Industrial Revolution and having a similar window arrangement can also be seen on the other side of the Pennines, and in Nottinghamshire and Leicestershire. The latter are of brick, but around Rochdale the material is sandstone from the Coal Measures. In many instances the windows are now partially blocked up.

of buildings in Richmond itself. The handsome triple-span bridge over the Swale, dating from 1789, shows it off to advantage.

The only English county in which Lower Carboniferous sandstones have figured prominently for building is Northumberland, where they occur over wide, scantily populated areas. They are hard and often difficult to work, but their colours, usually warm shades of pale yellow, buff and honey, can be very agreeable, as at Wallington (*129c*). This gracious house, later unfortunately re-roofed, was built in 1688 with local stone, now partly honey-coloured and partly grey, taken from a long-abandoned quarry at the adjacent village of Cambo. One of the best of these sandstones came from Woodburn on the Rede, a tributary of the North Tyne. Another was Prudham, quarried at Fourstones on the South Tyne, five miles north-west of Hexham. This was used in 1846–50 by John Dobson for Newcastle Central Station, which, although now much soot-begrimed, preserves to an admirable degree its sharp arrises and general crispness of structure. After a period of inactivity, Prudham freestone was worked again in 1965. Also in operation are Blaxter quarry near Elsdon, in the centre of the county, with a creamy-buff, coarse-textured, micaceous sandstone of medium strength, and Doddington near Wooler, in the north, an old quarry which yields a robust and attractive stone of a pinkish hue, flecked with purple and grey. Northumberland can provide the historically minded with a good example of Carboniferous sandstone employed as a building material: the Romans used it freely for the facing of Hadrian's Wall.

The Carboniferous sandstones of the south-western counties occur in three areas, two of which are associated with the small Gloucestershire coalfields. Forest of Dean stone, some of which belongs to the Coal Measures series, some to the Lower Carboniferous, is among the strongest (although by no means the most attractive) of the sedimentary rocks, and is still worked in a number of quarries to the east of Coleford. A new one at Bixhead was opened in 1967. The best stone here is at a depth of about 130 ft., which entails the removal of at least 90 ft. of 'overburden', a nearly impossible task before the invention of the tracked excavator. To-day it is quite feasible; the unwanted top covering is dumped in worked out quarries nearby, and blocks weighing up to ten tons are hoisted out of the quarry by a jib crane. What would not our old cathedral builders have given for such mechanisation? At Burnhill quarry the working face is at 70–80 ft. The basic colour is grey, but one variety has a dark bluish tinge. It is in demand for engineering purposes, and also for paving, as well as for building; in our own time it has been employed at Avon-mouth docks. Pennant sandstone, bluish-grey again, is much the same. This fine-grained Coal Measures stone was formerly quarried in the north-eastern suburbs of Bristol, where it was at one time used extensively. In the same neighbourhood there is a purplish-red gritstone which can be seen, in combination with oolite for the dressings, at the churches of Yate and Westerleigh. The Coal Measures stone has also been worked to a very small extent in north-east Somerset, between Bristol and Radstock.

In central Devon and north Cornwall, the third area, the sandstones occur in what are known as the Culm Measures, a name given to a series of hard shales and sandstones which contain in places thin beds of impure coal, peculiar to this region. Culm Measures stone has been used a good deal locally in the region between Dartmoor and Exmoor, and westwards to the north coast of Cornwall around Bude. It is a humbler stone than some of those described above, and is obtainable only in small, hard, somewhat rubbly pieces, often of a dark brownish-red. Perhaps its chief attraction is that lichens grow readily upon its surface; many walls which would otherwise look dark and heavy are appreciably lightened with spots of pale green and silvery-grey. Nowhere on English buildings have lichens played a more welcome part.

The Oldest Sandstones

The Old Red Sandstone rocks, probably formed between 345 and 395 million years ago, are of considerable importance for building in parts of Scotland, Ireland and Wales. In England they only occur in the Southern Marches and in a corner of Worcestershire. They may be a dense and even rather depressing red; but they can also be pink, purple, brown, greenish-grey, pure grey, or grey with a blush of pink, a delicious colour. The tint may change slightly almost from block to block, and sometimes within the single block of stone, yielding effects of much charm. Yet the Old Red sandstone, like the New Red, to which in appearance it is sometimes rather similar, is only moderately satisfactory for building. It varies a good deal, so that generalizations may need qualification; but if less friable than the New Red, it is also likely to reveal weaknesses when exposed to the weather. Some of it splits easily parallel to the bedding, which renders it useful for walling, steps and paving; on the other hand it seldom yields a freestone and generally comes from the quarry in rather small pieces. Its rough country face can none the less be very likeable and wholly appropriate to its surroundings.

The last Old Red Sandstone to be available for building purposes was the variety known as Red Wilderness, but by 1972 only very small quantities were to be had from a quarry near Mitcheldean in Gloucestershire. Red Wilderness is compact, strong and durable: an unusually good product of this formation. Many little quarry pits, long since abandoned, bear witness that it was once worked extensively in this area. It is the surface rock in much of Gloucestershire west of the Severn, in four-fifths of Herefordshire, and in most of south-east Shropshire. Often the soil is ruddy. Here and there the stone is of excellent quality, as luckily at Kilpeck, where one of the finest of our Norman churches is exceptionally well preserved. At Ross-on-Wye on the other hand, and particularly in Shropshire in the vicinity of the Clee Hills, the stone tends to be soft.

The Devonian rocks of the South-West were being formed during the same geological period as the Old Red Sandstone farther north, but are very differently constituted. They are by no means all sandstones, nor are they confined to Devon. They account for some of our most impressive moorland and coastal scenery. In west Somerset and north Devon there are the Quantocks, the Brendons, the whole of Exmoor and that splendid coast from Porlock Bay to Morte Point. The bold cliffs of south Devon and Cornwall are also largely Devonian. Most of these rocks are slate, with some limestone referred to earlier (p. 98); but here and there the sandstone is prominent and was once of some local importance to the builder, as at North Molton. In some places this stone weathers very well, and when the colours are peach pink or lavender it is a delight.

There are still older sandstones, belonging to the Silurian, Ordovician and Cambrian systems (395 to perhaps 575 million years old). In England they chiefly occur in the Lake District and the Welsh border counties, with small exposures in Worcestershire and Warwickshire. A great deal of Silurian stone was used for building, especially during the Victorian period, all the way from Ulverston to Hawkshead and Ambleside. In this area dark, flaggy sandstones—the 'greywacke' of the geologists—were readily accessible and quarried in many places. Their dour colouring, not at all attractive, is due to the embodiment within the hard stone of numerous particles of grey shale. The humble-looking late-fifteenth-century church at Hawkshead provides an unusually early example of the use of this material (among others). Its rubblestone walls formerly bore a covering of roughcast, which was whitewashed, so that Wordsworth, in 1788, was able to picture

> . . . the snow-white church upon her hill
> . . . liked a thronèd lady, sending out
> A gracious look all over her domain.

In 1875 this overcoat was heartlessly stripped off, and the effect is now decidedly crude.

The hard rocks from the early Ordovician series provide an uncompromising-looking building stone. They too can be very dark and sombre in tone, as can be seen at Keswick. But in southern Shropshire, in and around Church Stretton and under Wenlock Edge, the tints, mainly brown and buff, are more varied and more agreeable. The even older rocks of the Cambrian series include the micaceous, greenish Hollybush sandstone of the Malverns and the highly siliceous pink sandstone known as Hartshill quartzite, quarried near Nuneaton. The latter is useful as road-metal but has long ceased to be employed for building.

Sandstone Roofs

As a material for roofing, sandstone has been hardly less important than limestone: indeed, sandstone roofs are more widely distributed, and at one time may well have been more numerous. Most of the varieties of sandstone that have been discussed in this chapter have yielded roofing slates; to cite examples, Horsham slates come from the Cretaceous rocks, Northampton from the Jurassic, Rossendale and Pennant from the Coal Measures, Kerridge from the Millstone Grit, Northumberland from the Lower Carboniferous sandstone, Herefordshire from the Old Red sandstone, and Hoar Edge from the Ordovician. Sandstone slates, lovely as some of them are, do not achieve the perfection of the finest oolitic slates, partly because they are darker in tone and usually more sombre in colour, and partly on account of their greater size, thickness and sometimes clumsiness: they may be as much as 4 ft. wide and 3 ins. thick, and so heavy that two men working together can only just manage to lift them. It is because of their immense weight that so many of them have disappeared. Pitchford Hall in Shropshire is a half-timbered Tudor house which still preserves a splendid roof of sandstone slates (328b); some years ago they were all taken off and the whole roof boarded before they were put back.[1] More often these slates have caused the supporting timbers first to sag and then to collapse, only to be replaced by some lighter, cheaper, and usually quite inappropriate covering in another material.

Nevertheless, many sandstone roofs still survive in districts in which this stone was the regular building material. In some respects the characteristics which have already been noticed in the discussion of limestone roofs are equally in evidence here: for instance in the invariable laying of the slates in graduated courses. Or, to cite a more fortuitous affinity, we find a similar susceptibility to the attentions of mosses and lichens, stonecrops and even house-leeks; all these, when not permitted to flourish to excess, may add substantially to the visual attractions of a stone-slated roof. In other ways the character of the sandstone slates dictated a rather different architectural treatment. Because of their thickness, they were most satisfactory on a roof of simple form, as little interrupted as possible by subsidiary gables or dormers. Because of their size, the 'swept valleys' which are such

1 It should perhaps be pointed out that this procedure could be dangerous, for roofs covered with stone slates require ventilation. Denied this, the risk of encouraging beetle or fungi is increased.

a refined and delightful feature of the Cotswold roofs were difficult to achieve and were generally not attempted (although examples can be seen in Herefordshire at Staick House, Eardisland). And because of their great weight, a lower pitch was often essential; the oak pegs or iron nails could not have been trusted to hold them at the average Cotswold angle of 50°–55°. Nor was there any need for so steep a pitch, for sandstone slates are usually larger, and the larger and heavier the slates the less are they likely to be lifted off by a strong wind. Thus Horsham slate roofs which weigh even more than Purbeck (cf. p. 105), have an average pitch of only 45°, and in the North the angle averages no more than about 30° and may be as low as 24°. None of these features—the comparative absence of gables and dormers, the omission of 'swept valleys', and the lower pitch—is aesthetically to the advantage of the sandstone roofs, which do in fact lack the elegance and refinement of the best examples in limestone. Yet these rougher, heavier slates, usually fissile enough to respond to a tap from a hammer without any need of the assistance of frosting, often look wonderfully appropriate on the sandstone buildings for which they provide such sturdy roof-coverings. On half-timbered buildings in the West Country, whenever they have managed to survive, they have indeed a splendid presence.

If a roof is of stone (other than slate) in Sussex or Surrey, it will almost certainly have come from beds of hard but fissile sandstone in the Weald Clay. These great slabs, although known under the generic name of Horsham, were once obtained from many other places on the Weald Clay. There were parishes for which tithe maps show that almost every farm had its own 'stonepit field'; the slabs were wanted for floors, for field walls and sometimes for chimney caps as well as for roofs. These still survive in appreciable numbers over most of Sussex, in Surrey up to the line of the North Downs, and to some extent in Kent; and were it not for their great weight there would be many more. These slates, which turn dark brown after prolonged exposure, are almost too attractive to moss; this should be removed before it gets out of hand. It says much for the strength and durability of Wealden oak that many of the heaviest slates are on half-timbered buildings. Brewerstreet Farm at Bletchingley is a fine example (*314*a). At Horsham itself, in the Causeway, that charming, sequestered street leading to the church, No. 30 is also a timber-framed house; its brickwork and hung tiles have been renewed, but most of its wood and its dark brown roof are original (*130*b). Horsham slates demanded, needless to say, very massive support; rafters measuring 6 × 5 ins. were not unknown. Nor is it surprising that with such roofs a sagging ridge is the rule rather than the exception.

Reference was made earlier (p. 121) to the calcareous sandstone dug from the Northampton Sand in a number of places in the vicinity of Northampton. At Duston, these beds also yielded a dark-toned roofing stone which has not been obtainable for a long while but which was at one time in some demand locally. As at Collyweston, it was obtained by shallow mining.

In the west and north of England the sandstone slates are shaped from much older rocks. Some of them split quite easily, but here too the roofs are always thicker, heavier and darker than their limestone counterparts. Bristol in the Middle Ages was largely roofed with slabs of Pennant sandstone which might be as much as an inch thick. In the Southern Marches many old roofs have been replaced by red tiles or Welsh slate, or by other materials still less welcome; but where stone slates survive—and even to-day they are quite common in this part of the country—they will usually have come from the Old Red Sandstone, the colours ranging from brownish yellow to greenish grey, often tinctured with the greens of lichens and moss, as at Pembridge in Herefordshire (130c). Both the little houses illustrated probably date back to the fourteenth century, and in the course of time the rafters have sagged a good deal. Some repairs have unfortunately been effected with tiles. In southern Shropshire there are roofs of even older stone. The very striking, steeply pitched roof of the principal wing of the Prior's Lodge at Much Wenlock (124c) has shelly, calcareous Hoar Edge flags of Ordovician sandstone from long-abandoned quarries about eight miles to the west. For sandstone these slates are small (about 8 ins. deep with 4 ins. overlap), and are still held by oak pegs driven into the battens which traverse the rafters. About three-quarters of them are still the original ones fixed about 1500, and happily the owners of this remarkable and beautiful house have a stock of replacements obtained from barns and other buildings in the neighbourhood, the walls and roof-timbers of which could no longer support their weight. Slates of this type can be seen on other buildings in Much Wenlock and a few miles to the north-east at Madeley Court: this was a fine Elizabethan house built on the site of a grange of the priors of Wenlock, which is now falling into ruin. The slates at Pitchford Hall (328b), referred to above, are similar.

In Cheshire most of the sandstone is Triassic, but the roofing slates are of gritstone. Kerridge slabs, quarried near Macclesfield, were for centuries in steady demand in the county but they are no longer produced, because the demand is now small and ample supplies are available from old buildings that every year are being demolished. Although grey and heavy and sometimes a little sombre, they have given character to many Cheshire buildings. All the most notable 'black and white' buildings, such as Little Moreton Hall, Bramall Hall and Marton church, have dignified roofs of sandstone slates. Kerridge stone can be seen on the roof of the recently reconstructed Old Vicarage at Prestbury, and the rather similar slates at Little Moreton Hall (327c) may well have come from Tegg's Mill quarry, two miles east of Macclesfield.

In much of Derbyshire and the six northern counties sandstone slates from the Carboniferous rocks were for centuries the normal roofing material (*130a*). In the upper Colne valley south-west of Huddersfield, 'thackstones', as they were called, are known to have been in use as far back as the thirteenth century. The names used to distinguish the different sizes, of which something was said on pp. 101–102, show considerable local variations, and in the North three hundred years ago some of them were very quaint, like Jenny why Gettest thou, Rogue why Winkest thou, and Short Haghattee. Most of these very durable slates came from the Coal Measures or the Millstone Grit. Elland flagstones in the Huddersfield-Halifax-Bradford region and Rossendale flags from the other side of the Pennines, between Rochdale and Burnley, are well-known examples: the former were widely used in the West Riding and can be seen on the roof of the robust post-Reformation gatehouse at Kirklees near Brighouse (*129b*). Rossendale flags travelled over a considerable part of Lancashire. Farther north, roofing slates were produced in large numbers around Ingleton, in the Eden Valley, and at several places in Northumberland. During the last hundred years other materials, cheaper and flimsier, have tended more and more to oust stone slates; and there is no denying that the Northern flags, which may be more than an inch thick and are often somewhat rudely finished, can look formidable. But there rests the secret of their appeal. Large, hard, usually dark grey or dark brown, and often laid at a decidedly low pitch, these northern roofs cannot hope to charm the eye as do some of the stone roofs of the limestone Midlands and of the South, described earlier. What they do achieve is a complete visual harmony both with the architecture of the buildings of which they form a part and with the landscape in which they are placed. No one need ask for more.

5

GRANITE

Of the rocks of non-sedimentary character, the only one that has been employed at all extensively for building in Britain is granite. There are large areas of granite and some important quarries in parts of Scotland and Ireland; there are small workings of rocks akin to granite in North Wales; but until the Victorian period this stone was very little used in England except in the extreme South-West. Of the English granite quarries still producing building stone, one is in Westmorland and one in Devon; the other five are all in Cornwall. Yet as recently as 1957 the British Stone Federation was able to list no fewer than thirty-two working quarries in that county.

It always used to be said that granite was an igneous rock: that is to say, formed by the cooling of molten material. Much of it certainly seems to have originated in this way, but modern geological opinion suggests that other granites came into being at great depth, where intense heat and pressure, together with chemically active fluids, acted upon older rocks. The formation of granites has continued throughout geological time and therefore overlaps that of many sedimentary rocks; but whatever the process, the constituent minerals all have a crystalline character. The three essential components are felspar, quartz and mica. Of these minerals, quartz is so hard as to be virtually indestructible, and felspar only slightly less so. Mica, although comparatively soft and easily abraded (as can be seen when granite is polished), is also impervious to chemical weathering. Hence the distinguishing characteristic of this material is its great strength and durability. Virtually no tougher natural building stone exists.

The compact, crystalline and generally uniform structure of granite renders it not only exceptionally resistant to the polluted air of big cities but, as a rule, impervious to water. If the faces of contiguous blocks are worked slightly hollow, very fine jointing can be achieved. Hence for such undertakings as docks, breakwaters and lighthouses, and for some bridges, it is a magnificent gift: for these and many other public works it has been used on a very large scale in the past hundred and fifty years. Countless miles of English roads have kerb-stones and gutters of granite, often Welsh, Scottish, Irish (from the Mourne Mountains), Channel Islands, French, Belgian or Norwegian, but sometimes from our own quarries. With its suggestion of impregnability, it is also aesthetically a very suitable material for prisons. But for buildings of a more intimate character it must be recognized that granite, apart altogether from its high cost, has several artistic limitations. It is a stone ill-suited to decorative enrichment. This can be achieved, as at Launceston, where every square inch of the south and east exterior walls of the granite church is covered with carving.[1] These carvings are something of a *tour de force*, for the actual cutting must have been a work of much labour. Yet they do not stand up well to close inspection. There is no undercutting, not much refinement, and very little subtlety. In fact, their only artistic value is in the creation of an all-over texture. They serve to confirm rather than to deny the view that granite is not readily amenable to detailed enrichment through the agency of the chisel. Undercutting must be avoided; delicate projections must not be attempted; all ideas of fine or elaborate mouldings must be renounced.

What then remains? Not, as a rule, any compelling attractions in the field of colour. The chief determinant of colour in granite is the nature of its felspar, since this is the pre-dominant component. The colour range of the felspar crystals is limited: they are red or pink, grey or white, or occasionally slightly greenish, and these tints, sometimes combined to produce a mottled effect, are virtually the only ones which our granites can provide.

Texturally, despite certain reservations, there is more to be said in favour of granite. Being to a large extent an igneous rock, it is not stratified; although the coarseness of the grain varies considerably, it normally has rather a regular, even texture, somewhat reminiscent of granulated sugar that has gone hard. This can be very agreeable, especially when used internally over not too wide an area, as for example for a chimney-piece, a doorway, an arch or a pier. For a whole wall this even texture tends to monotony, which is still more marked if the stone is polished. Granite will take a very high polish, as was already well known in ancient Egypt. With the collapse of the Roman empire, either the practice of granite-polishing was abandoned or the method was forgotten; it was not rediscovered until 1803. Since the beginning of the nineteenth century it has been employed a great deal; latterly as a facing material over reinforced concrete. For this purpose it is required in big slabs no thicker than $1\frac{1}{2}$ to 2 ins. In days when the mason's only tools were hammers and picks, the large-scale employment of granite for cladding would have been quite impracticable. Because of its toughness the sawing processes still take much longer with granite than with most sedimentary rocks, but the introduction of many new machines, and in particular frame-saws and circular saws with blades that have cutting rims of

1 This sculpture was commissioned in 1511 by a Cornish squire, Sir Henry Trecarrel (or Trecarrell). The death in that year of his infant son and heir led him to discontinue work on what was to have been a fine house, Trecarrel, and to divert his wealth to the building of Launceston church. His own arms, quartering those of his wife, Margaret Kelway, are over the south porch.

carborundum and, in some cases, diamond-impregnated segments, combined with the use of pneumatic tools for various kinds of dressing, have enabled this stone to attain a new and widespread popularity. Granite cladding is often highly polished (there are three degrees of polish: sanded, egg-shell and full-gloss), and for industrial towns this finish is undoubtedly the most practical; rock-faced, punched and even axed surfaces all harbour dirt, whereas the smooth glossy stone is easily washed and stands up to the severest weather conditions. Polished granite can certainly look very handsome, and is appropriate too, for the clean lines and bold geometry of modern architecture. Yet one cannot altogether suppress a feeling that when it loses its roughness, that granular roughness which is natural to it, the most attractive quality of granite has been sacrificed; and there can be little room for doubt that, with the exception of Carrara marble, no stone has contributed so much as polished granite to converting many English churchyards, once so attractive, into ghoulish eyesores.

There are, on the other hand, many granite buildings before which, from the artistic standpoint, our awareness of texture becomes excessive. One of the reasons was, and still is, the high cost of granite ashlar, which places a premium on rock-faced and other rough finishes. Because it is also uneconomical, granite masonry seldom has regular coursing; and walls which are but a patch-work of squared stones of uneven size and shape faced at the quarry only look well in the roughest of country, while if the stones are not squared at all, the effect is crude (147b).[1]

A complete town constructed of granite is seen at its best when the sun comes out after a shower of rain, for then the scales of mica in the stone sparkle delightfully. Under most weather conditions, although one gains an impression in such places of timeless strength and of almost excessively good weathering properties, one's spirit, as those familiar with Oporto or Rennes or Aberdeen will know, is not uplifted. The reasons are not far to seek. Large areas of granite nearly always appear absolutely uniform in tone; unlike many varieties of limestone and sandstone, they do not readily acquire with age a rich patina. Nor, compared with many limestones, is unpolished granite a good reflector of light. Moreover, because of the shallow cutting and the absence of crisp mouldings, dictated by the refractory character of the material, there is often an unfortunate scarcity

1 Therefore Sir Charles Barry and his three colleagues who framed the *Report of the Result of an Inquiry . . . with reference to the Selection of Stone for Building the New Houses of Parliament, 1839* could say:

'We have not considered it necessary to extend our Inquiry to Granites, Porphyries, and other stones of similar Character, on account of the enormous Expense of converting them to Building Purposes in decorated Edifices, and from a Conviction that an equally durable and in other respects more eligible Material could be obtained for the Object in view from among the Limestones or Sandstones of the Kingdom.'

GRANITE AND SLATE
a. *Cotehele, Cornwall*   b. *Mountsorrel, Leicestershire* (demolished, 1958)
c. *The Old Rectory, Cossington, Leicestershire*

of shadows. Too frequently therefore, the prevailing colour can only be described as a 'dead grey'.

For these reasons, granite is best used in towns in combination with some other stone, preferably limestone. A granite-faced base can look extremely well on a building that is otherwise faced with limestone. In Dublin there are a number of buildings, including more than one in Trinity College, which are of grey Wicklow granite with Portland stone dressings. Both in colour and in texture this combination is telling. The muted grey of the granite is an excellent foil to the more brilliant, whitish hue of the Portland, and the smoothness of the limestone is admirably set off by the roughness of the other rock.

Both because of their imperishability (no buildings cost so little to maintain) and on account of their dearth of revealing details, granite buildings are sometimes difficult to date with any certainty. All that can be said is that, because of the daunting difficulty of cutting the stone in pre-industrial days, the older buildings tend to have the larger blocks. Sometimes these are enormous: blocks weighing ten or twelve tons are not unusual. The granite which we can still see in Perpendicular churches in parts of Devon and Cornwall, and in many a farmhouse, both in this region and here and there in the Lake District, was usually what is known as 'moorstone'. This was surface stone, lying about on the moors just as the sarsens lay on the downs of the South and South-East. It had been used, unworked, from the most ancient times. We see it, for example, at Chun Castle, on a hill a mile south of Morvah in the Land's End peninsula. This was a circular Iron Age fort protected by two concentric rings of ramparts, constructed of granite moorstone. Cornwall and Devon are still full of prehistoric remains in this stone, some going back to the Bronze Age. By the fourteenth century the masons had learnt to dress their 'presents' (as these exposed blocks of granite plucked from the surface of the moors were called) sufficiently well for rough church-building. At Altarnun, on the north side of Bodmin Moor, each pier, capital and base of the fifteenth century church consists of a single piece of worked-over moorstone. In humbler buildings it was not unusual to build without mortar; these cottages would frequently be whitewashed, as can be seen at such Cornish fishing villages as Polperro and Mevagissey, and also in Eskdale, Cumberland. But it is not without significance that wherever, as in parts of Devon, a choice was offered between granite moorstone and some other stone, say a limestone or a sandstone, the latter was almost always preferred, the moorstones being reserved for bridges, troughs, gate-posts, stiles and sometimes walls. In the late-sixteenth and seventeenth centuries, the methods of dressing improved, yet the usual granite was still moorstone. A notable example is provided by the Almshouses at Moretonhampstead, near the north-east corner of Dartmoor, which now belong to the National Trust (148b). At this long, low building, erected in

GRANITE IN THE SOUTH-WEST
    a. *Bonython, Cury, Cornwall*
b. *Almshouses, Moretonhampstead, Devon*

1637, the end-walls have only a jumble of stones, but on the front the big blocks were carefully squared, and along the whole length of the ground floor runs an open loggia. This has stumpy granite columns between the arched openings. The decoration is of the simplest; the workmanship is decidedly crude: yet it is perfectly in tune with the uncompromising material. It was an achievement, at this date, to have built so well. It should be added that, with all its limitations in the field of carving, granite did lend itself very well to any bold form of moulding not involving undercutting (for example, the cornice in plate *148a*), and that throughout all Cornwall and much of west and north Devon this stone long provided the principal material for essential architectural members such as door and window heads, dripstones, string courses, mullions, sills, steps and plinths. Most of these can be seen at Cotehele (*147a*).

Geographical Distribution

The best British granites for building come from Scotland and from Cornwall. Cornish granite, usually light silver-grey, is mainly concentrated in four areas between Bodmin Moor and Land's End. The most important occupies the triangle between Falmouth, Camborne and Helston. At least three quarries to the west and south-west of Penryn (Trenoweth, Trolvis and Bosinjack) still supply building stone, in blocks up to 6 × 3 × 3 ft. Godolphin House, just to the west of this triangle, offers an early example of the use of this stone for domestic purposes. Many more quarries were formerly working. It was probably one at Constantine, half way between Falmouth and Helston, which provided, about 1790, the finely jointed ashlar blocks, now delicately lichened, of Bonython, Cury (*148a*), a gracious house near Mullion on the Lizard peninsula. But the principal developments occurred during the nineteenth century, mainly for engineering purposes. Pelastine granite is very familiar to Londoners for it is the material of which Tower Bridge is constructed, and several other Thames bridges upstream as far as Kew. Until 1939 these included John Rennie's Waterloo Bridge, the finest that London has ever possessed. Virtually the whole of the Land's End peninsula is of granite, and so is every old building on its surface. Cornish granite walls are usually between 2 ft. and 2 ft. 6 ins. thick and built in more or less random courses. The quarries in Lamorna Cove, south-west of Penzance, were at one time important; some of the stone from here went to St. Michael's Mount. The other specifically granite districts are the St. Austell-Par neighbourhood and Bodmin Moor. The latter has well-known quarries on both its eastern and western flanks. Cheesewring, on the east side, now closed, was exceptional in Cornwall in yielding a pink granite as well as the usual grey. The only two working, De Lank and Hantergantick, are both to the west, close to St. Breward. De Lank is a black-pepper-and-salt looking granite of coarse grain, not very likeable but immensely serviceable. The present Eddystone light-house is built of it, and it is also well seen nearby at Blisland, that 'sweet grey granite village around its green'[1] with 'not one ugly building in it' and 'the most beautiful of all the country churches of the West'.[2] Much of this stone is now broken down into chips, but there is still some demand for masonry, and blocks weighing as much as 15 tons can be handled.

Formerly Cornish granite was in great demand for street paving and for setts. Plenty of granite pavements can still be seen at such places as Helston, Penryn and Penzance; to prevent it from becoming slippery it was often dressed in a pattern of concentric quarter-circles, or occasionally more elaborately. Setts were not only laid in the streets of every town in the South-West during the nineteenth century but sent all over the country too. Normally they measured about 10 × 4 ins., with a depth of at least 6 ins. They gave an excellent surface for horses drawing heavy loads in railway yards, docks and harbours as well as in urban streets. But with the coming of tar macadam and the substitution of pneumatic for iron tyres they were no longer needed, and many have been tarred over.

Dartmoor is the largest single area of granite south of the Border, but such is the abundance of less intractable building stone in Devon that its grey granite was hardly quarried before the beginning of the last century. Quarries were opened up in 1806 for the building of Princetown gaol, originally erected to house French prisoners-of-war, and this was the granite used for the London Bridge built in 1823–31 and recently replaced. Merrivale quarry, between Tavistock and Princetown, can supply blocks or slabs up to 8 ft. long and weighing ten tons, but they are mainly wanted now for engineering works. On the other side of the moor, some four miles from Chagford, stands what will almost certainly be the last big English house to have been constructed entirely of granite. This is the dramatically sited Castle Drogo by Lutyens, built between 1911 and 1930. Pevsner aptly terms it 'this baronial stronghold of the twentieth century: an extravaganza in granite'.

Lundy Island is entirely granitic and for local needs the rock was long worked on a very small scale. The graceful old lighthouse in the centre of the island, built in 1819 and abandoned in 1897, shows how well this material can look. Lundy's granite was first quarried commercially in 1864, and large blocks of it were sent to London for the first section of the Thames Embankment. But granite from Dartmoor and especially from Cornwall proved more accessible, and after 1870 export virtually ceased.

1 A. L. Rowse, *A Cornish Childhood* (1942).   2 John Betjeman, *First and Last Loves* (1952).

The only granite between Devon and the Lake District is to be found, somewhat unexpectedly, in Leicestershire. This is predominantly, as we have seen, a county of Lias and Trias. Towards the north-west, however, much older and harder rocks mostly belonging to the Pre-Cambrian Era lie denuded of their later Triassic covering. These rocks now stand revealed in the Charnwood Forest area as a group of small 'islands' of an entirely different character from the formations which cover the rest of the county. Among them, on the east and south sides of the Forest, are the well-known slates of Swithland, to be discussed in the next chapter, and a small intrusive mass of granite, quarried principally at Mountsorrel, about six miles to the north of Leicester.

The granite of Leicestershire has been worked on a sufficiently important scale to have inflicted all too evident scars on some of the picturesque Charnwood hills, yet practically the whole of the development has taken place only since the eighteen-twenties, when new methods of cutting were introduced. Previously the intense hardness of this stone rendered dressing so difficult that it was not suitable for high-class building, although in a random rock-faced fashion, without any attempt at squaring or shaping the blocks, it had long been employed for cottages, farmhouses and even churches. This rough granite, like the moorstone referred to above, seems to have been used almost as found. In its dressed form, the most considerable building is in Mountsorrel itself: Christ Church, built in 1844. In the past hundred years this granite has been much more important as an engineering material and for road-metal than as a building stone. In the Victorian age, like Cornish granite, it was in great demand for setts; but the task of preparing them was so hard that it used to be said that, if a man could earn a living at sett-making in Mountsorrel, he could do it anywhere. The quarry is still operating, but manual work has entirely ceased; it now produces nothing but granite crushed by machine for roadstone and to provide aggregate for concrete. The colour of this granite varies: some of it is pink, some grey. The grain of the latter being somewhat larger, it is not quite so arduous to work and therefore slightly more suitable for masonry. But when houses in this neighbourhood were constructed of granite their walls were usually only rubble, the stone either having been broken with hammers or built in with the natural face exposed. A particularly good example of this type of masonry, a range of houses abutting on to the Market Place at Mountsorrel, which mainly dated from 1705 (147b), was unfortunately demolished in 1958. Some of it can still be seen three miles away at the Old Rectory, Cossington (147c).

In Cumberland and Westmorland the granite areas are much more restricted than in the South-West, and are all on the periphery of the Lake District. They are of about the same age as the Old Red sandstone. Most of this granite is in Eskdale, to the south-west of the Lake District proper, and southwards from there to near Bootle. Here granite buildings are not rare. The colours range from grey to light and dark pink and red; most of the field walls are grey with lichen, but the buildings, usually dating only from the last century, are generally pale pink. This stone is, regrettably, no longer worked, but visually it is the most attractive granite in England. A similar stone can be seen in farm house walls around Ennerdale Water. At Threlkeld, a little east of Keswick, the granite has some pink patches but is mostly grey: a slightly bluish-grey. This excellent stone is now only crushed for road-metal. The tower of a church in Keswick, completed in 1965, is likely to be the last building in Threlkeld stone.

In Westmorland the concentration is small but important: Shap is the only granite in northern England to be worked to-day. But the quarrying of granite on Shap Fell did not begin until about 1868, and the cost was always such that in the county itself it would be difficult to find even one building constructed of it, outside the confines of the company's works. Of the two quarries, only the 'Red' produces building stone. The granite from this quarry is in fact bi-coloured: pinkish-red and grey. There are two distinct shades, 'Light Shap' and 'Dark Shap'; but the difference between the two is far less than between them and all the other English granites. The distinguishing feature of Shap granite, which gives it a very interesting appearance, if more curious than beautiful, is that it harbours large, very prominent crystals of red felspar, sometimes as much as 2 ins. long. So, although most of the stone is more grey than red, from a little way off the colours blend into what might perhaps be described as a 'dusty pink'.

In its unpolished state Shap is one of the most pleasing of the English granites. It is therefore unfortunate that the 'best' stone (i.e. the most uniform in colour and grain) is kept for the monumental masons, who polish it until it looks like potted meat, which, oddly enough, many people still choose (in the happily diminishing number of places where they are still permitted to do so) for gravestones. In the later Victorian period, when there was a considerable vogue for Shap granite outside its own county, it goes without saying that the polished surface was the favourite; and in the smoky towns of that era it was also no doubt the most serviceable. A demand persists for blocks, both for underwater construction and for facing the base storeys of large buildings, as well as for framing their doors and windows. For the latter long pieces can be produced specially. From time to time huge blocks can also be obtained, measuring up to 8 ft. × 3 ft. 6 ins. × 3 ft. 6 ins., and weighing as much as eight tons, or even more. The use of this stone for cladding—or 'slabbing', as the masons term it here—is a comparatively recent development. The invention of the new saws referred to earlier has opened up an entirely new market.

Granite also occurs in the Isle of Man, where it is still used for road-metal. This yellowish-grey, mottled stone was never quarried for domestic use, but for cottage-building it was collected from the streams in the form of boulders.

Other Igneous Rocks

There are some other igneous rocks which have made a modest but interesting contribution to the rich visual pattern of English building. All of them were once molten and have solidified on cooling. Where this occurred far beneath the earth's surface, the cooling process was slow, and the outcome was the formation of a crystalline rock of relatively coarse grain such as granite. If on the other hand the molten material reached the surface as the lava of volcanic eruptions, it cooled much more quickly, producing a variety of rocks of finer grain.

Most of these rocks are extremely hard and difficult to work, and mainly for that reason are no longer in demand for building, for which none of them has ever had more than a local importance. Their localities are usually not far removed from those in which we have already found granite, and in some places are identical. As the term 'granite' has only acquired a precise definition with the development of geological science, quarrymen and builders are still liable to apply it loosely to some of these allied rocks.

Those most closely related to granite are syenite, diorite, and porphyry or elvan.

Syenite is a crystalline rock mainly composed of hornblende and felspar, and sometimes quartz. It can be seen in the Charnwood Forest area of Leicestershire, where the rough, hard granites, syenites (quarried at Croft, Enderby and Stoney Stanton, all to the south-west of Leicester), porphyries and slates are often referred to collectively as 'forest stone'. The abrupt slopes of this interesting region still have beautifully constructed dry walling of this 'forest stone'. Many cottages and barns were also built of it, and some large houses like The Brand at Woodhouse Eaves, of 1875; but this refractory material could not be dressed, and sometimes the rubbly walls were plastered over to give a more finished effect. To-day it is only quarried for roadstone.

Diorite is sometimes described as 'black granite', but it is not a true granite, as it usually contains no quartz. It is heavier than granite and much darker in colour. This stone is not common in England, and I know of no instance of its use for building, but it is quarried for road-surfacing in Cornwall, near St. Austell.

Nor do we usually think in English terms of porphyry, so abundant in Minorca and on the west side of the Adige valley below Bolzano, in North Italy, as well as in Greece and Egypt. But this rock, so highly valued in antiquity, does occur in some areas, as for example near St. Columb Major in Cornwall, at Bardon Hill on the west side of Charnwood Forest, and on the Northumbrian slopes of the Cheviots. It has a distinctive texture with large crystals of felspar and quartz embedded in a fine-grained matrix; its colour varies, but in this country is usually light and often reddish. It was used internally in the 1840s, to most curious effect, at Place, Fowey, where the 'porphyry hall' has polished walls of this red stone. It too is only employed now for road-making.

Elvan is the name applied in Cornwall to the local quartz-porphyry which was once in demand for building both there and in the south-west corner of Devon. The most important of the Cornish elvans was Pentewan stone, formerly quarried on the cliff-top north of Mevagissey, but no longer worked. It is still more laborious to cut than granite and lacks the large visible mica flakes that are characteristic of the more familiar stone, but its fine texture renders it suitable for ashlar and its colour, usually light grey with a hint of buff, can be very pleasing. At Trewithen, near Probus, a gracious house begun in 1715, it is a surprise to find that the Pentewan stone on the south front is predominantly pink; this is due to the profuse growth of a very smooth lichen. This stone can be seen at three Cornish houses owned by the National Trust: Antony House at Torpoint (1711–21), charmingly sited in gardens landscaped by Repton, and the restored Elizabethan manor house of Trerice near Newquay, are both largely built of it, while a small quarry in the woods near the house yielded elvan for Cotehele (147a), of which there will be more to say in the next chapter.   *
It is also the material of the imposing church tower at Fowey. Elvan from the long abandoned Tartan Down quarry at Landrake was used as far back as the twelfth century for the once magnificent but now sadly decayed west doorway of the nearby priory church of St. Germans.

The basic igneous rocks differ from the granites both in composition and in colour. The two commonest are basalt, which is a volcanic lava, and dolerite, which is similar but has cooled below ground in relatively thin sheets. Owing to their quick rate of cooling they crystallized rapidly, which produced, by comparison with the granites, smaller crystals and a finer grain. These two rocks are together known locally as whinstone. They are dark grey or black; olivine dolerite sometimes has a greenish tinge. They are quarried in the western Midlands (notably on Brown Clee, in Shropshire) for road-metal. To see them used in a geologically unaltered condition, one must journey to Northumberland. Part of the Roman Wall stands on dolerite, and was constructed with enormous blocks of it; this stone was also used for most of the houses at Craster, including the south front (1769) of Craster Tower, for which, exceptionally, the blocks were all carefully squared (although not of course ashlared), a very laborious undertaking. At

Dunstan Hall nearby, the rubblestone walls are of mixed sandstone and whinstone. The long isolated rock that carries Bamburgh Castle is solid dolerite, nearly black and hard as iron, but not the building itself; the Norman keep, the least restored part, is of sandstone, which the builders preferred to bring by sea from North Sunderland Point, five miles away, rather than face the formidable task of digging out and cutting the stone that was on the spot.

Akin to dolerite, and another member of the group of rocks loosely termed green-stones, is catacleuse, a rare material deriving its name from the only place where it occurs, Cataclew Point, west of Padstow (so perhaps originally Cataclew's stone?). This can also look greenish in some lights, but normally it is almost black, slightly mottled, and with many spangles of a dark mineral known as augite. Since it is of finer grain and not as hard as most of the basic igneous rocks, it can be tooled and even carved, as can be seen, surprisingly enough, in the effigies of the first Lord Marney (d. 1523) and his son (d. 1525) at Layer Marney in Essex. The explanation is that Lady Marney came from Mawgan-in-Pydar, a few miles south of Padstow. It was also chosen for the fine effigy of Prior Vyvyan (d. 1533) at Bodmin. As a building stone it is best seen in the church closest to the quarry, St. Merryn. There the seven bays of the arcade are composed of it, and the font. The stone is bluish-grey in colour, but without a hint of green or of any augite. Catacleuse seems also to have been used for much of the window-tracery in the church of Padstow.

Isolated outcrops of basaltic rock occur in a weathered and somewhat altered state in Devon and Cornwall. According to Prof. Hoskins,[1] this stone was used by the Romans for the town walls of Isca (Exeter), and again by William the Conqueror when he built Rougemont Castle there in 1070. Subsequently it was in considerable demand locally for churches, and continued in use for houses and other buildings until well into the nineteenth century. Aeons of weathering have turned it into a brown stone of various shades, not particularly attractive; its distinguishing feature is the network of thin, whitish veins which thread through the body of many of the blocks. There is also a bluish-green variety. Dunchideock quarry on the eastern slope of Great Haldon is now closed, but basalt quarries are still working at Trusham on the west side, also at Buckfastleigh, Kingsbridge and Tavistock. Their stone is only used, however, for road-metal and concrete aggregate.

Hurdwick quarry has been closed, alas, for well over half a century, and is now much overgrown. This supplied the very distinctive greenish-grey stone of which much of the

1 W. G. Hoskins, *Devon* (1954), pp. 258ff. Prof. Hoskins has a wide knowledge of these slightly freakish building stones. It is indeed a fortunate circumstance that his writings should have been largely centred on Devon and Leicestershire, the two counties in which, with Cornwall, these little known materials were most frequently exploited.

town of Tavistock is constructed: a basaltic lava which earth movements have changed a good deal since its original formation. In its altered form it is softer, with a less resistant texture and some lines of cleavage. Hurdwick stone was quarried, on and off, for nearly six centuries before about 1900 for buildings of all kinds in and around Tavistock. Especially when viewed from its western side in the slanting light of a fine winter afternoon, this little Devon town, although by no means architecturally beautiful, takes on, from the special character of its stone, a vivid, strange, almost unearthly aspect.[1]

1 Mr. Ted Masson Phillips describes Hurdwick stone as 'a volcanic ash with a pitted texture which simulates decay'. He adds: 'Another volcanic ash (or tuff), reddish brown in colour, was quarried at Totnes and used extensively for walls of buildings but not for architectural features.'

6

SLATE

Slate is a metamorphic rock: that is to say, a rock which owes its present state to the action of some tremendous natural agency, such as great heat or long-continued pressure or both. In the process, such changes have been wrought in the mineral composition and fabric of the pre-existing rocks as to produce a quite different material. These metamorphic processes have usually accompanied the building up of great mountain ranges, and have operated at a considerable depth below the earth's surface. It is not always possible to say what a given metamorphic rock was originally: it could have been igneous or sedimentary. Slates from various areas differ considerably not only in colour, texture and general consistency, but also in age. Usually they have been formed either from clay or shale,[1] or from fine-grained volcanic ash.

There is, of course, an abundance of slate in Wales (mainly in the counties of Caernarvon, Merioneth and Denbigh but also in Montgomeryshire, Pembrokeshire and Carmarthenshire), and until almost within living memory it had for centuries been the chief building stone over most of the Isle of Man. In England it is confined to much the same three areas as granite: Cornwall and Devon, Leicestershire and the Lake District, with, in addition, Furness. For the builder it has had less importance as masonry—for which the term 'slate-stone' is convenient—than in the slab form with which it is specially associated. For, owing to the manner in which it has been transformed (the flaky mineral particles in the rock having been forced, under pressure, to lie parallel to each other), slate, on being struck, can be split without difficulty along the parallel planes of its natural cleavage lines. To builders this has long been a priceless asset. In the slate areas for generations the stone served many different purposes. As well as for roofing it was used for paving floors, for steps and stairs, for window-sills and surrounds, for copings, chimney-pieces, shelves, water-tanks (before galvanised iron supplanted it early in the present century), cheese-presses, salting-troughs, curriers' slabs, mill stones, fences, and on a large scale for grave-stones. Later, when damp-proof courses became the rule, slate proved the ideal material.

---

1 Shale may be defined as a clayey sediment which, owing to pressure from above, gradually becomes fissile as it gets harder.

In recent years it has found a new use: as a facing material for steel and concrete structures. The beautiful Lake District slates, in particular, are ideal for cladding, and the introduction during the past thirty years of modern methods of quarrying and sawing has brought to the enterprising stone industry of that area a new and unparalleled prosperity. For this type of work sizes, needless to say, are standardized; slabs not too large for convenient handling—2 ft. 3 ins. × 9 ins. and about an inch thick, for example—are usually preferred.[1] But much larger panels can be supplied: up to 6 ft. × 2 ft. 6 ins. by regular production methods, and far bigger still if specially required. In the last few years Lakeland slate has travelled to many countries on the continent of Europe and to some far beyond,[2] while here in England it has been employed on a number of important projects far removed from the slate regions. Although this ignores the *genius loci* it is a good example of something which is always a pleasure to see: the use of old and well-tried materials to supply the requirements of the new building techniques.

For paving, slate was formerly of great importance, especially in the South-West. Slate from Delabole, called for this purpose bluestone, was widely used in Cornwall and Devon for flooring kitchens, sculleries, dairies, still-rooms, passages, and sometimes for living rooms too. A little is still employed in this way, and it is not unduly expensive. The National Trust has recently refloored a room in this fashion at Saltram House near Plymouth; the slabs of slate, about 12 ins. square and laid diamond-wise, were not sawn nor polished but riven, which gives a very pleasing texture.

For low field walls the slate was also hand-riven. These were at one time not uncommon in the Lake District and in North Cornwall. Not very many survive to-day, but several good examples can still be seen in the vicinity of Hawkshead and Ambleside (167b).

Gravestones, on the other hand, were always sawn and polished on one face; the thinner, later specimens were smoothed on both sides. Here, although there are plenty both in the South-West and in the North-West, one thinks first of the Swithland slate of Leicestershire. In the eighteenth and nineteenth centuries thousands of tombstones, some with splendid lettering, found their way from Swithland not only into almost every old churchyard in Leicestershire but into all the adjoining counties too; for, being considerably lighter than the local limestone and sandstone slabs, they could travel more easily. This highly laminated stone was usually supplied in lengths of about 6 ft., of which 5 ft. showed above ground; the width varied according to the client's requirements. In the

---

1 Some of these slabs are only ¾ in. thick; but when they are so thin the great problem is cutting a slot in them or a hole for fixing. (Information from Mr. A. S. Ireson.)

2 A 600 ft. high bank in Montreal displays about 125,000 sq. ft. of slate cladding, and a bank at Portland, Oregon, about 100,000 sq. ft. For both buildings the Broughton Moor Co. was the supplier.

churchyard at Belgrave there is a headstone dated 1824 which measures 60 × 42 ins. above ground, yet is only 1½ ins. thick.

In the Isle of Man there were quarries which yielded immense 'beams', occasionally as much as 24 ft. long, and about 2 ins. thick. These possess an elasticity unusual in stone: it is said that a 2in. slate 'beam' 15 ft. long will bend a further 2 ins. without breaking. Castle Rushen, near the southern end of the island, has heavy stone-flagged floors supported on 'beams' of slate which have carried this considerable weight for over five hundred years. These 'planks' of slate also serve, here and there, as footbridges and gate-posts, and for lintels of doorways.[1]

Slate-Stone

Despite its durability, which is one of its most valuable properties, slate is not a difficult stone to work, on account of the ease with which it can be split. There are in fact places where it does not need to be quarried at all, since sizeable lumps, lying about as scree, can be picked up beneath every rock-face. It has not, however, been used for English buildings except in the localities in which it is found.

A typical slate-stone wall can be seen at St. Columb Major (*167*d). The pieces of stone are very roughly dressed on the wall-face and are of many shapes and sizes; none is squared and most of them tend to be wedge-shaped and rather long and thin, splitting to points, which imposes the need for a good deal of mortar. The colours are pleasant: a mixture of browns, fawns and greys, forming a patchwork in which there is also room for a few lumps of Cornish granite.

On account of its excellent cleavage slate is the ideal material for dry-stone walls. In Leicestershire it was employed extensively for this purpose when the Charnwood Forest was enclosed, about 1812. But because it splits so easily it is unsuitable for quoins, which involve cutting across the grain on one face, a task both laborious and unsatisfactory.

A few examples of slate masonry can still be seen in Leicestershire (for instance, Nos. 73 and 75, King Street, Sileby), but it was only in two regions of England, the North-West and the South-West, that slate-stone achieved any real popularity as a building material. In both areas the principal products were thin slabs for roofing and for the various other purposes mentioned above, but since the quarries supplied building stone too, if only in some cases as a by-product, this may be the best place for a short description of them.

The slate-producing area of the North-West extends from the Burlington quarry

---

1 The authority for these interesting examples of the use of slate, which I have not myself seen, is Canon E. H. Stenning's *Isle of Man* (1950), p. 100.

above Kirkby-in-Furness, a few miles north of Barrow, northward to the neighbourhood of Keswick. The Burlington slate, sometimes described as blue, is in fact closer to lead-pencil grey. This belongs to the Silurian period, but most of the slate of the North-West is Ordovician. An outcrop of specially high quality runs along the north-western fringe of Lancashire and into Westmorland near Ambleside. The grey-green slate of the Tilber-thwaite Fells was renowned in the eighteenth century, and it was one of these quarries, Moss Rigg, which provided the slate used at Coventry Cathedral. Operating conditions vary, but in 1970 seven quarries along this outcrop were still working, several having only been reopened quite recently. All but one are in Lancashire. Broughton Moor, the most southerly, is also much the largest; this quarry, situated 1300 ft. above sea level, towards the southern end of the ridge that sweeps up to the summit of Coniston Old Man and only accessible by a road with a gradient of 1 in 5, was first worked about the middle of the nineteenth century. Like Bursting Stone, on Coniston Old Man, it produces slate of two distinct shades, marketed as 'light sea green' (but more accurately described as grey with a slightly bluish tinge) and 'olive green' (which is really a greenish grey). Nearer to Ambleside Moss Rigg, Spoutcrag, Elterwater and Brathay quarries are all again in operation. Spoutcrag slate, also mostly grey-green, is notable for its beautiful markings. Brathay is a dark-toned slate obtainable, by request, in massive sizes: a single sawn slab can measure as much as 11 × 4 ft. In Westmorland the Kirkstone slate quarry, which has also seen a notable revival in recent years, mainly produces the 'light sea green' stone. Farther north again, and in Cumberland, another memorable outcrop bestraddles the Honister Pass: the slate of Buttermere and Borrowdale. Here olive green really is the predominant shade: this is among the most attractive of the Lake District slates. Finally there is the dark grey slate of Skiddaw, a stone of immense antiquity, which is neither very slaty nor reliable, and was used only for the most uncouth kind of building.

In addition to the quarries just mentioned, the region also had a great many small ones, now disused, from which slate-stone was once prised for building. This was usually a very rough stone, robust and durable, but unamenable to the refinements. At Fell Foot Farm in Little Langdale (181c) and in numberless field walls, such as the one near the Kirkstone Pass (167a), slate-stone is seen in combination with random lumps of volcanic rock (lavas and tuffs), some of which are 'cobbles' or 'cobble stone'. This term is employed in the Lake District in a somewhat special sense. Cobbles are lumps of rock brought down by glaciers and their meltwaters into the valleys during the Ice Age—which only ended here about ten thousand years ago—and collected from the beds of becks or from what are now fields or moors. The turbulent waters smoothed their surfaces and rounded their forms, but some of these lumps of stone are very big, and so difficult to break that the majority were used unbroken and laid random. Cobblestone walling is, of course, the reverse of urbane, but visually it suits the country to perfection, being in fact part and parcel of it; and in the construction of field walls, barns and some of the humbler cottages cobbles in this area have played an important part. Building with cobbles is very hard work, if only because the larger stones are so heavy, and although I have been told that a cobblestone wall is one of the easiest to construct, it is evident that some are much better built than others. Usually the stones were laid dry, which conveys a very rough-hewn appearance. Yet so well do such buildings look in their mountain setting that to-day in the Lake District National Park a favourite method of handling rather small random slate-stone rubble is to keep the mortar so well back from the wall-face that it is scarcely visible, giving the effect of a dry-stone wall. On the older buildings it is not unusual to see a large stone projecting here and there from the plane surface of the wall: this is what the builders call a 'through'—a stone large enough to extend through the whole thickness of the wall, which helps to give it strength. With dry-stone walls an excellent effect is obtained if the topmost stones are selected to be laid not horizontally but diagonally or vertically, so that they yield a vigorous serrated edge, which has also the practical advantage of acting as a deterrent to jumping sheep (*167a*).

When slate is used for walling in the Lake District to-day it will probably be 'greenstone'. That is the term used in this part of England to describe the high wastage (not by any means always green) which is inevitable in the production of roofing slates, sills, steps and panels or slabs for cladding. These pieces, lopped off in the trimming, are often rather small, but that is no reason for discarding them, since many, after being hammer-dressed on the site, make excellent walling stone.

In Devon and Cornwall the slate belongs to the Devonian rock-system and is therefore somewhat less ancient. In parts of Devon the rocks are very much intermingled, so that slates and schists, quartzites, limestones and sandstones are found in close juxtaposition. In Cornwall, where the Devonian rocks actually cover a larger area than the granite, slate has made an important contribution to the county's visual picture. Two miles west of Camelford, at Delabole, close to the Atlantic coast, is the largest slate quarry in England, a mile in circumference and in some places 400 ft. deep. The depths in different parts vary considerably, and access is by inclined ramps. The quarry has been active since the time of Elizabeth I, and though much of the interior of this huge hole (a dramatic sight) is now overgrown, workings in some areas continue. Much of the slate quarried at Delabole to-day is ground down, but there is still a demand for this stone for roofing and for other purposes: notably, as already indicated, for paving.

Cornwall used to have many other slate quarries, and slate-stone, although by no means as monumental as granite, could provide a less intractable and more colourful alternative material, as at St. Columb Major, referred to above, and at Lerryn near Lostwithiel (*167c*), where the masonry, although not laid in regular courses, has nothing in common with the plum-cake-like effect of random granite as seen, for instance, in the photograph of the demolished house at Mountsorrel (*147b*). The tints of the slate-stone in this part of England are warm: browns and fawns predominate. At Cotehele,[1] that secret, intimate, lovable house, so remotely placed, so beautifully sited, dressed granite (centre of plate *147a*), elvan (right) and slate-stone (left), can all be seen in the courtyard, in addition to slate on the roofs.

Devon's slate-stone is now very little used, but for seven centuries, from Norman times to Victorian, its virtues were continuously appreciated. A few large and a great many small quarries, now mostly overgrown, serve to remind us of the stone's former importance. Of the large ones, the Mill Hill quarry west of Tavistock, still not entirely closed, offers a memorable experience to the lover of stone, with its fascinating colours and the still, silent pool which to-day fills the deepest part of the workings. Equally important were a number of quarries between Dartmouth and Kingsbridge, especially Charleton, two miles south-east of the latter town, for which the proximity of the estuary meant convenient water-transport. Other quarries of Devonian slate, darker and less agreeable, may be seen in the north of the county between Barnstaple and Lynton. Their legacy is a great variety of buildings, including not only farms and miles of field-walls but numerous churches, especially between Start Bay and Plymouth Sound, and some excellent houses. An example is Collacombe Manor, near Tavistock, built in the fifteenth and sixteenth centuries; in its rough way the brown and grey front has plenty of character.

Slate Roofs

In the story of the English house, slate has much more importance as a roofing material than as a building stone. Unfortunately most people, when a slate roof is mentioned, envisage one covered, probably in the nineteenth century, with thin, smooth Welsh slate, which reveals this stone in its least attractive guise. England can show some much more agreeable roofing slate than this.

Although brittle, slate is often extremely hard and close in texture, non-porous, quick drying, wholly resistant to frost and capable of withstanding indefinitely even the most smoke-laden atmospheres. But what specially pointed to its employment as a material for roofing was its peculiarly fissile character. The Romans used Swithland slate for this

1 Pronounced 'Co-teel'.

purpose in Leicester and other kinds elsewhere. After their departure this practice fell out of use, and there are no further indications of slate roofs until the latter part of the twelfth century. From that time onwards there are many records of the use of slate for roofing, and not only in Cornwall and Devon, Leicestershire, Furness and the Lake District, the districts in which it was quarried. In addition, it is now known that during the Middle Ages roofing slate was brought, if only in small quantities, to places on or near the South coast from Brittany and from the Ardennes. Later, other sources of supply became accessible. In the last two hundred years, large quantities have come into England not only from Wales but from both Ireland and Scotland, and more recently from Norway and from Newfoundland.

English roofing slate, especially in the North-West, bears more resemblance to the limestone and sandstone slates that have already been described than to the all-too-familiar Welsh slate. Some of the best of the Lakeland slate was formed of volcanic ash of fine consistency, tremendously compressed so that it can be riven quite easily, albeit with an appalling rate of wastage (between 75% and 95%). Riven slates are seldom absolutely smooth and often quite rough; although much thinner and lighter than any limestone or sandstone slates, they weigh more—Lakeland slates considerably more—than the modern Welsh product. They were generally prepared and laid in graduated sizes, the average of which is markedly smaller than the Welsh slates; and there is considerably more colour variation, normally from grey through blue-grey and greenish-grey to quite a bright green, but including also a certain amount of rust-brown and, in Leicestershire, purple with a distinctly pinkish tinge, as well as grey-green. It is only fair to add that North Wales also produced at one time small, comparatively thick slates that were very pleasing. Roofing-slate sizes, no less than those of stone slates referred to on pp. 101–102 and 143, have their picturesque names, which apply in Wales too; it was indeed at the Penrhyn quarry that they are said to have been first introduced, about the middle of the eighteenth century. For some reason many of these names (about twenty are generally recognized in the industry) are drawn from the female aristocracy. There are princesses, duchesses, marchionesses, countesses, viscountesses and ladies. There are also small duchesses, wide countesses and narrow ladies !

In Cornwall a very high proportion of all the roofing slate has come from the great quarry at Delabole, which reached the climax of its productivity during the middle years of the nineteenth century. These slates are of fine grain, compact and strong, yet not very heavy. They are often described as blue, but the usual colour is dark grey tinged here and there with green. They were, and still are, available in various sizes up to 24 × 12 ins. The most popular are the small slates, known, because of the method of hanging them, which was with oak pegs over battens, as 'peggies'. To-day copper nails are often substituted. Random widths are used, but the majority are between 8 and 12 ins., and sometimes the underside will be torched with lime plaster. Except in north Cornwall and the north-west corner of Devon, where the big thick rag slates (to be referred to later) were sometimes preferred, peggies are the favourite type all over Cornwall and south-west Devon. They can be seen on the roof at Cotehele (*147a*), renewed by the National Trust in 1955, where the range of sizes runs from 10 × 20 ins. at the eaves to 4 × 8 ins. at the ridge.

Unfortunately, in order to counter the force of the Atlantic gales Cornish slates are often laid in cement, and the roof is washed over periodically with a cement slurry, a procedure known there as grouting. Or, particularly in fishing ports, red lead and tar may be used; these look more agreeable than might perhaps be expected. Nevertheless, this is a bad practice, because when a roof is deprived of proper ventilation the supporting timbers will be more prone to be attacked by beetle, and presently to rot. Eventually the whole roof is liable to slide off in one piece.

Devon also produced large quantities of roofing slate in former times, a stone which often has a slightly brownish tinge and attracts lichens freely. Research, particularly by E. M. Jope and G. C. Dunning,[1] has revealed that after about 1170 roofing slates were despatched by sea in considerable quantities from Devon and Cornwall to many places in southern England farther east, throughout the Middle Ages. By 1187 over 800,000 slates had been brought from Devon to Winchester alone, for the King's buildings. The trade extended at least as far as Dover and perhaps up the Thames, for slates from the South-West are recorded at Windsor in 1481. These slates came from quarries near the South coast, from Charleton westwards to the neighbourhood of Fowey. Other quarries near the North coast of Cornwall, around Padstow and at Trevalga between Tintagel and Boscastle, probably sent slates up the Bristol Channel, perhaps for the roofing of Taunton Castle and Glastonbury Abbey, and also to Bristol itself.

The richly textured Devon roofs are very attractive, but the slate has not the strength nor the hardness of the best Cornish products and has scarcely been quarried for over a hundred years. By the end of the nineteenth century, even in Cornwall, only three slate quarries were still working, all near Tintagel; and two of these had to close shortly afterwards. Delabole can now easily supply all the requirements of Cornwall, and most of its slate goes elsewhere. When a Devon roof decays and is replaced by Delabole slate, no serious harm is done, but unfortunately the replacement is often carried out in Welsh slate for reasons of cost. The effect of this is all too evident at Sydenham House, Coryton, a few

[1] See their important paper, 'The Use of Blue Slate for Roofing in Mediaeval England', in *The Antiquaries Journal*, vol. XXXIV (1954).

miles south-east of Dartmoor. The east wing has so far managed to preserve its original early-seventeenth-century covering of warm-hued Devon slate; the rest of the roof, since the nineteen-twenties, has been of smooth, blue-grey Welsh slate, shiny and regular, which is quite out of character with the rough, tweedy walls of the house, built of a mixture of the local brown shale and sandstone rubble, with plenty of mortar. In the south-east of the county another example is furnished by the church at Torbryan. Here the chancel is roofed with large, smooth pieces of Welsh slate, while the nave retains the Devon product, smaller in scale, roughly cut and richly lichened. The visual contrast provides an object lesson in right and wrong roofing materials.

The Pre-Cambrian slate of Leicestershire, to the formation of which reference was made on p. 152, was quarried along the east and south sides of Charnwood Forest, at Groby, at Woodhouse Eaves and above all at Swithland, the name by which all this slate is generally known. Roofing slate, as was indicated earlier, was even before the age of canals and railways much more easily portable than blocks of masonry; and except along the south-eastern fringes of the county, where oolitic slates were available from Northamptonshire, Swithland slate became by the end of the eighteenth century the characteristic roofing material of nearly the whole of Leicestershire. It was also in demand in adjoining counties: for instance, in the southern part of Nottinghamshire. Its use by the Romans has been mentioned; quarrying started again in the thirteenth century. By 1600 a Swithland roof, with slates rough-hewn and about $1\frac{1}{4}$ ins. thick, was probably the rule rather than the exception for the larger houses. During the Georgian period even the humblest cottages would often be so covered, to their great aesthetic advantage, for these blue-grey roofs, tinged with green and often spotted with moss and lichens, are not only splendidly durable but richly textured (147c). The purple variety is not so pleasing. In the nineteenth century Leicestershire became predominantly a county of brick, and for roofs the massproduced Welsh product, which alone could cope with the demand, completely captured the market. The last quarry of Swithland slate ceased working in 1887, and with its closure England was provided with yet one more example of the visual harm inflicted by the Industrial Revolution. To-day all that can be seen in Swithland woods are seven huge pits, half-full of water.

If a roof is good, a fairly steep pitch is usually welcome, since the covering material will be better seen; and here and there, both in Leicestershire (147c) and in the South-West, this is what we find. The North, on the other hand, as we have already noted in the descriptions of limestone and sandstone roofs, preferred rather gentle slopes, and in this respect the slate roofs are no exception (168a and b, 181c). The pitch is usually between 30° and 35°. But it was for roofing that this slate long made its greatest contribution.

SLATE CONTRASTS
Lake District walls
a. *Near Kirkston Pass*   b. *Near Ambleside*
Slate in Cornwall
c. *Notts Mill, Lerryn*   d. *House (formerly known as Bishop's House), St. Columb Major*

Within the confines of the Lake District itself, whatever the material of the walling, every self-respecting roof is still of slate. The roof of quite a modest building may weigh as much as ten tons, so the supporting rafters, in the old houses usually of oak, had to be of lusty strength. Their slates were always fixed with oak pegs, but later iron nails were used; in time, needless to say, these have rusted and given trouble. Nowadays the nails are of copper, galvanised iron or aluminium-alloy, inserted through pairs of holes punched in the head of the slate, and in addition the larger slates—those over 13 ins. long—have two more holes for nails in the long sides, to furnish further support; but of course none of this is visible, for every slate overlaps not only the next course below it but a part of the next but one, so that if, for example, the length is 1 ft., only about 5 ins. will be exposed. As with the Cornish slates, the widths are random (168b and c)—they can vary from as much as 24 ins. at the eaves to as little as 6 ins. below the ridge—but, following the usual excellent English practice, whatever the stone, the courses are always graded.

   Not all the Lake District roofing slate looks the same, nor is it geologically identical: some is very rough (168c), some comparatively smooth (168a). There are also considerable variations of colour: the blues and greens are the most attractive, but they are not ubiquitous. Before the end of the seventeenth century, however, the fame of this slate was already sufficient for Wren to have it brought to London for Chelsea Hospital and Kensington Palace. A good local roof of Wren's time is seen at Crackenthorpe Hall near Appleby (363b), built in 1685. The Silurian slate known as 'blue Westmorland' is to-day neither the one nor the other: the quarries, as we have noted, are in Lancashire, close to Kirkby-in-Furness, and the usual colour is a rather sombre grey, as can be seen at Hawkshead (168b). But the still older Borrowdale and Buttermere slate of the Lake District, which is of volcanic origin, is a very different material: this is the loveliest roofing slate in Britain, fine in grain and unforgettable for its green colour. When the sun breaks through after a shower of rain, these Cumberland Green roofs are a source of special delight. It is a great pity that during the last fifty years the demand for every kind of roofing slate has declined substantially.

   The ridges of these slate roofs were originally formed from pieces of freestone (usually sandstone) chiselled into shape and bedded on with lime mortar. The lengths of the ridge-pieces were random: usually between 2 ft. and 4 ft. Later these gave place to purpose-made dark grey-blue ridge tiles of Staffordshire clay in standard lengths (168b, 181c), which was undoubtedly a change for the worse. In the last few years ridge tiles of reconstituted stone have become available in half-round or plain angular sections 18 or 30 ins. long: the usual formula is three parts of greenstone dust to one of cement. These are an improvement, as they can be made to match the roofing slates. But another method

SLATE ROOFS IN THE LAKE DISTRICT
a. *Blea Tarn House, Westmorland*
b. *Hawkshead, Lancashire* c. *High Goody Bridge, Grasmere, Westmorland*

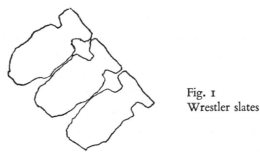

Fig. 1
Wrestler slates

was evolved in the Lake District, in which ridge pieces were unnecessary. Wrestler slates are so called because they interlock at the ridge. Slots were cut about 2 ins. below the top of each slate, into which were fitted other slates, similarly cut, from the obverse roof slope. In order to prevent rattling when it was windy, the slates were bedded down in lime mortar (nowadays it would be cement), and more was placed within the V joint, to a depth in the centre of about $1\frac{1}{2}$ins. (not visible from below). Provided the slate is not too hard, an old slater told me, wrestler slates are not difficult to produce, using a slate hammer. Those from Langdale are excellent for the purpose. To-day, nevertheless, they are a rarity. But Grasmere has several examples: for instance, on the churchyard lych-gate and on the interesting bee-wall in the garden of the Wordsworth Museum. Several 'wrestlers' are also preserved in the museum itself. They are no longer used, but there is no obvious reason why. There are still plenty of skilled stone-workers in the Lake District, and if the demand were there it could be met.

Slate from North Wales had been used at Chester as early as the fourteenth century and in Shropshire before the end of the Middle Ages; and it went as far as Williamsburg, Virginia, for roofing the Governor's Palace in 1709. But it was not until the reign of George III that its appearance in England became widespread. Architects and builders, let it be said, welcomed it with enthusiasm, for undeniably it had some great practical advantages. It was strong, reasonably durable (although in this respect not comparable with any of the English slates), completely non-porous, and already standardized in the matter of sizes. Most important of all, it could be split into extremely fine laminae: as little as $\frac{1}{8}$in. in the finer-grained varieties. Welsh roofing slate is thus much thinner and smoother than any other, and weighs less: compared indeed with a limestone or sandstone roof, the difference is remarkable, for a roof of Welsh slate will weigh on an average only about one-fifth as much. Thus the supporting walls could be less strongly built and wooden rafters and roof battens also substantially lighter. Moreover, the thin slate would lie quite happily upon roofs of very low pitch (22–26°). This particularly commended it to the Georgian builders, who frequently liked to conceal their roofs as far as they could behind parapets. Among the first to take advantage of the opportunities for economy offered by Welsh slate were the brothers Adam, for whose tall London houses its adoption meant quite a substantial reduction in costs. Others were not slow to follow suit. 'By 1792', says Sir John Summerson, '12,000 tons a year were being exported from the Penrhyn quarries alone, and London rapidly became a slate-roofed city.'[1]

The first Welsh slate had reached London by sea, for the quarries were close to the coast. Within a generation, advantage was being taken of the new canals to carry the slate to inland towns previously less accessible to it; fifty years later, the railways carried it all over the country. Where it was used behind parapets, there was no need for grading the sizes; when employed to roof factories and the humble dwellings of artisans, there was no call for such a refinement. But soon this slate was playing a far more prominent part; when roof timbers carrying heavy stone slates decayed and reconstruction became necessary, there was every temptation on practical grounds to substitute the newly available product (308e). In the nineteenth century Welsh slate replaced thatch, too, in all parts of the country. From the economic standpoint it was bound to triumph over all its rivals, even without the tremendous fillip given to this industry in 1831 when the tax on slate was removed while that on tiles remained.[2] Well might the millionaire builder of Penrhyn Castle acquire, about 1840, a four-poster bed carved entirely out of his own slate.[3] Only within the present century has the demand for Welsh slate declined substantially in the face of rival products, some of which (asbestos tiles, for instance) are visually still less attractive.

Yet there is no good reason why Welsh slate should be as unpleasing as it usually is. The 'machine look' of nearly all Welsh slate roofs derives from two causes. On account of its geological structure this stone can be trimmed (and from the purely practical standpoint this has doubtless been a great advantage) into standard rectangles of debilitating regularity. And since the end of the eighteenth century it has for some reason never been the practice to lay Welsh slates in courses of diminishing size, as with other natural slates.[4]

1 *Georgian London* (1945), p. 65.

2 But the tax on tiles was removed only two years later, in 1833.

3 This is in a smallish bedroom in the Keep. The much bigger four-poster in the State Bedroom, one of the most fantastic pieces of furniture in the British Isles, is, although stated in the *Country Life* article of July 28, 1955 (p. 194) to be of slate, in fact—unfortunately for the story—of oak.

4 During the middle years of the nineteenth century even Delabole slates were not always laid in diminishing courses, as can be seen at Notts Mill, Lerryn (*167c*). This was no doubt a re-roofing of an older building, and it will be evident that aesthetically much was lost.

They are dressed to a number of sizes (of which 24 × 12 ins., 20 × 10 ins. and 16 × 8 ins. are the most usual), but it has always been customary to sort the sizes into separate stacks, and to sell them thus sorted, different prices being charged for 'duchesses', 'countesses', 'ladies' and the rest. This serves to render Welsh slates easier to use: obviously, if a standard size is available, it is possible to calculate exactly how many to order for a given roof, while the task of laying them becomes much less skilful, and money is saved. Un-happily, the one thing which such methods can never produce is a lovely roof. Employed in conjunction with walls of robust red sandstone, as can be seen frequently in Hereford-shire, these thin, monotonously regular slates look particularly ungenerous and unworthy.

Care in the choice of colour is of great importance, and here the Welsh slate industry offers a far wider range than is generally known or recognized. In the great Penrhyn quarry at Bethesda (which in its heyday provided work for between five and six thousand men), the predominant colour is purplish-grey, but besides this there are purple, purplish-red, pure grey, green and blue. Although all these colours merge into one another, the Welsh practice has been to sort them just as uniformly for colour as for size. The two latter are the best colours, and also unfortunately the scarcest and therefore the most expensive. The green slate also costs more because it is the hardest, so hard in fact that, to its great artistic advantage, it cannot be trimmed to a smooth edge. Unfortunately it is the less attractive colours which have travelled throughout England. Purple is a particularly difficult colour to employ successfully, and when seen in combination with bright red brick it is painful. The greyer slate is better, and with walls of yellow brick or flint or some shades of applied colour-wash, seems to me preferable to red tiles. Yet how seldom, aesthetically, can even grey slate vie with a local roofing material. At Wallington in Northumberland, the original sandstone slates were replaced not with Welsh but with Scottish slate, brought in horse-drawn waggons across the Cheviots. The outcome was a roof of faultless efficiency, which is nevertheless too smooth for the stonework (*129c*). Only the pleasant grey colour partly redeems it.

It is usual to think of roofing-stones of every kind as being rectangular, but in the case of slate this is not always so. The South-West formerly made extensive use of scantle and rag slates, of which only the parts that show are trimmed and squared; but as the ragged edges are covered by subsequent courses this is not evident. Scantles and rags are of random widths and comparatively rough, and in their irregularity, sometimes involving additional cutting on the site, lies their virtue. The only difference between them is in size, rags being the larger, thicker, and more rectangular. The usual practice with rag slates was to nail them direct to the rafters.

The Romans are known to have cut their slate into a variety of shapes, which included elongated hexagons and even rough ovals. Later the French, with their *penchant* for circular turrets capped with roofs of tapering or conical form, found wedge-shaped slates very convenient, and also cut many of their slates to make scale-like and saw-tooth patterns.[1] In English buildings circular roofs of this type are seldom encountered, but slates curved at one end, to produce over a whole roof an effect suggestive of greatly magnified fish-scales, can very occasionally be found. (One of the standard sizes is 24 × 12 ins.) A roof of good slate cut in this fashion can look uncommonly attractive.

Slate-hung Walls

John Evelyn, writing in 1666, not long before its demolition, about the royal palace of Nonsuch in Surrey, recorded that there were two courts, 'one stone, castle-like; the other timber, Gothic, covered with scales of slate, fastened on to the timber as pretty figures.' (The timber-framing was on the upper storey only.) But this very interesting early instance of slate-hanging in England was entirely unlike all that was to follow. At Nonsuch, as at a number of places in Normandy, the slabs of slate were attached only to the timbers; the plaster infilling (900 ft. of it, moulded here into elaborate scenes from Classical mythology in the French Renaissance style) remained unmasked. The slates did not over-lap, and their surface was enriched with elegant bunches of flowers and fruit, carved in shallow relief and partly gilded. The carving, the work of Italians, was done in England, but the bluish-black, non-fissile slate used is believed to have been imported from France: perhaps from Angers.

Slate-hanging did not begin to become popular until the time of the Stuarts; its hey-day was the later Georgian age and especially the Regency. Examples can be seen in a good many of the older seaside towns, where the impervious character of slate affords valuable protection against the salty air, but the part of England in which there is far more than anywhere else is South Devon and Cornwall. Little towns such as Topsham, Ashburton, Totnes, Launceston, Liskeard and Padstow can still show numerous examples.

Sometimes the slates were hung upon timber-framed walls of lath and plaster; this even applies to the projection above the porch at Fell Foot Farm in Little Langdale (*181*c). An attractive example of this type is a range of old houses at Dunster in Somerset known as The Nunnery (*181*b). This building, part of which goes back to the fourteenth century, has

1 See Georges Doyon et Robert Hubrecht, *L'Architecture Rurale et Bourgeoise en France*, 2nd ed. (1957), pp. 196–197, and illustrations.

three storeys, of which the lowest is of red Devonian sandstone whilst the two upper are timber-framed and hung with slate. Between the windows on the top storey this is arranged, effectively, in diamond patterns. But timber-framed houses are not common in Devon and unknown in Cornwall; in these counties the walls to which the slate is attached are either of brick or of some rough stone, such as slate-stone (*167*d) or granite. This is also true of the North-West, where the hung slates are larger and thicker (*181*e). In some cases it was necessary to fix wooden battens and counter-battens on to the wall upon which, with the aid of long nails, the slates would be hung (cf. *278*e), and often their concealed upper ends would be bedded in mortar. The battens are not of course in evidence as there is a considerable overlap, but a glimpse of a side-wall, as at Ashburton (*181*a), is often sufficient to establish their presence. With brick walls they could usually be dispensed with, for the slates could be nailed directly into the mortar courses. Nowadays in exposed positions the slates are sometimes bedded in mastic. Occasionally, they have been applied to a wall without any overlapping. This can be seen at Pillar House, Hawkshead (*168*b) where both nails and mortar help to secure them, and also, in a very sophisticated example, probably by James Wyatt (*c.* 1797), at Soho House in the Birmingham suburb of Handsworth. Here the large slates, affixed to brick and stone-coloured, were intended to suggest finely-jointed ashlar masonry, for which they were an economical substitute.

The object of slate-hanging was always to provide additional protection against the elements; but, as so often when the pace of living was less hectic than it is to-day, the opportunity of turning an essentially practical device to aesthetic advantage was not neglected. Another house at St. Columb Major furnishes a pretty if rather timid example of decorative slate-hanging (*181*d). This craft is attractively displayed in the old Devon town of Totnes, although even here one cannot pretend that slate is used with anything approaching the resourcefulness to be seen in parts of west-central Germany. At Goslar, for example, this stone is handled with brilliant virtuosity, in window-surrounds, in wall-patterns of many different designs, and in swept valley effects upon the roofs, not to mention the charming blending of colours: light, dark, greenish and brownish greys. At Biedenkopf near Marburg, in the Upper Lahn valley, one can even see an heraldic shield, and below it a winged eagle, all represented in hung slates; and everywhere in this area at least one edge of nearly every slate is curved. Moreover, the craft is still very much alive in this part of Germany, in contrast, unfortunately, to England. A visit to Hesse and the Harz Mountains leaves one doubtful whether we have shown enough enterprise in our use of slate. Nevertheless, a stroll through Totnes affords many pleasures for those interested in slate-hanging. Some of the slating is staid and plain, but on a few houses, mostly appearing to date from the late eighteenth or early nineteenth centuries,

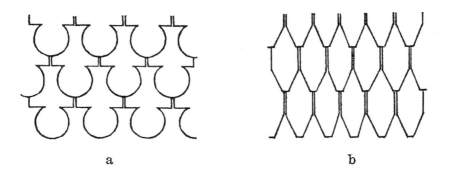

Fig. 2 Patterns of slate-hanging at Totnes

the patterning is gay and fanciful. (Yet the most familiar pattern, the simple fish-scale, does not seem to have been favoured here.) Contrasts of natural colour are also exploited: two colours, such as purple and grey, will be effectively arranged in horizontal bands of, say, three courses each.[1] Whitewash and colour-wash are also quite common, both in the South-West and in the North-West (*168*b). On hung slates these should be applied with circumspection, but in the right place they can look surprisingly well.

1 In 1977, however, the author could find only two houses in Totnes with slate-hanging in patterns, in both cases Fig. 2a; no example at all of 'b'.

7

MARBLE

'Marble' in this chapter is used in its popular as opposed to its geologically exact sense, for upon a strict interpretation there is no English marble. There are certain places in the world where long ago, as a result of the action in the earth's crust of natural forces such as great heat or pressure or both, pockets of limestone have become transformed into this somewhat different, crystalline substance which is known as marble. This is therefore, like slate, a metamorphic rock. Chemically there is no difference between marble and limestone, for both possess a high calcium carbonate content. The essential difference is in their structure. A limestone only becomes a marble when, under heat or pressure, it has been completely recrystallized. Stresses may produce fissures in the limestone which become filled with calcite, sometimes stained by other mineral colouring, and thereby veining is formed.

The attraction of this crystalline stone for builders has always been its ability, not normally shared by any sandstone nor by any but the hardest limestones, to take a high polish. The best varieties of marble are fine-grained, compact and even throughout, with no impurities and no flaws. In practice it is not always easy to draw a hard and fast line between what is marble and what is not. The confusion arises from the popular practice of describing as marble any limestone which will take a polish, for there are in England quite a number of limestones, and of widely differing age, which can not only be polished but brought to a sharp arris. It is usually said that there are only two true marbles in the British Isles: one quarried on the island of Iona, and the other the Connemara marble from near Clifden in County Galway. Both are metamorphosed dolomitic limestones, predominantly pale green in colour, with white markings. But with some of the polishable limestones effects can be achieved which are similar to those of the true marbles in their general aesthetic character. In addition to the attractions, for decorative purposes, of polished surfaces and a wide choice of colour, these stones lend themselves to a refinement, precision and delicacy of detail that can be a great embellishment to a building.

In the Middle Ages Purbeck marble and its substitutes were used outside as well as within, and in the localities in which they occur, all the more important English marbles (so-called) have been used externally in their unpolished state, as ordinary building stones.

In this country marbles resist the weather, and especially smoky air, no better than most other limestones, and in our climate a stone which will take a polish, even an imported true marble, cannot be relied upon to retain it for very long, so that for external usage the labour involved in polishing will scarcely be worth while. Even internally, the polish on a marble will not last long if the building is damp, as many, probably most, mediaeval churches in England were. Nevertheless, if we wish to gain some idea of the distinctive character of the English marbles in the Middle Ages it is in the cathedrals and churches that we must look; and more recent instances of marble and other 'dressy' stones in this country must also (with some modern exceptions) be sought indoors. In England in fact, marble, unlike polished granite, is essentially a stone requiring protection from the elements, which is why in the present short chapter I am departing from my general resolution to confine this book to external materials.

Some English marbles are extremely rich in shell-fossils, and it is when these fossils are most closely crowded together that the stone will polish best. In the younger marbles, including Purbeck, the predominant fossil-shells are of a freshwater mollusc, the water snail *Viviparus*.[1] The appeal of these stones, when polished, owes not a little to the elaborate figuring produced by the conglomeration of tiny petrified shells. In houses these marbles were most frequently coveted for chimney-pieces, some of which, especially in Elizabethan and Jacobean days, were carved with an exuberance which cannot always be admired. In churches, until well into the Stuart period, English marbles were much in demand for effigies, and still more, between the closing years of the twelfth century and the first half of the fourteenth, for small shafts. They were especially suitable for recumbent effigies in fairly low relief because whereas many, perhaps the majority, of our marbles can be dug out in lengths of 6 or 8 ft., they are seldom more than 1 ft. thick and sometimes no more than 2 or 3 ins. For colonettes, on the other hand, there was a disadvantage: the stone could not be laid in the direction of its natural bed. Upturned, as can often be seen in thirteenth century churches, it was very liable to split length-wise along the shafts.

The English marbles exhibit a good deal of colour variation. In its pure form marble, like the limestone from which it derives, is white. Pure varieties of either stone are, however, rare, and it is the impurities, which vary greatly both in kind and degree, that are responsible for the range of colours. As with the other limestones, iron oxides are responsible for many of the warm colours: the creams, yellows, browns, russets, reds and pinks. These impurities may permeate an entire block uniformly or they may affect certain spots only. Hence the figured character of much (though not usually the most pleasing) marble and the frequent occurrence of thin streaks and veins.

1 Formerly, and by some palaeontologists still, known as *Paludina:* I am assured that the two are synonymous.

Where English marbles can be obtained in reasonably large pieces, as with the Devon and, until recently, the Derbyshire groups, the current practice is to use them in slab form for laying on floors and for facing walls built of coarse materials, such as ordinary concrete, breeze-blocks or common brick, which require masking. In the last few years many foreign marbles have been brought in, true marbles, much more expensive-looking and usually more beautiful than any English variety, for the enrichment of public and commercial buildings of every kind.

In the employment of marble, therefore, a minor revolution has taken place during the present century. What has already been said about the use of granite and slate as sheathing materials applies here in some respects with still more force. Marble has been described as 'the precious stone of building', and through the centuries true marble, especially in England because we have none, has always been regarded as evidence of wealth and a symbol of luxury. Nowadays the stone is extracted, sawn, planed and polished mechanically, and good marble is structurally so cohesive that it can be sawn into slabs no more than $\frac{3}{4}$ in. thick, and with some foreign varieties even less. This has reduced the price considerably and thereby introduced a new aesthetic hazard, for few human temptations are more difficult to resist than the opportunity of achieving an expensive looking effect at a moderate cost. There are many modern buildings in which marble facings have been employed to great advantage; but in some of the temples of big business it is otherwise. In these we cannot suppress the feeling that the marbles have been introduced solely because they look suitably costly. They evoke the opulent insensibilities of the Roman Empire.

The Varieties of English 'Marble'

The geological pattern of the English marbles follows the progression with which we are by now familiar. The 'youngest' group occurs in the South-East: these are the shelly limestones of the Weald Clay. The principal quarries were at Bethersden in Kent, between Ashford and Tenterden, and at Kirdford in Sussex, to the north-east of Petworth. There were also the Gorlinger quarries near East Grinstead, and others at Petworth itself, at Laughton between Lewes and Hailsham, and in Surrey at Charlwood, Outwood and Ewhurst. All these belong to the same geological formation and are in appearance closely similar.

Bethersden marble is the most important member of this group and the only one to have been dug, albeit on a very small scale, in recent times. This interesting stone is found in thin, somewhat irregular slabs, not more than four feet below the surface. The strata are never more than 7 ins. thick, and often under half as much. In its natural, rough state it has a somewhat mottled appearance, owing to the shell fossils; in colour it is usually a medium grey, but sometimes brownish. It was formerly in much demand for paving, for which it was obviously well suited; the whole of Bethersden church is paved with it, and so is the path across the churchyard, both here and at the neighbouring village of Great Chart. Plenty of it can be seen on the local field paths, and it weathers well, as is also demonstrated by a number of Georgian tombstones; but although the fossils are visible they do not make much effect in its unpolished state. To see how decorative Bethersden marble can be, one must go indoors. Protected from the weather, beautiful damask-like effects could be realised by carving delicate floral and other patterns on the surface of the stone, polishing, and then cutting away the background so that the ornamental parts appear to stand out in very shallow relief. Since this stone, like all the English marbles, looks darker when polished, there is also a tone contrast: the darker grey carving stands out most effectively from the silver-grey ground, as on the monument to Lady Margaret Palmer (d. 1619) at Chilham, an outstanding example of what could be achieved with Bethersden marble. Less ambitious instances of the same technique are provided by two early seventeenth century fireplaces (in the hall and dining room: both apparently introduced from elsewhere) at a nearby house, Godinton.

Sussex marble, grey and brown, sometimes with greenish or bluish tinges, was in steady demand for ornamental purposes, not only in the churches of the Middle Ages but for long after: it can be seen, for instance, in Petworth House. On at least one occasion   * it travelled as far as Cambridge, where it was employed in 1583 for the porch of the old chapel of Corpus Christi College which no longer survives. The once popular Sussex name, 'winklestone', is an indication of the profusion of small snail shells (winkles) in its composition. It is also much in evidence in the older churches on the southern fringe of Surrey.

With Purbeck, far and away the best known and most widely used of the English marbles, we move back into the latest phase of the Jurassic age. The immense vogue for this shelly limestone during the Early English and Decorated phases of our Gothic architecture is confirmed by its survival in church interiors, and to a much smaller extent also externally, throughout the country. It is said to have been originally taken from a reef of rocks running out into the sea near St. Aldhelm's Head. When this was used up, the quarrymen followed the seam back under the cliffs. Information about these early quarries is scarce, but several of the best were Crown property. The proximity of the sea was a great advantage in establishing the popularity of Purbeck marble. Some of it was loaded into ships on the spot, but where carving was required the stone was carried to the yards in the village of Corfe Castle, where most of the masons lived, and thence to quays (which still exist) on the southern shore of Poole Harbour. Some of it was also loaded at Swanage. Round the coast it travelled, and up the rivers, to Exeter, Salisbury and Winchester (for the church of St. Cross, an exceptionally early instance of its use), to Canterbury and Westminster, Ely and Lincoln, Beverley and York, and even to Durham, where, surprisingly, it would seem to have been used at an earlier date than in any other English cathedral (in the Galilee Chapel, built c. 1170–76).[1] It was employed for a variety of ornamental purposes, and above all at this time for thin shafts and colonnettes. Less often it provided the facing material (not of course the rubble core) for piers on a majestic scale, as in Westminster Abbey and at Exeter (cf. p. 65). In its unpolished state the colour is generally light grey, but often with hints of several other colours: green, blue, red, brown and fawn. When polished it becomes considerably darker.

Purbeck marble can be seen in great profusion in the cathedral of Salisbury, for which it was very conveniently placed, shipment up the Avon presenting no difficulty. The contrast between the aesthetic effects of the polished and the unpolished stone can be specially well seen in the Chapter House, which, like the church itself, is built of Chilmark stone liberally enriched with Purbeck shafts. Most of the latter are unpolished, and of a pale slate-grey; but round the interior of the building there runs a stone bench, the seats divided by short colonnettes of Purbeck stone bearing an arcade. These came in for a great deal of rubbing, especially towards their lower ends, which are shiny and much darker. The unpolished Purbeck certainly tones better with the Chilmark stone, but it reflects no light. In the church itself, the thin shafts of Purbeck stone and the capitals and bases of the piers were all highly polished before being placed in position. It may be true that the application of varnish to the Purbeck stone during the nineteenth century has served somewhat to exaggerate both its shininess and its blackness; but there can be no doubt that this contrast of colour as well as of surface-texture was an effect deliberately sought by the original builders. The nave of Salisbury, to-day so light without its stained glass, has often been said to hold no mystery; but on a sunny day we can find much to compensate us for the absence of mystery in the beauty of the reflections. I do not know any other church in England in which, under the right conditions of light, reflections count for so much. Here is polished stone contributing what for England is a most unexpected and vivid pleasure.

1 The use of Purbeck marble here has been questioned, but was kindly confirmed for me by Sir Kingsley Dunham, F.R.S., Director of the Institute of Geological Sciences and formerly Professor of Geology in the University of Durham. Only the north and south shafts of each pier are from Purbeck: the east and west shafts, added later, are sandstone.

SLATE-HANGING
a. *North Street, Ashburton, Devon*   b. *The Nunnery, Dunster, Somerset*
c. *Fell Foot Farm, Little Langdale, Westmorland*
d. *St. Columb Major, Cornwall*   e. *Hawkshead, Lancashire*

To some eyes the tone contrasts in English church interiors in which Purbeck was profusely employed may seem over-emphatic; certainly this stone is more agreeable when it is not too aggressively black. Nevertheless, contrast was of the essence of its appeal. 'The dark colour which accentuated the precise shape of colonnettes, capitals, and mouldings', says Professor Brieger, 'was a welcome quality where it was desired to set up screens in front of a lighter wall. . . . The richest screen design was given to the triforium arcade. The polished dark marble shafts, lavishly used, glittered and shone against the deeper darkness of the openings and the lighter walls.'[1] The production of Purbeck marble dressings became a most flourishing industry during the thirteenth and the first half of the fourteenth centuries. Often, apparently, they were delivered at the site all ready for use, having been shaped and polished before leaving the quarry: an interesting instance of early prefabrication.

This stone was, however, always something of a luxury which the smaller churches and secular builders, except locally, were usually unable to afford; hence the introduction of various substitutes of which there will be more to say shortly. After about 1330 taste began to change: in the Perpendicular churches, with light flooding in through their huge windows, the tall staccato accents provided by the dark shafts were no longer appreciated. For some while longer, Purbeck marble continued to be used for effigies, but its great heyday was over for ever. After three centuries of neglect there was, it is true, something of a revival in the use of this stone in the Victorian period mainly to meet the needs of widespread church restoration;[2] and even in our own day it has been worked when required, as for Exeter Cathedral and the Temple church in London after the second world war. But it has not been in regular production for many years, and in domestic architecture its part has always been small.

At a number of churches in Somerset, and to some extent elsewhere, Blue Lias, because it was so much more accessible, was brought into service between c. 1180 and c. 1300 as the local substitute for Purbeck marble for colonnettes, capitals, bases and tombs: indeed its use for ledgers continued long after 1300. The final smooth finish was obtained by abrasion and polishing, which with the only tools then available must have called for arduous labour. But except in the Chapter Houses at Wells and Exeter, this stone was not used for figurative nor foliage carving; it was too liable to fracture. When employed externally, as on the west front at Wells, needless to say it decayed, and most of the shafts there were

1 Peter Brieger, *English Art, 1216–1307* (1957), pp. 12–13.

2 An outstanding example of its use by a Victorian architect, and not for restoration, can be seen in the remarkable church which G. E. Street built for the third Earl of Eldon at Kingston in the Isle of Purbeck.

ALABASTER AND SCAGLIOLA
Kedleston Hall, Derbyshire

replaced in 1871 by black Kilkenny marble (really a polishable Carboniferous limestone) from Ireland.[1]

There are about two dozen other Jurassic limestones which will take a polish and have accordingly been described as marbles. In the pre-machine age, most of them could only be worked with difficulty. The only one that would ever seem to have had more than local importance is the marble quarried beside the River Nene at Alwalton in Huntingdonshire, four miles south-west of Peterborough. This is a hard medium-grey stone formed in the oyster beds of the Great Oolite, which until recently was constantly confused with Purbeck marble. Yet its appearance is really very different; in place of small snail fossils it contains fossilized oyster shells, which are both larger and more interesting. Alwalton marble was first employed by the Romans at nearby Castor, and in the late twelfth and early thirteenth centuries, after the Abbey of Peterborough had acquired this quarry as well as those at Barnack, it was the material chosen for several recumbent effigies of the Abbots preserved in what is now the Cathedral. It has also been identified during the last few years at Ely, Bury St. Edmunds, and notably in the wall arcade of the north choir aisle at Lincoln, where the Alwarton shafts have worn better than the Purbeck.[2]

None of the other marbles in this group, so far as I am aware, was ever used outside its own locality, and many are all but forgotten. In houses they were principally in demand for chimney-pieces, steps, plinths and paving-stones.[3]

1 For full details, see 'The Stone Insets of Somerset Churches', by Professor D. T. Donovan and Dr. R. D. Reid, in the *Proceedings of the Somersetshire Archaeological and Natural History Society for 1962–63*, vol. 107 (1963). Besides Wells and Exeter, they identified the use of Blue Lias in this manner at Bristol Cathedral, Glastonbury and Cleeve Abbeys, and at such churches as Curry Rivel, Portbury and Compton Bishop.

2 For Alwalton marble, see Donovan Purcell, 'A Forgotten English Marble', in *Country Life*, Sept. 9, 1965, and the same writer's *Cambridge Stone* (1967), pp. 71–75.

3 As to the best of my knowledge no complete list of the Jurassic marbles is available, a few readers may care to have one. The progression is along the limestone belt from south to north.

DORSET and SOMERSET
    (1) Purbeck: see above.
    (2) Portland stone, although not described as a marble, is nowadays sometimes polished for internal use.
    (3) All within a few miles of the Dorset-Somerset border:
        (a) Bothenhampton (close to Bridport), Long Burton (S. of Sherborne), Haydon (E. of Sherborne) and Bowden (near Gillingham), all from the Forest Marble. Fossil-rich paving from Haydon quarry, on the far side of Sherborne Park, can still be seen on the refectory floor at the Hospital of St. John, Sherborne. The soft-soled, heelless slippers of the pensioners keep it well polished.
        (b) Melbury (near Evershot), from the Oxford Clay.
        (c) Lyme Regis, Ilminster and Marston Magna (N.E. of Yeovil), from the Lias: all rich in ammonites. Long Burton and Marston are both sometimes known as Yeovil marble.
    (4) Street, Shepton Mallet and Radstock, bluish-black, from the Blue Lias.

The remaining English marbles are of much greater antiquity: nearly all belong either to the Carboniferous system or to the Devonian. The former are the northern marbles, products of the counties of Derbyshire, Lancashire, Yorkshire, Durham and Westmorland.

The Derbyshire marbles belong to the hilly portions of the county at the southern extremity of the Pennine chain, especially to the region around Bakewell and south of Miller's Dale, but also to the Wirksworth neighbourhood. In their unpolished state, several of them were referred to in Chapter 3. The best known is Hopton Wood, which was lately used for a new floor in Birmingham Cathedral. It was formerly available in two colours, light cream and grey. The latter was used by Robert Adam in combination with white Italian marble for the handsome floor of the great hall at Kedleston. The somewhat similar Derbydene marble (a trade name), with many fossils, can be seen in quantity on the floor of Coventry Cathedral. 'I felt,' wrote the architect, 'that these creatures who lived million of years ago could make their contribution to the life-span of the building.' Also grey, with large, lighter-coloured fossils, is the marble known as Derbyshire Fossil, from Monyash near Matlock; quite a lot of this stone was used at Chatsworth. Another grey variety, sometimes with veins of purple, comes from the hills to the west of Bakewell. A very handsome chimney-piece in this material can be seen in the dining room at Belvoir Castle. The uniformly textured black marbles of Ashford and Little Longstone, close to Bakewell, were formerly popular: Derby Black,

(5) A quarry in the Lias, not identified, provided the original stone for the profusion of small colonnettes, etc., at Wells Cathedral: see above.

GLOUCESTERSHIRE
Campden: from the Inferior Oolite near Chipping Campden.
    Used for the reredos of the church at Brailes, Warwickshire, about 8 miles to the E.

WARWICKSHIRE
Binton and Temple Grafton: from the Lias west of Stratford-on-Avon.

OXFORDSHIRE:
(1) Bletchingdon, a greenish-grey stone with yellow markings from the Forest Marble formation some eight miles north of Oxford. This stone was used externally in 1636 for the 7 ft. high columns in the Canterbury Quadrangle of St. John's College, and eleven of these, out of the original sixteen, are still *in situ*.
(2) Forest of Wychwood. Also a rather coarse Forest Marble.
(3) Banbury, a brown and grey stone from the Lower Lias, which at one time enjoyed a considerable local reputation.

BUCKINGHAMSHIRE:
Buckingham marble, a shelly stone from the Great Oolite.

NORTHAMPTONSHIRE:
(1) (*a*) Culworth, whitish, and (*b*) Byfield, nearly black: both thinly bedded stones from the Great Oolite, a few miles N.E. of Banbury. In the Stuart and Georgian periods these two marbles were used in

as it was called, will take a high polish and is the best of its kind in England. But as all these marbles occur only in very narrow beds (never more than 10 ins. thick), their usefulness was always virtually confined to internal cladding and paving; none is any longer procurable.

A curious marble occurs in north Lancashire; the quarry, long closed, was at Stainton, about five miles south-west of Ulverston. It is grey-green with mainly brown fossils, some very large: a 'dressy' stone but not specially pleasing. Some of it was brought across the estuary of the Leven for use in the reconstruction of Holker Hall after the fire of 1871. In Yorkshire the slopes of the Pennine chain have yielded marble both on the west side, from the Deepdale quarry near Dent (cf. p. 98), and on the east side in Nidderdale. The

conjunction in a number of country houses, for floors. Byfield stone, or another very like it, sometimes called Northamptonshire marble, can also be seen to good effect on the Queen Anne staircase at Cottesbrooke Hall. Like Purbeck it is quite a light grey before polishing.

(2) Watford (on the M.1), a shelly stone from the Lower Lias, resembling Banbury.

(3) Stanwick and Raunds, bluish-grey Forest Marbles, once in much demand locally.

(4) Weldon ragstone. See p. 81.

HUNTINGDONSHIRE AND PETERBOROUGH:

(1) Alwalton: see p. 184. (Pronounced 'awl-walt'n'. Formerly it was 'allerton', spelt and pronounced thus.)

(2) A shelly Forest Marble resembling Alwalton, at one time quarried in the Soke of Peterborough.

LINCOLNSHIRE and RUTLAND:

All from the Inferior Oolite.

(1) Stamford: from the lowest and hardest of the three beds in the Stamford (Casterton) quarry suitable for building. Average thickness about 2 ft. Formerly in local demand for steps and pavings, this hard, cream-coloured stone still serves these purposes in several of Stamford's churches. In the past few years limited quantities have happily become available again, and it has been employed for floor-paving at York Minster, Norwich Cathedral and Halstead Hall, Lincolnshire. Several outsize blocks have been quarried for altar slabs in new churches, for which this attractive material is also well suited.

(2) Clipsham: from the base of one of the quarries. Sometimes known as 'Suties' marble. Has good figuring and polishes well, but has seldom been used.

(3) Grimsthorpe Park. In the Middle Ages a black marble was quarried here, but exactly where is no longer known. The fine patterned stone floor of the Vanbrugh Hall in Grimsthorpe Castle incorporates some black marble which may well have come from this quarry.

(4) Ancaster. Big-figure Weatherbed from the top of the quarry, the hardest and shelliest stratum, has a marble-like appearance when polished. There is now a sizeable demand for this stone in slabs 2 ins. thick for internal wall-facing, and also for paving. The polishing is done at Mansfield. Cf. p. 182.

This is perhaps the best place to mention also two older English marbles, both formerly quarried in the South-West:

Cotham, a brown Rhaetic stone found just north of Bristol.

The dull red and yellow brecciated marble found at Draycott, near Wells and at Bleadon, known locally as 'wonder-stone'. This is a dolomitic conglomerate belonging to the Permian series. The three western piers of the north nave arcade of Wells cathedral were formed of this stone.

latter was known at least as early as the thirteenth century when some of it found its way to Fountains Abbey, only a few miles distant. Leland, in Henry VIII's time, noted that in the Chapel of the Nine Altars the angles of the tall piers were enriched with thin ringed shafts 'ex nigro marmore albis maculis magnis intersperso' (of black marble with large white spots). These tall shafts disappeared long ago, but some shorter ones, wholly black, survive.

The other celebrated Chapel of the Nine Altars, in Durham Cathedral, also has slender dark shafts, in this case from Frosterley. As was noted earlier, Purbeck marble had been brought to Durham for the Galilee Chapel at an exceptionally early date; but it was very much simpler just to float the required stone down the Wear. Dark grey, with many pale grey fossils, the marbles of Frosterley and Stanhope, adjacent villages, soon became the regular substitute-materials for Purbeck in this northern diocese. Frosterley marble had already been used just before 1200 in Bishop Pudsey's Great Hall, now the Chapel, in the Palace at Bishop Auckland, which Pevsner had described as 'the most magnificent piece of English domestic architecture of its century' (i.e. the twelfth). Bishop Auckland, it should be observed, is also on the Wear. The industry flourished: the quarries became the largest in England after Purbeck, for the working of marble. But the remaining beds are very thin, and at Frosterley marble production is no longer considered practicable. The other Durham marble, quarried at Egglestone on the Tees near Barnard Castle, was never of any importance.

Westmorland's Orton Scar stone (cf. p. 98) is another that polishes well. Formerly it was seldom used in this way except for monuments, but latterly its scope has been broadened. It can be seen to excellent effect on the hall floor laid a few years ago at Abbot Hall, Kendal. The decorative markings in this stone, with its oatmeal and grey tints, are due to fossilized crinoids, some of which are very large. Crinoids are animals rooted on the sea-bed with long stems and a number of feathery-looking arms; their popular name is sea-lilies.

Among the English marbles, it is those from South Devon referred to in the discussion of limestone (see p. 98) that approach most closely in character to true marble. There are quite a number of them: Happaway from Stentiford Hill, Torquay and Petitor from St. Mary Church, just to the north of it; Ipplepen, Stoneycombe and Ogwell, all from south-west of Newton Abbot; Ashburton; Kitley, from south-east of Plymouth. They are all very hard stones, which polish brilliantly and often show the characteristic veining and figuring generally associated with true marble. Some polished slabs reveal the intricate patterns of coral colonies and other reef-building organisms. There is a wide range of colours, from deep red to light grey, from shell pink to dark green and black.

There is, so far as I am aware, no evidence that the Devonian limestones were ever polished and employed as marbles during the Middle Ages. To use it in this way was a post-Renaissance, and especially a Victorian, development; the nineteenth century church restorers were attracted, almost inevitably, by the rich and elaborate markings so characteristic of much Devon marble. As any visitor to the South Devon churches will know, the introduction of pavements and fonts, pulpits and reredoses in the more florid of these materials, with their streaks and patches, specks and splashes in so many different colours, is usually far from welcome artistically. Chosen and employed with discretion, these marbles can be a great embellishment; in the quiet setting of the English village church, they are often, to modern eyes, very much the reverse. Ashburton marble, almost black with thin pink and white veinings, is the only one still quarried; the preparation and polishing are carried out at Torquay. This is another stone which has been used to good effect in Guildford Cathedral. Slabs up to 8 ft. × 4 ft. 6 ins. are obtainable, and can be as little as an inch thick. Substantial quantities are now exported.

The term marble has also been employed to describe some of the still earlier rocks of Shropshire and Herefordshire. To the Silurian epoch belong the limestones of Wenlock and of Ledbury. The former, from a nearby quarry, provided the stone for the Priory church at Much Wenlock, now a charming ruin. Although it shows no signs to-day of polish and probably never had much, it is sometimes known as Shropshire marble, and has weathered a great deal better than the New Red sandstone also used there. Clee Hill marble is a basaltic stone which can be seen at Hopton Court on the eastern slope of Titterstone Clee Hill, but its introduction here only dates from 1812. To see a very hard 'marble' used domestically on a truly vast scale, one must go to Penrhyn Castle in Caernarvonshire, which in the early nineteenth century was built entirely of light grey Mona marble, the local name for what is really a serpentine, from Anglesey. This is a fine stone which has weathered admirably.

Serpentine and Polyphant

It is said, and Cornishmen are often the first to confirm, that in many ways Cornwall is not England. Think for example of these delectable and wholly special Cornish saints: St. Enodoc and St. Carantoc, St. Wymp (or Wennapa) and St. Kea, who came floating over from Ireland, mysteriously, upon a granite boulder. There are stones here which are no less special and no less unusual; such are two which we have already encountered (Chapter 5): elvan and catacleuse. Two other varieties peculiar to Cornwall are better known:

serpentine and polyphant. These are somewhat alike, and as both will take a high polish they are often classed with the English marbles. Both are compact rocks of great antiquity, but principally composed of magnesium silicate.

Serpentine, which is in some degree similar to the stone familiar on the continent of Europe as *verde antico*,[1] occurs on the Lizard peninsula, where it is one of the principal building materials. It can be dark red or grey, sometimes veined or mottled with brown or black, but the usual colour is dull green, with dark markings allegedly resembling those of a serpent's skin. (It would be agreeable to learn that the Lizard itself derived its name from the resemblance, but this is not so.) It can be seen all over the little peninsula: at Landewednack, for example, where the church is quaintly dedicated to St. Winwallo, we find it not only mixed with granite in the fabric of the walls but employed for some of the tombstones, and within for the pulpit. Serpentine is not a reliable building stone: it is very prone to flaws, and hard blocks may contain soft pockets or weak veins which only become exposed when it is cut up. Large pieces are therefore difficult to obtain and it is not suitable as a rule for external work, nor should it be used in quantity: its prettiness could become cloying. But in moderation it can fascinate, and it is not surprising that during the past hundred years some has been used in public buildings in London and elsewhere.

Polyphant is a dark-hued stone, green or grey with a bloom of blue, and sometimes spotted with dull reds and browns, deriving from iron. The quarries were a few miles to the south-west of Launceston. The name of the hamlet was formerly written Polyfant. Despite its rather sombre colouring there was for many generations a local demand for this material, which stands up to the weather much better than serpentine. The churches of St. Stephen-by-Saltash, Sampford Courtenay near Okehampton, and the south arcade at Launcells near Bude all show polyphant from the Tudor period. It was employed elsewhere for the mullions and tracery of church windows. In the last quarter of the nineteenth century, polyphant and serpentine were both used by J. L. Pearson in his cathedral at Truro.

Alabaster

England has one other building material that will take a high polish: alabaster. The white or nearly white stone employed for sculpture in ancient Egypt and elsewhere, which is often called alabaster, is in fact a soft variety of marble. Alabaster, as the term is used

1 I have long cherished this ancient description of *verde antico*: 'It is in parts fresh green as the sea or emerald stone: in other parts like cornflowers in grass, with here and there a flake of snow.'

to-day and as it is found in England, is not marble but gypsum: that is to say, sulphate of lime. This substance occurs at various places in England, mainly in the Triassic formations. In the later Middle Ages it was worked at Tettenhall in Staffordshire, at Humberstone just east of Leicester, where it can still be seen in the church, and even as far south as Dorset and Somerset; but it has long been a speciality of the marls of the Trent valley. From Tutbury in Staffordshire (on the Dove, a tributary of the Trent), from nearby Hanbury, and above all from Chellaston, four miles south-east of Derby, very large quantities of alabaster were quarried (and partly mined) from about 1400 onwards and were either carved in the surrounding villages or carried down the river to the famous sculpture factory at Nottingham. (Factory is, I am afraid, the correct description.) Fauld mine at Hanbury is still worked: blocks of up to two tons can sometimes be obtained if specially ordered. But for building this stone, so lacking in physical strength, so soft that it can be cut with a pen-knife, so vulnerable to wind and rain, is useless out of doors. Internally where finely wrought detail is required it is excellent, but it can easily draw too much attention to itself both in colour and texture; at its best it is nearly white, yet much of it contains red veining produced by staining from the Trias. What has been said about the addiction of Victorian church architects—and sculptors—to Devon marbles applies with still greater force to their unfortunate enthusiasm for 'streaky bacon' alabaster. For red and white variegated alabaster to look well, the character of the architecture should be aloof and ceremonious; this is a very 'dressy' stone. England has two notably fine examples of its proper use: the columned halls (both, incidentally, known in the house as 'the Marble Hall') at Kedleston (182) and at Holkham. For Kedleston in Derbyshire, the ivory white alabaster, veined all over with dull red and grey, came as it happened from just within Nottinghamshire; for Red Hill, where the Soar flows into the Trent, was a family property. There are twenty huge columns, each 25 ft. high.[1]

For the slightly earlier and still more magnificent hall at Holkham in Norfolk, a Derbyshire alabaster was used, with lighter red markings on a ground of almost pure white. Here the red introduces a note of warmth which in this austerely classical setting is very congenial. Nor could anyone who enters either of those two extraordinary rooms fail to recognise that a smooth, polished, and in other environments distinctly ostentatious stone is wholly appropriate to Palladian grandeur.

[1] Edwin Smith's photograph (182) is taken looking into the great hall from the saloon. The pilasters in the foreground are not stone but grey-green *verde antico* scagliola. This was a polished plaster composition (consisting of sand, lime, gypsum and crushed stone or some other agent of the required colour) which was much used internally in the grander houses of the reign of George III. The craftsmen were often Italians, and such was their skill that one sometimes has to look very carefully to distinguish scagliola from genuine stone. For further details see R. B. Wragg on 'The History of Scagliola', *Country Life*, Oct. 10 1957.

TARRED COBBLES AND CHEQUERED FLINTS
a. *Pavilion Parade, Brighton*   b. *The Marlipins, New Shoreham, Sussex*
c. *Ugford Farm House, near Wilton, Wiltshire*

8

FLINT

England has perhaps no more curious material than flint, a stone of obscure origin quite unlike any other in colour and texture, and not used for building in any other country on so extensive a scale. For architectural purposes it has many limitations, but it has also distinctive qualities, much in evidence in East Anglia[1] and the South-East.

Geologically, flint is one of the purest native forms of silica. It is therefore extremely hard and virtually indestructible; on the other hand it can easily be fractured, and in any direction. When freshly dug, lumps of flint are practically black, but usually have a kind of white 'rind' over their surface which has been developed over a long period within the chalk. Their true habitat is in the upper layers of the Chalk formation, where they have sometimes been quarried; the well-known Grimes Graves in Norfolk, which date back to Neolithic times, cover several acres. More than two hundred pits were dug through the Breckland sands and into the chalk; some of the flint seams, which were worked with red deer antlers, are as deep as forty feet. From time immemorial flints have also been gathered, to the benefit of farmers, from the surface of the fields. Where the chalk reaches the sea, as for instance between Blakeney and Cromer, the hard flints are dislodged by the action of the waves from the softer material in which they lie and piled up on the foreshore. For building purposes, if it is desired to use whole flints, those which have been washed by water are much to be preferred because of their smoother and more regular surfaces; lumps of flint that have not encountered the action of water are usually nodules of very irregular and indeterminate shape (compare plates *192*a and b with c and d). Water-washed flints are also found in certain places near the coast where the soil is to-day alluvial or gravelly, and on the edges of some of the fens as in Cambridgeshire.

Comparable, from the building standpoint, with water-washed flints are pebbles and

---

[1] The limits of East Anglia, which because of its shortage of stone has hardly been mentioned so far, need to be defined. Before Egbert united all England into one kingdom in 829, Norfolk was the country of the North-folk, and Suffolk of the Southfolk, of the kingdom of East Anglia, of which Essex, which had been occupied by the East Saxons, not the East Angles, did not form a part. Nevertheless many writers, including geographers, are now in the habit of employing the term 'East Anglia' to include Essex, and this convenient practice is followed throughout the present book.

TYPES OF FLINT MASONRY
a. *Burgh Castle, Suffolk: south wall*   b. *Cottage at East Raynham, Norfolk*
c. *Morston, Norfolk*   d. *Mighell Street, Brighton*

cobbles. These derive from a great variety of rocks and geologically, therefore, may differ substantially from flint, but for our purposes it seems convenient to consider all these together, since they have much in common, both aesthetically and functionally. The distinction between pebbles and cobbles is one of size only. Pebbles are usually less than 3 ins. in diameter; cobbles—always called cobblestones in America—vary greatly in size, from about 3 ins. to a foot or more across (and the cobbles of the Lake District, as noted on p. 161, are often much larger still). They are always fragments which have broken off from the parent rock and been transported elsewhere by glacial ice or water, and during the process have become more or less rounded. Sometimes, they lay about in the fields and the farmers were only too anxious to be rid of them; in the alluvial plain of Holderness (East Riding of Yorkshire), where cobbles were at one time much used for domestic buildings and even for churches, they were collected from the boulder clay, and are known as boulder stones. Elsewhere they were gathered from the beds of streams or from beaches, as at certain places along the west coast of Cumberland between Millom and St. Bees, notably near Bootle, where the local name for them is 'cobble-ducks'. In France, both in Burgundy and in Roussillon, field and stream cobbles were used for church-building (the technique was known as *opus spicatum*) as far back as the tenth century. Excellent examples of coursed cobblestone masonry dating from the second quarter of the nineteenth century can be found in America, in Ohio, Michigan, Vermont and particularly upstate New York. Cobbles were once much used in England, as elsewhere, for paving. A cobbled street, although delightful to look at, means hard walking or riding (349b and c). So cobbled paving is now more likely to be found in domestic courts and gardens (*147a*).

The geographical limits of English flint building have already begun to emerge. It is a common material in all the chalky downland regions of the South and East, and in the adjacent Tertiary areas of still more recent geological formation which are deficient in other forms of stone: in the river gravels of the Thames valley, for example. There is a great deal of it in Surrey, Kent and Sussex, while in rural Berkshire and Hampshire it is easily the favourite building stone. Farther west, it is still abundant on the Wiltshire and Dorset downs and in the intervening valleys, and where Somerset, Dorset and Devon meet there is chert, a material that has much in common with flint; but beyond this, to the south-west, there is nothing in the least comparable. North of the Thames, there are innumerable flint buildings of all kinds between the centre of Essex and the chalk line of the Chilterns and Gogmagogs, and indeed for a few miles beyond; but as soon as the oolite is reached, they cease altogether. The counties concerned are therefore Essex (especially the western half), Middlesex and Hertfordshire, and the southern and eastern portions only of the shires of Oxford, Buckingham, Bedford and Cambridge. In Suffolk and Norfolk, flint architecture can be seen at its most ambitious and best; and part of the Norfolk coast is as famous as the Sussex seaboard around Brighton for its beach-pebbles and cobbles (*192c*). Farther north, all these stones become increasingly scarce. There are no flint buildings on the chalk wolds of Lincolnshire and East Yorkshire, but Holderness has its big, bumpkin-looking boulder stones; there are cobbles also in Lancashire, from Blackpool northwards around Morecambe Bay, and along part of the coast of Cumberland. With perhaps a few minor additions, that is the complete picture.

In south-eastern England flint, so easily portable, was already being used for building purposes in the Early Iron Age. Lowbury Camp in Berkshire is one example, and it has been suggested that Royston Cave in Hertfordshire may once have been a flint quarry. The Romans made extensive use of flint, especially in the construction of thick rubble cores for their walls but sometimes for facing also, between lacing courses of thin tile-like bricks introduced to give added strength and stability. The 'forts of the Saxon shore', erected towards the end of the third century to protect the south and east coasts against Saxon invaders, furnish several imposing examples, among them the castles of Porchester, Pevensey, and, in Suffolk, Burgh (*192a*). During the Saxon and Norman periods flint again became a building material of paramount importance in the South-East. Many churches were constructed of it, including all the round towers of East Anglia, of which there are still 5 in Essex, 41 in Suffolk and 119 in Norfolk. (Some of these towers have been much restored, but most of them date back at least to the twelfth century, and an appreciable number, constructed for defence against the Danes, to the Saxon period. A few can be found elsewhere, as at Welford in Berkshire.) The flints at this time were nearly always used unfractured, but as a rule they were roughly coursed because with this stone and plenty of mortar it is actually easier to build a wall in more or less regular layers, even when the lumps are quite shapeless.

Flint-building continued throughout the Middle Ages. In Surrey, most of the old churches from the ridge of the North Downs northwards are faced with flint: it was the obvious material to use. Sometimes it was mixed with chalk rubble, and finished with a thick coat of white plaster. To-day this has seldom survived, and the coarse texture of the walls stands revealed; as we see them now, Surrey's churches, it must be admitted, often lack graciousness. In coastal districts beach pebbles, where available, were also in demand. Dr. Salzman[1] cites an entry in the Dover Castle accounts for 1354 relating to payments for the carriage of no fewer than 3464 cartloads of stones from the sea-shore.

The Gothic era witnessed a steady series of improvements in the technique of flint-

1 *Op. cit.*, p. 139.

building: arranging the facing flints in more deliberately regular courses became widespread after about 1250, while knapping and flushwork first appeared soon after 1300. But before passing on to a survey of these developments, all of which were long confined to high-class buildings, principally churches, in the more prosperous areas, it might be well to consider in a little more detail the essential character of the material.

Flints are intensely hard, but generally small: the great majority measure between two and five inches in their largest dimensions. Their shape, unless they are split and dressed, is either rounded, if they have been subjected to the action of water, or amorphous. The latter can certainly be rather fascinating. Miss Olive Cook, in a charming passage in her *Breckland* (1956), writes that 'even more than their colour, it is the outlandish forms of the flint which transfix the eye. The curving shapes that Henry Moore loves are among them: some are knobbly and bronzed like trunks: some resemble great gulls with black beaks or with black feathers in their tails; and there are long-necked swans among them and heads of pure, white oxen with eyes like sloes.' Yet, however inviting such shapes as these may sound to those in search of *objets trouvés* to mount and place upon the book-case, it will be evident that they are not, to put it mildly, ideal for the builder. Hence, the user of whole flints always had to bed them in a great deal of mortar: so much so, in fact, that it is not unusual to find a building in this material which shows more mortar than flint (*192b*).

The strength or weakness of a flint wall, therefore, depends directly upon the nature of the mortar in which the stones are embedded. That such flint buildings as Porchester, Pevensey and Burgh Castles, or the long stretches of wall at Silchester, should have survived even in part for nearly two thousand years is evidence of the tremendous strength of Roman mortar. Later builders were not always so skilful. Much more even than with blocks of squared stone, the great danger was from damp. On the external face it was necessary that each flint should be completely ringed with mortar. And since they did not have the quick-drying Portland cement which would be employed to-day, but only deep clay, or at best lime mortar which dried slowly, the process of construction was somewhat laborious. After every few feet of wall had been completed, a dozen at the most, it was necessary to pause to allow this to dry out properly before further pressure could be applied from above. Flint-building in the winter months was not feasible at all. The water-rounded flints were in one sense less difficult to handle than the nodular ones, but under pressure there was always a risk of their slipping and rolling, which could prove troublesome.

Nor were these the only potential sources of weakness. Where a rubble wall was faced entirely with flint, large boulders would be inserted at intervals if and when they could be found; otherwise there could be nothing but the mortar with which to tie the outer skin to the infilling. The facing, in fact, was no more than a veneer. There was also the

SQUARED FLINTS AND FLUSHWORK
a. and c. *The Gatehouse, St. Osyth's Priory, Essex*
b. *The Hall, Southwick, Sussex (before alteration: see p. 203)*

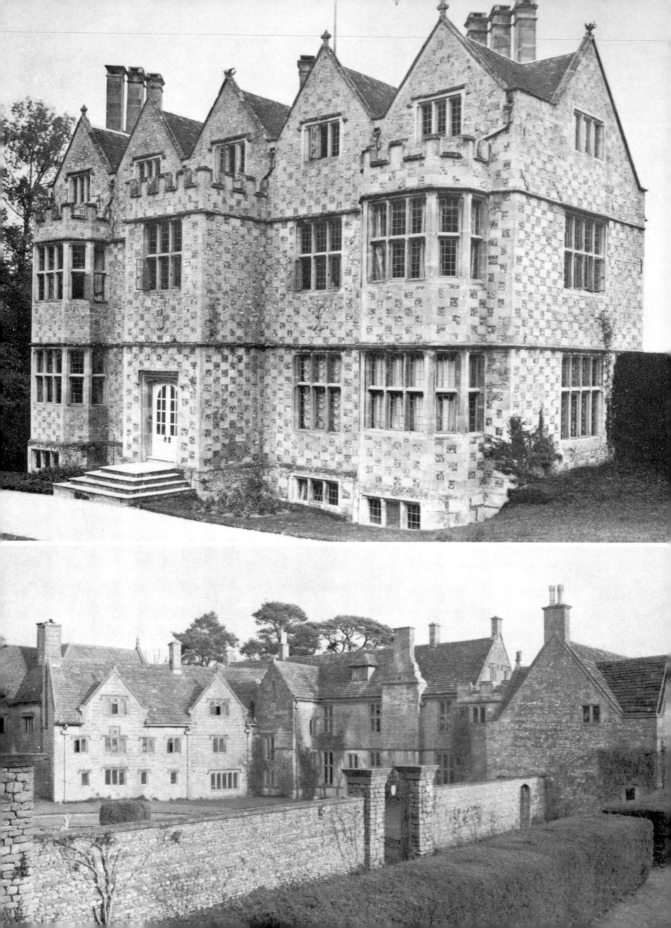

problem of the corners, whether they were the angles of a wall, a door, or a window. It was to obviate the need for these that so many flint-built church-towers, and a few chancel-ends also, were given rounded forms.

It will be evident that the usefulness of flint was greatly increased when supplemented by other materials, particularly materials obtainable in larger units. The Romans had introduced lacing-courses of stone or tile-like brick at set intervals, which helped to tie in the facing with the rubble-built core, and thereby greatly to strengthen the walls (*192a*). Later, in the flint churches, stone was obtained at least for the base of the tower, for quoins, door and window frames, and internal arcades; in north-west Norfolk this was generally carstone, while to the rest of Norfolk and to Suffolk it was usually brought either from Barnack or from Caen, both of which were accessible to many East Anglian towns and villages by water. Later still, when bricks again became available, they were widely employed in all these positions and for bonding. It was delightfully characteristic of our Gothic builders to combine structural devices with decorative effects. In East Anglian churches of the fifteenth century, for instance, it is not unusual to find voussoirs of red brick and flints in alternation. Good examples are the rather grand aisle windows at Rickinghall Superior in Suffolk and the clerestory windows of St. Wendreda at March in Cambridgeshire. Or again, the chance would be seized of arranging in simple chequer patterns the exposed ends of bricks required for bonding. Long after church building practically ceased in Norfolk and Suffolk, brick, and less often ashlared stone, continued to provide dressings for flint-built houses and cottages over a wide area (*192c*). Flint itself, even if it had been available in larger pieces, was much too hard to respond to the attentions of a freemason.

Outside these two counties, builders did not usually attain quite the same level of accomplishment in the use of flint, but the resort to stone or brick for the dressings became all but universal. Often, as can be seen on the Barbican of Lewes Castle, where greenish sandstone from the Weald was introduced for the dressings, the stone is now in much worse condition than the flint. Nevertheless, on aesthetic grounds the introduction of a certain amount of stone is invariably to be applauded. The larger scale of the pieces of stone, generally placed at the edges, provides welcome 'punctuation' just where the eye demands it. Then there are the all-important questions of colour and texture. It is in truth not easy to become enthusiastic about the colouring of a wall of unfractured flints, which all too often reminds us of school pudding, with black currants, brown sultanas, and plenty of dun-coloured suet where the mortar is. Many flints are yellowish-brown,[1]

1 This is very much in evidence on the modern additions to Chelmsford Cathedral, where the external colour-effect is only one degree better than that of pebble-dash.

CHEQUERS AND BANDS
a. *Lake House, near Amesbury, Wiltshire*
   b. *Chantmarle, Dorset*

due to staining with iron in places where the water has receded; there are also steel greys and, less frequently, bluish greys; and there is plenty of white. That is about as far as the colours range. Where the whites are dominant, the effect can be shrill: where the browns, greys and blacks prevail, the general tone may well be sombre. Stone dressings, therefore, if carefully chosen, can give a flint wall a comeliness which it may badly need, by introducing both a warmer colour-note and a quieter, less 'busy' texture. Many buildings which are mainly flint-faced would be less appealing than they are, had not some gracious stone been able to give them the finishing touches.

These considerations do not apply with so much force where the dressings are of brick. A small quantity of red brick introduced with discretion, for instance to provide the quoins and window surrounds of a Georgian house, as in Mighell Street, Brighton (192d), can be delightful; but broad areas of red brick juxtaposed with flint almost always look too 'hot'. In fact, there are few more disagreeable combinations of colour than that produced when flint and red brick, or flint walls and red roofing tiles, are employed in about equal proportions, as can often be seen in Norfolk. If it is desired to use bricks in any quantity in juxtaposition with flint, yellow or white are certainly preferable; and where a flint building, probably dating from the nineteenth century, already has a good deal of red brick, the application of a good oil-bound distemper over all the brick surfaces is well worth considering. Some striking examples of whitened brick in combination with tarred cobbles can be seen at Brighton (191a). Another good instance is the Manor House adjoining the churchyard at New Shoreham. For roofing, slates, and especially blue slates, tone far better with flint than red tiles. Texturally, too, brick is by no means so effective as dressed stone in conjunction with flint, because with the small-scale jointing and tight mesh of mortar the telling contrast cannot be achieved.

The aesthetic value of dressings in either stone or brick can, however, be vividly appreciated if one spends a little time in a building such as Framlingham Castle, which is devoid of them. No material, lacking stone or brick dressings, is more unpicturesque than flint; none makes such utterly shapeless, unlovely ruins; no masonry, in decay, is more sternly rebarbative. Even when not in decay unknapped flint can look unattractively porridgy, as can be seen at Goodwood House in Sussex, which the third Duke of Richmond expressly instructed his architect, James Wyatt, to build entirely of flint because it could be obtained locally. For once the local material was certainly the wrong one. The white lumps of coursed flint are laid in ample mortar; their irregular shapes rendered this essential. The size of the 'mesh' is about the same as that of a brick wall but far more insistent, as the grey mortar is much darker in tone than the flints. The effect is extremely undignified for so large a house, for which indeed this material was quite unsuitable. The slightly earlier stables, by Sir William Chambers, faced externally with knapped and squared flints, set off with whitish limestone dressings, are altogether better.

Aesthetically, the rendering and colour-washing of an unfractured flint surface, if decently maintained, can hardly fail to be an improvement. An effective example can be seen at Charminster close to Dorchester, where a range of thatched cottages along a curving street has been given a unity which could not have been achieved if the broken surface of the flint had been left naked. How frequently did this occur? Flint rubble walls were always plastered internally, and so they should be. On entering a flint church, or house, one half expects to find oneself immured in a rocky cavern, and to encounter instead smooth, gentle walls always gives a sensation of relief and pleasure. But evidence of external rendering is not widespread. Relics of it can be seen now and again, as on that sturdy little church, mainly dating from the twelfth century, which nestles under the South Downs at Ford near Arundel; and the more rough-and-ready the craftsmanship, no doubt, the more desirable it was felt to be. Yet when carefully built, the external rendering of flint rubble walls is from the practical standpoint unnecessary, and in East Anglia at any rate a great deal of the flintwork has always remained exposed.

Allied to flint in character but distinguishable from it is chert. This is a kind of silica which occurs in nodule form, or sometimes in narrow beds of its own, in many other rocks besides chalk, including the Upper and Lower Greensand, the Portland Beds (under the Portland stone), and the Carboniferous Limestone. Whereas flint, when fresh, is always black or dark grey under its white or brown 'rind', chert, although it may be black, is more frequently brownish. It also fractures somewhat differently. Chert is found in the Lower Greensand along the northern fringes of the Weald. But the best area in which to see it used as a building stone is where Devon, Somerset and a corner of Dorset meet. Here the chert comes from the Upper Greensand. Plenty of it can be seen at Colyton, also at Shute Barton near Axminster and at Awliscombe north-west of Honiton. The old Grammar School at Chard was mainly built of chert boulders from the hill at Combe St. Nicholas, a couple of miles away. They are roughly squared, and as large as bricks: some in fact are larger. Their colour is elusive: milky-brown mainly, with suggestions here and there of amethyst, and something of the shiny, semi-transparent look of horn. They furnish yet one more example of the infinite variety of England's pattern of building materials.

Rough undressed flints continued in use for the humbler types of building long after the appearance of the technical advances and refinements that are about to be considered. It was indeed only after wood began to grow scarce in parts of East Anglia about the time of Elizabeth I that flint construction became usual for cottages and farm-buildings. The walls of such buildings are sometimes decidedly crude, with flints, brick fragments and

dollops of conglomerate stone all jumbled in together. Some have also been disfigured by
inept modern repointing. Yet for comfort a flint cottage was certainly a great advance on
lath and plaster and timber-framing. With their solid walls and small windows,[1] such
cottages may seem to be built for winter rather than for summer, and they are usually
devoid of charm; but they can be very snug. Many date from no earlier than the nineteenth
century.

Refinements

The flint buildings which have been discussed so far, although often extremely well constructed, are, if large, generally austere, and if small, unpretentious. As time went on
men who often had to build with flints, beach-pebbles or cobbles, because nothing else
was available, developed new techniques which were to add substantially to the visual
effectiveness of these materials.

It was possible to make one great improvement without even breaking the stones, by
devoting more careful attention to the coursing. (Compare plates *192c* and d.) Since, as
already noted, it often made construction easier, rough coursing was a common practice
both with the Romans and with the Normans; but to form a really regular course it is necessary to select stones of approximately the same size, which no doubt gave more trouble.
By the fifteenth century, beautifully controlled surfaces were being produced; and, once
achieved, this became the permanent practice of the more accomplished builders. There
were many variations. Along the Sussex coast one may even find rows of kidney-shaped
flints set in broad mortar courses. Usually, it was the eggshell-smooth ovoid stones that
were preferred. These might be carefully set up on end in even rows, or inclined alternately to right and to left, to produce a refinement of the rough herring-bone type of
masonry also favoured, on occasions, by the Normans. Pebble walling has a long tradition
in the Cromer, Cley and Blakeney district of Norfolk. Many of the pebbles, carefully laid
in level courses, are no larger than eggs. They were formerly taken from the beaches, but
in many places this is now prohibited. At Blundeston near Lowestoft, the church wall has
coursed and rounded pebbles which project substantially beyond the plane of the mortar,
a good method of obtaining a texture. On the Cumbrian coast, rows of round 'cobble-
ducks' can sometimes be seen looking like small cannon-balls. For such a wall-facing
stones of nearly uniform size are essential. The outer surface of the rough rubble core is

---

1 The frequent meanness of the fenestration is an unattractive feature of many flint-built cottages. Aesthetically, this material cries out for white paintwork, for which sash windows with glazing bars, even if quite
modest in scale, offer an ideal opportunity.

thickly coated with strong mortar, into which the wet cobbles are hammered and left to set firmly. In Cumberland thin courses of slate were sometimes introduced at intervals, as 'levellers'.

Many examples of coursed pebbles and cobbles occur in and around Brighton, Shoreham and Worthing, where most of the buildings so faced date from no farther back than the Regency. The results are often excellent (192d). Sometimes a whole wall, cobbles and mortar, was coated with black tar, as a protection against the salty air. The dressings of these Sussex buildings are usually of brick, which is often lime-washed, thereby reversing the 'black and white' relationship that presently we shall meet in the half-timbering of the West Country; there it is the structural members that are black and the infilling white: here the quoins and window-surrounds are white and the infilling black (191a). Without the careful, rhythmic coursing, however, the effect would be very different. Basil Champneys's church of St. Mary Star-of-the-Sea at Hastings, faced with beach pebbles and split flints arranged in random fashion, is externally unattractive. On the other hand the coursed cobble facings at Basildon New Town (Orsett End), introduced at first floor level to produce a lively, dark-toned texture in contrast to the relatively smooth, light-toned white brick below, are a notable success.

More important aesthetically even than regular coursing, and often combined with it, was the introduction of fractured flints. Although the work requires skill and practice, flints can be split open quite easily, and squared on one face or trimmed to more elaborate shapes if required. This process is known as knapping, and such flints are used with the split face showing. They are scarcely found before the fourteenth century, but knapped flints played a great part in East Anglian church architecture during the later Gothic age. They were always a speciality of Norfolk and Suffolk, and particularly of Breckland on the border of the two counties; in a modest way this ancient industry still continues around Brandon. Flints are now prepared to order in any traditional way required.

Squared flints are the most urbane of any. The shaping is confined to one face, but the art of producing them was gradually developed to a high pitch of technical perfection. The usual dimensions are about 4 ins. square; some are rectangular and look like small bricks. These flints can be seen not only in Breckland and southwards towards Mildenhall and Bury St. Edmunds, but elsewhere in East Anglia, in Kent (for instance at Sandwich), and, very notably, on and near the coast of Sussex. The exterior of the south aisle of St. Michael's church, facing on to the main street at Lewes and built in 1748, is a fine example; others, a little farther west, include Court Farm at Falmer and the Hall at Southwick (197b),   * both eighteenth-century houses, and, in the heart of Brighton itself, No. 69 Ship Street. This Georgian house is faced with knapped and squared flints laid with such regularity that only the very shallowest courses of mortar are visible between them. Such fine craftsmanship involved a great deal of labour, and for this reason was always expensive; but, although I have heard the view expressed that such perfection is tedious, an isolated example here and there is in my view always a pleasure.

Both in colour and texture, knapped flints differ quite considerably from unfractured flints. When freshly broken they are often jet black; as they weather their blackness tends to fade and they become greyer, but the general effect of flint-knapping is undoubtedly to darken any wall and to impart to it a more even hue. Any suggestion of greater sobriety on this account is, however, instantly dispelled by the change which also takes place in the surface-texture. Freshly knapped flints shine like crystals and are therefore highly susceptible to the play of light. Although in time they may lose some of their pristine lustre, the weathering process is a very slow one.

Allusion has already been made to the introduction of stone or brick to provide the dressings for flint buildings. Sometimes these other materials play a much larger part; and in my view it would be true to say that flint is seen at its best in combination with generous quantities of stone. It should be added that in the patterned walls about to be described the flints are not always nor of necessity knapped, and that in some cases they may have only been very roughly broken; but in all the most refined examples they are both knapped and squared. The favourite patterns were two: horizontal bands and chequers. In the Chalk and Greensand areas of Dorset and Wiltshire, as also to some extent along the Thames estuary, bands and chequers were methods of making the local stone go further, the blocks of stone at the same time ensuring a stronger wall than one composed solely of flints.

At the church of Cliffe-at-Hoo in Kent the black and white stripes—knapped flints and ragstone—dating from the early fourteenth century are altogether too strident for visual comfort. Far better is the effect at Chantmarle near Cattistock in Dorset, a village whose delightful name alone suffices to tell us that it is in the Hardy country (*198*b). Here the employment of flint bands in conjunction with Ham Hill limestone on the south-west wing, a refacing in 1910 of the only surviving portion of the fifteenth-century house, is echoed in the banding of the garden wall and foreground building, erected about the same time. The variable sizes of the roughly dressed slabs of stone and the difference in scale between all of them and the much smaller flints are very satisfying. In East Dorset and Hampshire, where they are also fairly common, the alternating bands are usually brick, which can look quite attractive when the flints are carefully worked and the bricks not too red; but often, as already suggested, this colour combination is not satisfactory. Neverthe-less the Victorians, with their passion for polychrome effects, lost no opportunity of using flint and red brick in conjunction, not only in stripes but in other ways besides; for instance, at Ludgershall just within Wiltshire, large diamonds of red brick were inset into flint walls. They were doubtless thought to be very pretty.

The combination of flints, usually knapped, and squares of ashlared limestone to form a chequer or chessboard pattern became a popular decorative device in most of the flint areas. In the early examples, such as the Marlipins at New Shoreham, Sussex (191b), a certain irregularity still prevails. This mainly fourteenth-century building, now a museum, has a south front faced with a chequer pattern of knapped flints and pale creamy-yellow Caen stone. The pattern is a bold one, requiring up to ten flints for each of the dark squares; and here some of them were only rather roughly shaped. In the fifteenth century the tendency was for the squares to get smaller and more regular, although on humbler buildings or in less important situations, such as the end wall of Ugford Farm House near Wilton (191c), built in 1635, only an irregular patchwork was attempted. Wiltshire has many examples of flint and stone chequer-work: the stone might be oolite, or come from the Greensand, as here at Ugford and at Tollard Royal, or from the Chalk, as in the Wylye valley and at Quidhampton, Burcombe and Barford St. Martin, villages west of Salisbury. Chequer-work is in evidence on Wiltshire churches too, as for example on the south front at Amesbury; here the blocks of stone vary in size considerably, but the flints are all carefully squared. An admirable domestic example near by is Lake House at Wilsford (198a), at which the chequer patterning was carried out about 1580.

There is also plenty of chequer-work in Norfolk and Suffolk. Two of the best known but not perhaps most enjoyable examples are the fifteenth century Guildhalls of Norwich and King's Lynn. At the former the squares, very black and very white, are arranged diagonally. Chequer patterns frequently appear on church parapets and on the side-walls of porches, as for instance at Woolpit. Sometimes, as at Potter Heigham and on the tower arch of the Norwich church of St. John Maddermarket, the squares of stone have given place to red brick. But in East Anglia, when we think of flint and stone in combination, there is no temptation to linger over the chequer-work, for this is the region of a much more brilliant and resourceful type of decoration: flushwork, the cutting of designs in ashlared stone, with knapped flint as a foil. For the more ambitious designs the process was to slice a block of freestone into slabs about 2 ins. thick, out of which the desired pattern was cut. This was then mortared on to the surface of a flint rubble wall and the interstices were carefully filled in with split and, where the design permitted it, squared flints, which were nearly always black (197c). Only the face of the flints is flat; the backs are rounded or sometimes conical. Their thickness at the centre is no more than $1\frac{1}{2}$ ins., and usually less. For the smaller designs the method was simply to hollow out a slab of stone to the required shape and mortar in the flints wherever they were needed. The stone was cut into a great variety of forms: heraldic shields, monograms and single initials, interlacing knots, crosses, stars and crowns, trefoil-headed panels, pinnacles with an efflorescence of crockets, tracery with every little cusp crisp and sharp, and purely geometrical shapes such as the quatrefoil. Wavy, foliated stems may run the whole length of a plinth or a parapet, or there may be an inscription in boldly-cut Gothic lettering that is itself very decorative, as at the church of Stratford St. Mary on the Suffolk-Essex border. At Chelmsford there is a conventionalized lily. Where the stone ornamentation stands out beyond the knapped flint infilling as on the buttresses at the east end of the striking church at Lowestoft, the technique is known as proudwork: this is rare. In nearly every case the cut-out stonework and the flint infilling are on the same plane: hence the name, flushwork.

Flushwork had appeared early in the fourteenth century, notably on both faces of the gatehouse of Butley Priory near Orford, now a private house; but it was not until the second half of the fifteenth century that suddenly, in the Eastern counties, it became all the rage. Its costly exuberance, lavishly displayed over the exterior of the church at Long Melford (one of the half dozen finest village churches in England) was very much in tune with the early Tudor taste for all that was rich and sumptuous. This was its time of triumph; on buttresses and battlements, on porches, plinths and parapets, between clere-story windows, and even here and there over the whole face of a tower, as at Eye, no church-builder who could afford flushwork failed to have it. In the domestic sphere it is much rarer; it was too great a luxury for all but the rich. Yet there is one quasi-domestic example of great splendour. About 1481 a wealthy ecclesiastic, the Prior of St. Osyth's, erected for his Priory, situated between Colchester and Clacton, a new gatehouse (197a and c). Although in its outline it recalls the fortified entrance of earlier days, its purpose was very different. It was built to provide comfortable private rooms, away from the other monastic buildings, for himself and his guests. It was designed in the form of a battle-mented gatehouse purely for picturesque effect. There is, on the outward-facing front, a little sculpture around the principal arch, including an animated St. George and the Dragon in the spandrels, but the whole of the rest of the ornamentation is in the form of flushwork. So liberal is the use of ashlar that the harshness of the flint is admirably counteracted. Indeed, the sight of those split flints, flickering and sparkling in the sunlight, is a delight in so rich a setting, above all when the sun suddenly catches them after a shower of rain.

East Anglia has other gatehouses elaborately adorned with flushwork, among them that of St. John's Abbey at Colchester, the only portion of that monastery to have survived. But taste changed, and before the middle of the sixteenth century the interest in flushwork

lapsed. Only during the years of Victorian church restoration were there hints of an imita-
tive but harmonious revival of the craft. An example is the chancel wall of the church of
St. Michael Coslany in Norwich, carried out on the lines of the fifteenth century flushwork on the adjacent Thorpe Chapel. Georgian builders found other ingenious ways of
using flints: for instance, on the front of his little 'Temple' (now a cottage) in the park of
Euston Hall, Suffolk, William Kent employed them very effectively to simulate vermicu-
lated stone! And galleting, the insertion of flint chips into the mortar courses, usually with
a purely decorative intention (see p. 52), although fairly infrequent, seems to have been
undertaken at widely different dates.

Remarkable successes were achieved with flint, yet it will be found that as soon as
brick became readily available, this was nearly always preferred in all the flint areas by
those who could afford it. This was true of the Stuart and still more of the Georgian
periods. By the well-to-do, flint was now usually reserved for tenants' cottages, farm and
garden buildings, and for follies such as Sir Francis Dashwood's hexagonal Mausoleum on
the hill above West Wycombe. The Regency and Victorian periods witnessed a revival
of interest, first in cobbles and then in flint, although by then it was actually cheaper to
build in brick. To-day, although in certain places flints can still be obtained, the labour
for knapping and squaring is difficult to procure, and ordinary flint-facing, requiring both
time and considerable skill, is seldom thought to justify the cost: in my judgment rightly
so. For despite the fascination of squared and knapped flintwork, and the real beauty of the
best flushwork, the usual flint buildings can quickly pall. After, say, a week among the
flint churches of Suffolk or Norfolk, and despite their wonderfully rewarding experiences
in other directions, it is a joyous moment when one is at last confronted, as at Beccles,
with an ashlar-faced tower. Flint proved a great blessing where there was no other suitable
material, and, if properly constructed, a flint-faced building will stand up to the English
weather much better than will many varieties of stone. But aesthetically flint has needed
all the help which the most skilful and refined craftsmen have brought to it, to enable it to
hold its own.

Pudding-Stone and Septaria

With the conglomerates and concretions we really do 'scrape the barrel' in our survey
of English building stones, and they will not detain us for long. Conglomerate stones are
composed of fragments, usually rounded by the action of water, of previously existing
rocks, held together by some kind of natural cement. Concretionary stones include not

only flint and chert but nodules of impure limestone which sometimes occur in clays. The only two that concern us are pudding-stone and septaria, products of the Tertiary epoch and therefore among the 'youngest' natural building materials that we possess.[1]

Pudding-stone largely consists of flinty pebbles and small lumps of sandstone, united into a very inedible-looking dark brown 'pudding' by a natural cement of iron oxide or some siliceous material. Sometimes, as in Hertfordshire, it is very hard, but often so crumbly that pieces can be dislodged with the fingers. Nevertheless, this coarse stone has been employed here and there for building, for want of anything better, in all the Home Counties with the exception of Kent. It is a product of the pebble beds of the London Basin and of the gravelly region of north-west Surrey and the adjacent corner of Berkshire. Reference was made on p. 115 to its use for much of the church at Chobham, in contrast to the far more attractive sarsens of the tower. Pudding-stone is also the material of the much restored tower of the parish church at Wokingham. In south-east Dorset it underlies parts of the heathlands which surround Poole Harbour and run westwards nearly to Dorchester (e.g. Hardy's 'Egdon Heath'). The church at Wool displays this unlikeable dark-rust-brown conglomerate, and so, in combination with a greensand stone which was probably floated down the Stour, does Wimborne Minster. (It is perhaps worth observing that the combination at this church of two kinds of stone so different not only in colour but in *tone* has produced a 'spotted dog' effect which is not at all happy.) There is a little pudding-stone in Buckinghamshire around Slough and High Wycombe, where it proved of value for the foundations of flint churches, and it was used for parts of certain Hertfordshire churches and of the Hall at Great Gaddesden. But it is in the eastern part of Essex that one encounters it most frequently: Beeleigh Abbey near Maldon, largely built of pudding-stone rubble, is a characteristic example.

Whilst pudding-stone is closer to sandstone, septaria mainly consist of nodules of marl (calcareous clay). The name is said to derive from the old belief that these nodules were habitually seven-sided. It was, incidentally, because of the lime in their composition that, between 1796, when the first patent was taken out, and about 1850, when Portland cement superseded it, septaria were much in demand for the material known as Parker's Roman cement, of which there will be more to say later. Much of the stucco of the Regency period was produced from them. As a building stone septarian nodules have a long history, but only in the Thames estuary, north-eastern Essex and along the Suffolk coast as far north as Orford. The Romans used them freely, and they were turned to account by William the Conqueror for his castle at Colchester, where plenty can still be seen, especially

1 Septaria do also occur in the Jurassic clays, but have never been needed for building in those areas.

internally. About a hundred years later this intractable material was employed again for Orford castle, where on the keep, the only surviving part, it still figures prominently in conjunction with the dressed limestone which serves to set it off. Between the Orwell and the Stour, septaria were freely resorted to for the churches of Erwarton and Harkstead (tower); they can also be seen at the church of Herne in Kent. A much later example is the lofty and striking tower which Lord Darcy built at St. Osyth's in Essex about 1553, after the Priory had become a private house. This is entirely faced with a chequer pattern of limestone and brown septaria, almost certainly obtained from demolished monastic buildings. Similar chequer-work survives on a ruinous building a few feet away, below a fine group of Tudor chimneys (261d).

Strange sights can be seen near the coasts of Essex. So scarce were building materials that people would even dig up yellow mud from the beaches and compress it into amorphous lumps. Septaria and pudding-stone were not always much better. Small wonder, then, that this is the part of England in which are to be found some of the brickmaker's earliest and most considerable achievements.

9

BRICK

'England', wrote Karamzin at the time of the French Revolution, 'is a land of brick.'[1] The Russian writer was no great admirer of ours and, although Russia is also a land of brick, it was not intended as a compliment. 'The British passion for brickwork', a more recent commentator has observed, 'is admirable for smaller buildings, but for power-stations and other gigantic structures can be overdone.'[2] For the Main Block alone of the B.B.C. Television Centre at Wood Lane, London, the number of bricks used was about eight million. To-day England is indeed a land of brick. It was not always so.

History and Geographical Distribution

Men have made bricks for at least six thousand years. The earliest bricks were sun-baked, not hardened in the heat of a fire, and these bricks, used extensively in ancient Egypt and Babylonia, can still be seen in many parts of the world; in Spain, Argentina, the Indian reserves in the United States and elsewhere, the Spanish word *adobe* (signifying an unburnt brick dried in the sun) is familiar. Such bricks can be found in England, as will be described in Chapter 11, and have the advantage of being cheaper than burnt bricks, but they are best suited to drier climates than ours. Fired bricks were already being produced in the Near East by 3000 B.C., and, needless to say, it was this more durable form which chiefly found favour with the Romans, by whom the first bricks were introduced into this country.

The typical Roman bricks are broad and flat, and more like tiles than the bricks which are made to-day. Dimensions vary considerably: $12 \times 6 \times 1\frac{1}{4}$ ins. are typical, $18 \times 12 \times$

---

1 Nicolai Karamzin: *Letters of a Russian Traveller*, translated by Florence Jonas (1958). Karamzin (1765–1826) is the earliest Russian writer on England. His letters, first published in the *Moscow Journal* in 1791, were re-printed in *Russkaya Proza* (XVIII Veka, Tom. II), Moscow, 1950. He found London houses in 1790 'small, narrow, built of brick, unwhitewashed (so that the eternal soot from the coal may be less noticeable on them), and presenting a dull and gloomy uniformity. But their interiors are charming.'

2 Mr. Robert Harling, in April 1959.

$1\frac{1}{2}$ ins. not uncommon: and some are square. The thinness of these bricks, which is sometimes only 1 in. and rarely as much as 2 ins., enabled them to be very well burnt, which is the principal reason for their remarkable durability. The heat of the open stacks or 'clamps', in which faggots were the principal fuel, would have been insufficient to penetrate a brick of to-day's thickness. Normally the Romans only used their bricks for bonding courses introduced at intervals into flint or stone rubble masonry (192a). Nevertheless there can be no doubt that they established brickyards in many places in England and that the craft flourished. Numerous examples of Roman brickwork can still be seen, generally re-used; these hard bricks were in continual demand during the Middle Ages for positions such as the angles of church towers, where a particularly strong material was needed. They are frequently to be found in the neighbourhood of flourishing Roman towns, such as Verulamium (St. Albans) and Camulodonum (Colchester); besides St. Albans Cathedral, at least five other Hertfordshire churches, including two in St. Albans itself, incorporate Roman brickwork. But they also occur in the vicinity of quite small settlements, such as Ashtead in Surrey; Roman bricks are built into the church walls not only at Ashtead but at Mickleham and especially at Fetcham and Stoke d'Abernon, all in the neighbourhood. They can be encountered, too, at least as far north as Leicester.

With the departure of the Romans, English brick-making ceased and did not flourish again for nearly a millennium. The reason is unknown: the history of English brickwork until near the end of the mediaeval period is scantily documented. Yet if we think of the great brick churches of Northern Italy, and of southern France, of northern Germany and the Low Countries, many of which date from the twelfth and thirteenth centuries and some, like the eastern part of St. Sernin at Toulouse, from the eleventh, it is curious that England can show virtually no brick architecture of comparable date. The earliest examples of non-Roman brickwork in this country are in what are by no means wholly brick buildings, all within a dozen miles of Colchester. At Polstead in Suffolk, close to Stoke-by-Nayland, the much restored Norman church is mainly flint, but it was found more convenient to construct the chancel arch and the nave arcades of thin bricks. At Little Coggeshall in Essex, an outbuilding of the former Cistercian abbey dating from about 1190, and the plain rectangular chapel which was once the *cappella ad portas*, of about 1225, are also principally flint, but have badly weathered brick dressings which are clearly part of the original structures. And of about 1275 is Little Wenham Hall in Suffolk, a small fortified house constructed of many different materials: flints, lumps of yellowish solidified mud dug from the seashore, a little dressed stone for the buttresses, and at last plenty of bricks, variously coloured—red, pink, orange and especially cream and greenish-yellow. Whence came these bricks? The old belief was that they were all brought over from Flanders, perhaps as ballast. Very large quantities of Flemish bricks were undoubtedly imported: one shipment alone, required for the Tower of London in 1278, numbered over two hundred thousand.[1] But in the country districts around Colchester, with good clay on the site and examples of Roman brickwork still very much in evidence, importation from Flanders seems to me unlikely. There are no documents. We do know, however, that immigrants were coming from the Low Countries before the end of the twelfth century and settling in parts of East Anglia. Bricks are heavy; roads were bad; none of the three buildings cited above is on a river nor by the sea. Is it not much more likely that the bricks were baked on the site, even if, as is not improbable at Little Wenham, their makers were Flemings? The predominance of the yellow there renders this almost a certainty, for the right clay to produce yellow bricks was at hand locally. At Polstead and Little Coggeshall the colour is red but the size decidedly larger than that current in Flanders, which may well point to English brickmakers.

To the following century can be dated several more examples of the employment of English bricks in and around Colchester, and at least two brick vaults at Norwich go back to the same period; small quantities went up the Ouse to Ely in 1335–37, and to Cambridge for a vault in the church of St. Mary the Less a few years later; and there was also a small brick-field at Ely itself. But the first evidence of anything resembling a brick-making industry in this country occurs during the first half of the fourteenth century in Yorkshire, around Hull and Beverley. The trade of the port of Hull was principally with the Netherlands and the Baltic, the very regions in which brickmaking now flourished most. It is not difficult to imagine the seamen returning with descriptions of the vast brick churches they had seen in the Hanseatic towns; their home town had no stone but, as was quickly discovered, unlimited quantities of excellent brick clays. The very large and dignified church of Holy Trinity at Hull is still the leading example of fourteenth-century English brickwork. Between about 1315 and 1345 the eastern part of the building was constructed almost wholly of this material. Concealed in the Georgian period by rendering, the very notable early brickwork now stands revealed again: on the exposed south side there has been a good deal of later renewal, but on the north side of the chancel and on the north face of the transept it is surprisingly well preserved. The bricks are in part red, in part blue: small, regular, and laid with broad mortar courses, but not arranged to form diapers or other patterns. They were undoubtedly made in the vicinity. To the second quarter of the same century belongs the vault of the nave of Beverley Minster which, apart from the ribs, is again of brick, although few people realize this as it has been plastered over. During the latter half of the century local bricks were used to rebuild most of the

1 L. F. Salzman, *op. cit.*, p. 140.

houses in the town of Hull, and found their way a few miles eastwards to Roos, where the church was given a fine clerestory which is principally of brick. Across the Humber at the Augustinian Abbey of Thornton in north Lincolnshire, a big gatehouse, conceived for purposes similar to that at St. Osyth's and ante-dating it by just a century, was constructed about 1382 of reddish-brown brick with Tadcaster stone only for some of the facings. This desolate but imposing structure still rises in solitary splendour from the Lincolnshire flats. In 1409, 112,300 bricks of local manufacture were used in the erection of the gateway at Beverley known as the North Bar. The brickwork here exhibits some graceful refinements, including on both faces three blind windows with heads of cusped ogee form and a saw-toothed string-course, admirably suited to the material, at the base of the crow-step battlements. Nowhere else in England was brick used with such urbanity at so early a date.

It was only in the fifteenth century that the word 'brick' came into general use in this country. Previously the usual word had been 'waltyle' (wall-tile). Many more bricks were made now, but the method of manufacture remained primitive. Suitable earth having been found, it was dug, and trodden out upon a piece of hard ground strewn with hay or straw to prevent sticking. The treading of the clay, as of the grapes in sunnier climes, was done with bare feet: a laborious but a very necessary proceeding, since any pebbles not extracted would be liable to cause the clay to crack and split in the course of firing. It was then chopped up into convenient sizes, laid out to dry (heavy rain could do great damage at this stage), and burnt. As yet the dimensions were not standardized, but averaged at this time about $9 \times 4\frac{1}{2} \times 2$ ins.

Although the fifteenth century saw a substantial increase in the employment of brick in England it was, except at Hull, almost wholly confined to buildings of importance such as churches, schools and colleges, and a few large houses. In this sphere great strides were made. Eton College, founded by Henry VI, was, apart from its chapel, entirely built of brick. The earth[1] was dug at Slough on a site acquired expressly for the purpose; a kiln was constructed, and between 1442 and 1452 it supplied the school with about two and a half million bricks. Brick had already been employed a few years before this at other royal manors, notably Sheen, and to a small extent at Windsor Castle.

---

1 Earth it was, here: but this word is frequently misused in connection with brickmaking. Geologists apply the term brick-earth (which they write brickearth) only to those rather silty clays of the Pleistocene period, deposited as wind-blown dust during the last Ice Age in some parts of the Thames and Kennet valleys, Middlesex, East Anglia, the northern fringe of Kent including the whole of the Isle of Sheppey, West Sussex and the Portsmouth-Southampton area. In a geological context the term is not employed for the major clay formations; these are quite different in character, and are classified among the 'solid' rocks.

A few really splendid examples of fifteenth century brick architecture survive. Tattershall Castle in the centre of Lincolnshire was mainly erected between 1434 and *c.* 1448 by Ralph Cromwell, Henry VI's Lord Treasurer, on the site of a small castle of two centuries earlier. He was a rich man and he built lavishly: to-day his church is much denuded, his collegiate buildings gone, his almshouses rebuilt. His house, too—for it was a castle only in name—has lost its outbuildings, apart from a pretty little gatehouse. Deprived also of the great hall which once adjoined it, what confronts us to-day is a single huge tower, 112 ft. high, rising from a moat (*221c*). Although it may superficially suggest a Norman keep, it was in fact very different and not built to be defended. The windows are comparatively large. The four chimney-pieces within are magnificent. They are of Ancaster limestone, as are the dressings of the exterior, but everything else here is of rich red brick. For the tower alone 322,000 bricks were needed, together with several thousand more of a specially small size for particular purposes such as parapets. It has been established beyond doubt that all these were made at Edlington Moor, only nine miles away; but Cromwell, taking no chances, brought over an expert from Germany to superintend their manufacture. Unoccupied since 1692, Tattershall appeared to be in a very sorry state in 1911 when it was sold to a syndicate: the wooden floors had fallen in, the moat had filled up. The chimney-pieces were taken out, to be sold to America. But before this occurred, the syndicate went bankrupt, and the Castle passed into the hands of the Official Receiver. At this point Lord Curzon dramatically intervened. He bought both the Castle and the chimney-pieces, and then set out to find the latter. He had a Bill rushed through Parliament to prevent their leaving England, and arranged for all the ports to be watched. After three months they were discovered in packing cases at Tilbury. At the restoration which followed, the condition of the brickwork was found to be on the whole remarkably good. No other English brickwork of this date shows such fine quality nor such beautiful craftsmanship. Particularly striking are the ribbed vaults of moulded brick in some of the upstairs window recesses and lobbies, and over the lofty corridor on the second floor.

Much more extensive, and still more fascinating externally, is Herstmonceux Castle in Sussex (*222a*), now occupied by the Royal Observatory. This was also the creation of a court official, Sir Roger de Fiennes, Treasurer to the Household of Henry VI. But Fiennes had been a soldier, one of those who fought for Henry V at Agincourt, and now, a quarter of a century later (1440), he sought to give his house a military aspect. Here, more obviously even than at Bodiam, it was the old soldier playing at soldiers; and as every small boy is aware, to play at soldiers properly one must have a fort. The royal licence to 'embattle and machicolate' was in view of Fiennes's record of service readily forthcoming, and he must have greatly enjoyed imparting to his mansion (for that is what it really was) its assertive, pseudo-military swagger. Herstmonceux also fell later upon evil days: in 1777 it was dismantled and internally gutted, and when restoration was begun in 1913 it was an ivy-infested and unkempt ruin. But even the thick mantle of ivy had not yet destroyed the excellent brickwork of which the great house was entirely constructed. The brickmakers may have been Flemings; the clay had certainly been dug near by. Indeed, it may even have come from the site itself, for the wide moat had to be excavated. The restoration, which was not completed until 1935, caused much heart-burning among the archaeologically minded because within the courtyard no attempt was made to re-erect the buildings on the original plan. The aim of the restoration was to render the place not only lovely again but also usable, and the old plan would by modern standards have been very inconvenient. I for one, therefore, decline to be shocked: for, in sharp and welcome contrast to what had happened a generation earlier at Arundel, the restoration here was carried out with great sensibility in the handling of materials. And although, when Horace Walpole visited Herstmonceux in the summer of 1752, he concluded that it could never have been quite finished because 'almost all the walls, except in the principal chambers, are in their native brickhood', the external brickwork, a high proportion of which is original, is a delight. Seen across its broad moat on a warm afternoon, preferably through a slight haze, this great pink and grey building, which seems to be floating at anchor in its hollow, looks singularly poetic.

Another show-piece of fifteenth-century brickwork is the gate-tower of Oxburgh Hall in south-west Norfolk, erected in 1482 (*221a*). Most of this house was badly spoiled by later alterations and reconstructions: there can be few better places in which to take cognisance of the vast aesthetic gulf separating typical early Victorian brickwork, dressed with harsh-looking terracotta, from the genuine late-mediaeval article. This gatehouse was an early, but not the first, example in brick of those purely ceremonial entrance towers, intended to impress the approaching visitor, which were to become such a feature of our domestic and collegiate architecture under the Tudors. Apart from Herstmonceux, which has a tremendously consequential tower originally approached, as at Oxburgh, across a draw-bridge, there are the fine one at Queens' College, Cambridge, erected in 1448, and Middleton Tower near King's Lynn, built a year or two later. This last, the sole relic of a moated country house, is only a few miles from Oxburgh, but very inferior to it in proportions, besides having been considerably restored in 1856. There may also have been one or two others by 1480, but the Oxburgh gatehouse is the most imposing: indeed a work of outstanding distinction. The tall turrets flanking the entrance are enriched with sunk panels crowned by triplets of cusped arches, the bricks for which had to be specially prepared in moulds, two for each trefoil. These are best seen in the close view of part of the inner face of the gate-tower (*221*b), which also shows the characteristic scale and texture of this early English brickwork. Within the right-hand turret, the spiral staircase has a handrail of moulded brick and a vault in 'ploughshare' forms which, for its date, was a remarkable piece of virtuosity. The colour is a delight: an exquisite old rose that has acquired with age a rich patina. It is not merely mellow: it is as if dusted with silver, and not of course uniformly. The Oxburgh gatehouse is one of England's most enchanting pieces of architectural pageantry.

These three short descriptions must suffice to suggest the progress made in brick building during the fifteenth century. So far, all the examples to which reference has been made are in the East or South-East. The employment of brick on the other side of the limestone belt as early as this was extremely rare. I can point only to four instances. The oldest is in south Derbyshire: Prior Overton's tower at Repton, now part of the Headmaster's House in Repton School. This was erected about 1440 and, with its corbel-supported turrets, is a remarkably accomplished piece of brick architecture to find in this part of England at so early a date. Leicestershire has two examples, both near the county town and both unfortunately in ruins: Kirby Muxloe Castle, built in 1480–84, and Bradgate House, begun a decade later. At each the bricks were made on the spot: the craftsmanship at Kirby Muxloe in particular was of high quality.[1] The fourth instance is internal: bricks were used in 1499 in Durham Castle, where a big kitchen was constructed within the Norman building which was perhaps the original keep.

South of the Thames, brick was also at this time a rarity. Until the last forty years of the century Herstmonceux was probably the only brick building of any importance in this part of the country, unless we include the manor house at Dent-de-Lion, Garlinge, close to Margate, which on the evidence of the heraldry was finished before 1445. Here brick and flint were used in combination; on the front of the roofless gatehouse, all that survives from what must once have been a house of some importance, bands of dull red and pale yellow brick alternate with others of knapped flint. Edward IV's reign saw three important brick undertakings in Surrey, all associated with great ecclesiastics. To his Palace at Croydon Archbishop Bourchier added, in brick, the chapel, lengthened westwards by his successor at Canterbury, Morton. Bishop Waynflete of Winchester built Esher Palace, of which only the gatehouse remains, in red brick with blue diapering, and a few years later (*c.* 1470–75), in the same materials, the much more imposing tower with mock machicolations at Farnham Castle (*222*b). In the last decade of the century about 480,000 red bricks were made for that most glorious of all England's towers, the central tower of

1 Part of the Abbey wall at Leicester itself is also of red brick, with some blue too. The Abbey buildings have completely disappeared, but the wall, added by Abbot Penny between 1496 and 1509, survives.

Canterbury Cathedral. Not that its beauty owes anything to them, for Bell Harry was
entirely faced with Caen stone, but its core is of brick. In Berkshire bricks had been made   *
even in the fourteenth century, but only on a very small scale, and there is no major
example to record.

An early instance of the use of brick north of the Thames, dating from 1425, was at
the original Moor Park near Rickmansworth, of which nothing now remains, and a still
earlier one was at Stonor Park in Oxfordshire, for which 200,000 bricks were made at
Crocker End near Nettlebed in 1416–17. Another Oxfordshire example, also well away
from the limestone belt which gives the north-western part of the county its abundance
of splendid stone buildings, is at Ewelme. Here in 1434–36 William de la Pole, Duke of
Suffolk, erected not only a stately church, mainly in flint and stone although with brick
parapets, but a school and a hospital also, entirely in brick. The latter, which is really an
almshouse and still in use, has on its north side a very unexpected feature: above a doorway, within a recessed arch and under a crow-step gable, there is a large trefoil-design,
entirely carried out in moulded brick. Presumably this was the work of a Fleming,
for similar, and indeed more ambitious, decorative brickwork of this kind is to be found in
contemporary buildings at Bruges. But the bricks, now a good deal renewed, were certainly made locally.

In Buckinghamshire, Eton College embodies our only example of fifteenth-century
brickwork; and moving north-eastwards there is nothing of much importance until the
remains are reached of two ambitiously designed Bishop's Palaces, those of Ely at Hatfield
and of Lincoln at Buckden in Huntingdonshire, dating mainly from the fourteen-eighties.
The bricks for the latter may well have been brought up the Ouse from south-
west Norfolk. Of the original Hall built at Little Hadham in Hertfordshire in 1440
nothing survives above ground, but the bricks for it were made close by in a field still
called Bricklea. On approaching East Anglia examples begin to multiply. At Cambridge
several colleges besides Queens' were building in brick before 1500, notably Jesus. And
in the four coastal counties, Essex, Suffolk, Norfolk and Lincolnshire, far more fifteenth
century brickwork can be seen than anywhere else in England: the material was employed
there for parts of churches, especially in Essex; for schools, as at Wainfleet; and for important houses, some of which, like Caister Castle, are now in ruins, while large portions of
others, such as Faulkbourne Hall, are well preserved.

With the advent of the Tudors brick-making made rapid advances both in skill and in
popularity, so much so in fact that the reign of Henry VIII may justly be termed the first
great age of English brickwork. Remarkable feats of ornamentation were now accomplished, particularly in the designing and making of chimney-stacks, as will be described

presently. Socially this material was now in such high favour that both Wolsey and, a few years later, the King himself were perfectly happy to have their palaces at Hampton Court and St. James's constructed of it. Among surviving brick houses which date from the Tudor period are some of the most attractive in the country. In Essex, in addition to about a dozen porches and twice as many towers, including some, such as Ingatestone and Rochford, which are really imposing, whole churches were now built of brick, as at Layer Marney, Berechurch and East Horndon. Chignal Smealey near Chelmsford used often to be known locally as Brick Chignal because of its all-brick, early Tudor church.

Yet despite the success which brick now enjoyed, its adoption was still very far from being universal in England, either socially or geographically. The ordinary man, who could not afford stone, was no better able to pay for brick, except here and there for a chimney shaft. Very few small houses were built wholly of brick during the sixteenth century.

For more important buildings the four East Coast counties still held the leading place, but the horizon broadened. Brick now became an important building material in the three south-eastern counties, and in Middlesex, Hertfordshire and Cambridgeshire. Elsewhere brick buildings were by no means numerous, and in some parts of the country still quite unknown. West of the limestone belt, such houses as Compton Wynyates in Warwickshire (1520–27 : the roof of stone) or Plaish Hall, the earliest brick building in Shropshire (*c.* 1540), were altogether exceptional.

Although all but a few of our bricks were home-made, the builders at this time were certainly influenced by the Netherlands in some of their designs. This is specially seen in the taste for crow-step gables, which we have already met at Ewelme. These gables, for the steps of which specially moulded saddle-back coping-bricks were sometimes made (*222c*), mostly belong to the sixteenth century, and it is not without geographical significance that they occur most frequently in East Anglia and Kent. Later, curved forms were introduced; these were also derived from the Netherlands. Mr. Norman Scarfe has noted nearly fifty houses and farm buildings with curved Dutch gables in the county of Suffolk, erected between 1621 and 1700.[1] Red House Farm at Knodishall Green near Saxmundham, dated 1678, is one of the most imposing (*239b*). Mill House at Denham in Buckinghamshire has two curved gables and two crow-steps on a single front.

But this is to anticipate. Under Elizabeth and the first two Stuarts, the area of brick building continued to expand; the excellent clays around Southampton, for instance, were

---

1 *Suffolk: A Shell Guide* (1960), p. 19.

now exploited to such an extent that before long this town already had its official brick-maker. It is recorded that in 1574 a number of Southampton residents complained bitterly that this man was so pre-occupied with making bricks for the houses of the neighbouring gentry that their own requirements were being ignored.[1] In the seventeenth century Fareham became famous for the rich red bricks which have maintained their reputation ever since. Before the end of the Elizabethan age brick had also become general in Berkshire; every town in this county, except Faringdon which had its local limestone, came presently to be largely built of it. Brick made another appearance in Derbyshire, in conjunction with stone, at Barlborough Hall, and for the first time in Lancashire (and then only in the south-western part of the county). Other isolated examples elsewhere could no doubt be cited. But brick was not employed in Nottingham before the reign of James I, though it was occasionally used in Nottinghamshire during the sixteenth century. In the whole of Cornwall there is no known example earlier than Ince Castle near Saltash, which was built about 1640. For this the bricks were undoubtedly brought by sea.

Meanwhile in London, even before the Great Fire, as also in the Home Counties, brick had been steadily gaining in popularity among the mercantile and professional classes. Yet it was not until the last quarter of the seventeenth century that, thanks to falling prices, the taste for this material really gathered momentum, spreading downwards at last to the humblest cottage dweller, and fanning outwards over parts of the country that had up to this time possessed few or no buildings in brick. It might be well, therefore, to pause here and take stock of the progress that had been made by brick architecture in England up to the accession of Queen Anne.

Unlike all the materials which have been discussed so far, brick is a manufactured article, requiring skill as well as the presence of the right clay. Suitable clays were in fact much more widely available in England than the developments so far described might suggest; up to the closing years of the seventeenth century it was in many places not the clay but the will, and probably also the skill, to make use of it which were lacking. These clays differ widely in age. Almost every geological formation from the most recent alluvial deposits as far back as the Carboniferous system has yielded clays or shales useful for brickmaking, and in a few exceptional cases even older material has been used.[2] That is

---

1 *Victoria County History: Hampshire and the Isle of Wight*, vol. V (1912), p. 465.

2 At the present time about one-third of the total quantity of clay used in the production of English bricks is Jurassic (Oxford Clay and Lias Clay) and another third Carboniferous. Of the remaining third, one-half is Glacial and Alluvial Clay of the most recent geological formation.

not to suggest that all clays are equally good for the purpose. Some are far more cohesive than others. Some will not stand up to the required firing temperature. Others contain too much salt. Everyone must from time to time have noticed brickwork disfigured by the appearance of a white efflorescence on its surface; this is due to an excess of calcium or magnesium sulphate in the composition of the clay, usually brought to the surface by prolonged damp. In mild cases it will always cure itself in a few years, but if the quantity of soluble salts in the clay is considerable it can be very troublesome.

The best bricks depended upon two physically different clays both being readily available, the one as plastic as possible, the other sandy and non-plastic, to counteract the tendency of the plastic clays to shrink and warp during the process of firing. Further to offset this danger, it was for a long time a statutory obligation to dig the clay in the autumn and expose it to the weather before brickmaking began. The two clays, or it might be a single plastic clay and sand, were then blended and squeezed; by the date that we have now reached, this was beginning to be done in what was known as a pug-mill, instead of by men treading barefoot. The cylindrical pug-mill contained a central vertical shaft, from which revolving blades projected horizontally, as did another shaft, to which a horse or donkey could be harnessed to provide the motive power. The luckless animal, led probably by a child, was then walked round and round, and the coarse mixture, fed in at the top of the mill, emerged from the bottom as completely smooth 'dough', all pebbles and other impurities having been eliminated. The clay was then pressed into wooden moulds, each the size of a brick, left to dry for at least a fortnight, and then loaded into a kiln and fired, usually for about forty-eight hours. These kilns, even as late as the eighteenth century, were constantly catching fire. The fuel was still sometimes wood, but by 1700 it was generally necessary to obtain supplies of coal, much the most expensive item in the whole brickmaking process at that time.

The picture which emerges is of an intensely local activity, wholly unstandardized. Wherever possible the clay was dug on the site, and ideally, as at Ven House, Milborne Port, the first considerable brick house to be built in Somerset and dating from 1698–1700, the demands of mansion and garden went hand in hand. Over half a million bricks were needed for this house and for the embanking of its long south terrace. Stretches of water—originally straight canals—were required in the grounds. What better plan than to utilize the clay thrown out by the digging of the canals to make the bricks on the site? For humbler undertakings similar conditions applied. We have already noted how frequently, in the stone counties, small quarries would be opened to supply the needs perhaps of no more than a single farmhouse and its outbuildings. With brickmaking the same was now the case. Some parts of England are dotted with patches of irregular ground

FIFTEENTH-CENTURY BRICKWORK
a. and b. *Oxburgh Hall, Norfolk*
c. *Tattershall Castle, Lincolnshire*

which are all that now remains to indicate, to those who know what to look for, the former existence of a long-abandoned brick-field, if 'field' is not too grand a word for what may only amount to a few dozen square yards.

Thus up to the Industrial Revolution brick, no less surely than stone, exhibited its own local characteristics, in harmony with the land upon which it stood and out of which it came. It has been well said that at one time there were as many different varieties of brick in England as there were of home-made loaves. And in both cases the bakers were not all equally skilful. Because of the higher temperatures required, it was still more difficult in those days to estimate the right heat for a brick-kiln than for a baking-oven. The firing process was uncertain, the clay itself no less so. Some splendid bricks were made, and many others that were not so good. If we go, for example, to Charlecote Park in Warwickshire expecting to see the brickwork of 1558, we have a disappointment in store, for, although some portions of the original brickwork survive, most of it has decayed and has had to be replaced; so that the walls of the house are now an unattractive patchwork, largely dating from the Victorian period. For the detached gatehouse a different brick was employed and perhaps a different brickmaker; and this, although only slightly later, is in a much better state of preservation and far more pleasing in colour and texture than the house itself. Brick, properly made, and with the right constituents, is one of the most durable of all the materials of building. Where it has decayed, it is either because the wrong clay was used or because the methods of manufacture were defective. Before the Industrial Revolution there can be no doubt that both these conditions frequently applied. An example of brick decay can be seen at Knodishall Green (239b). Not surprisingly, it is almost always the chimney-stacks which require attention first. Sometimes these have to be completely rebuilt.

Nevertheless, with the accession of Queen Anne, England was on the threshold of the second golden age of her brick architecture. The material was still in the height of fashion: Wren had just used it for the King and Queen at Kensington Palace and, in combination with Portland stone to produce an effect of studied brilliance, at Hampton Court (239c). Within a few years, ornamental effects of extraordinary skill and refinement in both colour and texture were to be realized: some of these will be referred to later. Yet there were still no large centres of manufacture, and this held good throughout the whole of the eighteenth century. Itinerant brickmakers travelled about the country, testing the local clay and, if it proved suitable, settling down on the site and staying there until the brickwork, and probably also the tiles, of the required building were complete. It was an *ad hoc* development.

In London, the urge to abandon half-timbering and build or rebuild in brick had been

13*—P.E.B.

EARLY EXUBERANCE IN BRICK
a. *Herstmonceux Castle, Sussex*
b. *Waynflete's Tower, Farnham Castle, Surrey*   c. *Wallington Hall, Norfolk*

gradually gathering momentum since the time of Queen Elizabeth I, partly because people now feared the combustibility of wood, and partly because, whilst the price of wood was rising, that of bricks was falling. The Act for the Rebuilding of the City of London, the year after the Great Fire, made brick or stone walls compulsory in the capital. Fire devastated many other towns, among them Marlborough in 1653, Southwold in 1659, Northampton in 1675, St. Ives, Huntingdonshire, in 1680, New Alresford, Hampshire, in 1689, 1710 and 1736, Warwick and Gillingham, Dorset, in 1694, Dorchester in 1713, 1725 and 1775, Blandford and Tiverton in 1731, Stony Stratford, Buckinghamshire, in 1742, Crediton in 1743 and 1769, Wincanton and Honiton in 1747, Wareham in 1762, Honiton again in 1765 and Bradninch, Devon, in 1832. All these fires produced broadly similar results without any need for legislation. In each case, apart from a few special edifices, the rebuilding was largely or wholly in brick. All except Southwold and Alresford were places not far away from adequate stone quarries, and it might have been supposed that stone would have been preferred; bricks, however, were not only cheaper now but for a while, it would seem, still equally fashionable.

It is probable that, in all the counties to the east and south-east of the limestone belt, brick had already become the predominant building material by 1700. Many a timber-framed house in this part of England was provided in the eighteenth century with a new façade in brick, a Georgian veneer added to conform to the dictates of the Age of Taste. A striking instance is Lawford Hall near Manningtree (239a). Although at first sight one might not think so, this is a large timber-framed house built in 1583, which was given a fine 'face-lift' in red brick on the south and west sides in 1756. The lofty Elizabethan chimney-stacks will nevertheless be noticed, and the steep roof with its hipped gables rising far above the parapet, to yield most unGeorgian proportions. The effect, let it be added, is extremely pleasing. Some of these fronts in nine-inch brickwork two storeys high were only tied to the timber-framed structure behind them in the most perfunctory fashion. It is an odd sensation to pass through a Georgian doorway into a timber-framed house of a century or more earlier.

Numerous brick houses in the South-East were also felt to require a more dignified frontispiece. For its modest size a particularly swagger example is Sherman's Hall at Dedham (240c), where the new front, with its giant order and lofty parapet which curves up still higher in the centre to make room for a big sundial, was added about 1735. The transformation of the former rectory at Pertenhall in north Bedfordshire came later (239d). The fairly prominent roofs of the earlier, lower house can still be seen, but only from the back. The lofty front added in 1799 (it looks older) was provided with return walls along both sides to a depth of three bays. Several of the windows are dummies and must be, since at the top there is nothing behind them. The deception is fully justified by the result.

Elsewhere, the acceptance of brick came much more slowly, especially where there was plenty of stone but no suitable local clay. This particularly applied to the limestone belt itself. There were no brick buildings in the Cotswolds at this time, nor for long after, and rightly so. In regions where every building and every boundary wall is of stone, brick—and particularly red brick—is visually an intruder: the Cotswolds are an obvious example. The Pennines are another. This material looks perplexingly out of place amidst the hills and dales of the Northern counties, with their abundance of dark-toned stone and their subdued colouring, and it did not appear there until the Industrial Revolution. The South-West, so well provided with alternative materials, was another region in which brick had made very little impact when Anne ascended the throne. Exeter would seem to have had nothing in brick earlier than the Custom House of 1681. On the other hand, it had already made its mark in Newcastle upon Tyne, which Celia Fiennes in 1697 thought 'most resembled London of any place in England, its buildings lofty and large, of brick mostly or stone . . .'. In the West Midlands, with their excellent clays and their green, umbrageous landscapes, red bricks look perfectly at home. Brick buildings hereabouts dating from the seventeenth century are not very numerous; but in Cheshire, Staffordshire, Leicestershire and throughout the whole length of the country bounding the Severn and its tributary the Avon, as also at Ludlow, there is a profusion of Georgian architecture in this material.

The story of English brickwork under the Hanoverians is a tale of ever-growing dominance in nearly every part of the kingdom, in spite of the reaction in aristocratic circles, especially against red brick, of which something has already been said in Chapter 2. Of that the first *frissons* are to be detected in the fastidious coterie of the early Palladians. Colin Campbell's Mereworth Castle is built of brick, but the material was from the outset given a rendered surface, and the same procedure was adopted for Lord Burlington's Villa at Chiswick. At Holkham, Thomas Coke was more economical than his neighbour the Prime Minister at Houghton (cf. pp. 37 and 122), and at ease in the knowledge that the use of brick for villas had the imprimatur not only of Palladio but of Vitruvius himself; yet trouble was taken here, too, to avoid any visible hint of red. There must be many familiar with the sombre brownish-yellow face which the great house presents to the world who would be startled to discover that the inward facing bricks of the courts, never seen nor intended to be seen by admiring visitors, are bright red. The reason was purely practical: this good brick-earth had to be removed to get at the other, so it was obviously better to make use of it. The subject of brick colours will soon be discussed in more detail; meanwhile, as the fashionable pendulum was swinging ever further away from 'naked' brick, gracious 'middling' houses, usually red, were going up over wide areas. In addition to many country houses, some of our small towns—places such as Farnham, Blandford and Lymington, Abingdon, Bewdley and Pershore—were acquiring in red brick much of the distinguished character which happily they still preserve. Ancient cathedral cities like Chichester and Exeter, Salisbury and York, old market towns like Newbury and Devizes, Colchester and Shrewsbury, historic ports such as Bristol, Bridgwater and Portsmouth, were all building those Georgian houses for the merchant and professional classes which are even now among their principal adornments; and in every single instance the prominent material was red brick.

To explain the triumph of brick, not only in England but in almost every country in Europe[1] and in many beyond, is not difficult. It was a question of economics. When brick-making started in any given area, the initial cost of building in brick might still be more than in, say, wood and plaster, but ultimately one got better value in this than in any other material. Long before any bricks were made by machinery this was so, and for a number of reasons. In the first place, provided that the right clay was available, bricks were not very expensive to make. Although time and labour as well as reasonable skill were involved, the cost was much less than that of quarrying, shaping and transporting, even for short distances, heavy blocks of stone. Moreover, even in the stone areas, the skilled masons required for cutting and dressing stone could command substantially higher pay than the brickmakers. And if the cost of making bricks was not excessive, neither was the price of building in brick. Sizes of mould-made bricks were not regulated until 1571, but have in fact differed little during the last six centuries, because the determining factor has nearly always been the size of a man's hand. Bricks, therefore, are very convenient to handle. Normally too, whilst in any kind of stone or in wood the size of every piece will vary, bricks are more or less uniform; and standard sizes always reduce the cost of construction. Another consideration is maintenance. When towns grew smoky, brick, it is true, became begrimed with dirt and often very dingy-looking; one could wish that the mechanical washing and brushing process for cleaning brickwork were far more widely employed than it is. Yet whereas nearly all varieties of stone ultimately succumb to the acids of a smoke-laden atmosphere, a well-burnt brick hardly deteriorates at all. Repointing will become necessary from time to time, but good brick is a material of extraordinary

1 Scotland is a notable exception. Even as late as 1800 brick in Scotland was not common. Essentially a stone country, she has never developed, nor needed to develop, mastery of brick.

durability. (In this connection it may also be noted that early brick buildings—Thornton Abbey gatehouse (p. 213) is an example—sometimes survive where, had they been built of stone, they would undoubtedly have been pillaged by later generations. Brick, as any visitor to Rome will at once perceive, is far less rewarding to the vandal than the choicer materials.)

The foregoing do not exhaust the economic arguments that operated in favour of brick. There was also the question of safety. After the fires, to some of which reference has been made, the non-combustible nature of brick was a powerful argument in its favour. Chimney-flues and stacks had indeed long been built of it for this very reason, not only where the rest of the house was of wood and plaster, but also in combination with stone, as can still be well seen in the old Wiltshire town of Malmesbury, where nearly all the houses are of stone and practically every chimney-stack is brick. But there were other considerations besides the economic one. In addition to low cost, there was also high comfort. 'Brick', as its great protagonist, Nathaniel Lloyd,[1] observed, 'is a warm material.' Being porous, it is not a good conductor. Thus such a house, if well built, is warm in winter and cool in summer. In this respect brick is exactly the opposite of glass. Finally there was the question of appearance. This was probably not a primary factor operating in favour of brick, yet the Queen Anne and Georgian builders sometimes took so much trouble over details of colour, texture and ornamentation that there can be no doubt that its aesthetic properties were also appreciated.

English architects who worked during the eighteenth century in a strictly Classical style tended, whenever they had to use brick, to imitate stone forms as far as they could. A good example can be seen at Holkham, where from a distance an effect of rusticated stonework on the ground storey was produced by leaving a deep channel between every five courses of bricks, the edges of the bricks adjacent to the channels being chamfered off all along the face. The desired impression of greater scale at the base was further enhanced by the very precise jointing of the brickwork above. In less elevated circles, no attempts were made to disguise the fact that the character of brick is not grand but essentially friendly and practical; and these are the qualities which the smaller Georgian houses communicate, as much through the manner in which their brickwork was handled as by their quiet and gracious formality. Nor is it unusual to find that large stone-built country houses have brick outbuildings. This was not only done for reasons of economy, but because in the Georgian period it was widely believed that, owing to a tendency to sweat in damp weather, stone could affect adversely the health of horses. So for stables brick was in some places regarded as decidedly preferable.

1 Nathaniel Lloyd's *History of English Brickwork* (1925), although it could now be corrected on certain points of detail, is still the indispensable book on this subject.

It was not until the first half of the nineteenth century that the progress of brick really did for a while suffer something of a setback. This was due to two causes, perhaps not unconnected: taxation and fashion. The tax on bricks was first imposed in 1784. It was increased in 1794, and again in 1803. In some country districts it undoubtedly encouraged a revival of the use of wood for cottages, principally now in the form of weather-boarding. In towns, taxation does not by itself appear to have affected the situation very much. After the Napoleonic wars brick was used on a vast scale not only in fast-growing places like London and Brighton, where no stone was at hand, but also at Cheltenham, where there was any amount of good oolite available on Leckhampton Hill, only a mile or two above the town. The reason was that, despite the tax, brick was still decidedly cheaper, besides lending itself, because of easy handling and standard sizes, to speedier constructional methods. In all these places, however, as in many others, there was from about 1810 to 1850 a strong predilection, which now spread downwards socially at least as far as the lower middle class, for hiding all the brickwork that showed behind a coating of stucco. This was partly due to snobbery, the stucco being intended to suggest stone, the only material which was now completely respectable; but there was also a worthier motive. Regency architects aimed at broad, sweeping effects, and understandably found the small, neat mesh of a brick front inimical to their purpose. Brick, they felt, gave a poverty-stricken appearance and, given their aims, they were probably right.

The pendulum swung back again. The tax on bricks was swept away in 1850, and just about the same time (perhaps again there was some connection between the two events) people were beginning to feel that, although bare brick might look poverty-stricken, stucco was much worse because it was dishonest! Characteristically, in fact, the question had become a moral one. Stucco quickly fell out of favour; brick was now to achieve a hitherto undreamed-of commercial success. This was due to the introduction, for the first time on an important scale in the late eighteen-fifties and early eighteen-sixties, of mechanization in place of the old hand processes, which resulted in a great saving of time and labour. No longer was it necessary to expose the clay to the weather: the drying could be done by machinery. No longer were brickmakers solely dependent on the old pug-mills: grinding machines were not only much faster, but could deal with the harder and less plastic carbonaceous clays of the North Midlands and North which had formerly been considered unsuitable. Moulding also became a mechanical process, the clay being pressed by machinery into metal moulds; and in the wake of a commercially very important invention, the Hoffman Kiln of 1858, the fires no longer burned intermittently but continuously night and day.

The Victorians were delighted. Not only did costs fall considerably, but the general opinion was that the bricks were now much better. It was possible to make every wire-cut or pressed brick almost identical in colour and texture, precisely so in size, and perfectly true. This uniformity was so highly regarded that any bricks which varied were usually thrown out. Mortar courses accordingly became absolutely regular and sometimes extremely thin. Mass production had come to stay. Further inventions followed, rendering possible, from 1880 onwards, the commercial exploitation of the immense bed of Oxford Clay (so-called) which runs on the south-east side of the limestone belt from Oxfordshire through Bedfordshire to Lincolnshire. This is the clay that makes the bricks specially associated with Fletton, south of Peterborough, which by the beginning of 1889 was producing 156,000 bricks every day.[1]

Artistically the results were calamitous. Many of the old local brickworks could not compete with the new products, which in the second half of the century were sent, mainly by rail, all over the country. The distinctive character and colour harmonies of particular localities were completely disregarded: these smooth, insensitive bricks even found their way into stone districts in which visually they had no aesthetic justification whatsoever. This particularly applies to parts of the six Northern counties. In the South-West, Plymouth managed to retain the local limestone as its principal building material all through the nineteenth century, and brick is even now not very common in Cornwall.

The Cotswolds, being without industrial resources, also succeeded in remaining inviolate, and so for the same reason did Westmorland. But elsewhere in the North the fast-rising tide of industry brought with it a rash of red brick, so hideous that it almost seems as if lack of visual appeal had been deliberately sought. In the manufacturing towns and colliery villages of Lancashire and Yorkshire, Durham and Northumberland, cheapness now dictated that the building material should nearly always be brick, the effect of which is altogether lamentable.

To-day, on many English brick-fields, and above all on the outcrops of Oxford Clay at Fletton and to the south and east of Bedford (where a large proportion of English bricks are now made), the forest of chimneys, one for each of the great brick kilns, the water-filled clay pits, and the huge mechanical excavators tearing out the earth to a depth of anything up to 40 ft., are unlovable indications of the flourishing condition of the popular brick industry. Nevertheless, the artistic situation is better than it was. Some of the brick-fields are now producing much more attractive machine-moulded bricks: reference will be made presently to notable recent improvements both in colour and in texture.

---

1 Quoted from 'The Builder', April 27, 1889, by Dr. Marian Bowley, *Innovations in Building Materials* (1960), p. 69.

Furthermore, contrary to the expectations of many in the eighteen-sixties and seventies, the old local brickyards did not all have to close. Before the turn of the century, the requirements of several leading architects, notably Lutyens, were sufficient to re-establish a small but steady demand for the old, traditional, hand-made bricks, and for attractive new variants upon them. Even now, although every year sees new closures, in favourable areas such as Sussex, the Thames basin and the Suffolk side of the Stour valley there are brickyards which are still producing these sand-faced, hand-moulded bricks, with slight irregularities and subtle colour-variations. They are usually very durable, but take much longer to make, so inevitably they cost a lot more than the machine-moulded bricks; yet aesthetically they are so superior that, for facing, a few people are still prepared to pay the price. Particularly attractive are the rich brownish-red bricks made from the clay of the Sussex Weald at Burgess Hill, and at Chailey in the Ouse valley to the north-west of Lewes. In 1959 these beautiful narrow hand-moulded bricks were used to face Lord Holford's Arts Building at the University of Exeter. On the Ashburnham estate near Battle, fine bricks were still being made in a *wood*-fired kiln until November 1968. The general artistic superiority of the brickwork of the South of England and East Anglia to that of the Midlands and especially the North is partly a question of the character of the clays, but it is also due to the presence in the South and East of many more buildings faced with hand-moulded bricks, in all their rich variety of colour and texture.

Colours

Before mass-production yielded every year millions of bricks of a monotonous and standardized uniformity, one of the attractions of English brickwork was its many differences of colour, deriving, as has been indicated, from the highly localized conditions under which the bricks were made. Even among the reds alone, every shade may be encountered from orange-pink and salmon, and a warm terracotta that calls to mind some of the paintings of Pieter de Hooch, to the glowing crimson of a summer sunset, and beyond, through port-wine red to those deep plum and mulberry shades which hover on the brink of purple.

The principal colour determinant of brick has always been the constitution of the clay itself, and more particularly the presence of so-called impurities which act chemically as staining agents. Of these much the most important, as with stone, is iron. The fact that the vast majority of bricks are some shade of red is due to the very widespread occurrence of iron in the clay. Other colouring agents include manganese, cobalt, lime and sand: with hand-moulded bricks, the practice has been to sprinkle sands of different colours over the moulds. In modern times, especially in America, many 'new' colours have been produced by the deliberate addition of various metallic oxides in carefully controlled quantities, a practice which was unknown in pre-Industrial days. Another modern development has been exploited to excellent effect in this country. A good range of colours can now be obtained in machine-made bricks of the Fletton type by sandblasting them with minerals in finely granulated form. This is done under high steam pressure, and, on firing, each mineral gives its own colour and pleasantly varied texture.

The other traditional factor affecting colour was the process of firing. If, for instance, the clay were not too thoroughly mixed in the pug-mill, different lumps might burn to different shades. The bricks exposed to the greatest heat would emerge from the kiln the darkest, and the changes of colour might be considerable. Yellow bricks from the Gault would be turned into various shades of brown; red bricks from the Trias might assume the hue of a ripe plum, or turn purple-blue, or almost black. The character of the fuel might also affect the colour. 'Flared headers' could be achieved by burning large quantities of furze, the kilns being so constructed that the ends of the bricks came into direct contact with the flames. Later, with coal-fired kilns, the flared headers were produced by deliberate placing within the kiln close to the fire-holes. On emerging, these ends were always the darkest, and sometimes their surface had become partly or wholly vitrified. It is possible that the excellence of the bricks and tiles of the Tenterden district of Kent owed something to the hornbeams, common even to-day in local coppices, which once provided much of the faggot-wood for the kilns.[1] Certain kinds of wood yielded fumes containing potash, which was valuable in assisting the process of glazing. In the mechanized conditions of to-day, different colours can be obtained simply by controlling the quantities of air admitted into the kiln during the later stages of firing.

There can be little doubt that in the local brickfields differences of colour and tone were often accidental. The temperature of the kiln could not be accurately controlled, and the chemical composition of the clays was not exactly known. It did not matter. It has often been remarked that various colours of the same kind of flower will usually blend

[1] Mr. A. S. Ireson, in a personal letter, writes: 'There is a mid-eighteenth-century house in Somerset called Crowcombe Court where the building accounts have been carefully preserved. I saw these some years ago. The house is of pleasant red brick with facings and dressings of Ham Hill limestone, and the bricks were made on the estate. I was struck by the fact that whereas there were only three stonemasons, about the same number each of carpenters, bricklayers and brickmakers, there were twelve men and more sometimes "cutting faggots in the woods". The reason for the faggots (which were usually bundles of brushwood, undergrowth, tree toppings and hedge splashings) was not stated, being no doubt well known to the keeper of the accounts. One is left to infer that the only purpose for which they could have been used in connection with the building of a new house was for the firing of the bricks.'

happily together, whereas the mixing of two different species can be hazardous. So also with bricks: circumstances fortunately dictated that, although there might be considerable modulations of colour, they were all drawn from the same kiln; and the builders had the good sense to use almost all of them. More than anything else, it is this continual variation in colour which imparts to the brick buildings of the Tudor and Stuart periods their peculiar richness—a richness analogous to the palette of the Impressionist painters, who obtained their shimmering effects by the observance of not very dissimilar principles. Irregularities give life to a surface, and render it a pleasure to contemplate. This is a law of nature. The blades of grass in every field, the leaves on every tree, differ minutely from one another while adhering to a general conformity. The differences from brick to brick might also be scarcely perceptible, yet they were sufficient to break up the flatness of the finished wall and save it from dullness.

With the advent of a more Classical approach to architecture, such colour gradations became less acceptable. Wren, as can be seen at Hampton Court, liked bright red bricks that were almost uniform in hue in order to achieve as tellingly as possible the contrast with the gleaming white Portland stone so profusely introduced for the dressings, which is so excellent a feature of this building. In Classical architecture effects are always more deliberately contrived; the chance variation is not welcomed. Without a doubt something valuable was thereby sacrificed; but for a while there were many compensations. In the first half of the eighteenth century not only were the bricks themselves often of the finest possible quality, but interest would be given to a surface by deliberate changes of colour, as well as by other devices to be mentioned presently. At Bradbourne near Maidstone, for example, a Queen Anne house situated in a part of the country well known for the high standard of its brickwork, a lighter tone was introduced into the bricks of all the eight pilasters of the entrance front, while the central window, above the doorway, was given a frame of the deepest red, suggestive of a velvet curtain (240a). Thereby a design which could hardly in itself claim to be inspired was graced with a subtlety and a refinement that are altogether delightful. At Westwell, Tenterden (255d), built two or three years earlier (1711), all the brickwork was red as was usual in the South-East, but the builder achieved gentle variations both of texture and of tone which give much pleasure. (The cornice, pediment and keystones here are of stone.) At Dedham, on the other hand, white brick was as easily obtainable as red, and on the front of Sherman's Hall (240c) the emphatic colour contrast serves to underline the assertiveness of the design.

Patterning with bricks of different colours was practised in various ways at every period from the fifteenth century onwards, but since the intention was always purely decorative, this aspect of colour will be considered in the section devoted to ornamental brickwork. Meanwhile, it may be of interest to review rapidly the range of colours available in England and the changing attitudes towards them.

Clays from similar geological formations tend to burn to the same colour, and in pre-industrial days it was the marls of the Triassic system which produced most of the brightest reds. Hence the intense redness of much Georgian brickwork in the Midlands, especially in the area contained within a roughly equilateral triangle of which the angle-points are Tewkesbury, Grantham and Birkenhead. This red brick seems to become still brighter with exposure to the weather. And when at the time of the Industrial Revolution the shales of the Coal Measures were brought into service in the Northern counties for brick-making, an even redder product appeared, a red of almost unbearable density. These shales are very hard and provide bricks which will unfortunately wear for ever without weathering at all. Accrington in central Lancashire has the dubious distinction of having made some of the most durable and visually disagreeable bricks in the country. Not for nothing is one of the two principal varieties known locally as 'Accrington bloods'. By the end of the nineteenth century bricks of a quite relentless redness were being made in many other places besides Accrington. At Ludlow almost the only really hideous building is the Victorian market hall, in screaming red machine-made brick.[1] No one who travels in the Midlands or in the North can fail to be familiar with many lobster or tomato-red buildings, the hot smooth surfaces of which, usually now caked with grime, have done perhaps more to depreciate the aesthetic currency of brick as a building material even than those acres of pasty-faced Flettons, not originally intended to be used at all for facing, which are the twentieth century's most regrettable contribution.

It is also possible, even in an old house, for the redness to look overdone. The entrance side of Ingatestone Hall, a much restored Tudor house in Essex where even the mullions and transoms of the windows are of red brick, and where the tiles are of much the same colour, is an example: the 'brickiness' here becomes oppressive, and one finds more relish in the stable range, rendered with peach-pink plaster and incorporating some sash-framed Georgian windows, painted white. The density of the colour and the small scale of the individual unit lead us to welcome the introduction of some other material in which broader effects may be obtained and in which the concentrated redness can be relieved.

Yet how beautiful hand-made red brick can be. Among the more recent geological formations to the south and east of the limestone belt are clays that have emerged from the brick-kilns to make a most distinguished contribution to the English scene. The Weald, once dotted with brickworks, has often been said to provide the finest of all our brick clays; and in addition to imposing structures like the Tudor tower of Sissinghurst

1 Sir Nikolaus Pevsner aptly terms it 'Ludlow's bad luck' (*Shropshire*, p. 188).

Castle (*333d*), excitingly retrieved from a nearly derelict plight in the early nineteen-thirties, many cottages, farmhouses and busy little towns like Rye and Tenterden lend substance to the claim. Some of the Eocene clays dug in the Thames valley and around
Southampton Water are hardly less excellent. When correctly made, these warm-looking bricks have proved extremely durable and their glowing terracottas are a source of unfailing pleasure.

Apart from the reds, the brick colours most commonly encountered in England are yellow, buff and brown. One frequently comes upon references to white bricks, but applied to brickwork, as to wines, this has a connotation of elegance rather than of exactitude. White bricks, so-called, are produced when, in addition to iron, the clay contains a relatively high content of lime. Nowadays lime is sometimes added deliberately, but formerly white bricks were only made where the lime occurred naturally. The geological formations which can sometimes produce these bricks are the Pleistocene clays, as for example in Sussex between Worthing and Littlehampton, and at a number of places in Suffolk and Norfolk; the Jurassic clays, as seen over much of Bedfordshire and almost everywhere in Huntingdonshire, the Isle of Ely and the Soke of Peterborough; and between them the Gault. This is a name applied to the beds of stiff bluish clay which occur between the Upper and the Lower Greensand. One belt runs south-westwards from Cambridge, at the foot of the Chiltern hills and of the Berkshire Downs, into Wiltshire; this has produced white bricks intermittently throughout its whole extent, but especially at its north-eastern
end, in and around Cambridge. The other principal belt of Gault, equally narrow, encircles the Weald except on its south-eastern side, and is responsible for the white bricks produced to the north of Maidstone. The predominant colour of all the brickwork in this group is a rather washed-out or dusty-looking yellow. The time of its greatest popularity was the first half of the nineteenth century; the Winnats, a small house of *c.* 1840 at Keysoe in Bedfordshire, shows red brick at the sides but the front is entirely 'white'.

Brown bricks occur in widely separated areas, and notably in the Vale of York, but it is the reticent yellow-browns so widely employed in the London area that chiefly claim our attention. These, to add yet further confusion to our colour-descriptions, were euphemistically described in the old specifications as 'grey', a colour which, however desirable in imagination, was in fact seldom attained. These 'London stocks' were, nevertheless, high-grade bricks which have shown admirable powers of endurance. 'Stock' bricks were distinguished from 'place' bricks, which were cheap, underburnt red bricks, never employed in the Georgian age for facing. Beyond this it is not easy to define the term with precision. Originally they were bricks that had been carefully moulded on a stock, a wooden board upon which a small frame or mould was fitted to contain the clay. (The word is Old Norse, and has Teutonic associations.) Stocks were in use in England at least as early as the middle of the sixteenth century. In the Georgian period the term 'stock brick' still referred to its composition and method of manufacture without any connotation of colour: red and 'grey' bricks were both made in this way. More recently this term has come to be associated with what have been called 'London's sad and beautiful browns'—which in Georgian times were less sad-looking than to-day, because the bricks, fresher and cleaner, were not only lighter in tone but often decidedly yellow. There was an abundant supply of excellent brick-earth in the Thames valley to provide the substance of these bricks, which are still produced on both sides of the river's estuary, notably at Sittingbourne and at Shoebury-ness and also farther west, at Tilbury, Enfield and Hayes.

Yellow bricks of a very different character occur here and there in ports which traded with Holland. These are the small hard bricks known as 'Dutch clinkers', which in the last quarter of the seventeenth century were sometimes brought as ballast in ships coming to load grain or wood. These bricks measure only 6–7 ins. × 2½–3 ins. × 1¼–1½ ins., and one end may be pointed. Consignments were seldom sufficient to complete a house, but they can still be found not infrequently in Norfolk and occasionally in Kent. Because of their hardness they were excellent for paving yards and stables; sometimes they were laid in herring-bone patterns. Similar bricks, known as 'adamantine clinkers', were also formerly made in this country at Little Bytham in Lincolnshire. Manufacture continued until 1939.

If true greys are exceptional in London, other places have been more fortunate. The *sine qua non* is again the presence of lime in the clay. In south-east Hampshire, Wickham and Bishop's Waltham have a number of modest Georgian houses mainly faced with unvitrified silver-grey bricks. They are indeed a feature of 'this praty tounlet', as Leland called Wickham and as it still remains. Silver-grey hand-made bricks of much charm, some lightly vitrified, were produced over a long period around Luton. But far and away the best area in which to see these bricks is south Oxfordshire and Berkshire. From Thame to Hungerford examples abound. Nettlebed was at one time an important place for brickmaking (240b). 'Nettlebed purple headers', no longer made, are not purple at all but mainly silver-grey: the most completely vitrified bricks are grey-green, and very attractive. Many were also made in the Reading–Newbury district: Donnington Grove, a Gothick house of the seventeen-sixties close to Newbury is entirely faced with them, and Lutyens used them to great effect early in the present century at Folly Farm, Sulhamp-stead, where the surface of Reading greys has been justly compared to the bloom on a peach. And as with the white bricks at Keysoe, so with the grey at Cuxham, near Watling-ton: a cottage here is red at the sides but wholly grey in front. Another cottage here has grey and red in alternate courses. These grey bricks are often known as grizzles, although this term is also applied by some to underburnt bricks which would never be used for facing. Grey was held in such high esteem in the latter part of the eighteenth century that, where the necessary lime was lacking, red bricks might be given a thin 'skin' of grey by adding salt to the coating of sand before firing. Examples abound: they look silver-grey until they start flaking, as they sometimes do. Such bricks were also in demand for patterning.

Blue may also be no more than skin deep, as with some of the headers used for ornamental patterns by the Tudors (see p. 252). Wholly 'blue' bricks (as they are called: usually they are closer to slate-grey) are of comparatively recent origin. They are the products of some of the very tough clays of the Coal Measures, and their strength, hardness and ability to resist damp have rendered them specially suitable for works of engineering, for which they have been widely employed during the last hundred years. The most important region of their manufacture has always been the southern part of Staffordshire, but various other areas also make them, including County Durham, Lancashire around Wigan, and Almondsbury near Bristol. Needless to say, these engineering bricks are all machine-moulded; but Staffordshire blues have been occasionally employed with success for domestic buildings.

Even now, and leaving aside the new tints which range from tan to tangerine, our survey of brick colours is not complete. There is scarcely a limit to the colours that have been obtained. In Wallingford, for example, and in the unatomic parts of Harwell, a few miles to the west, one may see late-Georgian houses entirely faced with glazed bricks of a distinctly purplish hue, while to the north and west of Stone, in Staffordshire, the bricks are a dark purple-brown, the colour of old copper. A much older house, Anderson Manor near Bere Regis in Dorset, built in 1622, has a gracious front of brick with grey Purbeck stone dressings; the beautiful mellow brickwork comprises two stretcher courses of delicate pinks to one header course of deep purple (flared), carried over the entire surface. And in some of our early brick buildings, those of Tudor date in particular, purples and blues and greys may all be dotted about in the same wall with pinks and browns and several shades of red. Such brickwork, as Nathaniel Lloyd so happily expressed it, is our homespun, and to many eyes the more uniform colouring and smoother texture of what he called the faced-cloth brickwork of the late Stuart and Early Georgian period is no lovelier.

Before the eighteenth century brick buildings of any colour other than red were uncommon. There were many shades of red, some lighter, some darker, some pinker, some browner. Yet even when a wall incorporated bricks of several other colours in the manner just described, the general impression on stepping back was nearly always of redness.

Little Wenham Hall is an exception: here the cream and greenish-yellow bricks far out-number the red. Some of the mediaeval brickwork in the Colchester district and in Thanet is dull yellow, and just before 1500 a pale cream-coloured brick was used by Bishop Alcock at Jesus College, Cambridge. Of far greater interest in this respect is Hengrave Hall near Bury St. Edmunds (*84d*). Parts of the façade here, as was observed in Chapter 3, were faced with a fine oolite brought from King's Cliffe in Northamptonshire. For the non-stone areas a special variety of pale yellow brick was produced, to match the stonework. Technically this presented no difficulty, as suitable calcareous clay was at hand locally, but aesthetically it is noteworthy that even in Tudor times there were already people who did not like the combination of red brick and stone.

Hengrave, however, was an early swallow which certainly did not make a summer. Throughout the Elizabethan and the whole of the Stuart periods, the chances must have been not less than ninety-nine to one that, whenever bricks were used, they would be some shade of red or brown. Even after the advent of the Hanoverians the objections to brick, and particularly to red brick, were at first only faintly heard. Despite the inhibitions of the Burlington circle, even Palladian houses were frequently built of red brick until well into the third quarter of the eighteenth century: Wolterton (1724–30, by Ripley), Clandon (1731–35, by Leoni) and Brocket (c. 1760–70, by Paine) are but three examples among many. It was only in the seventeen-fifties that the fashionable reaction, aided and abetted by the writings of articulate architects like Isaac Ware and Batty Langley, really became influential.

The views of Isaac Ware, embodied in his *Complete Body of Architecture*, published in London in 1756, have often been quoted, but their relevance is such that they must not be altogether omitted from the present study. 'We see', he wrote, 'many beautiful pieces of workmanship in red brick, . . . but this should not tempt the judicious architect to admit them in the front walls of buildings. In the first place, the colour is fiery . . . and in summer has an appearance of heat that is very disagreeable; for this reason it is most im-proper in the country, though the oftenest used there, from the difficulty of getting grey. But a further consideration is that, in the fronts of most buildings of any expense, there is . . . stonework. . . . There is something harsh in the transition from red brick to stone, and it seems altogether unnatural. . . . On the other hand, in the mixture of grey bricks and white paint, the colour of the brick being soft, there is no violent change.' Even the grey stocks 'are to be judged best coloured when they have least of the yellow cast; for the nearer they come to the colour of stone, when they are to be used together with it, always the better.' Admittedly Ware either could not or did not always live up to his own principles: Wrotham Park, which he built in 1754 for Admiral Byng, is now entirely faced with a cement stucco that has lines incised upon it to suggest stone, but this only dates from about 1800 when the house was altered; the chief material was originally red brick.[1] Nevertheless, the renunciation of red brick steadily gathered impetus throughout the reigns of George III and his sons, not only in places like Cambridge, where the cooler colours could be obtained locally without difficulty, but for many country houses not so favourably placed geographically, such as Hale and Hackwood in Hampshire and Swallowfield Park in Berkshire, at all of which the red brickwork was (and still is) unhappily concealed under an overcoat of cement. In London itself red brick virtually disappeared from the more fashionable streets, as being in bad taste. It is remarkable to what lengths noblemen were sometimes prepared to go to rid their eyes of the offending prospect of red brick. At Althorp the second Earl Spencer employed Henry Holland in 1787–88 to cover the whole house with yellowish-white tiles (the so-called 'mathematical' tiles of which more will be said in the next chapter); and between 1786 and 1816 the third Earl Stanhope, impelled by an obsession with the danger of fire, did the same thing at Chevening. Both operations involved the owners in great expense, only to effect a change which most people to-day would deem to be visually for the worse. At this time there were those who really believed in the importance of buildings achieving in their materials not a contrast of colour but a harmony.

The making of white bricks now flourished in East Anglia, where some of the clays were excellent for the purpose. 'Cossey Whites' (which were light yellow) became popular around Norwich about 1830, by which time the Woolpit bricks of central Suffolk had already acquired a more than local reputation. One of the converts to them was Lady Dorothy Foster, daughter of the fourth Earl of Bristol, who in 1796 was pleading with her father to have Ickworth built of white brick. Lord Bristol, viewing the project from Italy, was to say the least not attracted. 'What!' he wrote, 'Build my house of a brick that looks like a sick, pale, *jaundiced* red brick, that would be red brick if it could, and to which I am certain our posterity will give a little rouge as essential to its health and beauty? White brick always looks as if the bricklayers had not burnt it sufficiently, had been niggardly of the fuel; it looks all dough and no crust. . . . No, my dear, I shall follow dear impeccable Palladio's rule, and as nothing ought to be without a covering in our raw damp climate, I shall cover the house with Palladio's stucco, which has . . . resisted the frosts and rains of Vicenza, and deceives the most acute eye till within a foot.'[2] Although not completed until many years after his death, the brickwork of the vast house was entirely faced with cement,

1 Formerly in Middlesex, Wrotham Park was transferred to Hertfordshire in 1965.
2 Vere Foster, *The Two Duchesses* (1898), pp. 116–117.

LATER STUART AND GEORGIAN BRICKWORK
a. *Lawford Hall, Essex*
b. *Red House Farm, Knodishall Green, Suffolk*   c. *Fountain Court, Hampton Court Palace*
d. *The Old Rectory, Pertenhall, Bedfordshire*

pretending to be limestone; since its surface is absolutely dead, the eye is neither deceived nor delighted.

The fashion for stucco during the Regency will be discussed more fully in a later chapter. Not infrequently, in towns, only the ground storey would be stuccoed, the brickwork of the upper part remaining exposed. This can look very well, whether it be red or some cooler shade. Which colours are to be preferred must always remain a matter of individual taste, perhaps even of the mood of the moment. It is probable that red has always been the popular favourite: red brick is warmer and more friendly. Some of the other colours are subtler and, it may be felt, better suited to Classical architecture. Our good fortune is that we have them all. Moreover, as mentioned at the beginning of this section (p. 231), we now have the means of producing a variety of agreeable colours by sandblasting. Aesthetically this is the greatest advance which has so far been made in this country on the mechanical side. Where for financial or other reasons it is not possible to use hand-made bricks, it can at last be said that most of the former objections to the machine-produced article, and especially its wearisome uniformity of colour and tone, have to-day been removed.

Careful choice of the right coloured mortar is no less important in brick than in stone buildings; it will not be necessary to repeat what has been said on the subject of pointing in Chapter 2. Whether the joints be wide or narrow, flush or recessed, there is one aesthetic principle which always holds good: the mortar, to look well, must be lighter in tone than the bricks. Black mortar, produced by mixing lime and sand with crushed clinkers or ashes and favoured sometimes in Victorian times, looks even worse with red brick than with stone. Fortunately a good architect to-day will always pay careful attention to the character of his mortar. The pointing of a brick building should always be 'part of the picture'.[1]

---

[1] But the pointing can capture too much of the picture, as may be appreciated by comparing plate 261b (much too white) with plate 261a (exactly right). Owners of old houses are sometimes faced with very difficult problems in regard to pointing. For instance, at Eggington House near Leighton Buzzard, a delightful building of 1696 which in recent years has been restored with much taste and care, an early morning peck at the original pointing had long been a favourite pastime of the local sparrows. As a result, many of the soft edges of the old red bricks had also perished, leaving wider joints to be filled than its builder intended. Great trouble was taken to match the colour and consistency of the new mortar to what remained of the old, but in relation to the scale of the bricks nothing could prevent the pointing from appearing, on completion, somewhat excessive.

On old (i.e. pre-Restoration) brickwork flush pointing is a mistake. It should always be slightly recessed and left fairly rough. One has seen old walls repointed so that the surface is now about one third mortar, which is altogether wrong. These early bricks owe so much to their irregularities of shape that if the mortar is allowed to creep over their edges the colour impact is changed and the potential textural appeal is entirely sacrificed.

BRICKS OF MANY COLOURS
a. *Bradbourne, East Malling, Kent*
b. *Nettlebed, Oxfordshire*   c. *Sherman's Hall, Dedham, Essex*

Textures

Builders to-day divide bricks into three broad classes: common, engineering and facing. The purposes of the two former are purely practical. Engineering bricks are notable for their strength, durability and resistance to damp. Common bricks are exactly what their name implies; produced to-day in vast numbers, they can only be used externally where a poor finish may be tolerated. The bricks which delight the eye all belong to the third category; it is only these which need concern us in a consideration of textures.

Important as is the nature of the brick surfaces themselves, the over-all texture of a brick building does not only depend upon this. The character and thickness of the jointing, the size and shape of the bricks, the bond: all these need to be taken into account. In every direction variations will be encountered, and we may be glad of it. Yet throughout all the changes, one factor remains constant: the smallness of the individual unit, determined by the size of the human hand. A brick wall is therefore essentially an aggregation of small effects. This implies a human and intimate quality not present to the same extent in stone architecture. But it also imposes a certain restraint. Brick is anti-monumental: it has not the impressiveness, the splendour sometimes, of stone. The smallness of the brick unit was not in tune with the grander or more pretentious aspirations of the Classicists.

In no respect is the intimate quality of brickwork more evident than in its texture. Like unpainted wood, another friendly material, and unlike the metals, painted stucco and some stone, most brick is not cold to the touch.[1] Sometimes creases or wrinkles may be seen on the surface where the clay has been pushed together; these call to mind the quiet hand processes by which it has been moulded. Bricks, unless glazed, do not call attention to themselves by reflections: here too we sense a reticence. Despite the gay reds of some bricks, this material has not the brilliance nor even, we may feel, the self-assurance of stone. Amateurs of stone are sometimes prone to decry brickwork as monotonous. It can be so. It can also achieve, presumably in an attempt to escape from this idea of its pervasive monotony, a fussiness and a flamboyance which are far worse. Sensitive builders at all times have realized that brick is a material that imposes its own clear limitations and have handled it accordingly.

---

1 The tactile temperature of building materials probably plays a greater part in our response to them than is generally recognized. The coldest are the smooth non-porous ones, which do not absorb the warmth of the atmosphere but reflect it back. Hence among the stones polished granites and marbles are the coldest, whilst the only cold bricks are the very hard, and particularly the glazed, varieties.

All clays do not behave in a similar fashion when subjected to burning. The red marls which overlie the small coalfield around Wrexham, for instance, contract very little with firing, and produce a smooth-faced brick of considerable density. Many facing bricks are made in exactly the same way as common bricks, except that more care is taken to remove all extraneous matter from the clay before firing. The best brick textures, however, depend upon the use of sand. The texture of good brickwork is by no means a matter of chance, occurring automatically whenever the clay is propitious. On the contrary, the best textures have almost always been consciously contrived. The sand was either dusted over the unfired lump of clay, or sprinkled into the mould, or both. Until the middle of the seventeenth century the sand used was nearly always coarse, and much of the appeal of the old brickwork depends on this. In the later Stuart and early Georgian periods, on the other hand, bricks of very smooth surface were sometimes required; to obtain these, sand of the finest consistency was employed, and to produce specially soft bricks, the proportion of sand to clay was increased. In the kiln these bricks were only baked, not burnt. The sand was often largely responsible for the colour of the finished brick, either from the nature of its composition or because of the deliberate addition of oxides (usually of iron or manganese) to stain it. Nowadays the moulds of some machine-made bricks are sanded, with good results texturally, but because of the special texture produced on the face of the brick by the act of throwing the clay into the mould, no machine process can rival these English hand-moulded, sand-faced bricks for richness of surface or subtle gradations of colour; they are among the most beautiful bricks ever made.

The soft bricks were required for dressings introduced in the form of pilasters, platbands, window-surrounds, aprons below first floor windows, panels inserted into parapets, and so on, as well as for what is known as gauged work, a term which embraces both cutting and rubbing. In the fifteenth and sixteenth centuries, when it was necessary to construct a brick arch, usually no attempt was made to have voussoirs (the wedge-shaped blocks of which an arch is composed) cut specially. The problem was solved in a somewhat rough and ready fashion with ordinary bricks, either by thickening the mortar joints towards the extrados (outer radius) of the arch, or by introducing here and there little extra pieces of brick or tile. Such improvisations, it need hardly be said, ran directly counter to the spirit of Classicism, which appeared in our architecture in the seventeenth century; so they had to be replaced by a procedure at once more precise, more fastidious, and more skilful. The whole arch, which might be semi-circular but was often segmental or, as over the doorway at Bradbourne (*240a*), semi-elliptical, would now be carefully set out on the drawing-board, the shape of each brick being exactly determined (*246a*). Every brick would then be cut with a special saw to the required shape, and rubbed down so as to make the finest possible joint. Another brick was commonly used to serve as a 'rubber'; to-day a piece of carborundum would be preferred. These specially soft 'rubbing bricks' came originally, in the first half of the seventeenth century, from Holland; one of the very earliest English buildings in which they were employed, with more skill than art perhaps, was Kew Palace (the Dutch House), built in 1631. By the end of the century they had become something of a Kentish speciality; and, although they cost much more than the ordinary facing bricks, there was a widespread demand for them under Queen Anne and the first two Georges. Admirable examples of their use can still be seen all over south-eastern England, and particularly in towns well endowed with brick buildings of this date, such as Chichester and Farnham. At Bradbourne (*240*a) the technique is exemplified to perfection. The centre of the south front of Chicheley Hall in Buckinghamshire is entirely faced with small rubbers, very finely jointed. An exquisite effect.

Hand in hand with the taste for gauged brickwork went a demand for much finer jointing, which directly affected textures. Until the seventeenth century the bricklayer used a somewhat slow-drying mortar compounded of burnt lime and sand, and because many of the early bricks were by no means true when they emerged from the kiln, broad mortar courses were essential. Their thickness was seldom less than $\frac{1}{2}$ in. and sometimes as much as a whole inch; the continual variations in width over the surface of the wall produce the reverse of a machine-made effect, and with hard, rough bricks are invariably pleasing (*221*b). Under the early Stuarts brick dimensions became more regular, to be followed in due course by a reduction in the thickness of the mortar courses, thinner joints being considered more urbane. With the appearance of cut and rubbed bricks, and still more with carving and moulding, the aim was as far as possible to suppress the joint altogether as a visual factor. Often the mortar was replaced by lime putty,[1] which cost more but, being of smoother consistency (because the mix had to be passed through a fine sieve), could be applied more thinly. Occasionally other devices were resorted to: for instance, the bricks over the windows of Twickenham parish church, built by John James in 1714, are said to have been laid not in mortar but in mastic. Another refinement introduced during the eighteenth century was what is known as 'tuck' pointing. By the addition of sand of the required colour and perhaps an oxide, a mortar would be mixed which was as close as possible to the colour of the bricks. The joints, having been pointed with this mortar flush with the wall-face, would be scored with grooves, not more than $\frac{1}{4}$ in. wide and sometimes as little as $\frac{1}{8}$ in., into which would be pressed flat narrow ribbons of a contrasting colour: either white, a chalk-lime putty, or (only after 1796) black, a compound of Roman cement and lamp black. The edges having been carefully trimmed, the effect produced, at a lower cost than by using rubbers throughout, was of that super-fine jointing

---

[1] Or, as it is sometimes called, putty lime.

COLOURED PATTERNS IN BRICK
a. *The Vyne, near Basingstoke, Hampshire*
b. *East Street, Rye, Sussex*   c. *North Pallant, Chichester, Sussex*

which was so much esteemed. It can be seen on many houses in London: for instance, in Bedford Square (*246*b). It was a laborious process which was still not cheap, nor very durable and, it may be felt, rather an overwrought artificiality.

The subtlety of gauged brickwork, with its fine jointing, is not in question. What is more difficult to decide is whether, on balance, it enhances or hinders our enjoyment of brick. Enthusiasts for rough-textured brickwork are liable to speak disparagingly of cutting and rubbing, on the ground that these smooth brick surfaces and thin joints involve a loss of texture, which is undeniable. But we do not always wish to be much aware of texture. The great virtue of gauged brickwork is breadth of effect; with fine jointing the smallness of the unit, the individual brick, is less in evidence. Furthermore, it is possible to obtain different and contrasted textures, as well as colours, on the same building, as many Georgian elevations amply illustrate (*240*c). The truth surely is that all these textures are welcome; to revert again to Lloyd's telling analogy, the Tudor homespun is obviously right for architecture of the Romantic kind, while the early Georgian faced cloth, with lapels of satin, is better suited to Classicism. Moreover, in the buildings of Wren and his successors the dressings are often of stone, to which the brick has to play second fiddle, and here a rough type of brick, with a rich tweedy texture, would be quite out of place. Let it be admitted that the brickwork in Wren's part of Hampton Court Palace has not the charm of the Tudor work, but there is no denying its radiance, nor the way in which it succeeds in showing off to the best advantage the stately white, and now in places nearly black, Portland stone (*239*c).

There is one type of brick texture which in England is never agreeable: the heavily glazed surface. I do not refer to the vitrified or semi-vitrified headers which can often be seen in diaper patterns, nor to the lightly glazed, purplish, Georgian bricks of Berkshire mentioned a few pages back, but to those shiny, dense, machine-moulded bricks so much loved in Victorian times because they seemed so eminently practical. Even the most ardent admirer of the Victorians can hardly claim that one of the virtues of their architects was sensitiveness to texture, and with the erection of buildings faced entirely with glazed bricks, usually bright red, they surpassed themselves. The special objection to these bricks, over and above one's general dislike of hot red machine-products, is that their hard impervious skin will always prevent them from weathering. Every vestige of texture has gone, and where the mortar courses are thin and of monotonous regularity, these brash, glossy surfaces assault the eye to a quite distressing degree. Their proper habitat is the public lavatory, and perhaps the dairy. Even there colour should be considered. There must be a good many people working in institutions (not to mention a well-known London club) who would like never again to have to look at those indestructible

GAUGING, POINTING AND BONDING
a. *Matfield House, Kent* (Country Life Photo)   b. *36 Bedford Square, London*
c. *48 High Street, Lymington, Hampshire*   d. *College of Matrons, Salisbury, Wiltshire*

glazed brown bricks produced by throwing salt into the kilns at intervals during the firing.

The addiction of some of these architects to glazed terracotta as a facing material produced results that were usually no less disagreeable. Before the nineteenth century its employment in England was for purely ornamental purposes; this will be referred to later. The new development was the production of glazed slabs, much larger than bricks, for use in facing. Some of the blocks were plain, others profusely ornamented, favourite motifs being the strapwork, cartouches, and other Germano-Flemish paraphernalia familiar from the days of the first Elizabeth. There was a wide range of colours and the material (here, it was felt, lay its abiding virtue) was imperishable. Halsey Ricardo, a pupil of Norman Shaw, who built a Mediterranean *palazzo* in West Kensington (8 Addison Road) in 1906–07 and faced it with brightly coloured and glazed terracotta, was not unaware of the material's aesthetic limitations. 'The fact', he wrote, 'that glazed bricks and glazed terracotta are virtually unchangeable—that the years that roll over the building will do almost nothing to blend and soften the sharp edges of the moulded work, to coax an interchange and play of colour from one brick to another—are limitations indeed', demanding compensatory advantages. These he thought he had found in its durability, in its non-absorbent surface, making cleaning easy, and above all in 'the charm of the colour'. Gay colour may be conceded here, however uneasily it shines upon its surroundings. Many of these late-nineteenth- and early-twentieth-century buildings faced with terracotta came to be remarkable less for their colour than for their soapiness, though it must be allowed that the Natural History Museum in South Kensington has been transformed since its cleaning in the late 1970s. Although shiny, or at least polished, surfaces are quite successful in countries where the light is bright and the atmosphere dry, in England, where the light is usually soft and the days often damp and a little hazy, glazed surfaces are out of place. Our climate demands matt surfaces, yielding quieter, gentler effects.

Some of the buildings of the last few decades show, especially in southern England, a renewed and very welcome awareness of the importance of texture. One has only to visit the Building Centre in London to see what a wide range of brick textures, as of colours, is now available. Some are pleasant, a few delightful; others are nauseous. Textures are now produced mechanically: bricks are given what is known as 'a rustic face' by the application, before firing, and only to one side and one end of each brick, of lightly incised striations, straight or wavy. Some people, no doubt, would regard such products as spurious, as in a sense they are; but where for economic reasons hand-moulded sand-faced bricks are out of the question, these artificially textured bricks may be the most acceptable substitute.

The texture of a building may owe far more to the dimensions of its bricks and to the way in which they are bonded than is sometimes realized. Very occasionally, one comes upon bricks which are the size of blocks of stone, as at Caversham, across the Thames from Reading, where at the end of the seventeenth century some measured 22 ins. long by 6 ins. broad. The 'great bricks', measuring $12 \times 6 \times 2$ ins., a speciality of Kent and Sussex, were used in the eighteenth century for pilasters and buttresses. But all these were freaks; since the thirteenth century, as observed earlier, the variations in the sizes in general use at different dates have been comparatively slight. Yet with so fine a mesh, a difference of only half an inch in the thickness of the bricks produces a marked effect visually. In Tudor times $9 \times 4\frac{1}{2} \times 2\frac{1}{4}$ ins. was somewhere near the average, and these dimensions—the width twice the height (or thickness), the length twice the width—are always pleasing. By the end of the seventeenth century, the average thickness had risen to $2\frac{1}{2}$ ins., and thereafter the measurements remained more or less constant until after 1784, when the brick tax was imposed. As the duty was payable per thousand bricks, sizes were at once increased, with bad results aesthetically: a thickness of 3 ins., and in the Midlands and North even $3\frac{1}{4}$ ins., which is very ungainly, became common. When at last the tax was repealed, in 1850, it was too late to retract. During the last hundred years small hand-moulded bricks only about 2 ins. thick have been used with beautiful textural effect for high-class work by architects of keen sensibility such as Lutyens; and in southern England one of the standard thicknesses for machine-moulded bricks is only $2\frac{5}{8}$ ins., which is visually acceptable. But in the North building with bricks measuring $8\frac{3}{4} \times 4\frac{3}{16} \times 2\frac{7}{8}$ ins. is still frequent, and these proportions are not so agreeable.

Bonding is the term used to describe the manner in which the bricks are arranged, and varying the bond is another excellent way of endowing a building with an interesting texture. When brick first came into use, bonding was usually quite irregular, and the appeal of old 'homespun' brickwork may owe not a little to this diversity. Where the courses do follow a regular pattern, it is always in these early buildings English bond—i.e. alternating courses of all headers (bricks laid with their ends to the wall-face) and all stretchers (those lying with their sides to the face of the wall) (256a). This bond remained general throughout the Tudor period, but under the Stuarts it gave place to Flemish (so called, although it is seldom found in Flanders), which comprises alternate headers and stretchers in the same course (255d). The change-over was very gradual; for example, the College of Matrons, a charming almshouse at Salisbury, was still keeping to English bond in 1682 (246d), more than half a century after the Flemish had been used throughout at Kew Palace. Since the end of the seventeenth century this has remained the favourite, while by no means the invariable, bond of English builders. For thin walls it is not in fact as strong

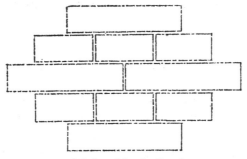

Fig. 3 English bond bricks 'breaking joint'

as English (because it involves more 'straight joints'); but it is both more ornamental and more economical, since in Flemish bond the proportion of stretchers is greater and fewer facing bricks are therefore required. Sometimes, to obtain a more interesting texture, for instance in a gable, the builder would 'break joint'. In every alternate stretcher course, that is to say, the joint would be moved half a brick to left or right (fig. 3): this is the distinguishing feature of English cross bond and of Dutch bond. There is of course no need to adhere to one bond throughout an entire elevation. Both English and Flemish can be seen, for example, on the front of Cromwell House, Highgate, and at Raynham Hall in Norfolk. Nowadays, because of the widespread preference for 11 in. cavity walls (i.e. $4\frac{1}{2} \times 4\frac{1}{2}$ ins., with a 2 in. cavity between, the two wall-faces being held together across the cavity with galvanized iron ties), buildings often show nothing but stretcher bond, apart from the headers at the quoins in alternate courses. Alas, the effect is always monotonous and dull. So no doubt would be houses faced entirely with headers, if we saw little else. In fact these are rare on account of the cost, so one always comes with pleasure upon a wall of headers, with its fine close mesh. There are several good examples in Hampshire, all, needless to say, from the Georgian period. One adorns the charming High Street at Lymington (245c); another is Church Hatch at the north entrance to the precincts of Christchurch Priory, a Georgian refronting of a seventeenth-century house. For obvious structural reasons, the most usual place to find only headers is in a curving wall.[1] Among other bonds which have been employed occasionally with bricks of one colour only may be mentioned English garden wall bond (three, or occasionally five, courses of stretchers to every one of headers) and Flemish garden wall bond (three stretchers to one header in each course); but

[1] The continuously curving or serpentine wall was a speciality of Suffolk; it is sometimes known as a crinkle-crankle. According to Mr. Norman Scarfe, there are forty-five of these walls, mostly late-Georgian, in Suffolk alone, and perhaps no more than twenty-six in all the other English counties. A notably fine example encloses the kitchen-garden at Heveningham Hall.

bonding also played an important part in the creation of ornamental two-colour patterns, to which we will now turn.

Ornamental Brickwork

Ornamental brickwork ranges from the simplest patterning to the most elaborate carving and moulding; and if the view advanced in this book is accepted, that the essential character of brick is homely, warm and intimate, it will come as no surprise to find that the less ambitious ornamental effects are often the best. What, in the right place, can be more charming than the arrangement of bricks in herring-bone patterns? To-day this is most commonly seen as a lining to slightly 'arty' open fireplaces, but formerly it was employed for the adornment of walls and chimney-shafts, and especially for nogging in conjunction with a timber framework, which will be considered in Chapter 12. Small bricks were the best for this purpose, and tiles also lend themselves readily to herring-bone patterns. Another simple but very effective example of patterning is afforded by the device known as brick tumbling. On end-walls and gables and sometimes at the base of chimney-stacks, the bricks would be laid diagonally to form a series of triangles, which were not only ornamental but practical also, as the bricks were laid at right angles to the slope of the roof and thereby provided a smooth base for the coping. This device, of which many examples can be seen in Holland, Belgium and Picardy, won considerable favour in the eastern counties from Kent to the East Riding of Yorkshire in the seventeenth, eighteenth and nineteenth centuries (fig. 4).

Fig. 4
Brick tumbling

The art of producing coloured patterns on wall-faces appears to have originated not in the Netherlands but in northern France, in the second quarter of the fifteenth century. It was taken up here soon afterwards, and a great many English buildings exhibit this kind of ornamentation in one form or another. Even when a builder was making, perhaps on the site, enough bricks for a single house only, he always had a choice of colours available as the bricks were not all burnt equally. Since the patterns were nearly always made with headers, the general practice at all periods was to select those bricks with the most heavily burnt ends. These might be grey, grey-blue, purple-blue, deep purple-red or nearly black; dark browns and reds were also used in some places. With flared bricks the stronger colour might only be skin deep. All that mattered was that these headers should be different in tone from the rest of the brickwork. In the Gault district of south Cambridgeshire and Bedfordshire, ordinary pink bricks, or sometimes bright orange-red, would give life to the familiar washed-out yellow. Heavily burnt bricks were usually rejected, especially in the Georgian period; very strong contrasts were not appreciated, for these made the pattern over-insistent. But much of the charm of Tudor patterning depends on the fact that the headers vary both in colour and in tone, as well as in the degree of their vitrification.[1]

In the very earliest English examples, Tattershall and Herstmonceux castles and Queens' College, Cambridge, the patterning is tentative and unconvincing. Bishop Waynflete's tower at Farnham Castle (*c.* 1470–75) shows the first important example of a regular all-over diaper, and very effective it is (*222*b). It was with the advent of the Tudors that ornamental patterning became fashionable; under Henry VIII there was scarcely a large brick building in eastern or southern England which did not incorporate sections of it, and here and there it persisted even into the Jacobean period, as at Kirstead Hall, Norfolk (1614). Easily the favourite pattern was the diamond; and a diaper of grey-blue diamonds, woven into the surface of a wall that is otherwise built of the small, mellow, red Tudor bricks, makes a delightful embellishment, as can be enjoyed at The Vyne (*245*a). Other patterns sometimes seen, particularly in Essex where they enjoyed special popularity, include the chequer, as on the gatehouse at Leez Priory, and the chevron, of which there is a bold example on the much grander tower at Layer Marney. A number of Essex churches also display this patterning. Seldom if ever was an entire wall covered with a consistent design, possibly because the supply of burnt ends was unpredictable and, on any given site, likely to be insufficient; but for Romantic architecture it may be felt that this was no disadvantage. Certainly the great fault of Victorian diapering (of which there is, needless to say, a great deal) is the impenitent regularity of the lattice pattern, carried out with machine-made bricks which do not vary by so much as a hair's breadth. For Londoners there is no easier place to see the difference between Tudor and Victorian diapering than the courtyard of Fulham Palace. The Tudor brickwork here has worn none too well, and the effect to-day is patchy, but the north-west, north-east and south-east ranges all preserve substantial parts of their pretty grey diaper patterns. The south-

1 In photographs blue or grey headers, if vitrified, often look paler than the brickwork that surrounds them, because of the light which they reflect.

west range is entirely Victorian and a model of how not to do it. The machine-made bricks, glazed above the doors, incorporate dark red diapers which look as different from their fellows as typing does from handwriting. (The tiled roofs present a similar contrast.)

In the matter of regularity, Georgian polychrome patterning strikes a happy medium between the two. As might be expected, the somewhat haphazard character of Tudor patterning and the preponderance of diagonal lines were not amenable to a more Classical style, which also called for something less intricate. The adoption of Flemish bond rendered it easy to produce an all-over chequer pattern, often with slightly flared grey headers, and throughout the eighteenth century this was the most popular form of polychrome patterning (245b and c). There are districts of England, as, for example, around Cranbrook in Kent, where almost every Georgian building down to the humblest cottage has its front faced with a simple diaper of blue headers and pink stretchers, and the effect is excellent. The restraint of the patterning is perfectly in tune with the character of the architecture. Where broader effects were desired, the usual way now was to insert complete panels of one colour into the face of another, the panel bricks often being of smoother texture and more finely jointed. Many other variations can be found. A charming example in Wiltshire is the front of The Moot at Downton, rebuilt in 1927 after a fire, but externally still a choice example of a William and Mary house. The brickwork of the slightly projecting central portion is wholly red, to which the rest of the front, faced with a chequer pattern of red stretchers and grey-blue headers, provides a gentle but effective foil. Here the limestone dressings and the white-painted woodwork add the strongest accents; the bricks and tiles, admirable as they are, supply the accompaniment.

References have already been made to the employment of red brick in combination with flint. The results are seldom very pleasing, but here and there, especially in Norfolk, flints were substituted for dark brick-ends to produce the desired chequers. When the flints are knapped and squared they serve very well. Ashlared limestone and sandstone have been very widely used to provide dressings for brick buildings, but seldom for flat patterning. An unusual example of brick making a chequer pattern with rough, unashlared stone occurs again in Norfolk: at Wallington Hall, close to Downham Market, the red brickwork at one end of the house was interspersed with lumps of the local brown carstone (222c: cf. p. 120). Patterns involving more than two colours, deliberately selected (as distinct from the delicate gradations mentioned above), usually look garish in England, where the weather is not right for them. The old builders were always well aware of this. It was above all William Butterfield who broke with tradition in this respect, with results which each may judge for himself.

One of the simplest effects of patterning results from the builder neglecting to fill in his putlog holes. A putlog (sometimes written putlock) is a short section of horizontal scaffolding, one end of which is inserted into the wall as it goes up. Putlog holes left open at regular intervals produce agreeable little accents of shadow upon a sunlit surface, as can often be seen in Italy; a famous example is the Torre del Mángia at Siena. Here in England the climate is an obstacle, and in buildings intended for domestic use the putlog holes have always been filled in with additional bricks or half-bricks as the scaffolding is taken down. It is in the walls of old barns that this agreeable form of patterning can still from time to time be found.

So far we have only been concerned with flat patterns, but raised decoration has also been a feature of English brickwork at every period. This did not necessarily call for the production of special bricks. The strapwork patterns which were popular under the Stuarts, for instance, could be achieved without difficulty by laying ordinary bricks with a projection of about an inch, to form ovals, circles, squares and so on. In the seventeenth and eighteenth centuries rustication was widely employed in brick architecture as in stone, and apart from the chamfering of some of the edges, this also did not call for specially prepared bricks. Although the purpose of rustication was usually to play down the smallness of the individual brick unit in a search for bolder effects of scale, this, too, is a form of surface patterning (255c). Among other simple but agreeable effects produced with ordinary bricks were dentilation (a course of headers with every alternate one projecting) and a variety of 'dog-tooth' achieved by laying the bricks diagonally, to produce a serrated edge; both these can be very effective in the topmost course of a wall, under the eaves or the cornice (262b). Various other raised patterns in monochrome brickwork have been in favour at different times and in particular localities, such as the panels of diamonds, their centres once whitened, which are occasionally to be seen on seventeenth-century houses in south Lancashire.

There were many requirements, however, which could only be met by the preparation of special bricks. These would clearly be necessary for highly individual features like the array of little brick columns which surround the chimney-stacks, and the frame of the niche over the front door, of The Old House, Blandford (255c). But such architectural members as window-mullions and transoms, labels, wall- and gable-copings, and, after the advent of the Renaissance, architraves for windows and doors, string-courses, pilasters, cornices, pediments—all these, and many other such refinements, although not ornamental in any elaborate sense, were an essential part of the design of every building. And all might be carried out in brick, as on the fine porch (c. 1586) of Flemings Hall at Bedingfield in Suffolk (255a). Such features called for special techniques, of which the chief were moulding, cutting and rubbing.

ENRICHMENT OF BRICK SURFACES BY MOULDING AND CARVING
a. *Flemings Hall, Bedingfield, Suffolk*   b. *Cromwell House, Highgate, London*
c. *The Old House, Blandford, Dorset* (Country Life Photo)   d. *Westwell, Tenterden, Kent*

Moulding was the usual method, because it was the least expensive, where a quantity of bricks of exactly the same section was required. The moulds were of wood and might be quite complicated. Bricks formed in this fashion are sometimes referred to as 'purpose-moulded'. A distinguished example of moulded brickwork (of *c.* 1637–40), easily access-ible to Londoners, is Cromwell House, Highgate (255b). The elaboration of mouldings around the windows and especially at the cornices is profuse, yet admirably disciplined: a marked advance aesthetically on Kew Palace. Often, however, it was not worth while making a special mould. When that was the case the hard bricks were roughly shaped with a brick-axe, a tool which is still sometimes used. Burnt clay is comparatively brittle, and will fracture quite easily if struck with force. Rough and jagged edges were then rubbed smooth with the aid of a piece of hard stone. For the more refined gauged work, there were the softer 'rubbing-bricks' already described, which lent themselves not only to rubbing but, when required, to the most sophisticated carving.

Even before the appearance of these softer bricks, considerable elaboration was some-times achieved, notably in East Anglia, and especially during the reign of Henry VIII. There were isolated instances well before the advent of the Tudors, such as that elegant cusped trefoil over the hospital doorway at Ewelme. Corbels formed of cusped trefoils, also moulded, appeared on some of the grand ceremonial gatehouses, as at Oxburgh (221b). Bands of purely ornamental trefoils and quatrefoils in panels adorn a number of early Tudor buildings in Suffolk (256a). Pinnacles with moulded crockets, carved finials, and even, on the gatehouse of the much restored Manor House at East Barsham in central Norfolk, a complete coat of arms in brickwork carved *in situ*, were not beyond the skill of these Tudor craftsmen (256b). Not all this work is pleasing. Sometimes specially large bricks, rising through several courses, were introduced, as for this coat of arms, and as can be seen on the central finial at Giffords Hall, Stoke-by-Nayland (256a). Usually these do not look well.

A few Tudor builders resorted to terracotta for their most elaborate ornamentation. This term (from the Latin, *terra cocta* = cooked earth) is applied somewhat loosely to any workable clay of fine consistency that can be fired, when mixed with sand, to a hardness and compactness not usually reached by brick. (Strictly speaking, it only becomes terra-cotta on emerging from the kiln.) The colour of unglazed terracotta varies in accordance with that of its clay: red, brown, biscuit and creamy-white are usual. It was widely favoured in Italy, both in close relationship with brick and also quite independently, by some of the sculptors. In England, until the Doulton era, it was very little used in con-junction with brickwork except during the Tudor period, and even on Tudor buildings it is not common. It varies a good deal from place to place. Sometimes, as at Sutton Place near Guildford, where it was employed lavishly to face turrets, enrich parapets and form

EARLY TUDOR ORNAMENTAL BRICKWORK IN EAST ANGLIA
  a. *Giffords Hall, Stoke-by-Nayland, Suffolk*
  b. *East Barsham Manor House, Norfolk*

the window-frames, it is quite clearly different from brickwork, and looks much more like a substitute for stone. This is also true of the very elaborate terracotta enrichment at Layer Marney (*262a*), where the craftsmen again seem likely to have been Italians. The intricate arabesque scrollwork and other Renaissance motifs on these two buildings, all moulded before the firing in biscuit-coloured terracotta, would have been impossible in coarse-bodied Tudor brick. Two and a half centuries later, architects and builders had at their disposal another remarkable species of terracotta in the form of Coade's artificial stone. This has no visual connection with brickwork and it has seemed best to group it with the patent stuccos in Chapter 14. But in other places it is not always easy to say exactly where brick ceases and terracotta begins.

The greatest elaboration of ornamental brickwork proper (that is to say, not terracotta) was achieved between 1660 and 1760, when prodigies of carving might be performed. The process involved very careful cutting, usually *in situ*, with wire-saws, files, and some-times strips of copper; and much gentle abrasion. The fronts of two fine Queen Anne houses in the South-East, Westwell at Tenterden (*255d*) and Pallant House at Chichester (*262b*), illustrate some of the typical refinements. At Westwell special attention was devoted to the aprons under the first floor windows, to the central window-head and the panels on the parapet. At Pallant House all the window-heads were exquisitely gauged and given a carved emblem at the centre, while on the parapet the heads of the sunk panels seem 'gathered' like a textile. To such consummate craftsmen elegances like these, and items in the Classical vocabulary such as egg and dart mouldings and Ionic capitals, presented no great difficulties. But the patience and skill needed to carve in brick a group of *putti*, a swag of fruit and flowers, or a Corinthian capital with all its acanthus leaves can well be imagined. Yet all these motifs, and others no less ambitious, are occasionally to be found. A very grand window pediment from a demolished William and Mary house at Enfield, which Lloyd regarded as perhaps the finest example of all, is preserved in the West Hall of the Victoria and Albert Museum. It embodies a pair of swags, two delicious *amorini*, and four large and handsome capitals, carved and gauged, together with much moulded brick.

It has unfortunately been necessary to make some harsh criticisms of Victorian brick-work in this chapter. This is therefore the place to offer some amends by adding that there is a profusion of carved brick ornamentation, dating from the last quarter of the nineteenth century, at Newnham College, Cambridge, much of which is of admirable quality. The architect was Basil Champneys. A characteristic which the flowers and fruit, the masks and finials, the Ionic columns and pilasters of Newnham College share with almost all the ornamental carved brick of the great period is that fine joints can be seen passing along and rising through them. Aesthetically this is important, for their identity with the buildings of which they are a part is thereby established; the spectator is left in no doubt that these enrichments are physically part and parcel of the fabric.

Brick Chimneys

The brickmaker had an important part to play in the construction of chimneys, especially in Tudor and Stuart times, and it was here, one often feels, that he enjoyed himself most. Here at last the stonemason could be outdistanced. Examples can be seen in many parts of the country of stone-built houses (reference has already been made on p. 227 to Malmesbury) with chimneys of brick.

Small houses and cottages seldom had chimneys before the time of Elizabeth I and, when they did appear, they were often only crude erections constructed of unfired clay. But for the larger houses brick chimney shafts were already regarded as a necessity in East Anglia by about 1450; elsewhere the demand for them began about half a century later. During the sixteenth and seventeenth centuries, in the South-East, East Anglia and the 'black and white' counties of the west and north-west Midlands, many brick chimneys were built into timber-framed houses of earlier date. For structural reasons these often had to be placed in the centre of the house, which was aesthetically very fortunate, for a well-built chimney-stack, centrally placed, can endow even quite a small house with unexpected dignity. Examples are specially numerous in the three south-eastern counties (*277c, 334c*) and in Suffolk (*342b*), and are almost always an asset.

The reason for this outburst of brick chimney-building was primarily practical: fire in the Middle Ages was an ever-present danger, and it was found that brick resisted heat better than almost any stone. Yet it will not be forgotten that the reign of Henry VIII was a very showy age, and chimney builders were not slow to seize upon the opportunities for high-spirited display presented by a feature of such prominence. Shafts which had begun by rising singly were soon being grouped in pairs, fours, sixes, eights and even, at East Barsham Manor, tens (*256b*). These exuberant clusters rise from well-moulded bases, and the shafts assume many forms: they may be octagonal (*261a*), hexagonal, square, circular, fluted, reeded (*256a*), or, strangest of all, spiral (*261b* and *c*). Their surfaces, moreover, are enriched with a wide variety of raised designs, embracing chevrons and zigzags, diamonds and honeycombs, lozenges and quatrefoils, even *fleurs de lis*, Tudor roses and other heraldic badges (*261c, d* and *e*). Most of this decoration was made piece by piece in moulds and fitted together as the chimney-stack went up. For very elaborate designs recourse was again had to terracotta, as at East Barsham, or the pattern might occasionally be cut *in situ* on the surface of the shaft. To render such complexities called for a very high standard of craftsmanship, which was not lacking. Skilled chimney builders were sometimes called upon to journey far afield.

Most shafts have at their upper end a projecting ring known as the necking, a fillet which, like the annulet at the top of a Classical column, is valuable as a 'punctuation mark'. Then they are all linked together by caps which are often of extraordinary intricacy. These caps are always corbelled out, frequently in several steps; and for the over-sailing courses, as for the necking, specially thin bricks or sometimes tiles are employed, to avoid any undue heaviness. Here moulded bricks are also the rule. Among many different designs, perhaps the scalloped octagon is the most fascinating, most of all when projecting 'spurs' of thin brick or tile are added at the angles (*261e*).

These effusive, fanciful chimney-stacks were a purely English development with which there is nothing comparable elsewhere. They were invariably carried out in red brick, even where, as at Hengrave Hall, the rest of the house was of stone and pale yellow brick. The great majority are in East Anglia, where the right materials were at hand and where men were rich enough at this time to indulge in such glorious extravagances. But a few of the best known and earliest are elsewhere. Hampton Court had a large array of such chimneys soon after 1515, and at Thornbury Castle in Gloucestershire two remarkable triple clusters in brick were raised as early as 1514. The illustration (*261c*) shows the stack on the south front. That on the north is less pleasing but more celebrated, on account of the shields of arms in terracotta and the knot, the badge of the Staffords, in brick, emblazoned on two of the shafts. (Both look rebuilt, and the present caps lack conviction.) It is significant that these two famous stacks should be in red brick, on a building where everything else is of limestone and in a part of the country where no other brickwork of so early a date is known. Here indeed is another striking indication of the social status of brick in the sixteenth century, when even so grand a builder as the Duke of Buckingham went out of his way to introduce it on to his roof for its decorative possibilities.

This ebullition of Tudor magnificence was, however, short-lived: it hardly outlasted the reign of Henry VIII. It is also necessary to add that most of these chimney-stacks have not been able to withstand unscathed more than four centuries of exposure to the elements. Many have needed restoration: not a few, including nearly all those at Hampton Court, have had to be completely rebuilt.

In some of the smaller houses of this period, such as The Cliftons at Clare, Suffolk (*261e*), there is a conspicuous contrast between the scale and elaboration of the chimney-stack and the simplicity and plainness of the rest of the building. Farther south this does

TUDOR CHIMNEY-STACKS
a. *Court Farm, Sollers Hope, Herefordshire*   b. *Layer Marney Hall, Essex*   c. *Thornbury Castle, Gloucestershire*
d. *St. Osyth's Priory, Essex*   e. *The Cliftons, Clare, Suffolk*

not occur because here the chimneys, although often lofty and of admirable proportions, are usually much plainer, moulded and carved bricks being seldom employed. During the reign of Elizabeth I such restraint became general for smaller houses, even in East Anglia. (This was the time when some of the stone-built mansions were resorting to chimney-shafts in the form of Classical columns with little pieces of entablature perched on top to serve as caps: not one of our happiest architectural fashions.)

In the seventeenth century taste changed again; there was now a fashion for setting the chimney-shafts, whether of brick or stone (*39a, 74d*), anglewise to their base. In brick a characteristic example can be seen in Sussex at Bateman's, Burwash, the home of Rudyard Kipling; this is a stone house of 1634 with a range of six lofty chimneys in red brick, arranged diagonally to the axis of the roof. Burwash also has a good example of the next development. This was the grouping of several flues into a single massive stack having long sunk panels and a boldly projecting cornice: the essence of architectural dignity. A pair of these are the dominant feature of the fine William and Mary house known as Rampyndene, a timber-framed building faced with bricks and hung tiles and with a lofty tiled roof. Another pair, of simpler and less striking design but not undignified, can be seen at Bradbourne (*240a*). The only flaw in both cases is the addition, in comparatively modern times, of chimney-pots.

These hardly seem to have been made before the early years of the eighteenth century, and at that time probably only in France. In stone districts the draught was sometimes 'improved' by simple devices such as tilting two slabs of stone against one another over the top of the shaft (*107c, 147a, 168a*) or raising a single slab on four corner supports (*198a*). All these might be regarded as the workaday heirs of the picturesque Gothic louvre, which was perched directly upon the roof; a reminiscence of the louvre, transferred to the top of an unusual stone shaft, can still be seen at Thornbury Castle (*261c*). Another common practice in the stone areas was to crown a stack with four thin, wedge-shaped slabs set at converging angles, either with pointed tops, as at Snowshill (*83a*), or more commonly cut to form a pyramid with the apex sliced off. Bath in the eighteenth century had many stacks crowned with these hollow truncated pyramids of stone. When under George III chimney-pots first started to become popular in England, good craftsmen took care to sink them within the flues so that they did not project more than about 2 ins., and were therefore invisible from directly below. This excellent practice is still sometimes followed to-day, but much less often than it might be, for it is fully consonant with both the essentials of good chimney construction, which are to reduce the size of the aperture at the top of the flue, and to contrive that the wind shall not blow across a horizontal plane but impinge against an edge.

ORNAMENTATION IN TERRACOTTA
   a. *Layer Marney Hall, Essex*

SUBTLETIES IN GAUGED BRICKWORK
   b. *Pallant House, Chichester, Sussex*
15+*P.E.B.

Tennyson was asking in 1830

> *Why the church is with a steeple built;*
> *And the house with a chimneypot?*[1]

But the large-scale introduction of these pots did not occur until the Victorian period, and was probably due to the widespread adoption of the Victorian kind of grate in place of the basket and hob types generally favoured in Georgian houses. Doultons' were making them from the eighteen-fifties and perhaps slightly earlier (the exact date has not been established), but the large majority were produced at the local brickworks. Tough clays made the best pots, and in time they became something of a Midlands speciality: great numbers were made in south and west Leicestershire and at Nuneaton. Presently 'tall boys' which could be as much as 7 ft. 6 ins. long were placed upon the market; perched on high shafts, these always look incongruous (*399*b). The special economic attraction of these elongated pots was that they could be used as substitutes for lofty stacks. Countless thousands of pots were added to existing stacks in the nineteenth century. The most acceptable, aesthetically, are those pots, often on small houses, which have been treated as an architectural feature (*284*d, *350*c). If large houses must have them uniform sets should be disposed symmetrically, as at Wootton Lodge (*123*a), although we may perhaps be thankful that castellated pots, such as these, were too expensive to command a wider currency. Some pots are a rich orange-red, an excellent colour in the right place; and there is a gay impudence about some congregations which can be rather endearing. Alas, these are the exceptions; the usual pot is an excrescence (*73*a, *84*a, *129*c, *148*a, *198*b, *267*d). Apart perhaps from a tangle of television aerials, nothing can do more to destroy the grace of a skyline than a prominent assemblage of pots and cowls; and I suspect that there are many people who may not have realized how much they could improve the appearance of their house by asking a builder to sink or remove these anomalous objects. In the United States, even on houses of the Colonial and Federal periods, chimney-pots are hardly ever seen, to their undoubted artistic advantage. On stone buildings square pots, with strong lips and if possible stone-coloured, are undoubtedly the best (*45*b, *90*b), but even these are generally out of character; and despite the identity of material, on a building with any pretension to style chimney-pots are usually little more acceptable in the company of brick and tile.[2]

1 *The 'How' and the 'Why'*, from *The Suppressed Poems of Alfred Lord Tennyson:* ed. by J. C. Thomson (1910).
2 A few people, I have found, disagree with this view. For them a bedside book has already appeared: *Chimney Pots and Stacks*, by Valentine Fletcher (1968), in which I am duly reproved.

10

TILES

Tiles, whether intended for roofing or as a covering for walls, have always had much in common with bricks. They are usually made at brick kilns; in fact it was formerly essential to fire bricks and tiles together, for those tiles exposed to the greatest heat would have warped, and banks of bricks were therefore arranged to shield them. For roofing tiles most of the better kinds of brickmakers' clay are suitable. The clay is baked harder, and the mix more carefully prepared: tiles are more uniform than bricks in both colour and texture. As with brickmaking, the production of tiles before the Industrial Revolution was highly localized. Now and again a place with the right clay and well situated for water transport, such as Woolwich in the later Middle Ages, might build up a flourishing little industry; but wherever the clay was good enough, a brick-field usually made its own tiles in sufficient quantities to satisfy local needs and no more. Sometimes these brick-fields were very small indeed, perhaps only supplying the materials for a single house.

The Romans used baked clay tiles for roofing in England, if less extensively than elsewhere; and, as we have noted, their bricks were often very little thicker than to-day's tiles. When tile-making began again in this country is not known for certain. In the Middle Ages the usual roofing material in the non-stone areas was thatch, with wooden shingles as a less common but important alternative. The first plain tiles were probably copies, in clay, of shingles. It is certain that their manufacture became widespread long before that of bricks. John Stow, in his *Survey of London*, published in 1598, cites the following passage from *A Description of the Most Noble City of London*, written by William Fitzstephen at the end of the twelfth century: '. . . As for prevention of casualties by fire, the houses in this city being then built all of timber, and covered with thatch of straw or reed, it was long since thought good policy in our forefathers wisely to provide, namely, in the year of Christ 1189 . . . that all men in this city should build their houses of stone up to a certain height, and to cover them with slate or baked tile; since which time, thanks be given to God, there hath not happened the like often consuming fires in this city as afore.'[1] A little later came the well-known Ordinance of 1212 specifically prohibiting the use of thatch

1 See C. G. Dobson, *Historical Notes on the Langley Museum of Roofing Materials* (1960), p. 14.

for roofing in London, and mentioning the available alternatives, which were shingles, lead, stone slates and tiles.

The spread of tile-making into at least fourteen counties of eastern and south-eastern England before the end of the thirteenth century is confirmed both by archaeological evidence and by the incidence of such surnames as Tiler, Tyler and Telwright.[1] To these counties can be added, in the second quarter of the fourteenth century, Somerset, the only one in the West that produced tiles in the Middle Ages. In places in which the clays were suitable, such as Nottingham, Coventry, Newbury and around Penn in Buckinghamshire, earthenware vessels, plain roofing-tiles, ridge-tiles and floor-tiles were all made by the same firm or individuals. Baked clay floor-tiles for internal use were produced on a considerable scale in England between the twelfth and the sixteenth centuries, but especially in the thirteenth and fourteenth. They were made of red clay mixed with sand and were sometimes given an ornamental inlay. For this the process was to carve a design in relief on a flat wooden block, which was then impressed upon the surface of the tile while the clay was still moist, the matrix being filled with white clay which turned yellow when glazed. Later it was discovered that by dipping the stamping block into white slip the pattern could be printed on to the surface in a single operation; but this method was not so durable. Sometimes the design on each tile was complete in itself; others were intended to be laid in groups of four or sixteen. Although they were glazed, the temperature of firing was low (seldom above 800°F.) and they had to meet the common wear and tear of floors, so the large majority perished long ago. The best domestic pavement to have survived was found during excavations in 1935 in the Queen's Chamber of Clarendon Palace near Salisbury. It dates from 1250–52, and is now in the British Museum. The undercroft of Clifton House at King's Lynn has two good tile floors of the early fourteenth century: a fairly recent discovery. The two most famous groups, both dating from the thirteenth century, are those on the floor of Westminster Abbey Chapter House (partly renewed) and those from Chertsey Abbey, now also in the British Museum. But to see much the largest surviving expanse of what may be regarded as the normal English church floor of the Middle Ages, one should go to the retro-choir of Winchester Cathedral.

In the fifteenth century another Benedictine monastery noted for the manufacture of tiles was Great Malvern in Worcestershire. The Priory church there has, behind the high altar, the only mediaeval wall-tiles in England. The colours, pink and golden brown, are most attractive, and there are nearly a hundred different designs, some in sets of four. Encaustic floor-tiles were also made in the fifteenth century at Barnstaple.

1 Cf. C. W. Bardsley, *A Dictionary of English and Welsh Surnames* (1901); P. H. Reaney, *A Dictionary of British Surnames* (1958).

BRICK-TILES
a. *Keere Street, Lewes, Sussex* b. *'The Railway Arms', Croydon* c. *Westgate House, Lewes*
d. *Patcham Place, near Brighton, Sussex*

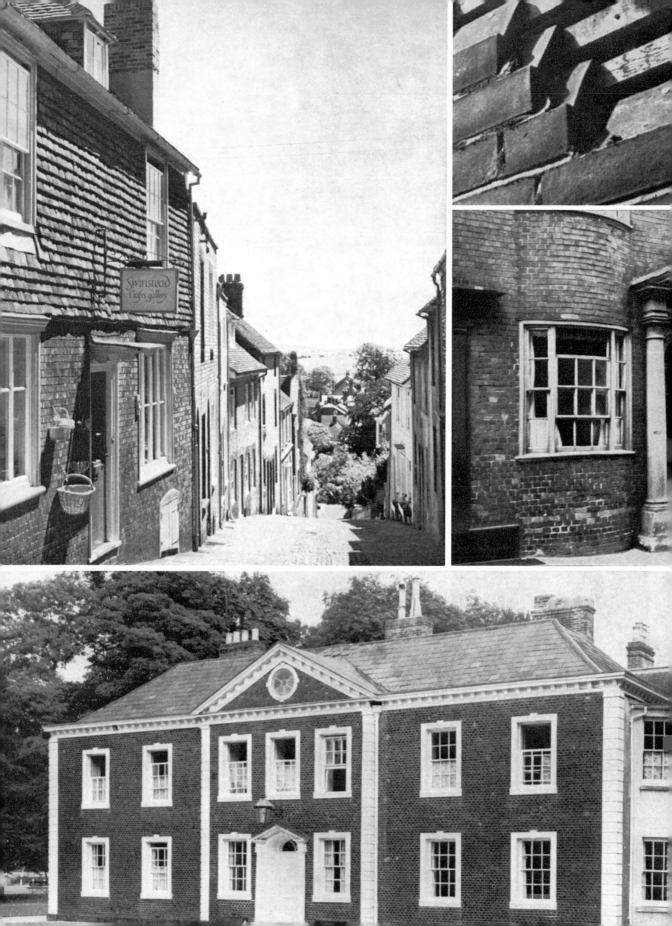

Many of the floor-tiles appear to have been the work of itinerant tilers who carried their patterned stamps with them and set up a local kiln at an abbey or at any other place where their services were needed. The designs varied considerably in style and quality, as did the tiles themselves in size. In roof-tiles there was also, in the early days, a complete absence of standardization. By 1300 it was not unusual for the better kind of house (that is to say, from the smaller manor house upwards) in the East and South-East to have a tiled roof; but, even allowing for the fact that some of these tiles were importations from Flanders, the variations were manifold. No doubt it was the inconvenience of this which prompted, in 1477, the statute of Edward IV that laid down precise methods for the preparation of the clay and standard dimensions, which were to be $10\frac{1}{2} \times 6\frac{1}{4} \times \frac{5}{8}$ ins. Whether the Act did much to improve the situation is doubtful, partly because with wood-fired kilns they were unable to regulate their temperatures with any degree of accuracy, so that underburnt tiles emerged from the firing too large and overburnt ones too small. Furthermore, local traditions died hard. For centuries plain tiles measured 9×6 ins. in Kent. In Sussex, on the other hand, the width was often $6\frac{3}{4}$ ins., while in Leicestershire most plain tiles have always measured 11×7 ins., and still do. Before the statute of George I, in 1725, reaffirmed the measurements laid down in 1477, the average size of a plain tile had diminished a little, to about $9\frac{1}{2} \times 5\frac{3}{4}$ ins. $\times \frac{1}{2}$ in. To-day $10\frac{1}{2} \times 6\frac{1}{2}$ ins. $\times \frac{1}{2}$ in. is the standard size.

References to mediaeval tile-manufacture beyond the limestone belt are scarce. It is recorded that there were tile-makers in Worcester in 1467 and that Nottingham saw its first tiled roof in 1503; but even under Elizabeth I it is probable that in the West and North thatch, stone slates, shingles and lead were all more commonly employed for roofing than tiles. Later the situation changed, and by 1830, largely owing to the making of the canals, Staffordshire and Shropshire had become two of our most important tile-producing counties. But except near the East Coast, the North still held back. Once again, in fact, we find the *genius loci* asserting itself. For there can be no question that 'tiles harmonize less well in the landscape where stone and slate are the material below the soil'.[1] One of the many who have recognized the truth of this was Thomas Gray. 'Not a single red tile', he wrote in his Journal in 1769 on first seeing Grasmere, 'no flaring gentleman's house or garden walls, break in upon the repose of this unsuspected paradise.' Since that time many parts of the North have been assailed by incongruous reds. Lancashire contracted a rash of bright red brick during the Victorian period, but at that time the usual roofing material was Welsh slate. This is certainly depressing, yet the

1 *The Architectural Use of Building Materials* (Ministry of Works, 1946), p. 32.

TILING, BRICK AND SANDSTONE IN THE SOUTH-EAST
Witley, Surrey

appearance in the present century of entire hillsides of red and pink roofs has been a still greater visual misfortune. In the hillier parts of Lancashire, tiles often look completely out of place—wrong in colour, wrong in texture, and wrong in scale; but this has in no way inhibited the widespread incursion, on grounds of cheapness, of smooth-faced machine-pressed tiles of altogether wretched aesthetic quality into places where they will never 'settle into the landscape'.

In recent years, with tiles as with bricks, great improvements have been made in the field of machine-production, and the best machine-made tiles, which are not flat but slightly cambered, are in attractive colours and quite satisfying in their appearance. Even concrete tiles are now acceptable. These, first made in Southern Bavaria as far back as the eighteen-forties, did not appear in England until 1893 (at Canterbury). They are now being made on a very large scale wherever the sand is suitable, which is in perhaps half the counties of England. About seven out of every ten tiles now made in this country are concrete, and some pleasant colours, notably greys and browns, are readily available. The colours of some concrete tiles have, it is true, proved fugitive, but it is believed that this weakness has now been overcome.

Happily, however, the making of sand-faced plain tiles by hand, although expensive, is not yet extinct. Few people, I imagine, would have them for choice on a stone building, but in combination with brick, tile-hung walls, or half-timbering either exposed or wholly coated with plaster, no roof-covering is more appropriate, and none at its best more beautiful.

Plain tiles, like slates, do not overlap their neighbours in the same course; so, in order to prevent water seepage, there must always be two thicknesses of tile over every part of the roof, and in the downward direction therefore, each course overlaps not merely the next course, but also the next course but one below it. Hence the term 'double-lap' tiles. In addition, for complete weather-proofing the tiles would usually be torched (pointed with mortar from underneath) or provided with some sort of lining. Modern practice favours a bitumen-filled felt which is very strong and virtually untearable, even with no supporting boards. The felt is fixed above the rafters and below the horizontally-running battens upon which the tiles are laid.

Slight variations in the size and shape of plain tiles, even if only as the outcome of rough workmanship, can be a great advantage aesthetically (*268*). Formerly, tiles were hung not, as is usual to-day, on sawn battens, but on riven oak laths which were seldom absolutely straight. Attachment was generally, as with stone slates, by means of small oak pegs driven through holes and hooked over the laths. Towards the end of the nineteenth century it became the general practice to provide tiles of every kind, before firing, with a small projecting clay hook on the underside known as a nib[1]; to-day practically all tiles are nibbed, and every fifth course—in better-class work, and always in windy places and on roofs with a pitch above 50°, every third course—will also be nailed. Good hand-made plain tiles always have a gently cambered surface, generally in both directions. ✻ This has practical advantages: the tiles lie better, conforming more readily to the minor irregularities of a timber roof, particularly on old examples; and since with the double camber the bottom corners of each tile repose on the centres of the two below, rain-water is led away from the vertical joints. Moreover, a roof composed of gently cambered tiles will be sensitive to light and shade as a dead flat roof can never be. Undulations may also be due to the sagging or warping of laths or rafters, or to the settlement of walls. Within reasonable limits, such irregularities are visually an asset (*239a, 277a, 334c*).

The addition of sand is with many clays a practical necessity, since without it the clay will be liable to stick to the mould. Aesthetically the introduction of sand, for tiles as for bricks, is also of great value, because of its ability to produce, upon firing, a pleasing texture. The usual procedure is to sprinkle both the mould and the unfired clay with coarse sand. A further attraction of sand-faced tiles is their amenability, under the right conditions, to mosses and lichens, which will not grow on smooth, dense surfaces. These natural growths, so long as they do not become excessive, serve to add still further textural and colour interest to a roof.

Colours, as with bricks, depend principally upon the composition of the clay. The ✻ Gault, for example, which in certain places is responsible for the local bricks being not red but pale yellow or dun-coloured, yields tiles of a similar hue, of which there are many examples around Cambridge. A speciality of Huntingdonshire and the western part of Cambridgeshire is the roof of variegated colours: yellows, browns, reds, pinks, greys—all in rather soft, pale shades. The tiles on these roofs are arranged haphazard and, as can be seen on many houses in the Cambridgeshire villages of Elsworth and Eltisley, their somewhat tweedy look is not unattractive. In southern Staffordshire the clay which produced the well-known blue bricks has also furnished the material for limited numbers of blue tiles. The very large majority of tiles, however, as of bricks, are some shade of red. In the right context, a roof of rippling red tiles affords unalloyed pleasure. The finest reds are to be seen in Kent and Sussex. The least enjoyable are the products of those Carbonaceous clays of the North Midlands and North to which reference was made in the preceding chapter. William Morris had a special aversion to the tiles made at Broseley, near Ironbridge in Shropshire: and with good reason.

[1] Nibbed tiles had very occasionally been made long before this; examples were found a few years ago in fourteenth-century kilns excavated at Boston, Lincolnshire.

In the last hundred years, and especially during the present century, there can be no doubt that red tiles have been employed in this country to excess. Usually, like bricks, they are no longer made from the local clays, so that the tiles on a street of houses, brought from different sources, do not harmonize with each other. They have also appeared in association with materials with which they can command no visual sympathy. On a building constructed of a rather yellow stone, like the abbey church at Pershore, they are far from pleasing. In combination with red sandstone they are even less appropriate. Ever since the fifteenth century plain red tiles have occasionally been used for church roofs in East Anglia and in the south-eastern counties as an alternative to thatch, in villages which could not afford lead. But when seen on old stone churches, such tiles are usually a Victorian or modern introduction for reasons of economy, and, especially when machine-made, they are unwelcome. F. G. Brabant, compiling in 1905 the *Little Guide* to Oxford-shire, observed that the church of Berrick Salome 'was restored in 1889, when the liberal use of timber and red tiles gave it a strange unecclesiastical appearance'. They look particularly incongruous on ancient spires.

With tiles, as with stone slates, an important aesthetic factor is the pitch of the roof. An angle of exactly 45° is for some reason ineffably dull: Lutyens termed it 'the ugly angle', and he was right. Plain tiles can be laid at 40° and pantiles at somewhat less, but for plain tiles a steeper angle than 45° is nearly always more pleasing (*277c, 349a*). As with Cotswold stone, the most distinguished tiled roofs will generally be found to have a pitch of between 50° and 60°. When, as sometimes occurs in Essex, Sussex and especially Kent, an old tiled roof is carried down to within a few feet of the ground, the effect can be memorable (*277a*); these gently billowing eider-downs of mellow terracotta red offer an experience of colour and texture of quite exceptional richness.[1] On some tiled roofs a slight change of pitch is noticeable towards the base: the fall becomes gentler and the eaves often correspondingly deeper. This was achieved by attaching to the rafters, near their lower ends, additional lengths of wood set at a shallower pitch, known as sprocket-pieces. The effect can be well seen on the gable at Kersey in the foreground of plate *349a*. The justification for this device was once again practical as well as aesthetic, for it provided a slight check on the flow of rain-water just where it might splash over the gutter. Visually it is particularly successful on buildings of somewhat formal character, such as Wolvesey Palace, Winchester, or Moyles Court near Ringwood, a pleasant 'middling' house of about 1655. To this kind of building sprocketing, as it is called, always adds a

---

1 They are familiarly known in the Wealden villages as 'cat-slide' roofs. Some of Lutyens's own most memorable roofs, like those at Folly Farm, Sulhamstead, were certainly inspired by them.

touch of distinction.[1] A mansard roof is contrived on the opposite principle: the pitch of the upper part is shallow, of the lower part—which may of course also be sprocketed, as in the Georgian example near Tenterden (334b)—rather steep. In this instance the roof is well proportioned and pleasing, but all too often with modern mansard roofs the lower slope is nearly vertical and the dormer windows too large, which is aesthetically unsatisfactory. This form of roof was a French invention, and little regret need, perhaps, be felt that, except in the eastern counties, especially Lincolnshire and the Fens, where most of the older examples occur, it has never been very popular in England.

In a variety of ways the tilers followed the traditional practices of the stone slaters. One was in the making of swept and laced valleys (see p. 102). These require time and skill and are therefore seldom seen on the roofs of to-day, but are always an asset. A valley (that is to say, the sloping angle formed by the meeting, generally at right angles, of two parts of a pitched roof) is nowadays usually leaded or, preferably, covered with tiles specially made for the purpose (278c). The angles of hipped roofs also require special tiles, known as saddle-backs or bonnets. The old 'granny' bonnet hip tiles, bedded in mortar, each with an assured 'lift', can give great charm to a roof (278b, 334c). So can another type made for a special purpose: the ridge tiles. These are sometimes designed to come up nearly to a point, but better effects are obtained with half-round or 'hog-back' tiles of generous proportions. Such tiles, also bedded in mortar, provide a simple but strong point of culmination for many of our most beautiful roofs (277c). Ridge tiles have been made in England at least since the fourteenth century. Dr. Salzman has recorded a few early examples of more or less elaborate cresting.[2] On some later buildings, one can see old ridge tiles that have been thumb-pinched to produce a wavy, slightly comb-like effect which can be pleasing; minor additions of the sixteenth and seventeenth centuries at Winchester College offer examples. But often absolutely plain ridges, with a slight upward tilt at the ends, are preferable. The addiction to serration and other forms of fussy cresting, usually carried out in terracotta, is a particularly irritating manifestation of Victorian taste; it occurs not infrequently on church roofs as well as on old houses restored in the later nineteenth century, such as Sawston Hall in Cambridgeshire.

---

1 Sprockets were not confined to tiled roofs. Among examples illustrated, they were used for stone-covered roofs at Snowshill (83a), Mickleton (83b) and The Old House, Blandford (255c). They were also employed in conjunction with slate, as at Eltham Lodge (c. 1664).

2 See *Building in England down to 1540*, p. 231.

Spanish and Roman Tiles

The plain roofing tile, the commonest form in England, is almost unknown in some countries, where other quite different types were developed. In Mediterranean countries, including the southern part of France, the normal kind is what is known here as the Spanish tile, which resembles our ridge tile except that it is tapered along its length. It is said to have acquired this form by having originally been shaped round the thigh. Later it was made with a potter's wheel in the form of a tapered cylinder which was split lengthwise to produce two tiles; but to-day it is usually moulded. It was introduced into Europe through Spain by the Moors in the seventh or eighth century. Each course of tiles is laid with the convex and concave surfaces facing upwards in alternation, producing the effect which has caused these tiles to be widely known as overs-and-unders. They were originally bedded in mud; to-day they are usually laid in mortar and nailed. The practical advantage of using these rounded tiles is that they can be laid upon roofs of very shallow pitch. Aesthetically they are extremely satisfactory, the convex surfaces yielding a strong texture, very sensitive to contrasts of light and shade. Nevertheless, such tiles are clearly unsuited to the roofing of gables, hips, dormers and the often complicated pattern of an English roof, and were not used here before the latter part of the nineteenth century. An outstandingly good example is County Hall, London, where the high roof has a boldness of scale and a textural interest which tiles of no other type could have given it.

The Romans, in England as elsewhere, were in the habit of using rounded tiles known as *imbrices* (singular, *imbrex*) to cover the joints between the flat tiles (*tegulae*). A Roman roof therefore, in England as elsewhere, looked like a compromise between one composed of plain tiles and one of overs-and-unders. It was from the combination of flat and rounded tiles that were developed, in the nineteenth century, the so-called Patent Roman and Patent Double Roman tiles, which were originally a speciality of Bridgwater. The latter are large tiles, about $16\frac{1}{2}$ ins. long and 14 ins. wide, with two rolls rising from a flat surface; they overlap in much the same way as pantiles, but their rolls are not nearly so bold. They are now widely used, and in places far removed from Bridgwater. Sometimes these tiles yield an agreeably textured surface, but often they look excessively mechanical.

Fancy shapes, such as fish-scale tiles, of which there will be more to say in connection with tile-hung walls, were, although not unknown in 1837, essentially a Victorian development. There is only one other traditional type of roofing tile in England besides the plain tile, and that is the pantile.

Pantiles

Pantiles differ radically from plain tiles in size, in shape, and in general appearance. In size they are substantially larger; it was decreed by Act of Parliament in the time of George I that their measurements, after firing, should not be less than $13\frac{1}{2} \times 9\frac{1}{2}$ ins. $\times$ $\frac{1}{2}$ in., and these dimensions have been retained without much variation ever since. In shape they are more complex. In the downward direction pantiles overlap one, not two courses below (thus, in contrast to plain tiles (see p. 270), they are 'single-lap' tiles), but they also overlap transversally, the down-bent edge of one pantile hooking over the up-turned edge of its neighbour. This, it might be supposed, would make them more weather-proof than the other type. In fact this is not so, because pantiles do not usually fit together very closely; hence with them some form of sub-roofing is more than ever necessary. Torching was general, and in Norfolk they used to rest upon a layer of reeds and hair mortar; to-day some sort of reinforced waterproof felting is regarded as essential. That does not affect their appearance, and so long as this precaution is taken they may be safely used on a pitch as gentle as $35°$ or even $30°$ (*284*d).

Although the shape was more complex, the need only for a single overlap rendered a pantile-covered roof considerably lighter than one covered with plain tiles, and this, combined with their amenability to a flatter pitch, meant a substantial saving on roof timbers. Thus, contrary to what perhaps its appearance would suggest, the pantiled roof, especially in those parts of the country where wood had become scarce, was the more economical form. Steeply-pitched roofs of pantiles are perfectly feasible, but for reasons of cost are not often seen; and when one comes upon a cottage with such a roof, as at Digby near Sleaford (*277*d), the probability is that the pantiles replace an original cover-ing of thatch. (This photograph also illustrates the fact that, unlike plain tiles, the appear-ance of pantiles changes sharply with the viewpoint.)

The pattern of English building has been determined primarily by geology, but other factors have also contributed their share, among them trading connections and local fashions. The incidence of pantiles in this country provides an excellent instance of the play of these two latter forces. For our oldest pantiles are only found in places engaged in commerce with Holland, whence their importation began in the seventeenth century. Although Charles I granted a patent for the 'makeing of Pantiles or Flanders Tyles' as early as 1636, it is generally believed that the first English pantiles may not have been produced until 1701—by a company at Tilbury in which Daniel Defoe held an interest. During the following sixty years the English products gradually supplanted the Dutch.

Yet, although there was a growing vogue for them throughout the Georgian period, wide areas of the country would have little or nothing to do with them. Old pantiles can be found at a few places in the South-West that traded with Holland, and notably Bridgwater, which presently started making its own. From the end of the eighteenth century Bridgwater was one of the principal centres of production in the country for this kind of tile. It is therefore frequently seen in Somerset (277b), and sometimes on the fringes of neighbouring counties, as for instance at Bradford-on-Avon. Otherwise, pantiles are rare in the West and Midlands; rare also in the South-East, where local kilns supplied all needs with the finest plain tiles. London absorbed large numbers of pantiles before the advent of Welsh slate early in the reign of George III, and travelling north, they are increasingly in evidence beyond Bedford. Huntingdonshire and Cambridgeshire have a great many pantiles, and so have Essex, Suffolk and especially Norfolk.

Continuing northwards, the picture again changes. Wherever there are old tiles in Lincolnshire, they are much more likely to be pan than plain—so long, that is, as they are not *too* old: at Aubourn, for instance, a pantiled village seven miles south-west of Lincoln, the sixteenth- and early seventeenth-century Hall alone has plain tiles (probably renewals here). Pantiles are also characteristic of the villages in the contiguous corner of Leicestershire to the north-east of Melton Mowbray, and of much of Nottinghamshire, whither Dutch tiles could easily be brought up the Trent. The East Riding too is a land of pantiles, beyond which we find them in places on or near the coast all the way to Berwick and on into Scotland. Apart therefore from Somerset, these tiles have markedly Eastern and North-Eastern associations. There are towns in Yorkshire (away from the hills) and in Lincolnshire in which one can sometimes chance upon a remarkably Dutch-looking view. The main constituents of such a scene are certain to be water, bricks and pantiles.

Texturally a pantiled roof can offer great enjoyment. The large size of each tile and the rhythmical surging of the courses combine to endow even the smallest roof with a surface richness which is often admirable (277b). The wavy line of pantiled eaves may also be delightful (192c, 277d). But with pantiles, hardly less than with Spanish tiles, simple roof-shapes are essential. Dormers can only be embodied awkwardly (277d), and valleys are quite impracticable.

Pantiles, like plain tiles, are usually red: sometimes, as in East Yorkshire, a strong, brilliant and in places perhaps rather harsh red. But as with plain tiles the range of colours is considerable: pink, orange, buff, brown, yellow, green, grey—shades of all these may be found in old pantiles. Glazing was not common before the present century, which was aesthetically lucky. The advantages of a glaze are practical: it gives additional strength and

PLAIN TILES
a. *The Manor House, Orlestone, Kent*   c. *Sedlescombe, near Battle, Sussex*

PANTILES
b. *West Harptree, Somerset*
d. *Digby, near Sleaford, Lincolnshire*

reduces the danger of frost-cracking. Some of the imported Dutch pantiles used in London in the early Georgian period were already glazed. Norfolk at this time specialized in blacks, often glazed; these can also be seen at Boston. When they reflect the sky they often appear dark blue. Towards the end of the nineteenth century pantiles started to go out of fashion, and hand-moulded pantiles are, I believe, now unobtainable. Two yards near Barton-on-Humber are still making clay pantiles by machine, and in the old town, a Conservation Area, their employment is rightly insisted on; but unhappily plain and concrete tiles have now invaded the traditional pantile areas on a large scale. (It was good to learn that a pub in the old town of Barton, which recently put on a new roof of concrete tiles, was forced to take them off again.) In the present century pantiles with brightly coloured glazes, blues and greens and yellows, have enjoyed a certain popularity. These look more at home in the crisp, bright sunlight of California than under skies which are often grey and rain-laden. Perhaps acceptable as a roof-covering for an isolated white house on the edge of a cliff, these exotic-looking tiles make bad neighbours in an English street.

Tile-Hung Walls

Tile-hanging first appeared in south-eastern England towards the end of the seventeenth century. Its purpose, like slate-hanging, was to afford protection against bad weather, especially driving rain, hence its alternative name: weather-tiling. Although it gradually spread to other parts of England, it has always remained a speciality of Kent, Sussex and Surrey, together with parts of Hampshire and Berkshire. There is tile-hanging also in Wiltshire in and around Marlborough, and here and there in Buckinghamshire. Elsewhere, it is not very frequent. When they are plain, the tiles used were, and still are, the same as for roofs.

Sometimes the walls which have been given this additional covering of tiles are themselves of brick. In such cases the tiles were either hung on wooden battens plugged into the walls or fixed by wooden pegs (or later, nails) directly into the mortar courses. But most of the older tile-hung houses are timber-framed, and here the procedure was closely comparable to that described on pp. 173–174 with reference to slate-hanging: the tiles were hung upon oaken laths, and the upper ends might be bedded into lime and hair mortar. A photograph of part of a house at Tenterden, stripped of its wall-tiles, shows the laths nailed across the closely spaced vertical studs (278e). They might also, for additional security, be fastened with wooden pins, generally oak, hazel or willow. More often than not the tiles are confined to the upper storey, and sometimes only to the gables

TILE-HANGING
a. *Burwash, Sussex*   b. *Bell Inn, Minster-in-Thanet, Kent*
c. *Witley, Surrey*   d. *Lilac House, Biddenden, Kent*
e. *Tenterden, Kent* (*this house, the Manor House, was demolished about 1959*)

(*268*), these being the most exposed parts of the building. The joints might be filled with mortar, but in all the best examples they have been left open, to yield little vertical shadows (*268*). There will also be horizontal shadows cast by the overhangs (*267*a), in addition to which every hand-made tile will be slightly curved. Hence a good tile-hung wall is a creation of infinite subtlety, an agglomeration of shallow and slightly irregular convexities, seemingly held in place, under the right conditions of light, by a fine mesh of shadow. Burwash in Sussex provides a rich display (*278*a).

Colour, as always, is of the greatest importance, and happily the Weald still abounds in gorgeous terracottas, often with minute variations of tint and gradations of density almost from tile to tile, some being a little more orange, others a little more vermilion. Much of this splendid colouring is traceable to wood-firing. Because these tiles hang vertically, rainwater runs off them at once, and unlike roof-tiles they do not remain damp for days and perhaps weeks at a time. Lichens, mosses, seeds and soot particles do not therefore adhere to wall-tiles as they often do to pitched roofs, and for this reason they seem to be able to hold their richly glowing reds to an incomparable degree. Elsewhere the colour may only be a dark reddish-brown, but for tile-hanging a warm hue has almost always been preferred. Sand-faced tiles suitable for this purpose are still being made at several Wealden brick-yards.

In contrast to slate-hanging, in which patterned surfaces seem to me more entertaining than plain, I feel that hand-made terracotta-coloured tiles are so beautiful in themselves that the simple rectangles, with their gently curved faces, are the best (*130*b, *267*a, *277*c). Nevertheless, the lower edge of the English wall-tile has often been given what has been regarded as a more ornamental shape. Probably the favourite variant, illustrated in Kent at Lilac House, Biddenden (*278*d), has been the half-circle, which is also known as the fish-scale or scallop. Among others may be found the fish-tail, the V, and more recently the arrow-head (fig. 5a) and the hammer-head (figs. 5b and c). Other shapes in favour in the South-East in the latter part of the nineteenth century are seen in (d) and (e). Sometimes these various shapes were combined to form further designs: (f) shows a favourite Victorian pattern, and a similar one, which is undeniably rich, is seen in plate *278*c at Witley. A wall of fish-scales may certainly look delightful, and the simple 'embroidery' on the front of the Bell Inn at Minster-in-Thanet (*278*b) is not without charm. But these ornamental tiles can be tiresome. With fancy tiles it is usually preferable to maintain the same design over the whole surface of the wall; five courses of this and three of that tend to be fussy and fidgety (*328*d). Needless to say, the least pleasing effects were obtained with machine-made tiles of the second half of the nineteenth century, which could only yield patterns of lifeless monotony.

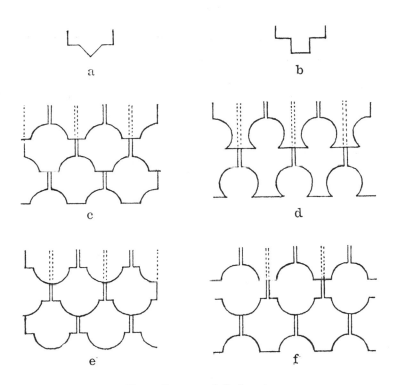

Fig. 5 Patterns of tile-hanging

Brick-Tiles

Tiles made to imitate bricks were an invention of the Georgian period. They were intended to deceive, and often did so with great success. One who lived in the house for many years has described how at Nunwell, close to Brading in the Isle of Wight, 'the southern front, originally built of stone, was given a new skin of red brick-tiles. . . . These imitation bricks, though less than half an inch thick, have stood the test of time exceedingly well, and are so deceptive to the eye that it was only some twenty-five years ago, when electric light was being installed, that the present generation discovered to their cost that the entrance front of their house was not built of brick but of particularly tough stone.'[1] The masking in this fashion of stone and brickwork was not unusual in the South and South-East, but a much more frequent use for these tiles was to give an inexpensive 'face-lift' to older half-timbered buildings. In such cases the brick-tiles were sometimes

1 C. Aspinall-Oglander, *Nunwell Symphony* (1945), p. 155. It should perhaps be added that the date given here for these brick-tiles, 1716, would appear to be at least half a century too early.

bedded into a plaster covering, but the usual practice was to nail them on to wooden battens, as with tile-hanging; a good example can be seen on the courtyard side of Guildford House, at Guildford. Plate 267b shows brick-tiles being fixed to the front of the Railway Arms inn at Croydon as recently as 1950. This building was originally weatherboarded; the wood had deteriorated and suitable replacements were at that time unobtainable. The tiles are seen after bedding, but before pointing.

What, it will be asked, were the reasons for resorting to brick-tiles? Initially, they were two: the desire to provide protection against the weather, and the wish to keep up with current fashion. At No. 47 Winchester Street, Salisbury, the latter alone counted: this is a good brick house of Stuart character, the front of which was transformed in the Georgian period by changing the windows and nailing tiles all over the earlier solid brickwork. It is likely that both motives often operated together; like the hung tiles, brick-tiles were also commonly referred to as 'weather-tiles' in the eighteenth century. Much care went into their making; there were headers and stretchers and even rubbed bricks for window-heads, all meticulously jointed. The game is only given away, sometimes, when one looks at the shallow window-surrounds or at the side walls of a building which has only been treated front and back, or where, with the passage of years, the nails have failed and the tiles have started slipping out, as can be seen on the fronts of a number of houses in Lewes (267c).

Brick-tiles were not particularly cheap, and they were not originally introduced in order to save money. With the imposition of the brick tax in 1784 the situation changed, for the tiles were not subject to it. There was now a strong incentive to use them for new buildings too; thus at Lewes the original Quaker Meeting House, dating from that very year 1784, is described as being 'in a local style requiring a framework of wood, with mathematical tiling hung on this'. With the rising cost of bricks the employment of these facing tiles became comparatively common in south-eastern England, and the large majority of such buildings belong to the period between 1784 and the repeal of the brick tax in 1850. By this time, as we have seen, red brick was no longer acceptable to fashionable society, and Henry Holland was busy persuading his clients to use those yellowish-white tiles to which reference was made in the preceding chapter in connection with Althorp and Chevening. These were rebated tiles specially manufactured and lending themselves to very fine bonding; and although in the Althorp Accounts they are called 'rebate tiles', they were usually known, somewhat mysteriously, as 'mathematical' tiles. They appear to have been originally made in the New Forest, and first employed by Holland, a few years before the introduction of the brick tax, to face Sloane Place, his own London house, long since demolished. This is the house which is said to have given the

DEVON COB (RENDERED)
a. *Hayes Barton, East Budleigh, the birthplace of Sir Walter Raleigh*
b. *Ashton*

Prince of Wales his idea for the original Pavilion at Brighton, built for him by Holland in 1786–88; and it was no doubt the use of 'mathematical' tiles here which did so much to render them fashionable.[1]

Within a few years they were accepted by other architects, such as Samuel Wyatt and John Soane; the former was using them in 1792 at Belmont Park near Faversham—yellow tiles carefully made to simulate gauged brickwork. For Chevening, the third Earl Stanhope had some singularly unattractive dun-coloured tiles (said to be waterproof and fireproof) made to his own specification. When in the course of time the nails by which they were secured rusted, the tiles started to fall off, until in 1970 the entire covering had to be removed. So, with its brick facing renewed, Chevening, after nearly two hundred years, has again become a red house. There were no standard dimensions. At Althorp   * the surface measurements of the stretchers are $8\frac{1}{2} \times 3$ ins. and the joints, in a hard white cement, are only $\frac{1}{8}$ in. thick. These tiles remain, to the building's considerable artistic disadvantage. That this was also the view of some contemporaries is suggested by Horace Walpole's barbed comment after a visit to Althorp in 1793. 'I am sorry', he wrote, 'that the pretty outside is demolished and that Mr. Holland has so much of the spirit of a lucrative profession in him as to prefer destroying to not being employed.'

Through two generations the vogue for brick-tiles was considerable, yet for reasons which have never been satisfactorily explained they were far more common south of the Thames, and especially in the coastal regions of Sussex and Kent, than anywhere else. The town which probably has the most of any is Lewes; here, as elsewhere in Sussex, it was the practice to use only headers (*267*a and c). Other places in which they were something of a speciality are Canterbury, Hythe, Tenterden, Rye, Brighton, Winchester and Salisbury. There are a few examples in London, in Cambridge, and around Durham,   * and there are isolated instances of their use elsewhere on large country houses, such as Althorp and Helmingham Hall, Suffolk. But many counties have no examples of the 'mathematical' tile. A possible explanation is that there was something about this form of wall-covering which was felt to be a trifle 'fancy', even dishonest. That might have rendered it less acceptable in the North than in the more sophisticated—and at this time richer—South-East.[2]

---

[1] Somewhat similar tiles had been used instead of bricks by George Steuart in 1783–85 at Attingham Park, Shropshire, with a different intention, which was to reduce the weight of a large and lofty building erected on foundations devoid of natural strength. (See an article by Michael Rix in *Country Life*, October 21, 1954.)

[2] For the geographical distribution of brick-tiles and for other valuable information on this subject, see A. Arschavir, 'False Fronts on Minor Domestic Architecture', in the *Transactions of the Ancient Monuments Society*, New Series, vol. 4 (1956), pp. 110–122.

PUGGED CHALK, MUD AND THATCH
a. *Broad Chalke, Wiltshire*   b. *Guilsborough, Northamptonshire*
    c. *Great Creaton, Northamptonshire*

CLAY LUMP AND PANTILES
    d. *Shipdham, Norfolk*

A special development of the brick-tile is in evidence at certain seaside towns, notably Brighton: the black-glazed facing tile. This was produced about the turn of the century with the specific intention of providing houseowners with the best possible protection against the depredations of a salty atmosphere. Such tiles, which were always laid in header bond, were only occasionally used on country houses; they can be seen at Patcham Place, a mid-Georgian building just north of Brighton, where the contrast between the black walls and the white wooden dressings is attractive (267d). But the most striking example is provided by the Royal Crescent in Brighton itself. This terrace of tall houses, erected by an unknown architect or contractor between 1799 and 1807, is of red brick, entirely faced with black-glazed 'mathematical' tiles, set in light coloured mortar with fairly thick joints. The effect is much better than might perhaps be expected. On sunny days, some of them reflect the sky and appear quite blue. And they certainly cost far less to maintain than the stucco facing of most of the buildings which surround them.

11

THE UNBAKED EARTHS

Mud, cob, pulverized chalk, wichert, pisé, clay lump: these are the materials which now claim a brief consideration. They are generally the stuff of rather humble buildings, mostly cottages, small farm-houses and their appendages, but in many parts of England their use was once widespread.

Mud is just wet earth; to be suitable for building, it must contain sufficient lime to enable it to set, and usually it needs to be mixed with chopped straw, and for preference also ballast (gravel or other small stones) and sand. Cob is the same: this is the word used to describe mud buildings in the South-West, and especially in Devon and Dorset.[1] If it contains chalk, so much the better, for chalk mixed with mud will make a stronger wall. So too will shilf, the name given to the little pieces of waste slate which are abundant in Cornwall: one part of shilf to two of mud and straw was the usual recipe for 'clob', as the Cornishmen generally called it. In a small area of Buckinghamshire, there is a chalky earth a foot or two below the surface which when mixed with straw is known as wichert. All these are semi-wet mixes; pisé is stiff earth that is kneaded or mixed with gravel (but not straw) and rammed between boards in a nearly dry state. Clay lump, an East Anglian material, differs from the others in that the earth, mixed with straw, is shaped with moulds into rectangular blocks and left to dry in the air before being used.

As materials for building, the unbaked earths have certain characteristics in common. The first and golden rule, which applies to all of them, is that they must be kept dry. If subjected to prolonged damp, they will certainly disintegrate. So long as they remain dry they may endure for centuries; and although liable to cracking in very dry weather, mud walls often get harder and stronger with the years. The essential precautions are summed up in that old Devon saying quoted by C. F. Innocent: 'all cob wants is a good hat and a good pair of shoes', that is to say, a solid plinth and some kind of roof or coping. The unbaked earths have always been provided with good plinths, at least a foot high and sometimes 2 ft. In Devon the plinths would generally be of stone or pebbles; in Leicestershire of boulders from the Boulder Clay; in Rutland of good rubble limestone; in Cumberland of sandstone; in Norfolk of flint or, later, brick. Sometimes, for additional protection,

1 It is also heard from time to time elsewhere, e.g. in Northamptonshire and in Kent.

this base would be tarred. It was needed not only to prevent the damp from rising, but also as an impediment to rats and mice and other vermin. As for the roofs of these buildings, they were usually of thatch: the coping of boundary walls, if built of mud, might only be clods of earth, but even these were often thatched (*191c*). Earth buildings are sometimes liable to attack not only from vermin but from bees, which burrow into the thick walls to make their nests, puncturing the surface with countless little holes. These can be very troublesome.

It seems probable that earth, cut into sods or trampled and daubed upon wattles, has the distinction, perhaps shared with wood, of being the oldest building material to have been in use in this country; and often, as in the next chapter we shall see, the two were employed in conjunction. It is known that some of London's houses in 1212 had walls of mud, and there is indisputable evidence of cob construction in Devon by the end of the thirteenth century. That county still has more 'unbaked earth' buildings than any other, some of which date from the sixteenth and many from the seventeenth centuries. Among these are several of considerable size, notably Hayes Barton near East Budleigh, where Raleigh was born in 1552 (*283*a). This pleasant E-shaped thatched house, although later altered and unfortunately rendered with cement, still has its walls of cob. Nor is this material rare in other south-western counties, particularly in the southern and western parts of Somerset and most of Dorset; whilst there are still numerous clay lump houses in East Anglia (*284*d). A hundred years ago mud cottages could be seen scattered throughout most of the English counties. Even to-day, especially in the Midlands, there are many more of them than the casual traveller might suppose, owing to the masking of the mud walls with facing materials: plaster, limewash, brick or cement. At Great Creaton in Northamptonshire (*284*c) ironstone was used for the front wall, up to first floor level, in order to support the joists for the upper floor, but beneath the rendered parts the walls are of mud.[1] Mud-built cottages, sometimes incorporating crucks, were also not at one time rare in the North-West, on both sides of the Solway Firth. In this part of Cumberland 105 'clay daubins' (as they were called locally) were recorded in 1956, ten bearing dates ranging from 1672 to 1825.[2] Since then several have perished, and this seems certain to continue: it is to be hoped that a few of the best will be preserved. A remarkable fact about these cottages is that the walls (but not the roof) were sometimes completed in a single day; for newly

1 See M. V. J. Seaborne, 'Cob Cottages in Northamptonshire', in *Northamptonshire Past and Present*, vol. iii, no. 5 (1964). This article covers the whole Midlands area (Northamptonshire, Leicestershire, Nottinghamshire, Rutland and Warwickshire) and includes a valuable distribution map. Mr. Seaborne has generously allowed me to reproduce two of his photographs.

2 See R. W. Brunskill, 'The Clay Houses of Cumberland', in *Transactions of the Ancient Monuments Society*, New series, vol. 10 (1962): pp. 57–80.

married couples the whole village might work together as a team and end the day by dancing on the freshly laid floor. These houses were single storeyed but lofty, usually with thatched roofs; and provided that they were given a protective covering of plaster and an annual coat of whitewash, they could be expected to survive for 150 or even 200 years.

Building in mud or cob was a laborious process, calling for at least semi-skilled labour. The mix had to be carefully blended; the treading was done by oxen, horses, or often by the men themselves. As in flint construction, plenty of time was essential, for each layer had to harden before another could be added. This might take several weeks if the weather were bad. Two years were needed for a two-storey house, and it is not surprising to find that many mud buildings, like the well-preserved one at Guilsborough in Northampton-shire, formerly used to store coal for the village poor (284b), have only a single storey. The mud here is of a rich brownish ochre, the roof of good straw thatch. In a well-known passage, S. O. Addy, writing in 1898, described[1] the erection of one of a number of mud houses formerly to be seen around Hornsea in the East Riding of Yorkshire, an account which would at one time have been applicable to many parts of the country. The layers of mud and straw were only from 5 ins. to 7 ins. thick. After each course had been given a thin covering of straw, it was left to dry out. In Devon the courses were normally about a foot high, and it was customary for one of the labourers to stand on the wall and tread down each lump as it was forked up and placed in position. No shuttering was used. Since the form was normally determined by the eye alone, these buildings often have about them an air of improvisation which can be attractive; walls may sway gently in and out; corners tend to be curved; ovens may be set in little semi-circular projections below the chimney stacks. The walls of these mud cottages were always very broad: seldom less than 2 ft., often 3 ft., and occasionally over 4 ft. When they were finished, the loose ends of straw were trimmed off, and then the whole was generally given a protective covering of plaster or limewash or both. Sometimes this was white, but in the West country it was often cream, buff or pink. The cottage at Ashton in Devon (283b) is pale blue. The usual, and certainly the most appropriate roofing for this type of building was thatch, with generously formed eaves. Another ancient roofing material, turf, once common in parts of Scotland and Ireland, hardly seems to have been used in England except to some extent in Cumber-land. Only the fireplaces, flues and chimney stacks had to be, as with all these unbaked earth buildings, of brick or masonry (284d).

Apart from applied colour washes, the colour of a mud or cob building also varies with the character of the clay in its composition. In the New Red Sandstone areas, for

1 In the first edition of *The Evolution of the English House*, p. 40.

example, as at Sampford Courtenay in Devon, the mud may look decidedly red. If lime is present in the form of chalk, it may take on a whitish hue. Chalk as a building stone has already been considered; something must now be said about its less masonic aspects. In eastern and southern Wiltshire and on into Dorset, also in the adjacent parts of Hampshire and Berkshire, pulverized chalk was at one time much in demand for mixing with the mud and straw. A good wet mix of 'chalk mud' might have as much as three parts chalk to one part clay: for durability, the higher the proportion of chalk the better. No shuttering was required, and the finished walls, often tiled now, were at one time always thatched in this part of England. At Ugford (*191c*) the chalk-mud wall keeps its 'hat' of thatch, whilst its 'shoes' are of brick. Elsewhere, as for instance in East Kent (where, however, cob was never a favourite material), small lumps of chalk, not ground down, seem to have been thrown into the mix. In parts of East Anglia, and especially in south Cambridgeshire, the marl (chalk and clay mixed) was moulded into large unbaked bricks very much in the manner of clay lump, to be described shortly. Yet another use for chalk was as a constituent of the roughcast with which some mud-built cottages were coated. For all these purposes, surface chalk was quite suitable, whereas chalk-stone, as mentioned earlier, usually had to be dug from the deeper beds.

In some Chalk areas, of which the Wiltshire Downs provide a good example, walls may be constructed entirely of chalk, which is nevertheless not masonry. Here the method was to 'pug' the chalk by adding water, and then to pour it between a pair of boards, ram it down, tread on it, and wait for it to dry out. The result, though inferior to the best clunch, was a wall closely comparable to cob, and requiring much less skill to construct (*284*a).

Wichert was dug from a belt of unwontedly hard earth up to a mile wide, which stretches from near Aylesbury westwards to Long Crendon, north of Thame. It owes its pale yellow colour to the presence of chalk. The earth was mixed with water and a little straw. The process of construction was as slow as with cob, and much the same: walls two to three feet wide on rubblestone plinths; no shuttering; the earth trodden down at intervals. The coping in Buckinghamshire is now usually of tiles, but thatch was once common. The rendering was generally of lime plaster or roughcast. Care had to be taken that this was not too heavy, or it would tend to fall away; garden walls were often left unrendered. Wichert is best seen at Haddenham, where most of the older houses are built of it, and at Dinton.[1]

1 As wichert is not widely known, I append references: *R.C.H.M.*, *South Buckinghamshire* (1912), p. xxiv; C. F. Innocent, *The Development of English Building Construction* (1916), p. 136; J. H. B. Peel, *The Chilterns* (1950), p. 23. It is sometimes written 'wychert', and occasionally 'witchit'.

Pounded chalk might also be the major constituent of pisé, but more often this was prepared in other ways. Building with pisé, or rammed earth, is traditional in Asia, Africa and America as well as in Europe. In France, where it was first introduced by the Romans, it became a popular method in the Rhône valley: it is known there as *pisé de terre*. Its distinctive characteristic was that the mix, which ideally consisted of earth of a gravelly or sandy consistency, with a little clay added for cohesive purposes, was kept nearly dry. For building in this fashion wooden shutter-boards were essential, but even so many will wonder what caused it to cohere. The answer is mechanical energy: 'When particles of soil are forced together into close contact by ramming, they are compelled to adhere together by molecular and capillary forces and to form a hard and solid mass which is excellent for building purposes.'[1] The process required, nevertheless, considerable experience. On a foundation of rubblestone, brick, or more recently concrete, the earth was thrown between strong shutter-boards and beaten down with almost scientific precision, to secure uniform compression; it was very important to avoid air-pockets. Until iron superseded it, the rammer used to be made of hard wood and was often heart-shaped. If there was any danger of vermin, broken glass could be mixed with the earth for the first foot or two. Since with pisé the material was already dry, building could proceed far more quickly than with mud or cob or flint: a height of 9 ft. could be reached in the course of a single day. Therein lay its great practical advantage over the other unbaked earths.

Much of the soil of England is very suitable for pisé: the red marls of the Triassic formation are especially good. Yet among our traditional building materials it occupies only a very minor place, partly, it may be suggested, because the need to employ wooden shuttering sent up the cost, and partly because for building in pisé dry weather is essential. A cob wall, when it has dried out, is very similar to a pisé wall and may last just as long. In England pisé, no less than cob, must always be rendered or at least limewashed. Yet within the present century pisé has been used as have none of the other materials discussed in this chapter. Acute shortage of the usual building materials after both the world wars, and their very high cost, prompted a number of architects to advocate, for single-storey cottages and outbuildings in those parts of England where the earth was serviceable, the use of pisé or its modern offshoot known as stabilized earth.[2] Furthermore pisé, alone among the unbaked earths, once enjoyed a short spell of fashionable patronage. This was due to the commendation of Henry Holland, ever an enthusiast even in Revolutionary days for anything from France. J. B. Papworth, in his *Designs for Rural Residences* (1818), stated

---

1 Clough Williams-Ellis and J. and E. Eastwick-Field, *Building in Cob, Pisé and Stabilized Earth* (Revised edition, 1947), p. 22.

2 Stabilized earth is pisé with the addition of a little cement, which makes a stronger and better-wearing wall.

that pisé was 'introduced into England by the late Mr. H.'. Holland used this method for the construction of some estate cottages at Woburn in the early seventeen-nineties, according to his own account with great success, although they long ago disappeared.[1] By 1819, states the *Cyclopaedia* published in that year, pisé was widely familiar in the southern counties. Some of these pisé walls may still survive, hidden under paint or plaster.

The Boulder Clays of parts of East Anglia (to be specific, of central and south Norfolk, north and west Suffolk, and south-east Cambridgeshire) were used extensively for several centuries as 'clay lump', which is the English version of *adobe*. Plenty of cottages in this material still survive in villages between Thetford and Diss (e.g. Garboldisham, Blo' Norton). Why clay lump is virtually confined to East Anglia is hard to explain, for there are many other places where local resources were suitable for it.[2] The work of preparation was simple. After the clay had been dug out, it was watered, and most of the large stones (flints) were removed; it was then covered with chopped straw (or sometimes spear grass) which was trodden into it, usually by a horse, in order to make it more cohesive. The material was then pressed into wooden moulds and left, probably for several weeks, to dry out. In character, therefore, clay lumps were like unfired bricks, but much larger: they measured 17 or 18 ins. by anything from 5 to 9 ins., and were 6 ins. thick if required for an outside wall. The mortaring was done with puddled clay of a somewhat finer consistency; lime was not essential. Some further external protection was then needed. The cheapest and least attractive was a coat of tar; this is found principally on farm buildings, where it had the practical advantage of deterring the cattle from licking the clay. If the tar were afterwards sanded, which for cottages was usual, it could be colour-washed; but rendering with lime plaster gave the most pleasing finish, and this is also quite common. The external facing often makes it difficult to recognize buildings of clay lump, especially when, as frequently occurred in the nineteenth century, they were given a 'skin' of $4\frac{1}{2}$ in. brickwork. I am therefore fortunate in being able to include a photograph of a pair of early nineteenth-century cottages at Shipdham, between Norwich and Swaffham, taken at a moment when their protective plastering had been temporarily removed (*284*d). Shortly afterwards there was nothing to be seen but unattractive brown pebble-dash. Shipdham is another village with a lot of clay-lump cottages.

1 For Henry Holland's interest in pisé, see Dorothy Stroud, *Henry Holland* (1950), p. 35; H. M. Colvin *Dictionary of English Architects* (1954), p. 292; and Christopher Hussey, *English Country Houses, Mid-Georgian* (1956), p. 22.

2 According to Dr. Norman Davey, clay lump was also used in the seventeenth and eighteenth centuries in the Black Country, notably at Lye, a mining place on the Worcestershire-Staffordshire border close to Stourbridge. See *A History of Building Materials* (1961), p. 22. And excavation has shown that at Leicester this material was employed by the Romans.

Although these clay lump buildings of East Anglia are not so picturesque as the more hand-moulded-looking cob cottages of the South-West, they were technically the most advanced of the unbaked earth buildings. Their walls have only about half the usual thickness of cob, yet for insulation they are just as efficient. Owing to the method of erection, repairs to the wall-surface of a cob building may present difficulty, but in clay lump construction it is comparatively easy to remove a defective block and replace it with another one. Nevertheless, in all the unbaked earth techniques, clay lump included, it is not unusual nowadays to come upon buildings in a state of wretched dilapidation, and every year some more of them are condemned. In Bedfordshire, for example, there were still quite an appreciable number of whitewashed and thatched mud-built cottages at the beginning of the present century. Now there is scarcely one. Should this, it may be asked, be a matter for serious regret?

It must not be supposed that any of these earth cottages date from the Middle Ages. Some belong to the sixteenth and seventeenth centuries; the majority, probably, to the eighteenth and early nineteenth centuries. In relation to the general level of domestic building in that period, they clearly occupy a very modest place. Yet in addition to their visual attractions when properly cared for, and despite all the hazards from mice and bees and damp, their amenities cannot be denied. I have been invited inside cob cottages in Devon, clay lump cottages in Norfolk, and mud cottages in Nottinghamshire; in every instance the occupants were enthusiastic: 'so cool in summer, so snug and warm in winter'. It was a pleasure to encounter such ardour for traditional building materials. It provides the answer to our question: the steady destruction, year by year, of these old clay-built country cottages is indeed something to be deplored.

What is nearly certain is that we shall see no new ones. The use of pisé is again in abeyance. Clay lump may still be used occasionally for farm buildings, and between the wars two council housing schemes in southern Norfolk were carried out in it; but the effect was ruined by applying cement for the external rendering. Unless the material is dug on the site, its use is no longer economic, and even then there may be no labourers with the requisite knowledge. How pleasant it would be to see cob revived, if only for garden walls. 'Cob walls for garden fruit', wrote S. Baring-Gould in his *Book of the West*, 'are incomparable. They retain the warmth of the sun and give it out through the night.' But cob has been virtually extinct for over a century, and so has wichert; this is now repaired with breeze blocks, for the old craft knowledge has been lost, probably for ever. As substances for building, the unbaked earths already belong to history.

12

WOOD

Wood has been used on an immense scale for building; indeed, a guess would be (and it can only be a guess) that in the course of history more buildings have been constructed partly or entirely of wood than of any other material except perhaps brick. At one time the world was far richer in forests than it is to-day, and of few countries is this truer than of England. In *The Making of the English Landscape*, Prof. W. G. Hoskins cites the estimate made by Gregory King in 1688 that the acreage of woods and coppices in England at that time amounted to about three million; and, having regard to the reckless felling of timber in the two preceding centuries for shipbuilding and fuel for iron-smelting, as well as for building and many other purposes, he estimates that in 1500 this country must have possessed at least four million acres of woodland. That is more than the total area of Kent, Surrey, Sussex, Hampshire and Berkshire. Earlier there was still more: Messrs. Knoop and Jones note that in J. C. Cox's *Royal Forests of England* over sixty genuine forests are listed as existing in England in the thirteenth century. In some parts of the country the ubiquity of the trees was an embarrassment. Parts of the Midlands were covered by oak forests so dense that the early settlers avoided them. In the Weald (and the word 'weald' meant 'forest' in Anglo-Saxon), which is still the most wooded part of England but is now notable for the rich variety of its trees, the oak was known as 'the Sussex weed'.[1]

Practically all our trees were hardwoods, and in this we were fortunate. In northern and central Europe the wood used for building is frequently soft: fir or pine. The grain is of little interest in itself, and the wood is not very resistant either to damp or to fire. Hence the practice of painting external timbers, which with hardwood is unnecessary. At Goslar, for example, a town notable not only for its slate-hanging (cf. p. 174) but for its abundance of timber-framed houses, the wood is almost all painted, sometimes green

[1] Hence the 'Song of the Sussex House-Agent', sung with and to an air of deep contentment. The refrain runs:

> *Four postes round ye bed,*
> *Oake beames overhead,*
> *Oake boardes on ye floor,*
> *No stockbroker askes more.*

but generally *café-au-lait* or a rather anaemic red. As the infilling is now more often than not cement, the effect produced by these streets of timber-framed houses is not very agreeable.

In England a wide choice of hardwoods was available; yet the wood which was almost always selected for the better buildings was oak. Much has been written about the beauty of English oak, and it is indeed a wonderful wood, strong, close-grained and very durable. Even warping and cracking, although not rare (*328c*), are less of a problem with oak than with most other woods. Planks and panelling are, it is true, very liable to warp, whatever the wood, if they are not properly seasoned, and oak beams may crack along the heart-shake if they embody the whole tree. But quartered logs do not crack, and oak beams, even when 'green'—that is unseasoned—show no inclination to warp. Oak church doors still in use include several from the thirteenth century and one, at Hadstock near Saffron Walden, which is partly of Saxon date. With age, if it is left unstained, it is likely to assume an exquisite silvery hue. Sussex oak was famous; Shakespeare's country bore, in the Forest of Arden, oak trees in profusion; the Welsh border counties were, for miles on end, one vast oak forest. With such an abundance of this splendid wood—and England is said still to have more oaks than any other species of hardwood tree—what need was there to look elsewhere?

So little, that F. H. Crossley was led to declare categorically that 'oak was invariably the material used in timber construction'. That, however, is not quite accurate, although on the subject of the employment of sweet (Spanish) chestnut as an alternative to oak there is some uncertainty even among the experts. The difficulty here is that, whilst chestnut never attains the strength of oak, it assumes with age a very similar appearance. It was thus long believed that the roofs of two late-fourteenth century halls, at Westminster and at Lord Leycester's Hospital, Warwick, were of chestnut, but in the present century it has been proved beyond doubt that in fact both are of oak. The roofs of Winchester College cloisters furnish another example of a similar belief now disproved. Nevertheless, a few examples can be cited in which the wood is at least traditionally thought to be of chestnut. There are the roofs of Framlingham church, of the south chapel at Ewelme, and of the nave of the former Augustinian priory church of Stavordale in Somerset (later used as a barn and now a private house), the arcade piers of the nave at Wingham in Kent, and a few of the timber-framed yeomen's houses in the same county. There is also documentary evidence for its use at Dover Castle in 1278.[1] In the former manorial barn at Bishop's Cleeve in Gloucestershire, converted in recent years for use as a village hall, the early

---

[1] See L. F. Salzman, *op. cit.*, p. 252.

fifteenth-century roof timbers are of both oak and chestnut. The probability is that resort was had to chestnut at places where this wood was plentiful and oak had become scarce. It was occasionally employed for floors, as in the late seventeenth-century parlour at Eye Manor in Herefordshire. Chestnut has one advantage over oak internally: it does not attract beetle. But it is not as durable.

Of the other varieties of English wood it is difficult to speak with certainty because so much has perished. It is known that elm was sometimes employed in the later Middle Ages and in Tudor times as an inferior substitute for oak, in places where the latter was beginning to become scarce. It also served for floors, and later for weather-boarding. Beech was widely in demand for laths. Willow and sallow (the goat willow) were sometimes used in the construction of cottages and barns because, like elm, they were cheaper than oak.[1] Other varieties of wood which also make an occasional appearance, as for instance in the Fenland villages in the sixteenth and seventeenth centuries, include poplar, lime, hornbeam (which William Harrison, writing in 1573, calls 'hardbeam') and even plum tree. But in the story of English building these are of small importance.

With such rich resources of our own it might be supposed that, before the seventeenth century, we had little need of imported timber. Yet from quite early in the Middle Ages large quantities of oak boards were brought here, principally for panelling, from Germany, through the Hanseatic ports, and from Riga; in times when the shifting of heavy materials depended so much on water transport, these places were probably more accessible to eastern England than many of the home woodlands. Pine was imported too; small quantities of Norway fir would seem to have been brought over, probably only for the Royal works, as early as the thirteenth century. But in mediaeval times soft woods were little used for building. With the rising price of English oak after the mid-sixteenth century the situation changed, especially in regions such as Yorkshire and the Fens, in which oaks were by now becoming rare. Moreover, for some purposes, mainly internal, soft wood was preferred to oak because it could be worked much more quickly.[2] So from this time onwards deal (pine and fir) from the Baltic and Scandinavia began to be imported on an ever-increasing scale, to be supplemented in the nineteenth century by vast shiploads of coniferous timber from Canada and the United States.

1 In 1317 John of Bytham, a carpenter, was sued in the Fair Court of St. Ives for putting alder and willow into a house which he had contracted to build of oak. See *Select Cases concerning the Law Merchant*, Selden Soc., vol. xxiii, p. 103: Roger of Moulton *v.* John of Bytham. This is but one of many references for which I am indebted to Mr. John Harvey.

2 Pine, under a protective coat of plaster, was used at Cambridge in the seventeenth century for the structural framework of part of the former White Horse Inn in Castle Street. See R.C.H.M., *City of Cambridge* (1959), Part I, p. cii.

Although carpenters' yards would doubtless hold stocks of timber for standard components like rafters and joists, the principal structural limbs of a timber-framed building
would have to be selected from growing trees, the shape of which could be seen.[1] Only,
in fact, after the building had been designed and ordered could the right oak trees be
found to produce it. This timber would of course be 'green', but that was no disadvantage
because oak in its unseasoned state is much more easily worked. Nearly all wood-framed
buildings were constructed of unseasoned oak. This largely accounts for the warping and
sagging of the timbers which so many of them display. But no loss of strength was involved, because as its sap dries out oak becomes harder. Where precision was required, as
with panelling, doors and shutters, seasoned wood, frequently imported, was of course
preferable. In the Middle Ages water sometimes played a notable part in the seasoning of
oak. The trees, after felling, would be stripped of their bark and, where it was not possible
to let them float downstream to the place where they were needed, they would be left
to soak for a year or more in the fresh running water of rivers or millponds. The water
gradually replaced the acids and saps in the timber, and when retrieved the water in the pores
of the grain slowly gave place to air. Shrinkage and warping were thereby reduced and much
time saved, for seasoning without the water treatment would have been impossibly slow.
To-day drying kilns enable the whole process of 'seasoning' to be accomplished within the
space of a few weeks, without regard to the seasons.

The three great dangers to which wood is prone are dry rot, wet rot and wood-boring
insects. Dry rot is a fungus (*Merulius lacrymans*), which only takes hold in still, unventi-
lated conditions. Wood attacked by dry rot becomes in time criss-crossed with deep fissures
and very light in weight, and ultimately crumbles away as soon as it is touched. Wet rot
is commoner than dry rot but much less of a menace because its effects are always visible
on the surface. This is also due to a fungus (*Coniophora cerebella*), which usually grows on
the external surface of wood (and sometimes plaster). Several of the wood-boring insects,
notably the death-watch beetle (*Xestobium rufovillosum*), only as a rule attack large timbers.
But this does not apply to woodworm, the name given to the larval or wood-boring stage
of the common furniture beetle (*Anobium punctatum*), a far commoner pest, which can only
be destroyed by chemical treatment.[2] Here again oak is advantageously placed, for oak

---

1 The only alternative was to reuse existing timber. This was a common practice in the case of the humbler
buildings, and is even now and again found in those of better quality. Cf. p. 300.

2 The eggs, which are only just visible to the naked eye, are laid on rough wood (never on painted nor on
polished surfaces) in July or August. Five weeks later, when the grubs emerge, they immediately burrow into
the wood, in which they remain for four years, moving about. They then enter the pupa stage. As soon as
the beetles appear they fly about, infecting new areas of wood as the egg-laying process is repeated.

heartwood is beetle-proof except under conditions of persistent dampness, as for example when wall-plates on the lower ends of rafters are set beneath a parapet not provided with a damp-course—which is unfortunately all too common in old buildings. Even into oak *sapwood*, which was little used before the seventeenth century, the furniture beetle rarely penetrates more than half an inch.

History

With the possible exception of earth, wood is our oldest building material; but because in comparison with most others it is so perishable, little is known about the early wooden buildings of this island. When the Romans landed in England it seems certain that they found the large majority of buildings constructed of wood or earth, or both. There were also, here and there, crude bricks of unbaked mud mixed with straw. The Romans introduced stone, but they did not abandon wood; on the contrary, the evidence provided by many of their sites shows that they made extensive use of it. They also used wattles and plaster, referred to disparagingly by Vitruvius. In Saxon times, although in some parts of England the peasants lived in mud huts and stone was employed for some of the churches, wood was the most desirable building material in current use. Excavations now leave no room for doubt that many Saxon houses were of the wattle and daub type. Only one wooden building from the Saxon period has survived: the nave of the church of St. Andrew at Greensted in Essex. Needless to say it has undergone extensive restoration, notably in 1848, but the walls are of great interest and in England unique. They are composed of half-trunks of oak trees, varying from about 7 to 15 ins. in diameter, split vertically, with the curved portion of each tree facing outwards. At their lower end the trunks were dropped into a horizontal plank, the wooden sill, while at their upper end they were fastened with wooden pegs into another horizontal plank, the wall-plate. Their inner faces were plastered. The nave of this church was built not later than 1013, and may be the original chapel erected here during the tenth century. At that time there was no brick base; the sill lay on the ground, and in due course this and the lower ends of the trunks succumbed inevitably to the damp. They have certainly been shortened: their height, originally somewhat over 6 ft., is now only about 4 ft. 3 ins. But given suitable conditions, such as in this case the protection of the sawn upper ends provided by the roof, oak will last for many centuries; and there is no reason to doubt that the Greensted oaks, apart from three on the north side which occupy the position of a former doorway, are original, and therefore more than 950 years old. As a sidelight on early methods of timber construction, derived here without doubt from Scandinavia, this constitutes a remarkable survival. It was an extravagant way of using oak, but in Saxon days this did not matter in the least. Greensted church is perhaps more curious than beautiful, but it is probable that externally the walls of many little Saxon churches resembled it.

Throughout the Norman period wood was used for the construction of many village churches still much influenced by Viking art, but none has survived. When these wooden churches had been rebuilt in stone, as many of them had been even before the end of the twelfth century, their belfries or spires and their porches continued in many areas to be constructed of wood. This specially applied to south-eastern England, where in some places good building stone was scarce. The timber belfries of Essex make a notable group. A considerable number of mediaeval wooden spires remain: although mostly quite small, in Sussex alone there are still about forty. Much the loftiest (228 ft.) is the famous crooked spire of Chesterfield. But other timber spires that have long ago perished, particularly those of Lincoln and Old St. Paul's, which survived for a long time, rose considerably higher than this. Wood also continued until the very end of the Middle Ages to provide the material for almost every parish church roof, because in England the stone vault was a luxury which, with rare exceptions, only the grand churches could afford. There is little here to regret. The wooden roofs of the Perpendicular period, particularly the hammer-beam roofs of East Anglia, offer one of the greatest delights of our church architecture; nor must it be forgotten that the abundant church furniture of the later Middle Ages— screens, stalls, benches, altar-tables, font-covers, pulpits—is nearly always of wood. There are moreover still surviving, albeit drastically restored in every case, about half a dozen timber-framed churches in the counties of the west and north-west Midlands and one in Hampshire; and about twenty stone churches could be cited, some in the western and some in the south-eastern counties and two in central Devon (Nymet Rowland and Dowland), in which the nave arcades are of wood.

In the secular field, the general use of wood persisted for much longer. Recent research has shown that for the keeps of their castles the Normans used stone from the outset more frequently than was formerly believed,[1] but the ancillary buildings continued to be of wood—which is why, so often, only the keep survives. Ordinary houses, when not of unbaked earth, were, even in a county like Gloucestershire, which had plenty of stone, nearly all timber-framed, and sometimes wholly of wood, until the latter part of the sixteenth century. In some counties wood still remained the commonest material for houses throughout the seventeenth century too. By this time more private bedrooms were

1 See D. F. Renn on 'The Anglo-Norman Keep, 1066–1138' in *Journal of Archaeological Assn.*, vol. XXIII (1960).

required, so the houses often have three storeys and an array of gables, which can be very picturesque. A good example is Aylmers near Sheering in Essex.

Where there was a choice of wood or stone, the former was usually preferred. Not only was wood more easily handled, but every area of cleared woodland offered an opportunity for more tillage. Prof. Hoskins points out[1] that at Northampton in the early part of the sixteenth century stone was actually being replaced by timber as the principal building material; in 1675, as a consequence, the place suffered a devastating fire. Mediaeval timber, although the oldest, is often the best. It is almost always heart-oak. There were more trees from which to choose, and fewer people to use them. Later, any available wood might have to serve, and sometimes the bark would be left on, which it seldom was in the Middle Ages. From Elizabeth I's time onwards, it was also a common practice to reuse old timbers from demolished buildings, including many rebuilt at this time by well-to-do people in brick or stone. Yet up to about 1600, and often later, the majority of English towns, not excluding London, were almost entirely filled with timber-framed buildings. Leicester was, domestically, all timber-framed (and in a bad state of repair) until brick was introduced during the last quarter of the seventeenth century.[2] Manchester, strange as it may seem to-day, remained a town of timber-framed houses until well into the eighteenth century.

All these English buildings are rightly described as timber-framed, but the significance of this term is generally misconceived. The technique of timber-framing depends on the use of *halved* or cleft timbers, as opposed to whole logs. The term therefore distinguishes timber-framing from other systems, such as post-hole construction (in which the building was erected on posts driven into the ground). It is of course also true that the large majority of these buildings were only partly timbered: that is to say, whereas the skeleton was of wood the interstices were filled with some other material such as mud or plaster, applied to a light wooden 'core' of sticks or laths. For timber-framed buildings wholly sheathed with wood one has to look, in England to-day, principally to the dwindling numbers of surviving windmills and watermills. In America, on the other hand, where there is an immense amount of wooden architecture, practically all the timber-framed houses are also wood-covered. Almost always this covering is weather-boarding (see pp. 331–335), but Mount Vernon, the home of George Washington and now the most visited house in the United States, is different. Here, although the entire structure, except for the red tiles, is of wood, the house is faced not with weather-boarding but with blocks of wood, painted and sanded and carefully chamfered at the edges to give the appearance of rusticated stonework.

---

1 W. G. Hoskins, *Provincial England* (1963), p. 81.   2 *Ibid.*, p. 104.

Building stone here was so scarce that none could be found even for the pavement of the loggia, which had in the end to be imported from England. Mount Vernon, although begun about 1740, dates mainly from the seventies and eighties. By that time wood was in greater demand than ever in England for roof-rafters, window-frames, doors and numerous internal requirements, and the heavy tax on bricks did result in the appearance of a number of wooden cottages, especially in Kent and Sussex, at the end of the eighteenth century and during the Regency; but no one erecting a large house would have wanted it to be timber-framed.

Geographical Distribution

The distribution of timber-framed buildings in England to-day does not reflect the all but universal employment of wood in this country in the Middle Ages, not excluding areas like Derbyshire or the Cotswolds, which had an abundance of good building stone. At that time the only county not well supplied with wood (generally oak) suitable for building was Cornwall. But it cannot be too strongly emphasized that the proportion of mediaeval domestic timbering which survives is very small indeed, and includes none of the humbler examples. The large majority of our existing timber-framed houses belong to the sixteenth and seventeenth centuries; only in Kent, Sussex and Essex is there still an appreciable number of houses of this kind earlier than 1500. In the North of England, according to Mr. Smith[1], timber-framed buildings dating from before 1600 are rare. In the West Midlands and in parts of Southern England there are even a few poorly framed cottages, and a greater number of barns, which are mid-Georgian. By the middle of the sixteenth century, however, partly owing to the low rainfall and strong coastal winds which made the replacement of felled woodlands more difficult there than elsewhere, oaks were no longer plentiful on or near England's eastern seaboard. Leland, travelling through Northumberland, records laconically, 'little or no wood . . . they burn sea-coal'. The growing scarcity of timber was certainly one of the factors that stimulated the rise of the coal industry, as also the increasing use of brick. By the time of Elizabeth I Lincolnshire was another county suffering from a shortage of oak-trees, and so were parts of Norfolk. The Fenland villages, in particular, which had frequently to be satisfied with inferior woods, were hard pressed to satisfy their timber requirements; and, as Sir Roger Pratt commented in one of

1 Mr. J. T. Smith's paper, 'Timber-Framed Building in England: Its Development and Regional Differences', printed in the *Archaeological Journal* for 1965, pp. 133–158, although all too short, is easily the most authoritative general study of the subject yet to have appeared. But there are many problems which have still to be resolved.

his notebooks, 'the carriage of timber' was 'very chargeable and troublesome'. In the Breckland area of Norfolk and Suffolk, now covered by mile upon mile of spruce plantations, a royal proclamation in 1604 ordained that new houses must henceforth have their walls and window-frames of brick or stone and that the cutting of timber for firewood must cease altogether. Hence in these areas timber-framing, as it decayed, was replaced with other materials, usually brick or flint, so that in some districts scarcely a single framed building can be found. By the beginning of the eighteenth century oak was in short supply nearly everywhere.

Frequent fires were another reason for the disappearance of timber-framed houses; these of course were a far more persistent danger in towns than in the country (cf. p. 224). The advent of the Industrial Revolution dealt timbering another blow, and this again fell mainly on town houses. Shrewsbury and Chester are the only English towns of any size which still display an appreciable number of timber-framed houses.[1]

The situation to-day, therefore, is that timber-framed buildings are mostly to be found in rural areas or in small country towns, and, with a few exceptions, only in those parts of England in which the supply of oaks remained plentiful throughout the sixteenth and seventeenth centuries at least. To be specific, those areas are (i) the whole of England south and east of the limestone belt as far north as a line drawn from Huntingdon to Cromer, with Essex holding pride of place as the county with the largest number of timber-framed houses; and (ii) the whole of England west of the limestone belt from the Severn estuary to Leicestershire, and thence east of the Pennine chain through Nottinghamshire and the West Riding as far north as York, and west of the Pennines as far north as the Ribble (central Lancashire). Outside these two regions, which together cover about half the country, timber-framed buildings now tend to be scarce, although 'pockets' can be found elsewhere; even at Stamford—in the heart, that is, of a great stone district—there is, as indicated earlier (p. 41), more timber-framed construction than a casual observer might suppose, for here the framework was plastered over, and nearly always so remains. Such buildings can be found in other predominantly stone towns too: Kendal, for instance, and Hawkshead. Local variations can be detected here and there, and considerable differences are evident between the practice of the West and North and that of the South-East; but it may be well to review first the basic types.

1 Of these two, Chester appears to have many more; but restoration of timber-framed buildings there has been drastic, and much of the city's 'black and white' is patently bogus. Even Mr. Ian Nairn, an enthusiast for Chester, has described it as a 'splendid half-timbered hoax; . . . after a look at photographs of the eighteen-sixties one can hardly believe that it is the same place'. This is, however, partly because in the eighteenth century many of the exposed timbers were covered with plaster. The modern addiction to plaster-stripping, both in its practical and its aesthetic aspects, is considered later in the chapter.

Cruck Construction

In the rudest structures no distinction was made between walls and roof; the framework consisted simply of pairs of tree-trunks rammed a foot or so into the ground (their butt ends having first been scorched, for better preservation) and tied together at the top, or sometimes just below the top so that they crossed. Thus in section the shape resembled an isosceles triangle. Repeated at intervals, and linked horizontally at the top by a lighter piece of timber known as the ridge-pole, and lower down by one or more slender poles called purlins, the main structure was already complete. The interstices were probably filled in with branches, to support a covering of straw thatch, brushwood or heather which stretched right down to the ground.

From this was developed, in England, what is known as cruck construction. The crucks were cut from trees with a natural curve whenever they could be found. In some cases a single tree-trunk would be sliced into two halves along its length, before trimming. This would not only make it lighter to transport, but would ensure a symmetrical arch. The crucks (or 'blades' as they were sometimes called) were usually set upon a sill-beam resting on a low plinth of rough stone or even on turf. Otherwise the construction of a cruck house was in essentials as described above.

At first, presumably, these were only single-storey houses. Presently, we may suppose, it was realised that the introduction of horizontal tie-beams about half-way up each pair of 15 ft. crucks not only increased their stability but made possible the insertion of an upper floor. The upper storey, reached by a ladder, would have been convenient for sleeping, but would have been deficient in head-room. Hence the next development: the introduction of longer tie-beams, the ends of which provided support for the wall-plates (horizontal timbers helping to support the roof). These ends were now directly above the bases of the crucks. This made possible, for the first time in this type of construction, the erection of

Fig. 6
The framework of a
Yorkshire cruck house, now destroyed.
From *Timber Building in England*,
by F. H. Crossley

vertical walls, and the pitch of the roof now became less steep. But the remarkable fact is that, as surely as in modern steel-framed construction, the walls, which were sometimes of stone but usually of wattle and daub or mud, were not themselves weight-supporting, and could have been, had the builders possessed it, entirely of plate-glass (cf. fig. 6).

This wooden skeleton was framed together on the ground (the pegs were always of wood), then reared (hoisted into a vertical position). If the plinth, the sill-beam, the crucks, the cross-members and the pegs were all prepared beforehand, a simple cruck house could be erected very quickly. It could also be dismantled again without much difficulty, and moved, and there are indications that occasionally this did occur. Sometimes the cruck blades would be worked upside down: since the longer portion would probably be the trunk rather than the branch, a wider span could thereby be attained. In the mature examples each pair of crucks was linked not only by a tie-beam but higher up by a collar beam, or even by two collars at different levels, useful for giving support to the purlins. At Leigh Court tithe barn near Worcester, the crucks are 35 ft. 3 ins. long. At the apex the crucks, in the mature type, were fitted into a short piece of wood known as the saddle, along which lay the ridge-beam, or rigg-tree as it was called in Yorkshire. Besides the saddle, there were various other methods of jointing at the apex; in one type, the crucks terminate in a collar, from which the roof end, usually thatched, slopes backwards to form a half-hip. The normal roof long continued to be of thatch, but sometimes tiles were substituted later. More often than not a cruck house only extended for two bays, but it could, and sometimes did, continue for several, and a barn still further. In fact, Leigh Court barn, which is 138 ft. long, has no fewer than eleven pairs of crucks, virtually unchanged from the time of their erection more than six hundred years ago.

Very little is known about the history of cruck buildings, which has accordingly provided a field for a wealth of learned speculation, ranging from Addy's suggestion that the idea may have originated in boat-building to the fourth Lord Raglan's theory that the cruck form began as a sophisticated imitation in wood of the Gothic arch in stone, and gradually filtered downwards.[1] Scandinavia is no longer considered a likely place of origin; recent writers, such as Geoffrey Webb and F. W. B. Charles, have found closer analogies in early Irish buildings, and in two tiny ruined churches in particular. Kilmalkedar on the Dingle peninsula, Co. Kerry, may date from the twelfth century, but the minute chapel on St. Macdara's Island off Co. Galway is believed to go back to about 700.

What is beyond doubt is that cruck construction was mainly employed in the West, Midlands and North; the form is indeed almost entirely absent from the three

[1] 'The Cruck Truss': article in *Man*, August 1956.

south-eastern counties and from East Anglia, Middlesex, Cambridgeshire and Lincolnshire, and is rarely found in any of the south-western counties from Hampshire to Cornwall.[1]   *
This was partly, perhaps, because the South and East were always more susceptible to influence from France and the Netherlands, in which this form of construction was not current, and partly also because, in the West particularly, it was easier to find suitable trees.[2] There are in fact, in the West, Midlands and North, still many more cruck frames than the casual visitor might suppose, because they were often plastered over, or masked altogether under a facing of stone, brick or clay. The insertion of floors, party-walls, chimneys and so on has tended to obscure the original structures; so that to find one's evidence it is sometimes necessary to penetrate into low-ceilinged bedrooms where all too often one is confronted with sad signs of cruck-mutilation. In Leicestershire for example, some years ago a group of patient researchers succeeded in discovering over forty surviving crucks, most of which were only visible internally.[3] Much the same is true of Lancashire, including Furness, and of parts of Yorkshire, counties in which cruck construction continued until after 1700. In north-western Cumberland crucks, admittedly of very poor quality and not matching pairs, were even being used in the first years of the nineteenth century for some of the 'clay daubins' of the Solway Firth area referred to in the preceding chapter. Except in the Outer Hebrides and the Shetlands, regions short of suitable timber, crucks were also normal for timber-framed buildings in Scotland (where they were usually known as 'couples') until about 1800, and considerable numbers still survive: but hardly one is exposed to view.

The county which has the largest number of cruck-frames visible externally is Herefordshire. Here there were at the beginning of the present century over a hundred cottages or small houses of this type, as well as twenty-eight barns. For this kind of construction north-west Herefordshire, from Weobley westwards to Eardisley and northwards to Dilwyn, Pembridge and Eardisland, is now unrivalled in England. Plates

1 See the distribution maps accompanying two important papers: the late Professor R. A. Cordingley's 'British Historical Roof-Types and their Members: a Classification', in *Transactions of the Ancient Monuments Society*, New Series vol. 9 (1961), pp. 73–129, and J. T. Smith's 'Mediaeval Roofs: a Classification', in the *Archaeological Journal* for 1958, vol. CXV (1960), pp. 111–149. In R. W. Brunskill's *Illustrated Handbook of Vernacular Architecture* (1970), p. 173, these two maps have been, very conveniently, superimposed.

2 Basil Oliver, in *The Cottages of England* (1929), p. 40, proposed another explanation: 'The more architecturally sensitive natives of the South-Eastern counties would never have tolerated so unsightly a form of construction.'

3 For these see the paper by V. R. Webster, 'Cruck-framed Buildings of Leicestershire', in *Transactions of Leicestershire Archaeological Soc.*, vol. XXX (1954), pp. 26–58. Most of them are in the centre or west of the county.

*307*a and b illustrate two typical Herefordshire examples, both from Weobley. *307*a shows a cottage adjoining the Red Lion Inn, once part of a large barn. It has been modernized in various ways but preserves remarkably well its original cruck-framed skeleton. So does the second cottage, illustrated in *307*b. After Herefordshire, the best counties in which to see cruck-framed buildings are probably Worcestershire, Warwickshire, Staffordshire, Shropshire and Cheshire. Over the whole of this area the house itself may well be of stone, while the outbuildings are timber-framed; most of these cruck-framed structures are therefore farm buildings or cottages. Internally cruck construction is undoubtedly seen to best advantage in some of the old barns.

Post-and-Truss and Box-Frame Construction

The very large majority of English timber-framed houses do not appear to be of the cruck-framed type. Yet in the cruck areas—mainly, that is, in the West, Midlands and North—the essential principle of cruck construction, which is that the entire load of the roof is conveyed to the ground through transverse frames placed at determined intervals, persisted until the end. In this type of building the curving crucks have given place to vertical posts, each pair of which supports a group of strong timbers arranged as a frame within the triangle of the roof, and known as a truss (fig. 7: p. 310). The base of the truss may be a tie-beam or a framed arch. The weight of the roof is conveyed to the trusses by purlins and wall-plates. Purlins here are longitudinal horizontal beams supporting the common rafters and framed into the trusses. Wall-plates run horizontally at the base of the rafters. In nearly all the mediaeval buildings of this kind and many later ones there are windbraces beneath the rafters which help to convey the load exerted on the purlins to the transverse frames. So here again the intervening walls are really no more than screens to keep out the weather.

In the South and East, often referred to by writers on timber-framing as the Lowland zone (which extends up the eastern Midlands as far as York), this type of construction was not favoured. Here, as can be clearly seen in plate *314*d, the side walls provide a continuous bearing. Thus there is no division into bays, and no concentration of thrust at fixed points. The roof need only consist of pairs of rafters joined by a light collar near their apex, to prevent spreading (fig. 8). The analogy is with early Romanesque rather than with Gothic, and still more closely with the early basilican type of building. In fact, it seems at least possible that this sort of construction was originally designed for stone-walled buildings and only

TIMBER-FRAMING: STRUCTURAL TYPES
Cruck-framed buildings: a, b. *Weobley, Herefordshire*
Post-and-truss: c. *Luntley Court, Herefordshire: dovecot*
Box-frame: d. *The Old Cottage, Cheam, Greater London*

applied later to timber ones. This is the kind of structure to which the label 'box-frame' should properly be confined.

In origin and in internal appearance it will be evident that these two types of timber-framed structure are very different. Yet to the average spectator they look much the same. A variation which the two longer walls may reveal externally is the occurrence in the first type of more massive posts at the bay intervals (*327a*). But the surest way of determining the difference is to look at the end-gables. Where there are purlins—that is to say, in all post-and-truss buildings—their ends always project beyond the gable-face (*130c*, *308c* (central gable), *333b*), although in the better houses it was customary to mask them with barge-boards (*308a*, *308c* (porch gable), *327a, b and c*). Usually, too, the purlin-ends will be linked by a heavy collar-beam crossing the face of the gable horizontally about half-way up (*308a*, *327a*), or, where there are two purlins, at one third and two thirds of the way up (*327c*). In the timber-framed buildings of East Anglia and the South-East, on the other hand, where purlins (although sometimes used) were less essential, the collar-beam is also less prominent on the gable-face (*314a and d*, *328a*), and for a roof of modest span may be omitted altogether (*308e*). Otherwise, the two types of construction often seem to be externally identical.

Hence it has become customary in recent years to group together all timber-framed buildings other than those of cruck construction under the 'box-frame' umbrella. This seems to me misleading, because it fails to take account of the diverse structural origins and character of the two types as described above. Older, and some contemporary, writers have preferred the general term 'post-and-panel', which carries the advantage of implying, what is undoubtedly true, that the aesthetic effect of timber-framed building depends hardly less on the treatment of the interstitial panels than upon the proportions and arrangement of the timbers themselves. But the only satisfactory course, in my view, is to preserve both terms, post-and-truss and box-frame; for both are needed.

Nevertheless, despite this basic distinction and many local variations, most of these buildings have certain essentials in common. These can be well seen in the photograph of the former Wool Hall at Lavenham, the building on the left in plate *313a*. First there is a base (the 'footings') of some solid material, such as stone, brick or flint, or sometimes large balks of oak laid horizontally; then a wooden sill placed along the top of this base. Strong upright posts or '*studs*' (the word derives from the Old English 'stuthu', meaning a pillar or post), often with the butt-ends uppermost, are mortised into the sill, whilst their upper ends are tenoned into another horizontal beam called a summer or bressummer (see p. 319) if it carries the floor-joists of an upper storey or a wall-plate if it supports the lower ends of the roof rafters. Here and there the whole lower storey will be of brick

(see p. 319)

'BLACK AND WHITE' IN THE WEST COUNTRY
a. *Reader's House, Ludlow, Shropshire*   b. *Moat Farm, Dormston, Worcestershire*
c. *Salwarpe Court, Worcestershire*
d. *Netherton, Pencoyd, Herefordshire, before 1960*   e. *Netherton, since 1960*

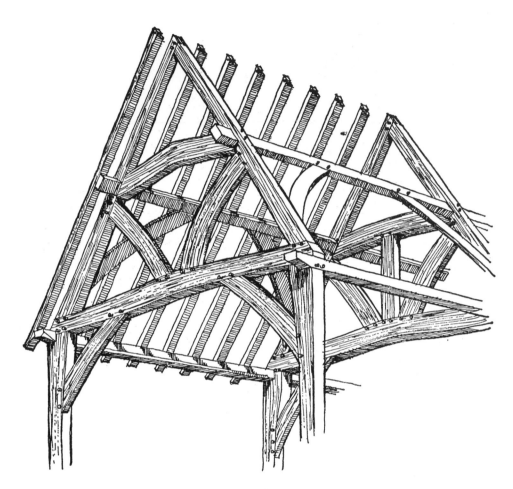

Fig. 7 A typical 'purlin' roof. Post-and-truss building.
From Chorley House, Droitwich, Worcestershire,
c. 1400: demolished, 1965

(277c: modern) or stone (129b); this is commoner in the North-West, especially in Lancashire, than in the South-East. If chimney-stacks were added, they were always of brick or
stone, brick being preferred because it is the more fire-resistant.

Frequently the upper storey projects on one or more sides; occasionally even on all
four, as in the gatehouse at Lower Brockhampton in Herefordshire (327a). An overhanging
storey was known as a jetty. The projection may be as much as 4 ft., and if there is a

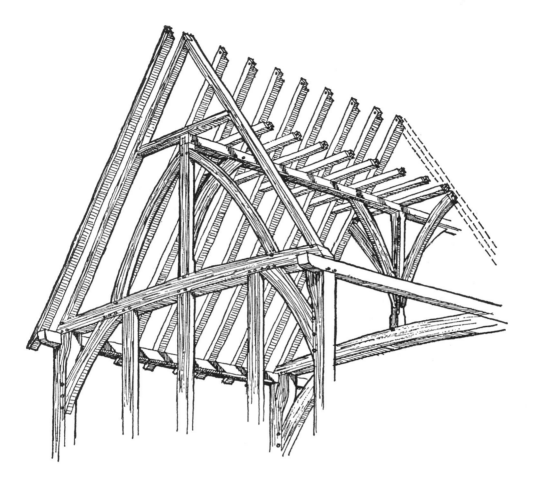

Fig. 8 A typical 'rafter' roof. Box-frame building.
From Severns, Castle Gate, Nottingham, *c.* 1450

second storey, this may overhang as much again (*40*b, *308*a, *327*c, *328*a). The reason for jettying is not definitely known; there are at least four possible explanations, all or any of which may account for it.

It has been held that the object was simply to gain increased floorspace, which was certainly desirable in the confined areas of towns; but the overhanging upper storey can frequently be seen in the depths of the country too. On the other hand, it seems possible, even probable, that the practice started in the towns, and country builders may have been following a fashion that had become popular.

The desire to protect the lower part of the structure from damp affords perhaps a more likely explanation. These buildings had, of course, no gutters at the eaves and no down-pipes, so without a jetty much of the water pouring off the roof would on windy days have been blown back against the walls. Not only was it necessary that the framing should be kept reasonably dry: the infilling too, frequently of plaster which was lime or colour-washed, would not have stood up for long to incessant streaking with rain-water.

Other possible reasons for the jetty are purely structural. One might be explained as follows. Imagine a heavy piece of furniture standing in the centre of an upstairs room. In time the joists which carry it will tend to sag. If, however, their ends project into space and are weighted by having to carry an upper wall and a share of the roof, the effect will be one of counterpoise. The result will be not to weaken but to strengthen the overall structure.

The other structural explanation turns on the problem of obtaining timbers long enough to run the full height of the building, which was often difficult. With jetties it was only necessary to have wall-posts one storey high.

But sometimes, when all is said, jetties appeared when they were not structurally necessary at all, as on the end-bays of the so-called Wealden houses (see p. 315). To account for these the obvious explanation must surely be the right one: men who could afford to pay for it could not resist a feature so charming in itself and, before the age of steel and concrete, impossible to achieve in any other material but wood. But during the reign of Elizabeth I jetties fell out of fashion, and for good.

Where the upper storey projected on all four sides, or indeed on two only if at right angles to each other, the construction had to be a little more complex. From an internal cross-beam, to which it was anchored, a horizontal member known as the dragon-beam ran diagonally to the corner-post, a very robust member often comprising the major part of a tree-trunk (328a). Into this beam were tenoned all the shortened floor joists in both directions, each pair making a right angle. Further support was often given to the corner-posts of timber-framed buildings by the addition of pairs of braces, sometimes curved, and carefully fitted into the vertical studs whenever they intersected them (307d, 313a, 327a). A local characteristic of Cheshire and Lancashire timber-framing is the introduction of a rounded cove under the overhang, and, below the roof, eaves with timbers shaped to the cove.[1] These were sometimes decorated, as at Little Moreton Hall

[1] The curved cove can occasionally be found elsewhere, e.g. at Stoneleigh in Warwickshire (Manor Farm House), but not often.

URBAN TIMBER-FRAMING
a. *Lavenham, Suffolk*
b. *Malt Mill Lane, Alcester, Warwickshire*

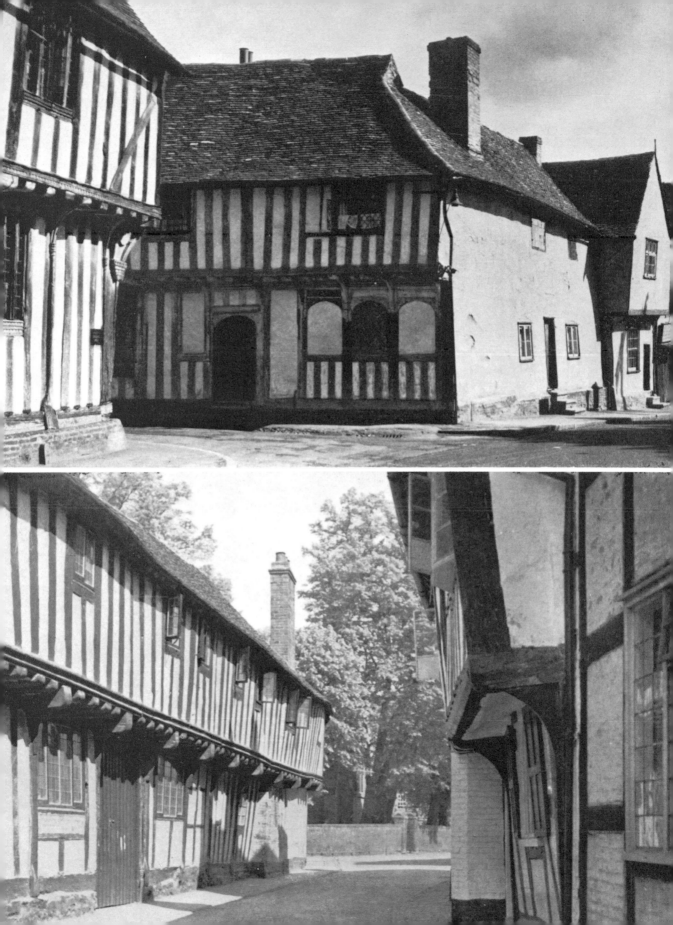

(*327*c). A few buildings in the west, such as Moat Farm at Dormston in Worcestershire, preserve tiled weatherings, at this house above both ground and first floor windows (*308*b). These can also be seen on the dovecot at Luntley Court (*307*c). Their purpose can only have been to throw the rain clear of the walls. A number of examples of storeyed weatherings can also be found in the Aegeri–See region of Switzerland.

Another and much more important local variation can be seen in what is known as the Wealden type. The characteristic Wealden house is a plain rectangular box (the perfect example of a true box-frame), in all the best examples close-studded, with a lofty hipped roof covering the entire structure. But as the two ends are jettied—even, in the grandest houses, on all three sides—the roof covers a larger area than the floor. Since the central hall is recessed between the jettied ends, the projection of the eaves beyond the wall-face of the hall is considerable, as can be seen at Corner Farm, Langley (*314*b and c), to the south-east of Maidstone. Additional support for the eaves is accordingly provided by curved braces rising from the jettied wings, in a direction parallel to the front. Of the 'standard' types of timber-framed house, the Wealden is easily the finest; most of these were built by well-to-do yeoman-farmers. Over a thousand examples survive, mainly in Kent; many of them belong to the later fifteenth and still more to the early sixteenth centuries, but a few are earlier. The name, as Mr. John Newman has pointed out, is a little misleading, since the thickest concentration of these houses is on the Greensand to the east of Maidstone, and not in the Weald. Outside Kent, houses of this type occur principally in Sussex, the south-eastern corner of Surrey and southern Essex, especially the Epping Forest district. Elsewhere in England there are no more than twenty in all, widely scattered.[1] The Kentish origin of the form is not in question; it is a pity that at nearly all of them the central hall was later divided horizontally and the tall windows removed. At a few of these houses, of which Corner Farm, Langley, is one, the intrusive floors have in recent years been removed and the large windows replaced, to their great artistic advantage.

Structurally the timber-framed house was, far more closely than any other, the forerunner of the steel and reinforced concrete framed structure of to-day. Although extended cantilevers and long-angle braces are admittedly out of the question in timber-framed buildings, the overhanging upper storeys are cantilevers in embryo. In the preparation of the parts of a timber-framed building, mediaeval documents also reveal a considerable amount of prefabrication. This does not of course imply mass-production;

1 See S. E. Rigold, 'The Distribution of the Wealden House', in *Culture and Environment: Essays in Honour of Sir Cyril Fox*. Edited by I. Ll. Foster and L. Alcock (1963), pp. 351–354.

CLOSE SPACING IN THE SOUTH-EAST
a. *Brewerstreet Farm, Bletchingley, Surrey*
b. and c. *Corner Farm, Langley, Kent*   d. *A Tudor house at Somersham, Suffolk, in course of demolition*

each frame was made to order by the carpenter for a specific client and site and, as Fox and Raglan discovered in Monmouthshire, 'though in their details of construction all our Regional style houses are very similar, in their main measurements of length and breadth no two are exactly alike'.[1] But usually the work of preparing the wooden skeleton was carried out away from the site. Mr. John Harvey tells me that almost every timber-framed building that he has inspected carries carpenter's position-marks, which can only be explained on the supposition that the wood was prepared in the shop or yard, in readiness for reassembly *in situ*. And, as Fox and Raglan also pointed out, 'such items as studs and panels, mullions and joists, were no doubt made in the workshops during the winter'. Because of transport difficulties, it is reasonable to suppose that the main timbers were prepared as near to the site as was practicable, but the actual distance might vary considerably. Thus 'the "framyngplace" at Eltham in 1401 was beside the gate . . . but the wonderful roof of Westminster Hall was worked many miles from its ultimate destination'.[2] In either event, the timbers seem always to have been framed together on the ground first, before being hoisted into position. For this reason, the dismantling of a timber-framed house can be accomplished far more easily than that of any other traditional type. The early-sixteenth-century house at Somersham near Ipswich, shown in plate *314*d during the process of demolition in 1955, was unhappily not re-erected elsewhere, but it will be evident that without excessive difficulty it could have been. Grange House at Leominster, now the Town Council offices, and notable for its profuse if unsophisticated carved ornamentation, was built in 1633 as the Market Hall. In 1853 it was offered for auction and purchased by a private citizen for the sum of £95! He had it set up again on its present site a few hundred yards away, at the same time filling in the ground storey, which had previously been open. Among other examples of short moves are Selly Manor House, near Birmingham, which in 1912–16 migrated about a mile to the village of Bournville; the Old Cottage at Cheam in Greater London (until 1965 in Surrey) (*307*d), which was taken to pieces in 1922 and re-erected in an adjacent street; and a little three-storeyed fifteenth-century house in Exeter, with a shop-front of that date (a great rarity), which, in December 1961, was not dismembered but manoeuvred on to a wheeled timber platform and winched along metal grooves to a new site a hundred yards away. Some timber-framed houses have made much longer journeys. Part of a house that stood until 1908 in Cow Street, Ipswich, was moved in that year to the Franco-British Exhibition at London's White City, and the following year was re-erected at Ashby St. Ledgers in Northamptonshire. Other examples

1 Sir Cyril Fox and Lord Raglan, *Monmouthshire Houses, Part II* (1953), p. 87.
2 L. F. Salzman, *op. cit.*, p. 200.

include a derelict yeoman's house shifted in 1910 from Benenden, Kent, to Northiam, Sussex, for the enlargement of Great Dixter; Coombe Wood House near Kingston-upon-Thames, brought in the same year from Colchester; and the transportation in 1926 of Agecroft Hall, Lancashire, to Richmond, Virginia. This last is a proceeding that makes some people very angry and one which, it is to be hoped, will not often be repeated; but it is surely preferable to obliteration without trace. Timber-framed buildings in danger of demolition now have a double chance of finding a new home. The Avoncroft Museum of Buildings at Stoke Prior, near Bromsgrove in Worcestershire, founded in 1963, and the Weald and Downland Open Air Museum at West Dean, Sussex, opened in the autumn of 1970, both have the preservation of threatened timber-framed buildings by removal and reconstruction as one of their objectives: at West Dean the main one.

Timber-framed buildings varied a good deal both structurally and ornamentally at different times and in different parts of the country, but a consideration of the surviving evidence, which is extensive, permits us to reach certain general conclusions. First, about the character of the timbers themselves. Of the humblest class of dwelling, the cottages of the poor labourers, we have scarcely any examples older than the eighteenth century because, where they achieved a wooden frame at all (and in some counties, as for instance Leicestershire, they were often only of mud), the timbers were usually flimsy and skimped, and probably not of oak, for oak was always relatively expensive. For this reason timbers, and especially corner-posts, of generous dimensions (or, to use the technical term, scantling), which always look best, were a mark of affluence. In some districts, such as the Weald, Cheshire, Lancashire and the West Riding, the better houses were habitually roofed with stone slates; these, being extremely heavy, naturally required very sturdy posts and strong rafters. In East Anglia, on the other hand, where oakwood was less abundant and roofs usually thatched, the framework could be lighter without any loss of efficiency.

There can in my view be no doubt that the most pleasing timber-framed buildings are those in which the studs (uprights) are closely spaced, and the panels just long, narrow rectangles, as in Malt Mill Lane, close by the church at Alcester (313b), a notably good, and now rare, example of a street largely composed of timber-framed houses. Brewer-street Farm, north of Bletchingley in Surrey, offers a particularly satisfying instance of close spacing (314a), and, in addition to several other buildings here illustrated, mention may be made of the distinguished stone-roofed Porch House at Potterne near Devizes, of the late fifteenth century, which was restored (and the timbers unfortunately blackened) about a hundred years ago. There most of the massive studs are only between 7 and 10 ins. apart. But close studding was a relatively late development. Most of it belongs to the years 1475 to 1600 or thereabouts, and is delightfully typical of Tudor extravagance. In the early post-and-truss and box-frame buildings the panels are broader, and sometimes absolutely square, proportions which for lesser buildings still persisted throughout the sixteenth and seventeenth centuries. In all parts of the country, in fact, the broad rectangle was the norm (*130*c). The reason why it is more often to be seen to-day in the West and North-West is economic: the East and South had more financial resources. The exact square is not usually a pleasing proportion in timber-framing (*308*c), although acceptable when the building itself is also square, as at Luntley Court, Dilwyn, near Leominster, where the charming dovecot, with a gable on each face, was not erected until 1673 (*307*c).

At Luntley Court—the house itself was built under James I—the timber framework still remained quite simple, but in houses of this date we do not always find such restraint. Panels in the western counties had by this time become not only broader but often smaller, and on some buildings very irregular. An orgy of decorative patterning developed; gnarled and twisted oak branches seem to have been sought out deliberately for the designs which they could be induced to provide, and where these were not to be had, short straight pieces were elaborately cut. Diamonds, herring-bones, criss-crosses, ogees, circles, trefoils, quatrefoils, star-patterns, chequers (with wood and plaster used in alternation)—all these are freely represented in the timber-framed buildings of the Elizabethan and Jacobean periods in the Midlands and North-West (*147*c, *327*b and c). An uncommon and specially entertaining example is the long barn erected about 1570 at Kenilworth Castle by Dudley, Earl of Leicester, which has cusped ogee struts within the panels.[1] Sometimes the design, a quatrefoil for example, would be gouged out of a broad piece of wood and filled in with plaster. It was all very exuberant and high-spirited, not, let it be admitted, in impeccable taste, and quite unstructural.

Although not so frequently as on the Continent, some of these timber-framed houses were greatly enriched, externally as well as internally, by carving as distinct from carpentry. Plate *328*c illustrates one of the oak brackets on the corner-posts of the timber-framed gatehouse added late in the sixteenth century at Stokesay Castle in Shropshire: an endearing object of fantasy in the Renaissance style. The carving is always more telling when confined to only a few members, as on the lofty porch, dating from 1616, of the nearby Reader's House at Ludlow (*308*a). Here the enrichments occur above and around the door, on the paired brackets below the windows, on the pair below the gable, and particularly on the barge-boards decorated with four dragons. There are still several excellent examples of ornamental woodcarving surviving at Ipswich, among which No. 7

[1] Could the inspiration for these have come from the fantastic west wall of Hartley Wespall Church, Hampshire?

Northgate Street (*328a*) is outstanding. This house, originally early Tudor, was plastered over and given sash-framed windows at the beginning of the last century, and restored as far as possible to its original state early in the present one. The carving runs in several directions: vertically on the corner-post, horizontally on the fascia-boards, and diagonally on the barge-boards; but it is by no means excessive. The structural importance of the corner-post has already been explained; the decoration here (which was not masked under the plaster) is exuberant, and includes a blacksmith with his anvil and a portrait head as well as a pair of heraldic-looking bird-heads. The fascia-board is the long horizontal board which masks and protects from the weather the ends of the joists that carry the studs of the upper floor, as distinct from the much more massive summer, which supports the joists at the back of the overhang. Where there is no jetty, the face of this beam is of course exposed: it is then known as a bressummer (bressumer, bresummer, or sometimes breast-summer: the word derives from the French *sommier* = a beam, and all these spellings are current). The ornamental forms appropriate to fascia-boards and bressummers are identical: trails of foliage, especially vines, were popular, while here at Ipswich there are a number of dragons, whose writhing, serpentine bodies are specially suited to this long narrow surface. The barge-boards are the planks which run up and down the gable, again with the object of masking and protecting the ends of structural timbers such as purlins. This is another instance, so characteristic of mediaeval art, of an essential structural member being given a pleasing decorative face; needless to say, the trailing vine was always a favourite motif for the adornment of long boards and beams. Because of their exposed situation, not many original barge-boards survive. The particularly fine set at Ockwells Manor (*333a*) (see page 325) is less than a hundred years old. On the pretty little gatehouse at Lower Brock-hampton (*327a*), the well-carved pair seen in the photograph date only from the restoration undertaken by the National Trust in 1952. The pair on the inner side, protected from the prevailing wind, are somewhat worn but genuine examples of external woodcarving belonging to the second half of the fifteenth century. Also original, and of similar date, are the north-facing pair on the gable at Clare (*355c*).

In a modern steel-framed building the skeleton is erected first and the filling of the interstices follows after. This is the obvious method where the dimensions of the skeleton are regular enough to admit of prefabrication. In timber-framed buildings such regularity was not possible: even in the most symmetrical frames, the panel sizes are always slightly different—and part of their appeal derives from exactly that. So in early examples the infilling was built in as the frame went up. To provide the necessary support for daub or plaster, more wood had to be introduced. Originally they used willow-sticks (withes or osiers), reeds or flexible twigs, normally of unbarked hazel or ash; at widely differing dates between the fifteenth century (in a few places perhaps even earlier) and the nineteenth, these gave place to laths. They were long, flat strips of wood, generally either of riven oak or beech, and usually narrow but sometimes several inches broad. In the photographs of the Reader's House at Ludlow (*308a*) and of the dovecot at Luntley Court (*307c*), taken before restoration, some of this wood is exposed to view. Where the panels were wide, as for the dovecot, upright staves were also needed: these were usually of cleft oak or chestnut, fitted into slots at the base and pegged into holes about 10 or 12 ins. apart at the top. Between them, horizontally, ran the thinner, more flexible sticks which were normally woven between the staves *in situ*, in the manner of a hurdle, and sprung into grooves cut into the sides of the studs. This primitive basketwork was known as wattle. At the Bell Hotel, Thetford, during decorations carried out some years ago in the gallery of the west wing, a section of wattle and daub was uncovered (and can still be seen) in which the wattles are held together with a thick string composed of twisted grass. Where the studs were close together, the vertical staves and the interweaving could be omitted; all that was required here was a succession of short horizontal sticks which could also be slotted into grooves. When laths were introduced, whether cleft or (as to-day) sawn, they were always affixed with nails. Both sides of each rough panel were then completely covered with daub, comprising wet clay or mud often mixed with chopped straw and sometimes cow-hair and manure: the consistency varied according to the district. Many old houses have in the garden, if not a moat at least a pond, recalling the place where the mud for the daub was dug out. The infilling panels were finished with a smoother coat of white lime-plaster or, in humbler instances, of an earth ochre wash, usually yellow or deep red. In a district where lime-plaster was something of a luxury the few owners who could afford it were sometimes tempted to notify the world of this fact by giving the name 'White House' to their farm.

With wood, however, it is impossible to avoid shrinkage. Wood is ever in movement, expanding in damp weather but contracting in dry, so that cracks are always appearing on the face of the timbers. Anyone who has lived or stayed in a timber-framed house will be well aware that such buildings are by no means inaccessible to draughts. So it was tempting to give the whole house another external coat of plaster, and in the South-East during the later seventeenth and eighteenth centuries this was commonly done. It undoubtedly helped to stop up the crevices that let in the draughts and the damp, but of course it also masked the timber-framing. Sometimes, as at Newport in Essex (*356a*), only the front was covered, so that on the side elevation the timber-framing still shows; but even where the visible wall-surface was completely masked, the underlying structure is as a rule easily recognizable, especially when the upper storey overhangs (*349a*, b and c, *355d*). In recent years, in obedience to the dictates of a possibly misguided romanticism, a great deal of this old timber-framing has been revealed again, the crevices being stopped up with new synthetic preparations which our forefathers did not possess. Rye, for example, which now has many timber-framed fronts exposed to view, had scarcely any in 1900, when the Mermaid Inn was still masked with brick-tiles, and other buildings with plaster. Not everyone applauds this practice.[1] From the practical standpoint there is this to be said for it: up to the seventeenth century the timbers were left uncovered because the carpenters knew very well that, exposed to the air and well ventilated, wood is much less vulnerable to boring insects and to fungi. But unmasked timbers seldom look altogether pleasing; the plastering process often meant driving in a great many nails to secure the laths or reeds, which leave unsightly holes when removed; and where it was the intention to plaster from the outset, the wood employed might be very rough. Each building, therefore, must be considered on its merits. In the West Midlands, although limewashing over timbers as well as plaster would seem at one time (especially in the eighteenth century) to have been prevalent, full plastering as at Netherton, Pencoyd, was not common. This Herefordshire farmhouse of *c.* 1570 was covered about 1750 with a 3 in. layer of plaster, and restored in 1960 as closely as possible (apart from the unfortunate nineteenth-century Welsh slate roof) to its original condition. Plates *308d* and e illustrate the transformation. The disappearance of cement rendering, an entirely untraditional material, is visually always welcome; otherwise the removal of plasterwork, although sometimes an improvement, needs to be accomplished with the greatest tact. The eighteenth-century view would have been that the plaster covering was in every way desirable, and that exposed beams were only a little less restless and disturbing than those Gothic flying buttresses which that age also so much deplored. Classical thinking to-day would agree with that attitude.

The casing of timber-framing with some other material was often carried out long after a house had been built. It was generally undertaken in the interests of greater warmth and comfort, but fashion might provide an additional motive. Of the desire to imitate stone, which could impart to a timber-framed house a very odd appearance (*40b* and d), something was said in Chapter 2 (p. 41). In Essex, Surrey and Kent, timber-framing sometimes hides behind eighteenth-century weather-boarding (*334d*), or behind hung tiles (*277c*, *278c*). When either of these, or indeed just lath and plaster, were intended

---

1 A lady in Suffolk who removed the internal plastering of her large living room, and who now looks upon beams inside and moats outside, remarked to me, 'I have been urged to strip off the plaster and show the beams outside too, but this I will not do; after all, one must have a *little* bit of comfort!'

at the time of building, it was no longer necessary to fill in the interstices between the timbers, and they were left as cavities. In many parts of England in the eighteenth and nineteenth centuries, the refacing of timber-framed houses and cottages in brick was a common practice. Where this occurred it is not always easy to discover that there is an oak framework underneath, often with the original roof-trusses. Even if there was a jetty, it usually disappeared when brick or stone were introduced.

In addition to those already mentioned, various other materials were employed in different parts of the country to fill the intervening panels. Among them may be cited pebbles from the Pebble Beds in the Triassic sandstone areas, boulders from the Boulder Clay, and sometimes, as for instance in Suffolk, clay lump (see Chapter 11). In Surrey there is flint infilling at Ash, whilst under the North Downs, as at Merstham, and in Sussex under the South Downs, as in some cottages below Bury Hill, it can be chalk. For the fifteenth-century gatehouse at Lower Brockhampton (327a), the original infilling was a composition of resin, beeswax and dried sawdust. Herefordshire (as at Withington) and Worcestershire (as at Wickenford) still preserve a number of barns having panels about 30 ins. square filled with broad oak slithers: the breadth of these thin strips, peeled from the tree's surface, could be, as at Bridge Sollers, as much as 7 ins. At Penshurst in Kent a late-fifteenth-century house by the churchyard gate has vertical oak boarding between its closely spaced studs. Where the spacing of the studs was wide, their sides might be grooved to receive boards, driven in horizontally one above the other. Tiles, slate and slabs of stone were also employed in this way, in close-studded buildings. Slithers of sandstone have been found in a number of Tudor buildings at Coventry; sandstone flags set in grooves were sometimes used in Lancashire, and were normal in the West Riding. In the Stamford neighbourhood Collyweston slates (see pp. 104–105) provided a favourite material for the infilling: these were usually 8–10 ins. wide, and plastered on both sides. Such an infilling, even in a stone district, was more expensive than the other materials here described, but the greater stability of stone meant that the braces, and indeed all cross-members except above and below windows and doors, could be dispensed with. A stone infilling yields a wall of exceptional durability.

Much the most important of these other materials, however, is brick. 'Nogging', as it is called, is to be found to-day wherever timber-framed buildings survive, for it is quite easy to remove a wattle and daub or a lath and plaster panel when it decays, and to substitute a brick one (307b). As bricks became cheaper, this occurred in many parts of the country. It is commonly supposed that thereby the owners of timber-framed houses greatly enhanced their comfort, but this is a delusion. The bricks were much heavier than what they replaced, and tended to overburden the wooden framing and so to cause structural trouble.

Moreover, $4\frac{1}{2}$ in. bricks are liable to project slightly from the oak framework, creating little ledges along which rainwater inevitably settles, in due course soaking the timber. And old bricks are usually more porous than properly rendered daub: here is another reason why the substitution of brick nogging has tended to encourage dampness.

Why then was it done? The probable explanation is that by the end of the seventeenth century good daubers were already beginning to become scarce. The old craft of daubing was a specialized one, and as brick became progressively more general for new houses, the need for daubers declined. There came a time, therefore, when it was both cheaper and much easier to find a bricklayer who could replace the old daub with nogging than a dauber with the requisite knowledge to choose the right wattles and clay-mix and replace the infilling in its traditional form. The change-over to brick took place at different dates according to the region: Warwickshire, for example, was a good deal earlier than Worcestershire. But according to Miss Margaret Wood,[1] there are no proven cases of brick nogging before the seventeenth century; and one has only to look at the bricks to see that more often than not they are Victorian.

The bricks are arranged in many different ways, of which perhaps the herring-bone or chevron pattern is the most attractive. Often this appears in combination with straight-forward horizontal courses (*333a and b*). Other variants include slanting courses and patterns of horizontal and vertical brickwork, both to be found in Essex. Elsewhere all the coursing may be of the normal kind (*130c, 191c*). And sometimes, as above the upper tier of windows at Sutton Bonington (*333b*) and over the whole front of the former Guildhall at Laxfield in Suffolk, the arrangement of the nogging will be haphazard, following no consistent pattern; but this is a mark of inferior workmanship.

In the Welsh border counties and in Worcestershire and Warwickshire there is far more brick nogging than a superficial observer might suppose, for on many buildings the brickwork was limewashed (*307b*). So great indeed is the passion for 'black and white' in this part of England that, far more reprehensibly, one finds many buildings which are entirely of brick, carefully whitened and blackened to simulate timber-framing. Why 'black and white' should have become so much more popular in the West than in the South-East is not easy to determine with certainty, but it may be due to the damper climate of the West, fostering the belief that it was necessary to protect the oak from the wet. What remains doubtful is how many, if any, old timber-framed buildings were given the black and white treatment when they were first set up. Documentary evidence on this point has so far proved elusive, but some specialists on timber building seem reluctant to

1 *The English Mediaeval House* (1965), p. 225.

go as far as Mr. F. W. B. Charles, who holds that all the 'black and white' which we see to-day is Victorian or later. Houses, he says, were sometimes decoratively painted in Elizabethan and Jacobean times, but with water paint; timbers were occasionally reddened (as at Pitchford Hall they still are) and plaster was washed over with ochre. But with water paint one could only have achieved a lamp black or charcoal black that would not have been durable. A permanent black did not become available until tar and pitch, distilled from coal, were marketed in the nineteenth century. To-day recourse is sometimes had to oil paint.

Artistically this blackening seems difficult to justify when applied to so sturdy a wood as oak. All that can be said in defence of it is that, if one is determined to have one's timbers black, then white plasterwork is the perfect foil. These buildings can look strident, especially in towns, where they consort ill with the often contiguous Georgian red brick; but in the heart of the country, standing alone in a field against an expanse of sky or half hidden among the trees which may be the descendants of those from which its own timbers were drawn, a black and white house can look attractive.

Nevertheless, most eyes will almost certainly prefer the gentler colour harmonies of the timber-framing in East Anglia and the south-eastern counties. Here the woodwork is scarcely ever blackened, although it may be given a coating of dark stain. But often, as in the former Guildhall at Laxfield referred to above, the oak will have weathered to a delicate silvery hue which is a joy to see. With oak of this colour, brick nogging looks far more agreeable than with blackened timber. And in this part of England the plaster itself is often coloured; the art here was to obtain a contrast of colour but not of tone. It is perhaps for their tonal unity, above all, that the timber-framed houses of Suffolk and Essex, Sussex and Kent, are such good neighbours. Their plaster panels may be pink or cream, buff or green, deep yellow ochre or muted apricot: the colours and the woodwork blend in sunny contentment, quieter and altogether less blatant than the 'magpie' houses of the West.

There can be no doubt whatever that our timber-framed houses hold a secure place in the hearts of the public, and there are some very good reasons why they should, for the best of these buildings are certainly excellent works of art. Yet certain reservations arise concerning them, which must have been felt by many students of architecture. Appreciation of them has not been assisted by the circumstance that, for nearly a hundred years now, their currency has been debased by the oakery-beamery productions of speculative builders; nor yet by the fact that such buildings, readily associated in the mind's eye with wheelback chairs, crazy paving, and ever-so-sweet rock gardens, have contrived to become one of the favourite symbols of what 'Beachcomber' has called Ye Olde and Fritefullye Merrye

Ynglande. But such excessively cosy associations are at least evidence of their widespread popularity, which is no ground for reproach. The two reasons for hesitancy are not dependent upon associations.

First there is the widespread feeling among the *cognoscenti* that timber-framed buildings are, to put it bluntly, largely fakes. There is a certain basis for this assumption. Reference has already been made to the present appearance of Chester, and there are a good many other town buildings, especially in the 'black and white' counties, upon which the work of restoration has been punitive. So also with some of the larger country houses. We go to a famous black-and-white house like Bramall Hall in Cheshire (in the village of Bramhall), and find ourselves standing before what is in effect a Victorian reproduction and a none-too-faithful one at that; for instance, all the chimney stacks are of terracotta, and much too red. We go even to Ockwells Manor in Berkshire, a picture-book house in a perfect setting (cf. *333a*), and often regarded as one of the most delightful timber-framed houses in England; yet here, too, the work of renovation has been formidable. One has only to look at the undeviating straight line of the roof ridge, or at a picture of the entrance front in 1838 showing no oriel windows, whereas now there are two. The need for restoration can often not be questioned, and sometimes, particularly in recent years, the work has been carried out with tact and skill. But this has not always been so, either in the treatment of the wood itself or, still more often, of the infilling. It is, for instance, not unusual in England (although less common than in France and Germany) to find decayed plaster replaced with cement, a practice which cannot be too strongly deplored. In the employment of traditional materials, too, there is plenty of scope for errors. Another National Trust building, Paycocke's House at Great Coggeshall, Essex, offers a good illustration. The appeal of the front here, despite the fascination of its discreetly restored silver-brown wood-carving, is quite seriously compromised by the unattractive bricks introduced about 1905 (before the National Trust took over) for the renewal of the nogging.

There are, then, many evidences of restoration, sometimes carried out with a thoroughly insensitive eye and hand. Yet England also possesses many thousands of timber-framed buildings—far more than is perhaps generally recognized—which have undergone comparatively little restoration. These are mostly smallish houses, often farmhouses or cottages, standing alone in the countryside, or maybe in villages. Usually they belong to the late sixteenth or seventeenth centuries, but some, at least in parts, are older. Good English heart oak, properly framed, will stand almost indefinite exposure to our weather in all seasons; it becomes nearly as hard as iron, and, if untouched, retains its exquisite colour. This oak has indeed greater durability than most varieties of English stone. It would probably be hard to discover an old timber-framed building which does not contain *any* new wood, but *mutatis mutandis* this is equally true of brick and of most kinds of stone. Yet when the structure of an oak-framed house has remained inviolate, a conservative restoration will usually be all that is necessary. The drastic and often deplorable renovations of which, particularly in the West, one cannot long remain unaware, have always been the outcome of later tamperings.

The other reason why some informed students of architecture are liable to be less than enthusiastic about timber-framing is perhaps best suggested by the story of those visitors from Spain at the time of the marriage of Mary Tudor to Philip II, who reported back that 'These English have their houses made of sticks and dirt, but they fare commonly so well as the King.' This was an impolite way of saying that what our timber-framed houses lacked (and it should not be forgotten that London itself was still at that time largely composed of them) were the social graces, the elegance of 'polite building'. On the whole this is true, especially of the West. In the timber-framed buildings of the South and East formal designing, as at Brewerstreet Farm, Bletchingley (*314*a), is often clearly in evidence, and at their best they achieved a refinement and subtlety, as can be seen in the graceful little shafts attached to the lower range of studs in the former Wool Hall at Lavenham (*313*a) and in many delicately moulded door and window frames, which were seldom matched in the West. (Pitchford Hall (*328*b) is a notable exception in this respect.) Western timber-framing might claim to be the more audacious; the overhangs are bolder, the timbers more robust, the roofs more frequently of stone. But as a rule the details in the West are undeniably cruder, the effects more obvious, the designs, owing partly to the many variations in the size and shape of the panels, more confused. The profusion of gables on such Worcestershire houses as Mere Hall, Hanbury, and Middle Beanhall Farmhouse, Bradley (*327*b), can certainly be entertaining; but one is aware that this is not 'architecture'.

To some this will matter little. It can certainly never be forgotten that for centuries wood was our principal building material, and that our inheritance of timber-framing is easily the richest in the world. What so many of these buildings have, and it is surely no trivial possession, is a closeness to the soil on which they stand, a down-to-earth honesty and lack of pretension, and often a true countryman's strength. When in addition to these are added the considerable charm which many still retain and the sheer lovability of some, there can surely be no question that whenever a decision has to be made whether to equip such houses with modern amenities or to destroy them and replace them with something entirely new, the former course of action should almost always be preferred.

WESTERN EXUBERANCE
a. *Lower Brockhampton Manor, Herefordshire*
b. *Middle Bean Farm, Bradley, Worcestershire*   c. *Little Moreton Hall, Cheshire*

Post-Restoration and Georgian Woodwork

When all who could afford it were building in stone or brick and no longer with a framework of timber, wood still remained a structural material of the first importance. Indeed,
until the evolution of the iron girder, all planning was normally governed by the length
of the available beams. At the Sheldonian Theatre, Oxford, as is well known, Wren
achieved a span of 70 ft. by an ingenious arrangement of interlocking beams suspended
from trusses, but an unsupported flat ceiling of this breadth was, at the time, a remarkable *tour de force*. Wood long continued to be the essential material of roof and of floor
construction, although externally this was usually only apparent at the cornice, a feature
which was sometimes treated very boldly (*356*b). In later Stuart buildings, the significant
part played by the white-painted wooden cornice can be well seen at the Salisbury College
of Matrons (*246*d) and at Bradbourne in Kent (*240*a). Dentilation, a Greek invention (the
dentils are the tooth-like blocks which form a miniature, rhythmic frieze under the cornice proper), adds charm to both these, in two quite different moods: sturdy at Salisbury,
finely wrought as jewellery at Bradbourne. In the Georgian period, the parapet often rose
above a brick or stone cornice of modest projection (*262*b), and sometimes the cornice
was omitted altogether (*245*b): but on the many buildings which preserved this feature,
it was always an embellishment (*267*d and *334*b). The wood used now was usually pine,
imported in great quantities from the Baltic and Scandinavia. It was invariably painted,
and the paint was always white; artistically it is important that this convention should be
observed. Externally the application of colour to Georgian wood cornices is almost always
unsuccessful, and may almost be regarded as a breach of good manners.

Apart from cornices, the features for which wood was habitually used externally in
the post-Restoration and Georgian periods were doors and door-cases, sometimes with
projecting hoods (*246*d and *356*a), window frames, and small pediments over doors and
dormers (*240*a). The door-case often became the most prominent feature of the elevation
and might be carved with great exuberance, as at Hill House, Cranbrook (*328*d). In
carpentry and joinery, as in so many other directions, this was a great age for craftsmanship: and although extensive use was now made of pattern-books, notably Francis Price's
British Carpenter, first published in 1733, many different designs of a Classical character
were evolved, some of which were very handsome. Space does not allow a discussion here
of these doorways; typical early eighteenth-century examples can be seen in plates *240*a,
*262*b and *381*d, whilst agreeable but less ambitious later examples are shown in plates *148*a,

CARVED ENRICHMENTS
a. *7 Northgate Street, Ipswich, Suffolk*   b. *Pitchford Hall, Shropshire*
c. *Stokesay Castle, Shropshire: Gatehouse*   d. *Hill House, Cranbrook, Kent*

*192*d, *245*c, *246*b and c.[1] The subject of the sash-framed window, for which wood had a contribution of great importance to make to the design of the Georgian elevation, will be considered in Chapter 16.

Shingles and Weather-Boarding

Wood, so often sheathed with some other material, is itself employed as a covering material in two ways.

Shingles are slices of wood used for covering both roofs and walls, in much the same way as tiles or slates. In some parts of the world they have been used very extensively; these include the whole of northern and the mountainous areas of central Europe, Canada, and some parts of the United States. In England they were widely employed for all types of roof from Roman times until well into the Middle Ages. But even in the twelfth century they had begun to be superseded by clay tiles, which were at once more durable, less inflammable and, from about 1300 cheaper too. In the eighteenth century, however, they were still being used in some places for the roofing of cottages. To-day they are principally to be seen on church spires (*278*c), and mainly in the three south-eastern counties, together with parts of Hampshire, Berkshire, Hertfordshire and Essex; there are also a few examples in Shropshire, Herefordshire, the Forest of Dean and elsewhere. Shingled spires sometimes develop a twist: the fine one at Cleobury Mortimer in Shropshire is an example.

Abroad, shingles are often of fir, larch or sweet chestnut, and in North America of red cedar: the best are of *Thuja plicata*, once known as arbor vitae, and now generally as thuya, a native of British Columbia, whence the tree was introduced to the East in 1853. In the South-Eastern States, as at Mulberry Plantation House near Charleston, South Carolina, built in 1714, the original shingles were of cypress-wood, to which the more recent cedarwood is regarded as inferior.[2] But in England the traditional wood for shingles, as for so much else, is once again oak. Cleft oak shingles are usually between 4 and 6 ins. broad and, as they are always laid with a considerable overlap, anything from 8 ins. to 1 ft. in length. The slice of wood is thicker at the lower end, which in the prettiest

1 For a short, well-illustrated survey of these Stuart and Georgian doorways, see Nathaniel Lloyd, *A History of the English House* (1931), pp. 311–326.

2 Shakes, also common in North America, are bigger and thicker than shingles, and always hand-hewn. They too are usually of cedarwood, but occasionally of oak. They are not found in England. Like shingles they are used as a covering for both roofs and walls.

examples is rounded, to produce an agreeable fish-scale effect. The traditional method of fixing was by means of wooden pins to laths or battens, but these have now given place to copper nails. The wood, which should be cleft with the grain to avoid disrupting the fibres, needs to be very well seasoned, and the pitch of the roof not less than 45°. Even so, a hot summer following a wet winter will cause a good deal of warping and splitting. The surface of an oak-shingled spire will require fairly drastic restoration, and perhaps complete renewal, at least once every hundred years, and may not last more than half as long. Thus no old shingles survive. Nevertheless, it is a method of roofing which gives unfailing pleasure.

Unfortunately the use of oak for shingling in this country has now become rare. Machine-sawn Canadian cedar shingles can be obtained in substantially larger sizes and at so much lower cost that the English wood has generally been unable to compete. Cedar has some sterling merits: with its close, straight grain, it is easier to handle than oak, at least as durable, and weathers to a very agreeable grey. Yet it cannot rival the beauty of oak, which after it has weathered (and this takes only two or three years) can look wonderfully silvery in full sunlight. An example of oak shingling can be seen at Sissinghurst Castle in Kent. Here the octagonal turrets flanking the Tudor tower, which were originally capped with lead-covered 'tips' of ogee form, were in 1839 given 'candle-snuffers' sheathed with Wealden oak. In 1958, under the direction of Sir Edward Maufe, these were renewed with shingles of exactly similar wood. The effect is admirable (333c and d).

Weather-boarding is the term used to describe lengths of board fixed, either horizontally or vertically, on to the surface of a building, generally but not necessarily a timber-framed building, to give additional warmth and protection against the elements. This is another method much employed abroad, for instance in Scandinavia, and on a big scale in Canada and the United States, where it is known as clapboarding (pronounced clabberding). In England weather-boarding, like shingling, has long been characteristic of the three south-eastern counties, and especially of the Weald of Kent. It also occurs widely in Essex, less frequently in Middlesex, Hertfordshire and Buckinghamshire, and rather rarely in the West. Even in the North, at least in Lancashire, it was once current. Three attractive examples can still be seen at Hampstead: Romney House, built in 1797, Heath End House and the former farmhouse of Wyldes (334a). Much more surprising is one survival in the very heart of London itself: a single wall only, at 27a Charles Street, Mayfair.

There are several different ways of constructing weather-boarding. The boards may be tongued and grooved, or rebated and beaded, or, as so often in Scandinavia, just juxtaposed and provided with narrow projecting strips to cover the joints; when employed vertically, these are the usual methods. Tongued and grooved vertical boarding can be seen, for example, on the lower stage of the steeple at Margaretting in Essex, but to make any artistic impression the boards require not only to be laid horizontally but to overlap, so that in the right conditions of light they cast a rhythmic succession of thin, straight shadows (334c). Weather-boarding, formerly of elm or less often oak attached with pegs, is now usually of some soft wood such as pine, which is nailed on. American red cedar is again the most practical.

Weather-boarding with the lower edge of each board chamfered and the upper edge 'feathered' (that is to say, cut away gradually to a very thin edge), the most refined type, does not appear to have been used in England much before 1500, except perhaps for a few timber-framed church towers. By about 1600 it was being applied to barns and other farm buildings, but most of what we see to-day belongs to the later Georgian period (334b). At Cobham in Kent, numbers of weather-boarded cottages, the excellent design of which still gives pleasure, date from the early years of the nineteenth century, and Thorrington Tide Mill near Brightlingsea in Essex (now disused) only from 1831 (334e). Cottages of this kind were in fact still being constructed at Tillingham, also in Essex, as late as 1881. Moreover, the last few years have seen a welcome revival of weather-boarding in southern and eastern England. In the words of Mr. Robert Harling, 'many of the younger architects find that timber not only emphasizes the spare and functional lines of their designs, but, when skilfully treated, either by paint or preservative, will act as a vivid visual foil to brick and concrete finishes elsewhere'. Sometimes the overcoat of weather-boarding is confined to the upper storey, and often it is much later than the house which carries it. Whitehall at Cheam (334d) was built at the beginning of the sixteenth century as a timber-framed house, the projecting porch and room over having been added about 1540. It was not until the end of the eighteenth century that, no doubt for greater comfort, the whole front was covered with boarding. Some would hold that aesthetically this was no advantage.

Architecturally weather-boarding is a modest material, without pretensions. It was never used on the great houses, and its employment in preference to tile-hanging or facing with brick was usually prompted by the need for economy. F. H. Crossley thought it 'cheap-looking and disagreeable', but this is surely much too harsh a view. It is principally to be seen on small houses, cottages, barns and especially on mills (334e), some of which are very large and picturesque. Oak and elm boarding may be left unpainted, and so may red cedar, but European softwoods require a preservative. In coastal districts, weatherboards are usually covered with black tar as a protection against the saltiness of the air.

BRICK NOGGING

a. <i>Ockwells Manor, Bray, Berkshire</i>   b. <i>Sutton Bonington, Nottinghamshire</i>

SHINGLES

c. and d. <i>Sissinghurst Castle, Kent</i>

Very quaint and, as a collection of shapes, amusing are the net houses of the fishermen under the East Hill at Hastings which managed to survive the fire of June 1961; these all-wooden buildings, lofty and gabled, are all roughly weather-boarded and wholly tarred.[1] Inland, too, tarring is very general, notably for farm buildings and barns: tarred boards are to be seen in East Anglia (especially Essex) and all the south-eastern counties, and look particularly well under a roof of mellow red tiles. For houses tar also has its enthusiasts,[2] but the usual Kentish practice of painting the boards white or cream, as seen in the Weald near Smarden (334c) and near Tenterden (334b), looks better. For the painting of weather-boarding I should like to see, in England, a more adventurous use of colour. Those who have seen some of the clapboarded houses of New England will know how charming they look in their liveries of grey or green, grey-blue, yellow, dark red or mushroom, usually with white-painted window reveals and sash windows with all their glazing bars. Portsmouth, Concord, Newburyport, Marblehead, Salem (the best of all): the effect of these and other little towns so largely built of wood really is, in the old phrase, as pretty as paint.

1 The two destroyed and three badly damaged net houses were most commendably rebuilt on the original lines within a few months by the Hastings Corporation.

2 Like ditchwater, which, as G. K. Chesterton once observed, is by no means dull: 'it teems with quiet fun'.

WEATHER-BOARDING
a. *Wyldes, Hampstead, London*   b. *Near Tenterden, Kent*
c. *Near Smarden, Kent*
d. *Whitehall, Cheam, Greater London*   e. *Thorrington Mill, Essex*

13

THATCH

The old word 'thack', which still survives locally in parts of Yorkshire, was originally applied to any kind of roofing substance, and the German *Dach*, once the same word, continues to have this connotation. It was because the material employed in early days was so frequently straw or reed or heather or some similar vegetable product that the later word 'thatch' acquired its more limited meaning.

Since scarcely any surviving thatch is as much as a hundred years old, this is not an easy subject about which to write with authority; moreover, because like turves and moss and ferns and other primitive kinds of English roofing this was essentially a humble material, a great deal went unrecorded. There can be little doubt that the use of thatch in this country, if the term be stretched to embrace the roughest brushwood, was formerly very widespread, as in many parts of the world it still is. The Venerable Bede, who died in 735, makes more than one reference to it, and it was probably in use long before then. The early records dwell upon its inflammability,[1] and here and there in village churches one may still see fire-hooks, reminders of the days when to tear off the burning thatch as quickly as possible was the only hope of saving the rest of the building.[2] In towns it was frequently the custom to give the thatch a coat of whitewash to protect it both from smoke-dust and from sparks, a practice still sometimes followed where thatch survives in Wales. In London a coating of lime plaster, to reduce combustibility, was made compulsory as early as 1212, when it was at the same time decreed that thatch was not to be used for any new roofs in the capital. Gradually town after town followed suit. Thatch was proscribed in Hull under Elizabeth I; in Cambridge by an Order in Council of 1619. To-day its use in towns is widely restricted by local bye-laws; and since thatch is essentially a country material which looks somewhat ridiculous in urban surroundings, no regrets need be felt on this account.

1 Margaret Wood (*op. cit.*, p. 292) gives many instances of early fires in towns for which thatched roofs were 'doubtless a prime cause': London, 1077, 1087, 1135–36 and 1161: Canterbury, 1161; Winchester, 1161 and 1180; Exeter, 1161; Glastonbury, 1184; Chichester, 1187; Worcester, 1202; Chester, 1140, 1180 and 1278.

2 There is also one at the Bedehouse at Lyddington in Rutland, and another at Eaton Bray, Bedfordshire. At Southill in Bedfordshire it is not so long since the thatch fire-hook was used to drag the lake for drowned bodies!

It is probable that by about 1200 thatch was already beginning to fall out of general use for the roofing of buildings of importance. For all but the grandest houses, however, some form of thatch provided the commonest type of roof in most parts of the country, until well into the Tudor period. We even have a record of thatching being undertaken in 1493 at, of all places, Collyweston.[1] Only at the time of what Prof. Hoskins has called 'the great rebuilding' (c. 1570 to c. 1640, except in the four most northerly counties), when all classes but the poorest were to a substantial extent rehoused, did thatch give place in some parts of the country to more permanent materials. Elsewhere it continued much longer, and in some areas, as we shall see, it is still quite common. Even for churches, thatched roofs have survived in considerable numbers in East Anglia. In the county of Norfolk alone, at the accession of Queen Victoria, it is believed that there were still about two hundred and seventy churches which were wholly or partly thatched. To-day there are between fifty and sixty of them in Norfolk and nearly twenty in Suffolk, and in the whole of the rest of England less than a dozen in all. It should not be supposed that there is anything undignified about a thatched roof for a church. On the contrary, a covering of Norfolk reed thatch over walls of flint is an admirable embellishment.

In order to understand why thatch has survived with some tenacity in certain areas and almost if not entirely disappeared in others, we need to be able to answer a number of questions. Did the area become industrialized, or retain a predominantly rural character? What was the nature of the local building material? Were there available any good alternative substances suitable for roofing? And could the locality itself satisfy the requirements of the thatcher?

Thatching can be carried out in many different materials, by no means all of equal merit. In mediaeval times the usual practice was to cut off only the ears of the wheat with the sickle. The stalks, although trampled on by the reapers, remained in the fields until the first frost of autumn, when they became brittle and could be broken off and gathered easily. These short straws were then stored until needed. The thatcher started, as he always does, at the eaves, and over each layer of stubble he added a 'daub' of wet clay. The result must have looked muddy and not at all elegant. Other thatching materials seldom if ever encountered nowadays include flax, formerly favoured in Derbyshire, and broom, in use in the seventeenth century on the Isle of Man. Sedge continues to be in demand for ridging roofs of Norfolk reed-thatch, and entire roofs are still occasionally thatched with sedge in the Fen country, where at one time it was used extensively. It can be seen in the Cambridgeshire villages of Stretham, Wicken and Fordham, all between Ely and Newmarket.

---

1 Cited by L. F. Salzman, *op. cit.*, p. 227, from the Accounts of St. John's College, Cambridge, vol. ii.

This coarse, grass-like, water-loving plant (*Cladium mariscus*), which is distinguished from the true grasses by having a stem devoid of joints, offers an excellent material to the thatcher.

The three principal substances employed have long been reed, straw and heather; and of these the first (*Phragmites communis*) is undoubtedly the best. This is not uncommon in wet places in Britain—on the margins of estuaries, rivers and canals, lakes and pools—and before the draining of the fens there were great reed beds in parts of Huntingdonshire and the Isle of Ely; but it is arduous to cut, difficult to use and expensive. In recent years its cultivation has been encouraged at Key Haven in Hampshire, at Radipole and Abbotsbury in Dorset and in Glamorgan, whilst limited quantities are also cut from the verges of tidal estuaries in Essex and Suffolk. 'We like reeds that grow in brackish water best', said Ronald Blythe's thatcher, who cut his own reeds from the River Alde at Snape; 'in the brack caused by the salt tides meeting the river waters every twelve hours. They're pickled a bit, I suppose'.[1] But the principal commercial beds are still where they have always been, in the broads and marshes of Norfolk. Reed thatch ('Norfolk spear' as it is sometimes called) costs the most initially, but in the long run the outlay is no more, because if well and closely laid it lasts sixty, eighty, and in a few rare cases even as much as a hundred years. (Nor is it usually necessary for many years to provide reed with that covering of fine-meshed wire as a protection against birds and mice which with the looser varieties of thatch soon becomes essential.)

In most parts of England, however, for many centuries the normal material for thatching was straw. This could be either wheat, rye, oats or barley, the two last only *faute de mieux*. Rye straw was usually regarded as the strongest, with an average life of about thirty years; this was the favourite material for roofing the timber-framed cottages of west and south Lancashire, and is still used occasionally where it is readily available locally: for instance, at a few places in Essex. But the straw generally employed in England was wheat, and this too might last thirty years if both the workmanship and the straw itself were of really good quality. Yet a roof of 'long straw', in fact rather short in the stem and liable to be attacked both by the weather and by birds, often had to be remade after only fifteen or twenty years. The thatcher always wanted straw that had not been beaten and bruised by threshing—haulm (or halm) as it was called. In olden days he got it. To-day the combine harvester crushes the straw and renders it useless for thatching, and scientific agriculture, with its concentration on short-stemmed corn giving heavier yields, has caused further difficulties for him. Many excellent examples of long straw thatching, like those at Long

---

1 See Ronald Blythe, *Akenfield: Portrait of an English Village* (1969), p. 133.

Crendon in Buckinghamshire here illustrated (*364c*), are still to be seen in the corn-growing districts of the Midlands and South, and a farmer growing an acre or two of long straw can more or less count on a grant; nevertheless, the unbruised long straw of hand-harvesting days is almost everywhere only a memory, and the shortage of straw suitable for thatching is now so great that in the last few years many craftsmen in long straw have been mastering the completely different technique required for thatching in reed.

In districts where the wild reed is not to be found in any appreciable quantity, thatchers are sometimes able to obtain threshed straw known as wheat reed. This term, like 'Spanish Burgundy', is misleading, for botanically there is no affinity with true reed; it owes its origin to a similar method of laying. Long straw is applied to a roof in 'yealms', small flat bundles laid in overlapping courses at intervals of 4 or 5 ins. Wheat reed is laid with the butts of the stalks forming the exposed surface (cf. fig. 9 on p. 346). The contrast between the two is seen clearly at Broad Chalke (*284a*). For wheat reed thatch the straw should be about 3 ft. long, and it may not be the kind of wheat that yields the most grain, nor must it be bruised, which means acquiring a special device known as a comber that can be attached to the threshing drum. Although expensive, combers give excellent results: the unbruised straw emerges stripped of ears and leaf, cleaned and tied in bundles ready for use, rendering possible the tight, smooth finish and the ornamental ridging which are also the special attributes, aesthetic and practical, of true reed. Combed wheat reed is a speciality of the South-West; until a few years ago the technique was virtually confined to Devon (where it was known as 'Devon reed') and Dorset (where to call it that would be a *faux pas*: there it is 'Dorset reed'). Its recent appearance in other areas is due to the commendable initiative of the Rural Industries Bureau. There are roofs of this type, such as on the Old Rectory at Winterborne Came near Dorchester, for over twenty years the home of the Dorset poet William Barnes (*341b*), which almost equal the best Norfolk thatch in appearance. Other examples may be seen on the Almshouses at Moretonhampstead (*148b*) and at Ugford Farm House (*191c*). A good roof of combed wheat reed can be expected to last half a century.

Thatching in heather, more properly ling (*calluna vulgaris*), was more widespread than is perhaps realized, and on commons and in moorland regions where no corn was grown it provided a useful alternative; it was also used purely ornamentally on a straw base. It is now mainly confined to sports pavilions and summer-houses, and only rarely found on larger buildings. In Sussex and in Devon, especially on the fringe of Dartmoor, its use was at one time general; in parts of Yorkshire, Durham and Northumberland too, and in Scotland, this long remained a favourite material. The heather was cut while still in bloom, and laid, for preference in the autumn, with the roots carefully entwined and pointing upwards. In parts of Scotland it was customary, in order to make it firmer, to bed it in clay. One might suppose that it was very intractable, but in fact with the aid of the shears a remarkably smooth finish could be obtained. Although so little heather thatching is done to-day, some people regard it as preferable to straw, as being not only cheaper but more durable and less likely to rot in a period of prolonged wet weather. Aesthetically the chief disadvantage of heather is its dark tone. A rich brown when freshly cut, it gradually changes to a sombre black, and this can look dreary.

From what has emerged about the requirements of the thatcher, and from what has been said in earlier chapters about the location of alternative roofing materials, we should now have some useful pointers on the subject of geographical distribution. One other factor was important here: the weight-bearing capacity of the walls. Of all the traditional forms of roof covering in general use, thatch was the lightest.[1] Moreover, it only required quite a modest framework: a foundation of laths sufficed, or of long thin battens no more than $1\frac{1}{4}$ ins. wide and $\frac{1}{2}$ in. thick, nailed across the rafters (which used nearly always to be of oak) at intervals of about 5 ins. This not only rendered it substantially more economical than tiles or stone slates; it made it the obvious, and on some buildings the only possible, roof where the wall construction was too weak to carry heavy loads. Thus wherever the unbaked earths were used, the roofs were almost certain to be thatched. It is the widespread use of cob in Devon which largely accounts for the extensive use of thatch in that county. Clay lump cottages, too, were generally roofed in this fashion; and although timber-framed buildings were sometimes given such a massive framework that the immense weight of a stone roof, whether of Horsham slates in Sussex or of Kerridge slates in Cheshire, could be supported with perfect safety, here also thatch was the natural material to choose.

Aesthetically this was a happy circumstance, for in country districts thatch is a very good mixer. It looks especially well with a plastered or limewashed wall, whether this be over cob or mud or clay lump, or over timber-framing with a lath and plaster infilling. It also looks well with exposed timber-framing, with flint, and with every kind of stone. It is less happy, perhaps, with tile-hanging, but this is a combination seldom seen, for where there are tiles on the walls, there will be tiles on the roof too. Neither gutters nor down-pipes are usually provided when this is of thatch, and looking at the effect of the gutter added in recent times at Moretonhampstead (148b) we may be glad that they were not. In order to ensure that rain-water is thrown off as quickly as possible, before it has time to sink in, a fairly steep pitch (not less than 50° for straw: a little less for reed) is

1 Lead sheets were equally light but much more expensive. See page 378. Copper would have been appreciably lighter still, but was hardly used in England before the nineteenth century (see page 383).

STRAW THATCHING
a. *Ampthill, Bedfordshire*

'COMBED WHEAT REED'
b. *The Old Rectory, Winterborne Came, Dorset*

thus essential, as well as pleasing. Sometimes in Southern England the thatch will be carried down in a steep slope almost to the ground, and will appear to swaddle an entire building much as a hedgehog is enveloped in its spines.

The geographical picture has now taken shape. To see English thatch at its best we must go to Norfolk, where, despite the presence of a distressing number of high-pitched roofs freshly covered during the present century with corrugated iron or asbestos, much still survives. In Suffolk a survey undertaken by the Rural Community Council in 1960 showed that there were more thatched dwellings in that county than in any other in England. Over wide areas of Essex, Cambridgeshire, Huntingdonshire and Lincolnshire thatch, though less common than formerly, is still a familiar sight. Moving westwards towards the limestone belt, through Bedfordshire, Hertfordshire and Buckinghamshire, it is becoming rarer, but is by no means extinct; and there is some, as might be expected, in the Otmoor region of Oxfordshire. Even on parts of the belt itself, especially in North-amptonshire, a substantial amount of thatch can still be seen: in and around Geddington, for instance, and at Rockingham (342a); also at Great Tew in Oxfordshire, another 'feudal' village. On the other side of the belt there is still quite a lot in Worcestershire. Because of the excellence of the local tiles, not much can now be found in Kent, Surrey or eastern Sussex; but from western Sussex all the way to Devon, and including the Isle of Wight, we are in the other major area of English thatch, and although true reed in this part of the country is still exceptional, the best combed wheat reed in the South and South-West is very good indeed. The fine fifteenth-century tithe barn at Place Farm, Tisbury, Wiltshire, 188 ft. long, possesses what is probably the greatest expanse of thatching on any building in the country: 1450 sq. yds.[1]

Outside these regions, thatch is now exceptional, and in some counties has been uncommon for several centuries. A little rye-straw thatch can still be found in the non-stone areas of Lancashire; but in the counties along our Welsh border (as also in Wales itself), in the North Midlands and North, and in the Isle of Man, thatching has now become rare. To some extent this may be a matter of climate: the West and North (and, still more, Scotland, where thatch, often of poor quality, was the normal roofing material until the end of the eighteenth century) are the wetter parts of the country and the great enemy of thatch is damp. No doubt the economic factor is also partly responsible: thatching is a skilled

[1] The smallest expanses also mostly occur in the southern counties, as copings to those boundary walls of chalk or cob surrounding gardens, orchards or farmyards (191c) which were several times mentioned in Chapter 11. Just a few survive elsewhere: for instance, at Ely. In some areas thatchers had to devote a good deal of their time to ricks. In East Suffolk, with a couple of boys to help him, a thatcher might do anything up to three hundred ricks a year.

REED THATCHING
a. *Rockingham, Northamptonshire*
b. *The Manor House, Brundish, Suffolk*
19* + P.E.B.

craft, its materials are dear, and it is no longer an inexpensive form of roofing. This explains why, even in the favourable areas, it is sometimes found to be in dire need of attention (*283a, 341a*).

Perhaps no building material exhibits so many variations in the actual handling as thatch. Whether these variations owe more to the traditions of the locality, or to the style of the individual thatcher or his family, is a difficult question; but such investigations as I have been able to make point to the conclusion that, except in so far as reed obviously imposes a different handling from straw, the second influence was the more potent. Before the Industrial Revolution the practice of many crafts was traditional in families, son following father from generation to generation. Some Devon villages once had as many as three or four thatchers *each*. To-day, with the decline of hand craftsmanship, this is much less general. With this craft, it is true, there is little justification for historical generalization, because, as has been said, scarcely any thatched roof is as much as a century old, and subtle changes are almost certain to take place every time a roof is rethatched. There is a dearth not only of written but also of trustworthy pictorial records before the invention of photography. It is nevertheless significant that, wherever the thatching in a village displays a stylistic unity, it will invariably be found to be the work of a single thatcher or family; often, too, the place itself will be in the ownership of a single landowner, as at Rockingham. Even where there is evidence of some regional thatching method, the good thatcher will not fail to add his own distinctive touches. Nor is it unusual to find two or three widely different styles in the same village. As for the singling out of regional or local characteristics, a good deal of caution is required. It has been said, for example, that in East Anglia the eaves of a thatched roof are usually continuous, as at Brundish (*342b*), whereas in the South-West the thatch is often brought down below the level of the upper window-heads as at Ashton (*283b*). As a very broad generalization this may be valid, but there are many exceptions. At Cavendish in Suffolk, for example, the thatch on the group of Elizabethan cottages to the south of the church familiarly known as 'Hyde Park Corner' comes well down between the upper windows. And the West Country has many examples of thatch halted at level eaves above the first-floor windows: several are here illustrated (*148b, 283a, 341b*).

It is in the treatment of dormers, gables and ridges that the thatcher has always found his best opportunities for the cultivation of an individual style. Not that these develop-ments are always pleasing: used in a fussy way, curving round a proliferation of little dormers and gables, thatching can be rather tiresome. Although the carrying up of the thatch over a window to make a very sharply pointed gable, perhaps with a cap and a little finial, can be attractive, a better effect can generally be obtained by embracing the dormers in a continuous roll. On many cottages what may appear at first glance to be dormers are really only upper floor windows set into a flat wall, the dormer effect being produced by bringing the thatch well down between them. In this type of roof, the thatch may be carried round the windows in a series of curved hoods, as in Bedfordshire in the neighbourhood of Ampthill (*341a*), and in Warwickshire at Meriden; or in a continuous roll; or, the most engaging way perhaps, by forming itself into a series of individual 'eyebrows' over the windows, as on one of the cottages facing the green at Frampton-on-Severn. Elsewhere, generally in the South, one may see the thatch fitting closely round the upper windows to produce a 'Little Red Riding Hood' effect, which no doubt looks very snug but can be 'just too sweet for words'. Another somewhat whimsy effect is produced when the thatch is brought down between the windows to provide a small canopy over the front door. There are many examples of this in the Isle of Wight, notably at Godshill.

The ridge is the most exposed part of a thatched roof, and has always required additional protection. In mediaeval times this was sometimes provided by extraneous material, such as clay or turves, comparable with the specially made ridge-tiles which now crown many thatched roofs in Holland. Another method which could be used with straw thatch was to make a crest by arranging the bundles so that they overlapped from each side alternately. Very occasionally one may see a decorative crest produced by twisting the ends of the straw into a succession of small knobs.[1] But the most interesting ridges are on roofs of true reed thatch. Reeds, being stiff and brittle, cannot be bent over a ridge, so here a further thickness of thatch was added along the apex of the roof, using sedge, tough grass or straw. These ridge-copings are not so durable as the rest of a reed roof: they need to be renewed every twenty-five or thirty years. But their lower edges could be, and often still are, finished off with considerable decorative elaboration. Zigzags and scallops are simple compared with some of the designs evolved, and here the individual thatcher really comes into his own (*342a*). More decoration may be introduced by the rods or spars of split hazel or willow which are often pegged on to the surface of the coping, and in straw thatching along the eaves and barges too, to give additional security (*341a*). These rods, known as liggers or ledgers, are commonly arranged in two parallel lines, with short cross-rods between, making lattice or more intricate patterns (*364c*). The ends of the roof are frequently 'stopped' by chimney stacks, but where these are absent the effect of a thatched roof may be greatly enhanced by giving the extremities of the ridge a

1 A glimpse of one at Chagford in Devon can be seen in *English Cottages and Farmhouses*, by Olive Cook and Edwin Smith (1954), pl. 270. This is one of the best books known to me on English vernacular building.

slight 'lift'. Elsewhere a hipped gable effect may be obtained, with delightful results when skilfully executed as on the out-building at Long Crendon (*364c*).

A further refinement, confined to reed thatching, is the contriving of decorative surface patterns. In order to understand how these are achieved, one must know how the reed is laid. A good thatcher always begins by stripping off all the old thatch, right down to the rafters; for if the new is piled on the old, as sometimes happens, the thatch may presently begin to slip, or, still worse, the roof may cave in. He then starts at the bottom and moves upwards. Each bundle of reed, which is about 2 ft. in circumference and may be as much as 7 ft. or even 8 ft. long, curves out from the rafters at its lower end so that the butts form the face of the thatch (see fig. 9). Except at the top the reed is not cut, but tapped into position first by hand and finally with a special tool called a leggett (also spelt legget, and leggatt), a small piece of board covered with horseshoe nails, with a handle set at an angle. Patterns such as that illustrated on the roof of Brundish Manor House in Suffolk (*342b*) are obtained by tapping up some of the reed a little more after the thatching is complete, and carefully trimming the edges. At Thurton in south-east Norfolk, where the church, not a small one, is wholly thatched, there are no fewer than three tiers of these decorative

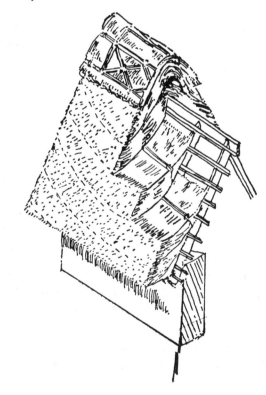

Fig. 9
Construction of a
roof of reed thatch
with sedge ridge

patterns. Many houses in Norfolk and Suffolk have one break about half-way down the roof, and there can be no doubt that they represent, technically, the most brilliant development of the thatcher's craft. Artistically the quality varies. Sometimes the effect seems incommensurate with the effort; elsewhere, as at Brundish, this patterning can be a delightful addition.[1]

Yet the appeal of true reed thatch, and to a less extent of wheat reed also, derives less from surface ornamentation, no matter how well conceived, than from the remarkably smooth and velvety surfaces which a skilled thatcher is able to achieve in these materials. There are roofs of reed thatch which are as 'strokeable' as a cat, and as beautifully groomed. It is indeed its 'organic' character which distinguishes thatch from every other form of roofing. Where they are in varying degrees hard and unresisting, a good fat cushion of thatch can evoke in us much the same tactile responses as the back of a sleeping animal. The art of thatching depends very much on the eye. The roof has got to *look* right. It must not be overloaded.

In the early nineteenth century, amateurs of taste valued thatch for its impeccably rural associations; and if in time it tended to acquire, in the words of Sir Uvedale Price, 'something of a damp dirty look', that was no disadvantage for a garden pavilion and, some would have said, no drawback either to the appearance of an estate cottage. Books such as W. F. Pocock's *Architectural Designs for Rustic Cottages, Picturesque Dwellings, Villas, etc.* (1807) and J. B. Papworth's *Rural Residences* (1818) are, needless to say, replete with thatch. And why did Barton Cottage, in *Sense and Sensibility* (1811), win no accolade?

> 'As a house, Barton Cottage, though small, was comfortable and compact; but as a cottage it was defective, for the building was regular, the roof was tiled, the window shutters were not painted green, nor were the walls covered with honeysuckle.'

Clearly the building was insufficiently Romantic: the roof should have been thatched.

Its aura of Romanticism has been no help to the appreciation of thatch during the present century. We are all familiar with jokes, usually well deserved, about thatched garages and petrol stations. Yet at its best, on the right building and in the proper setting, this material can give great pleasure. A smooth reed roof, unencumbered by dormers, with a slightly undulating ridge and good broad eaves, cut off cleanly with a pair of shears, can present a finely manicured effect, worthy even of crowning ashlared limestone walls without appearing incongruous. In addition to its artistic merits it makes a very

---

[1] 'We all have our own pattern', remarked the Akenfield thatcher; 'it is our signature, you might say. A thatcher can look at a roof and tell you who thatched it by the pattern.' (Ronald Blythe, *op. cit.*, p. 134.)

homely-looking, comfortable roof, cool in summer and warm (at least ten per cent warmer than a slate roof) in winter. It is also almost impervious to noise, which has encouraged its use in the neighbourhood of aerodromes. Nor is the fire danger nearly as great as formerly. Fires in thatched roofs are now generally caused by defective brickwork in chimney stacks, and not because thatch itself is so inflammable.

The present condition of the craft, although hardly flourishing, is not as desperate as some people appear to believe. In some districts there is a shortage of skilled thatchers, but not, for instance, in Suffolk. Several hundred are still employed full time in various parts of the country, and there is plenty of work for all of these and more, for it has lately been estimated that England still possesses some fifty thousand buildings roofed with thatch. Really serious is the difficulty of obtaining long straw, which is essential when repairs have to be made to an existing straw-thatched roof. A new roof will now generally have to be of reed, but for some the cost of this (£500 or more for an ordinary cottage) is prohibitive; and here there is also another problem. Reed from Norfolk would be available in almost limitless quantities if only the work of cutting it were not so laborious. This has to be done when all the foliage or 'flag' has withered, that is to say in mid-winter, working for hours in the damp and perhaps in an icy wind. The development of a motor scythe, and of an ingenious attachment to it designed to facilitate the collection of the reed in bundles, has helped, but some of our reed has now to be imported from Holland and from Denmark. Yet because of the shortage both of long straw and of combed wheat reed, and also because the beauty and efficiency of real reed are so apparent that owners sometimes want it now despite the high price, this kind of thatching is on the increase. So reed thatchers are to be found at work in parts of the country where their roofs were until recently unknown. Does this offend against the *genius loci*? Is reed an unwelcome intruder into traditionally straw districts? Here my answer is an emphatic 'No.' Thatch, with its quiet colouring (as soon as it has weathered) and, in the case of reed, its close texture, is visually so accommodating that, as suggested earlier, there is scarcely any material with which it does not look well—in country places. Please, in country places: not on the by-pass road; not in the residential street (where it always looks arty-crafty); above all, even if the bye-laws permit it, not at the shopping centre.

COLOUR-WASHED PLASTER OVER TIMBER-FRAMING
a. *Kersey, Suffolk*
b. and c. *Elm Hill, Norwich, Norfolk*

PLASTER

AND OTHER SURFACE MATERIALS

The motive for providing the walls of a building with some external covering, compounded basically of sand and lime, and later cement, may be practical or aesthetic to both. It is a custom which has been very widely followed in many parts of the world from early times. In England, owing to the widespread availability of more durable alternative materials, it is less general than in many other countries; but even so there cannot be many places without some buildings that have been (to use the familiar building term) 'rendered' in one form or another.

The terms *plaster*, *stucco* and *pargeting* were all used somewhat loosely in the past, but for present purposes, at the risk of pedantry, it would be well to define them as precisely as possible. Plaster and stucco are often regarded as synonymous; but bearing in mind that their ubiquitous employment internally is outside the scope of this book, it seems best to confine the term stucco here to those hard external finishes embodying some form of cement, widely used towards the end of the eighteenth century and during the first part of the nineteenth, generally with the intention of imitating stonework (*350*). This, it should be made clear, is directly contrary to continental usage. Throughout the continent the term 'stucco' is primarily associated with sculpture and ornamentation, largely to be found in Baroque and Rococo buildings, and often of a most exuberant character.[1] Pargeting (which is also written pargetting: both forms are current) is a word that was formerly applied to any form of coarse mortar-plaster introduced as an external wall covering. To-day it is only used in a more specialized sense, to describe ornamental designs in plaster, either in relief or incised. It is not usually applied to interiors.

1 Cf., for instance, John Bourke, *Baroque Churches of Central Europe* (1958), p. 247: 'In S. Germany and Switzerland there is a great deal of stucco statuary.... Stucco, though in itself synthetic, has the advantage of combining the visual appearance of stone and marble with a lightness in weight that made possible such boldly imaginative work as that of the Asams.' This sort of art is much less common in England, and where it occurs, as for example at Hagley Hall in Worcestershire, it is usually described as 'ornamental plasterwork'.

STUCCO
a. *Gloucester Gate, Regent's Park, London*
b. *East Street, Kimbolton, Huntingdonshire*   c. *Lodge at Hyde Hall, Sawbridgeworth, Hertfordshire*

Plaster

The finest kind of plaster is produced by burning gypsum, which is calcium sulphate combined chemically with water. Subjected to a low heat, so that most of the water evaporates, what remains is the substance known in this country as plaster of Paris, because its original source was the beds of gypsum underlying Montmartre. It was introduced into England soon after the middle of the thirteenth century at the instigation of Henry III, who visited Paris in 1254 and was much taken by it. Although the gypsum was at first imported from France, exploitation of our native deposits was not long delayed; these were chiefly situated in the Isle of Purbeck, in Yorkshire around Knaresborough, and particularly in the Trent valley, where the gypsum was much quarried and mined for alabaster (see p. 190). The waste from the alabaster workings and the inferior pieces (including, perhaps, all the red-veined stone, which was always rejected until the sixteenth century) were burnt for plaster.

The results were admirable. John Speed, in his *Theatre of the Empire of Great Britaine*, published in 1611 with maps and descriptions of every county, said of Nottinghamshire: 'Therein groweth a Stone softer than Alablaster [*sic*], but being burnt maketh a Plaister harder than that of Paris; wherewith they flower [i.e. floor] their upper roomes; for betwixt the ioysts they lay only long Bulrushes, and thereon spread this Plaister, which being throughly drie becomes most solide and hard, so that it seemeth rather to be firme-stone than Mortar, and is troad upon without all danger.' Along the Trent below Nottingham, in the Vale of Belvoir, and to a less extent all over the north-eastern Midlands and as far south as Northamptonshire, plaster was used both for floors and for internal walls: for the latter it was sometimes laid on reeds affixed to laths.[1] So hard did it become, and so beautifully smooth, that a great deal of it has survived in houses of the seventeenth and eighteenth centuries, from mansions such as Staunton Harold down to quite small cottages. This material is more durable than many kinds of stone. At least one complete building was constructed with it: in the fourteen-thirties 'Richard Beauchamp, the noble Earl of Warwick, . . . caused to be built at Warwick a stable of great size, of plaister de Parys, at a cost of 500 marks.'[2] In the nineteenth century plaster of Paris for structural purposes gave place to less expensive 'patent' gypsum plasters such as Keene's cement, which first appeared in 1836.

1 A few plaster floors can also be found in the Lake District.
2 L. F. Salzman, *op. cit.*, Appendix A, p. 408.

The usual plaster, however, was and is a much less refined and more economical material, compounded of common lime (or chalk marl where available, as in Cambridge-shire) and coarse, clean sand (normally from three to six times as much sand as lime), with the addition of various other substances to add toughness. There were many different recipes. Chopped straw and hay were often used, as were bullock-hair, cow-hair and feathers. Horse-hair was introduced when it could not be sold for upholstery. Cow-dung, road-scrapings and powdered tiles might be included, and in the present century it has also been a common practice to add a certain amount of cement. A mixture of one part cement to two parts lime to nine parts sand is to-day typical. For at least a thousand years plaster has been used in England as an external wall-covering, as well as on an immense scale internally. Although the primary object was to give additional protection from the weather, often the motive was also aesthetic: to provide a rough wall with a smoother and more agreeable finish. Before the eighteenth century, a dead flat surface was neither attained nor usually desired.

Various references have been made in earlier chapters to the materials of wall construction which it was the common practice to render with plaster. The applied surface could in every instance be roughcast, pebble-dash or cement and sand instead of lime-plaster; these will be considered shortly. All these are unfortunately more efficient than plaster as 'mackintoshes', but roughcast is seldom, and the other two never, as pleasing.[1] Rendering of the unbaked earths, although easily dispensed with in tropical or semi-tropical countries, was almost essential in a country as damp as our own. Except in the case of pisé (one of the advantages of this method) it could not be applied for some while, because it was essential to allow the earth to become thoroughly dry, which might take a year or even two. But when we think, say, of the cob cottages of Devon or of Norfolk clay-lump, it will usually be the external covering of plaster that will first come to mind. So also with timber-framed buildings. The coarse daub was always given a protective covering of smoother plaster (see p. 320). Later, when wattles gave place to laths, these too were plastered outside as well as in. And sometimes, particularly in East Anglia, the whole building would be given a further coat of plaster, concealing the timbers but also combating the draughts. In the lovely village street at Kersey in Suffolk (349a) not much framing shows, yet almost every house is built of wood. If the house is Tudor or Jacobean, it is probable that the framework was at one time exposed, but if a timber-framed house of the later seventeenth century is sheathed in plaster, the likelihood is that this was part of the

[1] In appearance, the dividing line between roughcast and the coarser kinds of lime-plaster is admittedly tenuous.

original building. In the eighteenth century a new timber-framed house in East Anglia would be given an all-over rendering almost as a matter of course.

It was not necessary nor usual to apply plaster (as distinct from stucco) over brick walls except where, with no local stone available for the dressings, a thin coating of plaster was used to simulate it, as noted at Giffords Hall gatehouse (p. 38).[1] With stone, on the other hand, a plaster finish was by no means uncommon. This was a custom which went back even to Saxon times: at Deerhurst in Gloucestershire, the walls of the chapel dedicated in 1056 were, we learn, originally plastered inside and out, 'to hide the projecting inequalities of the blue lias rubble-work'.[2] That Anglo-Saxon plaster was sometimes of excellent quality can still be seen at Hexham Priory, where in the relic chamber of Wilfrid's crypt a large part of the original plaster vault-covering, protected from the weather, has survived; it is intensely hard. Throughout the Middle Ages church walls, wherever there was no good stone, or no money to pay for it, were habitually built of rough materials which were then rendered internally with a thin coat of the mortar used in their construction, making them more or less smooth. The stripping off of this coat of mortar plaster during the Victorian period in numberless churches all over the country was ignorant historically, calamitous aesthetically, and dispiriting even from the aspect of amenity, as an interior treated in this fashion is almost always gloomy.

Externally, plaster was widely employed to cover the walls of both ecclesiastical and domestic buildings whenever the materials seemed themselves unworthy. A post-mediaeval domestic example may be seen at Gorhambury in Hertfordshire. The Elizabethan house, completed in 1568, abandoned in 1784, and surviving to-day only as a roofless fragment, was built of a mixture of materials, which included stone from a monastic foundation close by, flint, and brick made on the site. This hotchpotch obviously lacked refinement, so all was covered with plaster. As the stone window-frames project half an inch from the wall surface, it is evident that the rendering was no afterthought. Yet, externally also, it is not unusual to find these seemly coverings removed. The church at Odiham in Hampshire provides an unhappy but all too typical instance. The rubble walls, in this non-stone district, are composed of odd hunks of stone, some bricks, and plenty of flint. Their present untidy texture was certainly never intended by the original builders.

Another reason for adding an outer coat of plaster to a building was to reduce the danger of fire. As noted in the last chapter, the Order of 1212 prohibiting new thatch in the City of London also enacted that existing thatch was to be plastered and whitewashed,

---

1 This is a feature encountered in the Netherlands, and for similar reasons.
2 S. O. Addy, *The Evolution of the English House* (1933 edition), p. 135.

INCISED PARGETING
a. *Newport, Essex*   b. *Hubbard's Hall, Bentley, Suffolk*

RAISED PARGETING
c. *The Ancient House, Clare, Suffolk*   d. *The Garrison House, Wivenhoe, Essex*

a precaution which was extended to the walls of premises requiring constant heat, such as bakeries and cookshops.

External plastering, as distinct from roughcast or whitewash, was much less common in the North than in the South, mainly no doubt because of the harsher climate, but perhaps also because smooth finishes were usually no part of the aesthetic of Northern building.

The surface quality of plain lime-plaster is not seductive. Frequently it is rough-and-ready, and somewhat uninteresting. It is often less well kept than it should be (313a), for plaster, although cheap to apply, can be expensive to maintain. If neglected it soon becomes unsightly (277b). Perhaps its most attractive quality is its colour, which varies from cream to ivory-white according to the colour of the sand. If the natural colour is not what is wanted, another can be washed over the surface easily and speedily.   *

Pargeting

Ben Jonson wrote of a lady 'above fiftie' who 'pargets'.[1] Although no doubt the lady's intention was ornamental, it is evident that in Jonson's time the word did not yet have the particular meaning which it has since acquired. Pargeting, pargetting, pargetry, parget-work or parge-work are terms now used to describe ornamental designs in plaster relief or, by extension, incised. They are nearly always associated with timber-framing, but were also used on buildings of clay-lump. Although often restored, the original designs usually belong to the seventeenth century, when the craft reached its zenith. No examples survive from before the reign of Elizabeth I,[2] although earlier instances are recorded.[3] Pargeting, which is little known or practised outside England, declined in favour as the popularity of timber-framing waned under the Georges.

The incised decoration, also known as 'stick-work' or 'combed work', appeared first, and since it was much the easier to execute, was always the commoner form. The implements used were home-made: a pointed stick, a group of such sticks tied together in the

1 *Epicene, or The Silent Woman* (1609), Act V, Scene 1.

2 The only example known to me which has often been regarded as pre-Elizabethan is an elaborate coloured frieze which runs along the front of what are called Bishop Bonner's Cottages at East Dereham in Norfolk. This curious building, timber-framed, lath and plastered, and with a thatched roof of exceptionally steep pitch, is dated 1502. Although added later this date is probably correct, for thatched roofs of very steep pitch (60° or more) are almost always of pre-Elizabethan origin; but the pargeting would appear to belong to the seventeenth century.

3 See F. A. Girling, 'Pargetting in Suffolk', in *Proceedings of the Suffolk Institute of Archaeology*, vol. 23, Part III (1939), p. 202.

POST-RESTORATION PARGETING
a. *The Crown House, Newport, Essex*
b. *Sparrowe's House, Ipswich, Suffolk*

form of a fan, a wooden comb with five short prongs and a handle, or just a big nail. While the plaster was still wet, various designs, usually of a modest geometrical kind, were impressed into it. Among the simplest of all is what is known as 'sparrow-picking', consisting merely of rhythmic stab-holes produced by a triangular piece of wood with wooden teeth, affixed to a stick: it is not ineffective. Sometimes the entire front of a building would be covered with one design, but more frequently the surface would be divided into panels, in which doors and windows would take their logical place. The decoration might indeed go no further than a series of plain rectangular panels of different sizes, with moulded frames delicately incised. Or the panels might be 'pinked', that is filled with a variety of ornamental patterns: semicircles, scallops, lozenges, zigzags, herring-bones, scales, flowers, fans, or basket-work, as at Newport, Essex (355a) or Bentley, Suffolk (355b). This type of plaster ornamentation remained in favour until well into the eighteenth century; plain panels with multilinear borders, even when the execution was a little artless, consorted well with Georgian ideas of cottage building. About 1900 there was a revival of interest in this kind of pargeting, as can be seen at Letchworth: sometimes the designs were now impressed into the wet plaster from wooden blocks, and look rather mechanical.

Hard on the heels of the incised type of decoration, and in the wake of the Italian plasterers who had worked in England under Henry VIII, came the more interesting ornamentation in relief which some would alone describe as true pargeting. The early examples of raised ornamentation are modest: simple panels for the most part, diamond-shaped, square or rectangular, circular or oval, encompassing a date or a set of initials or a single ornament such as a Tudor rose (355b), a fleur-de-lis, a crown, a bird, a rampant lion or a two-headed eagle, inserted into plain or combed surfaces. These designs might be modelled free-hand with the fingers, aided by a few small tools, or impressed from moulds, which were normally of wood but occasionally beeswax. Pargeting was also used to decorate the surface of beams, bressummers and string-courses. For these, simple wavy patterns repeating about every eighteen inches were standard, but trails of grape-vine or honeysuckle are the best.

As the seventeenth century advanced, larger designs were attempted, particularly in Suffolk and Essex. Although the craft of pargeting never wholly lost its rustic character, with a good deal which, it must be admitted, has little artistic merit, the panels grew bigger, and here and there, as at the Garrison House at Wivenhoe near Colchester, the ornamentation—in this instance a kind of floral strapwork—was carried over the entire surface of the wall (355d). After the Restoration, we find the decoration more firmly disciplined by the architecture, which was all to the good. Another house at Newport offers a good illustration (356a): built about 1600, it was enriched in 1692 by the addition of a handsome shell-shaped wooden hood over the door and a good deal of gentle pargeting in the form of moulded panels, left blank below but filled with swags and foliage above. Elsewhere the ornamentation had now become bolder and rather more sophisticated. In tune with the times, its derivation was now more Classical. Bold acanthus-like scrolls and swags of fruit were favourite motifs; others were vines, honeysuckle, dolphins, vases, cornucopia, coats of arms and occasionally human figures, as at Sparrowe's House, Ipswich (c. 1670), the most elaborate example of the period[1] (356b). Single subjects might now be placed on cartouches, or surrounded by wreaths of flowers and fruit. Although some of the earlier, humbler examples may be more lovable, it was in the reign of Charles II that the craft is seen at its boldest. Style changed with the times, not to any extent with the locality.

The counties which preserve, and which always possessed, the greatest quantity of pargeting are Essex and Suffolk, especially south-west Suffolk. Next come the counties which adjoin them: Hertfordshire, notably the eastern part around Bishop's Stortford, which seems at one time to have been a flourishing centre for the craft; Cambridgeshire and Norfolk (not much here); and, across the Thames, Kent. Outside this south-eastern area pargeting occurs sporadically but infrequently. Its association with East Anglia is partly to be explained by the profusion of timber-framed houses in this part of the country, for which pargeting provided a suitable adornment, and partly by the wealth of these counties in the sixteenth and seventeenth centuries, which encouraged an indulgence in ornamentation seldom found on the plasterwork of the timber-framed houses in the West of England. And because the prosperity was mostly in the towns and large villages, it is there that we find the pargeting, displayed for all to see; on a house standing in isolation in the country upon which a Stuart nobleman would not have hesitated to lavish his riches, these less grand people would probably have regarded such expenditure as unjustified.

Like all other plasterwork, pargeting soon gets dirty, and every time its appearance is refreshed with a new coat of limewash or colour-wash the crispness of the outlines becomes a little more blurred. Moreover, the cumulative effect of coat after coat of limewash is to add substantially to the weight, so that after a time the wall may no longer be able to carry it, and pieces fall away. There can be no doubt, therefore, that the larger part of our seventeenth century pargeting has been lost for ever; and a great part of what is left has had to be renewed. Some years ago I watched two men repairing the seventeenth-century pargeting on the Ancient House (1473) at Clare in Suffolk, a house on the south side of the churchyard which is probably more often photographed for its plaster ornamentation than any

1 How much the pargeting here was 'recreated' in 1850 is a matter of some doubt.

other in England (355c). Under the aegis of the Ministry of Works, the two elderly pargeters, with a compound of lime and sand, horse-fat and horse-hair, were working away on a low scaffolding. Most of the existing plaster (which was itself a renewal, for it is known that this house once had a fabulous winged monster below one of its windows) had to be entirely removed. No moulds were used; they were relying on photographs. What we see now therefore is a reproduction, approximate and not exact, of what was itself not original. The work has been well done: the only alternative to renewal was destruction; and with such an essentially free-hand craft little may be lost when the plasterers are men of skill and sensibility. But it is as well to realize that a substantial proportion of the pargeting to be seen to-day, including many dated pieces, belongs to the late-sixteenth and seventeenth centuries in spirit rather than in fact; and furthermore that many examples which are now white (and all the better for it) would seem originally to have been coloured.

Roughcast and Pebble-dash

Roughcast (which is also written rough-cast) is another surface material with a very long tradition; it is variously compounded. Essentially it consists of a crushed aggregate containing coarse sand, washed gravel, or stone chippings, mixed with slaked lime and nowadays a certain amount of cement. The wall surface which is to receive it is given an undercoat, $\frac{1}{2}$ to $\frac{3}{4}$ in. thick, of lime and sand or, to-day, cement and sand, and upon this, while still wet, the semi-liquid roughcast is thrown with a trowel from a flat wooden board known as a hawk. Formerly another method was to throw it on from a brush. Now it will often be flung on mechanically. It is generally held that an application by throwing is more durable than one that is just laid on, and that roughcast is therefore externally superior, from the practical standpoint, to rendering with plaster.

It is probably fair to say that the widespread employment of roughcast in all parts of Britain has always had a practical justification. It may be hiding poor quality brick or any of the unbaked earths; the common use of chalk as a component of roughcast for mud-built cottages in the Chalk areas has already been noted. It might provide a covering for rubblestone masonry of all kinds, especially when so soft that additional protection was needed against the weather, or so hard that a dressed surface could only be achieved at the cost of much labour. Hence on the one hand the profusion of roughcast in 'soft stone' counties like Buckinghamshire and Bedfordshire, and on the other its extensive use over roughly constructed walls, whether of Devonian stone in the South-West or of Silurian and Ordovician stone in and around the Lake District. It is a material specially convenient for covering rounded surfaces (364a), the construction of which in masoned stone or brick entails considerable extra labour.

The artistic merits of roughcast vary widely. It can be very pleasing; it can also be quite the reverse. The differences depend partly on the composition of the roughcast, partly on its environment. The sand should neither be too lumpy nor too fine. In Scotland it is a common practice to use a beach shingle containing a generous proportion of sea-shells. But the besetting sin of most roughcast is the addition of too much cement, the reason being that cement gives a harder, more durable mix. Visually, unless it is painted, or at least given a fine matt finish with some such preparation as 'Sandtex', this is fatal; and to be pleasing a roughcast should not contain more than one part of cement to every three of lime. For town use the gravel or chippings, unless already of a uniform gauge, should be passed through a sieve in order to reduce the coarseness of the mix. Although in rainy weather it will soon become streaked, and will therefore require a good deal of superficial attention if it is to continue to look well, a smooth finish in a town is always preferable to a rough one, because in the hollows of the latter dirt will collect which it will be impossible to remove. In country districts a smooth finish may appear too urbane and a rough surface will weather more satisfactorily. It is in the country that this method of covering a wall is to be seen at its best, as for example at Cothay in West Somerset or at Westwood Manor, a National Trust house near Bradford-on-Avon in Wiltshire (363a). Both these houses have been roughcast over rubblestone ever since the fifteenth century; Westwood Manor, in particular, was a model example, with the roughcast seem-ing to 'grow' out of the fine limestone dressings and the colour a subtle blend of grey, buff and pale yellow. At Minster Lovell (107a) and at Crackenthorpe Hall (363b) the roughcast itself is by no means as good, but at the former we can enjoy a contrast of texture with the rubblestone masonry of the rest and at the latter an effective contrast of colour. Yet even in the countryside this material is often far from pleasing. At Packwood House in Warwickshire, another National Trust property, the depressing overcoat of mud-coloured roughcast which covers the whole building mars appreciably one's enjoy-ment of the exterior. Not far away is Corley Hall, a small Jacobean building, to-day a farmhouse, which is said to be the original of the Hall Farm in *Adam Bede*. Now, having been smothered in roughcast, it looks commonplace. The poor appearance of these and many other roughcast buildings (but not of course the fine ones, like Westwood) could certainly be much improved by the application of a fresh coat of whitewash, as at Hawks-head (168b), or of colour-wash—yellow ochre, for instance, as at Pembridge (130c); yet when the mix is full of cement, all that can usually be hoped for is that fresh colour will enhance the more distant views.

Although this book is not concerned with Scotland, the differing aesthetic estimates of roughcast North and South of the Border are of such interest as to justify, I hope, a short digression. In Scotland roughcast, which is there known as harling, is much more highly regarded than here. Probably no owner of a stone house in England would wish to see it covered with roughcast unless the masonry were so ragged or in such a poor state that additional weather-proofing was essential. In Scotland it is a common experience to encounter quite a different view. It is held that with masonry, even ashlar, the mortar courses, and often the slight variations of colour and texture between one block of stone and another, distract attention from the formal qualities of the architecture. As soon as one becomes conscious of the separate stones of which a building is composed, say the Scots, one loses the feeling of monumentality; whereas, on the contrary, the application of a uniform coat of harling, as well as providing the building with a good foil for any carved decoration, converts it into a single entity comparable with a piece of sculpture. The decidedly Scots-looking house at Penrith (364a) illustrates the point clearly. Great emphasis, it is true, is placed on the importance of good quality in the material (not much cement) and on the proper method of application. Since, as with fresco-painting, the joining up of a portion which has dried out to a new piece is not easy, it is desirable that an entire wall, from eaves to ground, should be completed in a single operation. Provided these requirements are fulfilled, the rough finish of a harled wall is greeted by the Scots with enthusiasm.

The practical justification for harling, on the ground that nearly all stone is more or less porous and that a coat of roughcast provides a valuable waterproof skin, is in fact of doubtful validity. It is not unusual to see harled buildings from the surface of which pieces have dropped off (and this can also be seen on the left of the Penrith photograph), making it all too easy for the wet to seep in behind; at Mellerstain in Berwickshire, where the harling formerly covering the wings has been removed, the rooms within are now said to be much drier. Here the central block was never harled, and in my opinion the benefit to the appearance of the house by the removal of the harling from the wings has been considerable. At Castle Fraser in Aberdeenshire, where part of the surface is harled and is of granite rubble which has been repointed with tact, Scottish enthusiasts expressed much regret that all was not harling; but there can be no doubt that to most English eyes it is the granite, even though undressed, which makes the more pleasing impression. One meets with a similar enthusiasm for roughcast in Ireland, where there is also a great deal of it—although here it is not called harling. Kilmainham Hospital on the outskirts of

TWO KINDS OF ROUGHCAST
·a. *Westwood Manor, Wiltshire*
b. *Crackenthorpe Hall, Westmorland*

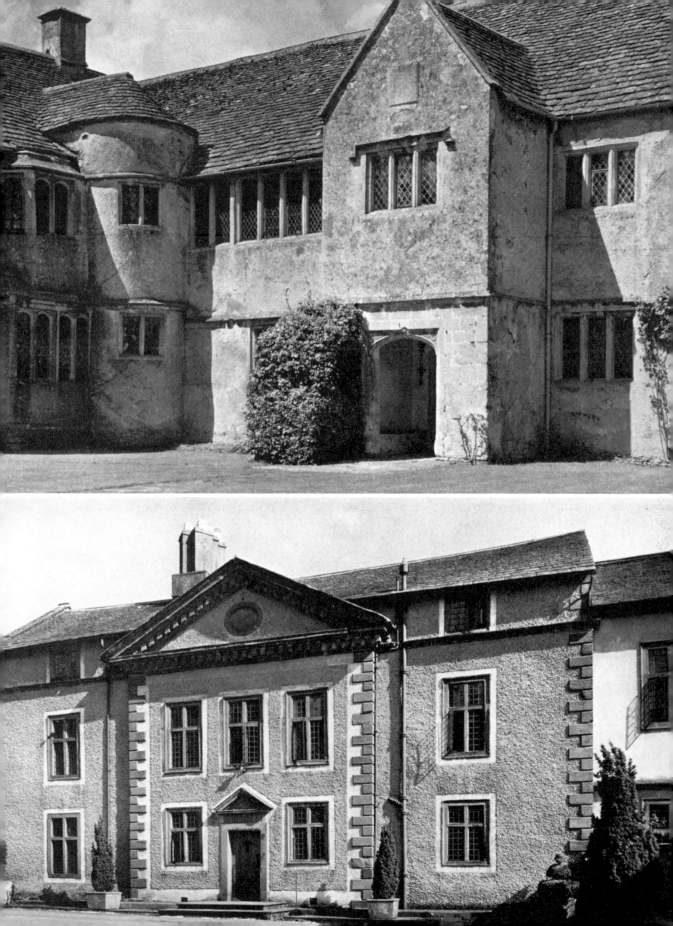

Dublin is a typical example: a brick building with dressings of granite but otherwise entirely covered with a decidedly pebbly roughcast. Dirty though it was, this was commended with evident pride by an Inspector of National Monuments; but English taste was not attracted, greatly preferring the unconcealed, albeit soot-laden, brickwork of Chelsea Hospital in London. On this question, therefore, there would seem aesthetically to be room for the most divergent views. Should a building be judged, and enjoyed, for the texture and colour of its materials, as well as for its design? Or are the former to be dubbed a Romantic 'extra', scarcely relevant to the central theme of architecture? The reader who has persevered thus far will know already how this author would answer.

Even when the roughcast is not very rough, and perhaps preferable on that account, its 'plaster' quality may be no asset. Before such South Devon churches as Ipplepen, Torbryan or Stoke Gabriel, which are entirely roughcast, one is conscious of a certain lack of definition. Their external wall surfaces seem everywhere to be soft and wavy, as if the buildings had been modelled in clay by some Brobdingnagian potter. Perfectly acceptable for a small house or a cottage, these gently undulating wall-surfaces seem on a large scale to entail some loss of dignity. On larger buildings roughcast may look best when employed over defined areas only, within a framework of stone. At Crackenthorpe Hall, apart from the rusticated quoins and the 'frame' of the pediment, the entire wall-surface was cement rendered, over which the roughcast was applied with careful discrimination (363b).

Pebble-dash resembles roughcast in that it is not trowelled but thrown, but here the mix consists of small washed pebbles only, with no lime. An undercoat of wet cement is therefore essential. It is at its least unpleasing when the stones are very small and not too brown, as at Strawberry Hill (364b). It must also be recorded that C. F. A. Voysey had a great affection for this material. Yet one often recoils with acute distaste from its coarse and lumpy texture and its drab yellow-brown colour. Because it is cheap and from the practical standpoint efficient, pebble-dash has been employed on a vast scale in all parts of the country during the past hundred years. When used to coat such buildings as the early round tower of St. Michael's at Lewes or Rufford New Hall, formerly a pleasing Georgian house in Lancashire, it looks wretchedly out of place. In rural districts where gravel is dug, as in many parts of Essex, village streets which were once delightful mixtures of grey oak, red brick, and much colour-washed plaster may now exhibit a characterless and depressing uniformity. In towns, the broken surface of a wall covered with pebble-dash is still more liable than roughcast to collect dirt particles from the atmosphere, which cannot be removed. Pebble-dash, as widely used in the last few decades, has made, in a word, one of the least cherished contributions to the pattern of English building.

ROUGHCAST AND PEBBLE-DASH
a. *17 Queen Street, Penrith, Cumberland*   b. *Strawberry Hill, Greater London*

WHITEWASH AND STRAW THATCHING
c. *Long Crendon, Buckinghamshire*

Stucco

The employment of various kinds of rendering, not merely for weather-proofing but with the deliberate intention of attempting inexpensively to simulate stone, has already been alluded to more than once in these pages. We have seen how, even as early as 1500, the appearance of stone dressings was being introduced in the non-stone areas by laying thin films of plaster over brickwork. With the advent of the Renaissance this practice became increasingly common on the Continent. In England one of the earliest full-scale examples is Inigo Jones's Marlborough House Chapel (originally the chapel of the Queen at St. James's). This building is of brick, with Portland stone for the dressings only; but the accounts preserved in the Public Record Office specifically refer to the rendering of the brick, which was to be 'drawn like ashlar'.[1] The excellence of the hard plaster quoins at Morden College, Blackheath, dating from the time of William III, was referred to on p. 38. A notable example in the next generation was Lord Burlington's brick villa at Chiswick (1725–c. 1730): here the base was faced with Portland stone, but the *piano nobile*, in the orthodox Palladian way, was given only a rendered surface, which was marked out in a masonry pattern with graphite. During the restoration of Chiswick by the Ministry of Works in 1952–58, the original procedure was followed. Two coats were applied, the mix being identical in each. This consisted of sand and lime in the ratio of five to one, with hair introduced as a binder. Since a smooth, even texture was now in demand, the sand was carefully washed and sieved before work was begun. The undercoat, having been allowed to set, was scratched to provide a key for the top coat, which was applied very thinly. Joints between one day's work and the next were carefully arranged to correspond with some architectural feature, to ensure an even texture. The colour was a light stone-grey.

It will be evident that we are now confronted with quite a different attitude towards plaster. Whereas with the old vernacular buildings the material had usually been employed for its own sake, on the more socially ambitious buildings of the Georgian period it was no more than an economical substitute for stone. The intention now was to obtain as smooth and hard a product as possible, the kind of plaster which in England has become known as 'stucco'. Although, as we learn from Vitruvius, the Greeks and the Romans had produced plaster fine enough to take a good polish, English plaster before the eighteenth century had been much coarser. The first patent for a stucco-type rendering to be

---

1 The rendering, renewed with cement, certainly does not suggest stone to-day, and the shallow trowel lines do nothing to assist the deception.

taken out in this country was in 1677, for Edisbury's 'Glassis', about which little is known. Almost another century was to elapse before a widely serviceable substance at last made its appearance, in the form of Liardet's cement, patented in 1773. This was immediately taken up in London by the brothers Adam and by Thomas Leverton. Its arrival was timely: it was the moment when London and a number of other cities were just starting to expand rapidly. For ornamental details another patent material also became available in the early seventeen-seventies: Coade's artificial stone (246b). Its composition, like that of Liardet's cement, remained a closely kept secret, and has never been precisely ascertained; it was not a stucco but a kind of terracotta of exceptional durability, produced from a mixture of certain clays and sands. Manufactured at Lambeth, it was taken up within a few years by almost every architect and speculative builder in London for the provision of ornamental details, often based on Greek prototypes. They have worn astonishingly well.[1]

By the end of the Regency, England was in possession of a number of patent external renderings which are generically classed as stucco. Among them were Dehl's mastic, patented in 1815, and Hamelin's mastic, 1817, but much the most important was Parker's Roman cement, which was patented in 1796. This was made, as mentioned earlier, from septaria: the nodules of calcareous clay were subjected to a process of burning. The principal centre of the industry—for an industry it became—was Harwich. No previous stucco had achieved its strength, durability, or power of withstanding damp, and although he used Dehl's and Hamelin's as well, it has been said that Parker's cement made Nash's architecture possible. The popularity of this stucco as a facing material for brick spread between 1810 and 1850 to all parts of the country. In London itself, apart from the spectacular achievements of Nash (that 'very great master, who finds us all brick and who leaves us all plaster') around Regent's Park (350a) and elsewhere, miles of streets and crescents

1 For Coade stone, see Katharine A. Esdaile in *The Architect and Building News*, January 19 and 26, 1940, S. B. Hamilton in *The Architectural Review*, November 1954, and a short summary in Sir John Summerson's *Georgian London* (1945), pp. 112–114. The Coades' factory was on part of the site occupied in 1951 by the Festival of Britain exhibition. In 1821 the firm was taken over by a cousin, William Croggan, whose signature occurs, for example, at the base of the splendid coat of arms erected in the following year over the big archway into the park at Easton Neston, Towcester. The business closed down in 1837. Mark Blanchard seems then to have bought some of the moulds, establishing his own business at Blackfriars in 1839. It has been said that J. M. Blashfield had been a sculptor employed by the Coades' firm and now bought some more; but neither of those statements seems to be true. Blashfield carried on at Poplar until 1858, when he moved to Stamford, where from the local clays and others brought from Dorset he began manufacturing terracotta both for ornamental purposes and as a building material. Stamford terracotta, although not quite such a clever deception as the original Coade stone, had a more stone-like colour and texture than is usual in this material. The business failed in 1875. (For many examples, see Rupert Gunnis's *Dictionary of British Sculptors, 1660–1851* (1953), under 'Blashfield', 'Coade' and 'Croggan'.)

and squares in such districts as Pimlico, Belgravia and Kensington were constructed in these years of brick, faced with one or other of these new patent renderings, and generally with Parker's cement.

In the middle years of the nineteenth century, 'Roman' cement gradually gave place to Portland cement. This was first patented, after many experiments, in 1824. The process consisted in firing pulverized clay and lime at a very high temperature (1400°C), and then in grinding down the resulting clinker which, mixed with water, set into an extremely hard and durable mass.[1] Its inventor, a Yorkshireman named Joseph Aspdin, gave it the name because he supposed that it looked like Portland stone. It is a material of great strength, and of immense importance because it forms the basis of modern concrete, yet it is seldom visually agreeable as a facing material. It is therefore fortunate that its production only became a major industry about the time that the facing of brick with stucco went out of fashion. Because it is easier to handle and so much stronger, however, Portland cement is now widely employed as a replacement for earlier kinds of stucco and also for the old lime-plaster. One has only to look, for example, at many of the houses in the main street at Odiham, or at every second church in some parts of Buckinghamshire, to realize what a disappointing substitute it makes.

In Nash's time, as mentioned earlier, every stuccoed house was covered with a network of meticulously incised lines intended to suggest mortar courses, which in many instances can still be clearly discerned (341a, 382e). In Cheshire, where there is plenty of sandstone, red, pink or buff, it was the practice to give stucco a wash of the same colour, before adding joint-lines carefully adjusted to the usual sizes of the local sandstone blocks. Hence, it will be inferred, the material was not at the time appreciated for its own sake; and when we now enjoy a Regency terrace of painted stucco not only for its design but also for the charm of its material, we are responding to a quality in the architecture which was not present in the mind of the designer. Not that this matters: a great deal of the world's art was ostensibly created for purposes quite different from those for which it is now esteemed. Nash, one can be sure, would not have minded in the least; but it is proper that this swing of the pendulum of taste should be recognized. There were in fact no terraces of painted stucco in London in Nash's lifetime, because, although paint was applied to external wood and ironwork, stucco walls were only colour-washed. The introduction of oil paint for walls and porticoes, which occurred in London about 1840, and the abandonment of the fake jointing both favoured those broad, 'picturesque' architectural effects in the attainment of which stucco is surely the ideal substance (350c). Especially when it has been freshly

1 For a detailed account of the process, see W. B. McKay, *Brickwork* (2nd ed., 1968), pp. 18–19.

painted—and the smoother and glossier the paint the better—there is no English building
material which is so light-hearted, so urbane, so well-mannered. Perhaps that is why,
outside London, one thinks of it especially in connection with those spas and watering-
places of the Regency and immediate post-Regency periods, where, as Alan Melville
once put it, fat elderly cats sleep in the sun and thin elderly ladies doze in the shade.

Nevertheless stucco is another substance which has been very variously estimated. The
Victorians, although they used it constantly, always seem to have had misgivings about it,
apparently, as intimated earlier, on moral grounds: they regarded it as dishonest. Pugin
of course was in the vanguard, stigmatizing 'all the mechanical contrivances and inventions
of the day, such as plastering, composition, papier mâché, and a host of other deceptions'
which 'only serve to degrade design',[1] and fulminating against 'the restless torrent of
Roman-cement men, who buy their ornaments by the yard and their capitals by the ton'![2]
But on the subject of stucco some architectural writers, even to-day, remain markedly
unenthusiastic. Sir John Summerson refers to it as 'in a sense a fake material'. For Mr
John Harvey it is 'a poor thing', following in the wake of Banister Fletcher, who bemoaned
the fact that Palladio so often worked in 'mean and commonplace materials, such as brick
faced with stucco'. Most plasters, certainly, are intrinsically dull, and need to be covered
with paint or at least distemper. But with the hard stuccoes of Regency architecture, this
was recognized from the outset. As a condition of their leases, the stone and wood and
iron parts of the Regent's Park terraces had to be repainted and the stucco portions re-
coloured and rejointed every fourth year, 'the colour of such stucco not to be varied or
changed at any time but always to be in imitation of Bath stone'. At Hove, presumably
because of the salty atmosphere, paint was insisted on; the houses in Brunswick Terrace
and Brunswick Square had to be repainted in a uniform colour every third year. Save in
times of war, and except with regard to the maintenance of the joint-lines, these conditions have, fortunately, always been enforced here. In London the Crown Estate Commissioners still impose a repainting of the Regent's Park terraces every four years. But in
less exposed places a stucco front may continue to look sufficiently fresh for six or even
eight years, especially if it is washed annually, which does not usually take long.

It cannot however be denied that constant repainting, apart from the cost, brings its
own problems, for in time the weight of additional paint on the plaster will help to pull
it away from the wall and cause trouble. Yet I am among those who continue to cherish
this material as one that has made a notable contribution to the English architectural scene,
especially in towns. If one takes a walk through the 'little' streets of a London borough

1 *Contrasts* (1836), p. 35.   2 *True Principles* (1841), pp. 56–57.

whose heyday was a century or so ago, a borough such as Camberwell, one can hardly fail to be struck by the much pleasanter appearance of the stucco-faced houses, when freshly-painted or washed (as many of them still are), than of those built of brownish-yellow stock bricks. The latter, mostly of early Victorian date, are now usually dreary; the stucco houses, built only a few years earlier, look far more mannerly.

Whitewash and Applied Colour

The covering of a wall with daub, plaster, roughcast, pebble-dash or cement endowed it, needless to say, with the colour of the material employed. This was often no advantage: it would be difficult to devise colours less attractive than those natural to cement or pebble-dash. It has therefore long been a common practice to apply whitewash, colour-wash or, much less often, paint. Nor have such applications been confined to the surface materials which have been the subject of the present chapter; in all parts of the country stone masonry, especially rubblestone, brick and the unbaked earths have been similarly treated. In America even the White House is of sandstone, painted.

The traditional covering was limewash. This was just mineral lime and water; and for old buildings, if there are no damp courses, limewash is still best, because it is porous, thus allowing any rising dampness to dry out. Modern whitewashes and distempers always include some sort of oil or glue size as a binder, which renders them more adhesive and more waterproof, but any damp in the wall itself cannot easily escape through such a covering, and is liable therefore to produce stains or blisters. The disadvantage of the old limewash was its impermanence: heavy rain quickly washed it off, and so it required constant renewal. The addition of tallow, often imported from Russia, made it less soluble and was therefore desirable; but tallow was not always available.

In former days the need to apply a fresh coat of limewash every year or two presented no problem. The material itself was very cheap and the labour was available. At slack times the farm labourers would put on smocks and old caps and get to work. First the lime had to be slaked and, especially when it was hot, great care had to be taken that it did not splash into the eyes. Then it was slapped on to the walls with brushes fastened on to long poles. Thereby cracks and flaws were filled up and buildings were kept in good repair. New whitewash was also a matter of personal pride, as in many places it still is. In sunny weather a freshly whitened house may be visible for miles, and set amid greenery can add a note of charm to a landscape (*168a*). So frequently has the process of limewashing been repeated that there are many farmhouses and cottages in the North and

West which now carry on their walls a crust more than ¼ in. thick. In East Anglia, clay lump walls not originally rendered have sometimes been limewashed so often that they now look as if they had been given a plaster rendering; and the same is true of many of the cob cottages of the South-West.

All through the Middle Ages houses, even of good masonry, were often whitewashed outside and in. So too were churches; according to the twelfth-century historian William of Malmesbury, this was already happening at York as early as *c.* 690.[1] The evidence of ancient church accounts leaves no room for doubt that even ashlar was normally lime-washed internally, and sometimes externally too. Inside, the main object of the limewash was amenity: the white ground kept the building lighter, helped to show up the wall paintings, and provided an excellent foil for the stained glass. But outside, the primary reason for limewashing was the protection of porous stonework from the elements, which included fire where the walls were of wood or the roofs of thatch. To-day one would not usually want to see ashlar thus treated, except perhaps in very smoky cities, where the whitewash would require incessant renewal. Applied to random masonry, however, particularly if the stone itself is somewhat dark in tone, a coat of whitewash often adds a welcome touch of brightness to a building (*181c*, *364c*). Several references have been made in earlier chapters to the pleasing appearance of whitewashed stonework, especially in the North. Around Norwich one occasionally sees walls of flint so treated, with excel-lent results. Nor is whitewash out of place on brickwork. Its use is more general now in Scotland, Ireland and Wales than in England, but we may be glad that some parts of this country still preserve the old tradition.

A limewashed interior can look cold and dreary if the tone is slightly grey; care must be taken during slaking to avoid this. The tint can be warmed by adding a trace of umber or other powder colour, but it needs to be skilfully done. To-day it is easier and often more satisfactory to buy natural stone lime, which need not be pure white: some of the best are off-white. Externally there is scope for almost unlimited colour variation. The pigments, which should be introduced in the course of slaking, add not only variety but also opacity to the limewash, which is very convenient. Small quantities of carbon black, for instance, produce a pale grey, and of Venetian red a light pink. Brighter colours need to be handled with rather more discrimination in the vaporous and often misty atmosphere of Britain than in the crisp, sparkling sunlight of the Mediterranean. There is, nevertheless, plenty of colour-wash to be seen in this country, much of it so succulent that one finds

1 'Age and weather had destroyed the comeliness (*decorem*) of the masonry; the bishop [St. Wilfrid] white-washed it with shining lime.' See L. F. Salzman, *op. cit.*, p. 356.

oneself turning out half the contents of the larder in order to describe it. There are tomato red, raspberry-and-cream pink, strawberry-ice pink, peach pink, salmon pink. We meet orange and apricot, lemon yellow, lime yellow, butter yellow, biscuit and cream. Apple and olive round off this gastronomic galaxy. It will be found that special colours sometimes enjoy a vogue in particular localities: shades of pink, for example, have long been popular in Suffolk. As was noted earlier in connection with Ingatestone Hall, colour-washed plaster may be much more agreeable than an expanse of unrelieved brick. Two particularly attractive East Anglian examples may be cited. Elm Hill at Norwich, a cobbled, winding street of old houses (*349*b and c), partly dating from the sixteenth century and all admirably reconditioned in recent years, is now a show-piece of colour-wash. There are blue, green and various shades of pink and yellow as well as white, while one house has brick nogging. The blending of colours is achieved with complete informality, and is notably successful. At Thaxted in Essex, Newbiggen Street leading northwards from the church has many timber-framed houses, of which all but one, in the usual Essex way, are wholly plastered. The use of colour-wash here is spectacular and, one is tempted to add, very un-English. Applied colour has turned it into what is, in my view, one of the prettiest streets in the country.[1]

With the advent of stucco and its frequent employment on Classical buildings in an urban context, the use of colour, naturally and rightly, became more sedate. The desire to suggest stone prompted the choice of stone colours. This, in London during the first half of the nineteenth century, meant, as we have seen, not the near-white of Portland but the yellowish hue of Bath stone, a tint which in distemper or paint does not improve with time. For architecture with a Classical character, a warm off-white is undoubtedly the best for England, with perhaps small accents of gayer colour and a harder gloss for doors. Terrace houses, the most elegant kind for towns, should all be painted not only the same colour but at the same time, for, as has been rightly observed, there is a neighbourliness in colour as in social life.

Oil-paint is one of the dressiest ways of providing a building with a protective and decorative external finish, and in towns especially, one of the most delightful. The house at Kimbolton in Huntingdonshire (No. 7 East Street: *350*b), with wide ground-floor windows lighting rooms which probably once served as shops, and a cement-rendered front painted white, with black 'toothing' at the quoins, is not perhaps altogether a 'good companion' and open to criticism on that account; but its effectiveness is beyond question.

---

1 By contrast, the interior of the fine church, entirely covered some years ago with an ice-cold grey-white limewash applied over every member without discrimination, is an example of how not to do it.

There is much to be said, too, for giving brickwork an overcoat of paint, especially if it is the over-patterned polychromatic kind or if it has become dingy and sombre, as has been demonstrated in a number of towns since 1959 by that admirable body, the Civic Trust. In streets well endowed with Georgian buildings colour is rightly used with restraint. In Magdalen Street, Norwich, on the other hand, and in the Market Place at Burslem, the Trust's first two major projects, the buildings provided a mixed assortment alike in style and in aesthetic quality; and, at Norwich particularly, much bolder colours were used, and in considerable variety. A few puritans cried 'chocolate box', but most people were delighted. Moreover, the street gained a unity which it had never previously possessed. 'The strong colours . . . were part of a deliberate plan to bring the upper parts of the buildings fully into play and thereby to persuade people to look at the street as a whole instead of being conscious only of shop windows and traffic. The brightest colours were used to mark either end of the whole area and intermediately to break the street into sections, thereby adding to the interest: they were also used to pick out buildings of special character and on buildings, such as public houses, where a gayer approach seemed more permissible than elsewhere.'[1] The influence of the Civic Trust's good work in Magdalen Street, Norwich, quickly spread to other towns in Norfolk such as Aylsham and Holt.

A similar project for Windsor was opened by the Queen, in the presence of over a thousand mayors and local authority representatives. This gave the required lead, and hundreds of other towns and villages have since followed suit, with impressive results. The Trust rightly concerns itself with everything which may affect the appearance of a street, such as planting trees and flowers, and protection from needless signs, advertisements and other clutter; and since the passing of the Civic Amenities Act in 1967 local authorities have the power, indeed the duty, to designate whole areas as worthy of special vigilance and control (Conservation Areas). In no direction has more enterprise been shown than in the handling of colour. The return of colour into English shopping streets, under the control of good architects (this proviso is very important), is a heartening event. Paint is unfortunately expensive, and must be kept clean, but it is much more durable than distemper, and for several seasons requires no more than washing.

Just as the appearance of concrete can now be immeasurably improved by using one or more of the fine range of new natural aggregates with interesting textures and colours which have been developed in recent years, so is it now also possible to use cement in a far more acceptable fashion than formerly. One way is to insist on white cement, which is manufactured with china clay instead of ordinary clay; it is twice as expensive, but well

---

1 *Magdalen Street, Norwich: an Experiment in Civic Design*, 1958–59. Civic Trust report (1960), p. 17.

worth it. The alternative is to add colour. When a somewhat rough finish is required, several good preparations are now available. Oil-paint costs a good deal more and needs to be laid over a priming coat in order to counteract the acids in the cement, but is much the best for smooth textures. No applied surface, in fact, can begin to rival the sparkle and sheen of fresh paint.

15

THE METALS

Lead

When we think of the tremendous place of the metals in the architecture of to-day, some effort of the imagination is required to realize that, no more than a hundred and fifty years ago, their structural importance was very small. The only metal which was much in demand by English builders before the Industrial Revolution, principally for covering roofs and containing window glass, was lead, a soft and pliable substance with no capacity for weight-bearing.

Lead is yet another building material with which England was well endowed, natural wealth which our Roman conquerors did not fail, nearly two thousand years ago, to exploit, especially in the Mendips. So rich were our resources that for several centuries before about 1850 the bulk of the world's lead supply came either from England or from Spain. Generally speaking our lead ores are found in association with the older rocks, but the distribution was widespread. One of the early attractions of lead mining was the quantity of silver which could be extracted during the process of smelting. All who walk in the Lake District will be familiar with the old Greenside mine on the Ullswater flank of Helvellyn,[1] and perhaps also with the former royal mines, exploited in Elizabethan times, at Newlands to the west of Derwentwater and near Coniston. On the main range of the Pennines, some parts of the fells, notably around the high, cold market town of Alston, are peppered with the remains of long-abandoned lead workings; in this parish alone there were no fewer than 119 mines working in 1768, and quite a number of them were still productive a hundred years later. In upper Weardale Bishop Pudsey of Durham is known to have been working the mineral for its silver in the twelfth century, on the strength of a charter granted to him by his uncle, King Stephen. In all the six northern

---

1 This mine yielded lead for hundreds of years, and was still employing over three hundred men between 1938 and 1945. It is now worked out and was finally closed in January 1962. At a cost of some thousands of pounds, all disfiguring traces were removed: ugly buildings demolished; streams turned back into their natural courses; dumps of waste carefully grassed over, after first being covered with sewage sludge. This is a fine example of what can and should be done whenever a mine ceases working.

counties, lead-mining has a very long, if not unchequered, history, and has left many scars. Reeth, in Swaledale, was one of the main centres: in the last hundred years, since the closing of the lead mines, it has lost three-fifths of its population. There was lead also in the Isle of Man; in Cheshire, near Alderley Edge; and in the Stiperstones district of Shropshire. In the South-West there were the famous lead-mines of the Mendips, whence came most, if not all, of the metal for a notable series of twelfth-century fonts scattered throughout the southern counties, and other mines at Marytavy and Bere Alston, close to Tavistock. Much the most important area of all, however, was Derbyshire, where as late as 1890 there were still over eight hundred men employed in mining lead. Some of the mines were near Hope, under the Peak, but the majority were in the centre of the county around Bakewell, Matlock and Wirksworth. In mediaeval times the metal was taken via the Derwent, the Trent and the Witham to Boston, whence it was shipped in considerable quantities to the Continent as well as to London and other places in the South. For a thousand years and more lead was, with the exception of tin, our most important metallic ore.

Until the closing years of the seventeenth century, all lead used in building was sand-cast, in rather heavy sheets (8–10 lb. per sq. ft.). The sand was spread out upon a table perhaps 10 ft. long and 6 ft. wide, with a rim, and if any relief ornamentation were required, models were made and pressed into the sand, over which the molten lead was then poured. The sandy bed left the lead with a lightly stippled texture which, while pleasanter to look at than a smooth surface, enhanced its susceptibility to surface oxidation and, later, decay: hence the thickness of the old lead. Milled lead was first produced in Wren's time and was rolled absolutely smooth and very much more thinly; indeed, at Greenwich Hospital in 1700 it was so light that it could not withstand the weather, with the result that the master plumbers pronounced it unfit for use on buildings, and its reputation remained under a cloud until the last century. Although cast lead is still produced in small quantities and is aesthetically much superior, nearly all the lead sheeting in use to-day is, for economic reasons, milled, and sometimes of foreign origin. Needless to say, methods of manufacturing have been greatly improved since Wren's day, and milled sheets may be as much as 40 ft. long and 8 ft. wide.

From the practical standpoint lead has a number of valuable attributes. It is easy to work: soft and malleable, it melts at a very low temperature, and can be used cold. It does not rust, and is therefore an excellent material for holding or repelling water. Nor is it easily inflammable; and if correctly handled it will endure for a very long time— two hundred, sometimes three hundred years or even more. Gradually, it is true, owing to the action of the weather and especially to the oxidation mentioned above, a lead roof will wear thin and require attention; but it can be patched, and when the decay is really serious it is quite feasible to remove the old lead and, with the addition of a certain amount of new, to recast it. It is nearly always laid over solid boarding, which in olden days was usually oak. It lasts much better, as the mediaeval builders understood but as the Georgians often failed to recognize, if laid in narrow strips, not over 30 ins. wide nor more than about 8 ft. long. Horizontal joints may be given a simple lap, but in all the best work the edges of adjacent sheets meeting vertically or diagonally are still rolled together in the mediaeval fashion. The use of large sheets in the eighteenth and early nineteenth centuries did not allow for the expansion and contraction to which, under changes of temperature, lead is especially prone, causing cracks and splits which have proved very troublesome.

Lead also possessed the important attribute of long being the only material in England which could be used externally on flat or nearly flat roofs. It was indeed, for several reasons, better used thus: lead on a steep pitch is always liable to 'creep'; laying is more difficult; costs are higher (because much more is needed) without any increase in efficiency; and more strength may be required in the supporting walls and timbers. Steeply-pitched lead-covered roofs are not rare, for they sometimes had to rise over vaults, or especially in East Anglia, over grand displays of woodwork; but there can be little doubt that many such roofs originally had some other covering, such as shingles or thatch, which demanded the steeper pitch. For other purposes, the ability of lead to provide a nearly flat roof which was completely watertight was a great convenience. In buildings of a military character such roofs, protected by parapets and battlements, were needed for defence purposes. Designers of Perpendicular churches were prone to favour elaborate and sometimes pierced parapets which could be seen better in combination with nearly flat roofs—although it may be that the parapets were felt to be aesthetically necessary for the very reason that so often no roof was now visible above the walls. Similar considerations apply from the middle of the sixteenth century to those great houses like Hardwick Hall (400) which adopted the 'lead flat'; the pioneer of this fashion was Protector Somerset's house in London, built in 1547–52 and demolished about 1777. With the advent of Classical architecture there were many demands for roofs of gentle pitch, for which lead was virtually the only answer. For instance, the roof behind the pediment added by John Webb in 1654 at The Vyne (245a) has a pitch of only about 28°, which is too little for the plain tiles that cover the main roof of the house, so recourse was had to lead. The same plan was adopted at the Salisbury College of Matrons (246d).

The exceptional pliability of this metal rendered it ideal for covering curved surfaces, whether of the ogee-capped turrets (or 'tips' as they were then called[1]) so popular in

---

[1] In most old documents the word is spelt *type*, and the identification with *tip* (= extremity) is not absolutely certain.

Tudor and Jacobean times, or of those delightful roof-lanterns (246d, 255b) which could be so useful for lighting a central staircase, or of the domes and steeples of Wren and his successors. For all these the underlying structure was normally wood.

The restraining factor on the use of lead was always the high cost. Thus, although it was employed by the Saxons for church roofs as early as the seventh century in at least two places (York and Lindisfarne), and for many, perhaps most, of the more important church roofs as well as for some notable spires in the seven centuries that followed (the fact that part of the workshop area at a big church or monastery was often known as the *plumbery* confirms this), it was not until the general increase in our wealth in the fifteenth century that lead roofs at length became more general. One reason why lead was desirable was its comparative lightness. It is not perhaps generally realized that lead sheets, at the normal thickness of 7 or 8 lb. per sq. ft., are no heavier than thatch, and lighter than tiles or slates. But even in the fifteenth century all the other roofing materials, stone slates included, were cheaper, and only the richer churches and very affluent private individuals could afford lead. Up to the reign of Henry VIII the attitude towards lead in England, in contrast to France, was purely utilitarian, and there can, I fear, be no doubt that Dr. Salzman is right when he observes that 'the mediaeval builders would have used corrugated iron if they had possessed it.'[1]

On the artistic effect of lead-covered roofs, opinions differ; in my view old cast lead can be a material of much virtue. In smoky towns lead roofs soon turn black and make little appeal. In a clean atmosphere, on the other hand, a cast lead roof will become steadily whiter. This is frequently believed to be because of the retention in the lead of a certain quantity of silver. In fact, it was usual from quite early times to extract the silver during the smelting process, and the whiteness derives from an insoluble (but fortunately non-staining) lead carbonate which is very commonly found on lead that has been subjected to long exposure. This whiteness, when it is still silvery, can be delightful. It can also be excessive, as at Ely Cathedral, where on a bright day the extreme whiteness of the vast, steep-pitched roof of the nave reflects too much light to be comfortable.

On a spire, 'standing like a frosted spear against the sky',[2] even very white lead is quite acceptable. Some English spires were covered with lead at a very early date, but the oldest have long ago perished. The doyen of the survivors is that at Long Sutton in Lincolnshire; the lead of course has needed attention more than once, but the structure belongs to the first part of the thirteenth century. Here, as often on spires, a rather complicated surface, with the strips of lead set on the diagonal and arranged in herring-bone patterns for the

1 *Op. cit.*, p. 263.   2 Lawrence Weaver, *English Leadwork* (1909), p. 86.

purpose of reducing the danger of 'creeping', helps to counteract the proneness to over-bright reflections.

Apart from roofs, lead played a very important part from the late twelfth century onwards in the art of glazing; here too, its pliability was invaluable when it was required to fit together small pieces, which for stained glass would be of the most varied shapes, into iron frames. Lead cames (grooved bars) can be seen in the church windows of every age, and in the domestic casement windows specially characteristic of the sixteenth and seventeenth centuries. These will be considered in a little more detail in the next chapter. Unlike the white-painted wooden glazing bars of the Georgian sliding sash window, leaded lights, owing to their small scale and neutral grey colour, do not play a dominant part in the impact of an elevation. On the other hand, they can enhance the textural appeal of an old house, especially as they are often slightly wavy. Unfortunately they are likely to need renewal after about two hundred years, so the temptation in the Victorian period to replace leaded lights with plate or sheet glass was often great. From the standpoint of good appearance this is always a mistake, as can be seen at Danny Park, an Elizabethan house under the South Downs.

From about the middle of the Tudor period, lead was also occasionally used for internal plumbing and more frequently for rain-water heads, down-pipes and gutters. Here it served both a useful and a decorative purpose. As early as 1240 lead down-pipes were ordered for the Tower of London, to save the freshly whitewashed walls from being damaged by rainwater.[1] The first reference to ornamentation in this type of English lead-work relates to the square pipes of the Palace of Westminster, which in 1532 were 'garny-sshid with the kinges arms and badges'.[2] Among Elizabethan and Jacobean houses which still preserve original rain-water heads of fine quality are Knole (which has fifty-seven of them, mostly dated 1605, and no two pairs identical) and Hatfield, and a great many were introduced at Haddon Hall during the same period. Some of them were painted and gilded: at St. John's College, Oxford, sufficient colour has survived for restoration to have been feasible, and the four heraldic rain-water heads here, dating from 1630, are among the most magnificent in the country. Towards the end of the seventeenth century the ears which project laterally at intervals to hold the pipes in position against the wall also became favourite places for decoration. The motifs often continued to be heraldic, as can be seen at Dresden House, Evesham (*381a*), and at Matfield House in Kent (*246a*). A rain-water head of complicated form—and by 1700 some were very elaborate—was cast in several pieces, which were soldered together. This was the most exuberant moment for the art of lead-work, as can be seen in the courtyard of Kimbolton Castle. Here the decoration covers not

1 Margaret Wood, *op. cit.*, p. 299.　　　2 L. F. Salzman, *op. cit.*, p. 267.

only the heads and ears but the whole length of the eight down-pipes (*381c*). In addition to some more heraldry, with shields of arms and supporters, there are lion-masks and dragon-heads, leaves of oak and bay and acanthus, and floral sprays. The effect is sumptuous. At Tullie House, Carlisle, the mood is more relaxed. The down-pipes (*381b*) show a repeating pattern of vines, vases, drops and minuscule angels, with more of the latter on the ears. One rain-water head here is dated 1689.

Yet within less than two generations English ornamental leadwork was already in sharp decline. It was the Palladians who killed it. To them even a richly decorated down-pipe was an offence, an excrescence not to be tolerated. And on their kind of house there can be little doubt that they were right.

Perhaps the most attractive qualities of lead are its softness and pliancy, and a suppleness of outline which may echo a sensitive hand and eye. Especially in the late seventeenth century, it was in great demand in gardens for statuary, fountain-figures, cisterns, vases and urns, as can be seen in the works of Jan van Nost (or van Ost) at Melbourne Hall in Derbyshire, Hampton Court and elsewhere. On buildings it might also be used in preference to stone for urns and vases, and as an alternative to copper or iron for weathercocks, which were often gilt. The Tudor palace of Hampton Court must have presented a delightfully gay spectacle when it still had its full array of ogee-shaped 'tips', each bearing a cluster of painted and gilded vanes. Nowadays in most places the gilding has gone, and sometimes, alas, the lead too; in the six years that followed the second world war, over eight hundred churches suffered thefts of lead from their roofs and many could not be replaced. Nor have common thieves been the only vandals. At Chester in the middle of the sixteenth century it was the dean and two of the canons! They actually stripped off portions of the cathedral roof and sold them for their own enrichment, an offence for which, it is satisfactory to record, they were all duly imprisoned.[1]

---

[1] The sale of cathedral lead by the canons of Lichfield in the seventeen-seventies prompted a scathing comment from Dr. Johnson. 'What they shall melt', he said, 'it were just that they should swallow'. On this occasion, however, the great Cham was under a misapprehension. Owing to the decay of the timbers, Lichfield's roofs were at this time in a serious condition, and the stripping off of the lead was a necessity. It was sold, and replaced by Westmorland slates, in order to pay for the re-roofing. Johnson's remark, which occurs in the first edition of his *Journey to the Western Islands of Scotland* (1775), caused great and understandable offence, and when the matter was explained to him he acknowledged that he had been unfair. From the second and subsequent editions it was removed.

LATE STUART ORNAMENTAL LEADWORK
a. *Dresden House, Evesham, Worcestershire*   b. *Tullie House, Carlisle, Cumberland*
c. *Kimbolton Castle, Huntingdonshire*

EARLY GEORGIAN WROUGHT IRONWORK
d. *Church Row, Hampstead, London*

Copper

Copper has been widely used for many centuries as a roof-covering material in Holland, Germany, the Scandinavian countries and Eastern Europe. Mines in the Wicklow Hills have also favoured its employment in Ireland; the domes of the Custom House and the Four Courts in Dublin, for instance, have always been sheathed in copper. In England, as in France, Spain and Italy, it is much less common than lead, for it was not used at all for roofing in this country during the Middle Ages, and only sparingly for three centuries after. It is sometimes held that the copper roof of the Chapel Royal, St. James's, goes back to 1540 but, whilst its predecessor may possibly have been made of this metal, it is now practically certain that the present roof of this chapel was only laid in 1837.[1] In 1708 there was a lively controversy about the covering of the dome of St. Paul's. 'The House of Commons was in favour of copper, which would have cost £3050; but it was finally decided by the commissioners and Sir Christopher to use the best Derbyshire lead, thus making a saving of nearly a thousand pounds. A broadside printed at the time discusses at length the respective merits of copper and lead, coming down heavily in favour of the former, which, it declared, would be lighter than the lead by above six hundred tons, and would last for ever.'[2] The choice of lead, made solely for reasons of economy, was surely fortunate aesthetically. It was not until the latter part of the eighteenth century that our copper ores, which occur in the Lake District and in Devon but principally in Cornwall, were for a while vigorously exploited. By 1800 we had become the world's largest producer of this mineral, but only because of our very early start with industrial processes. As the nineteenth century advanced, our production was overtaken by many countries far richer than ourselves in supplies of ore.

A few important English buildings were given copper roofs during the time that the native industry flourished. The north transept of York Minster is a notable example; although its present covering dates only from 1951, this has been roofed with copper since 1830. Except, however, for a short period after the last war when its cost became prohibitive, lead has nearly always been preferred in England, and perhaps not only because we possessed so much more of it.

---

1 See Robert Potter on this roof in *Church Roof Coverings* (1952), p. 12. (For fuller details regarding this very useful publication, see Bibliography.)
2 A. Tindal Hart in *A History of St. Paul's Cathedral*, edited by W. R. Matthews and W. M. Atkins (1957), p. 203.

REGENCY WROUGHT IRONWORK
Six gay balconies at Cheltenham, Gloucestershire
21*—P.E.B.

It must be acknowledged that, for roofing, copper has a number of practical advantages over lead. It is much lighter, one of the lightest, in fact, of all forms of roof covering, and therefore useful for buildings weakened by age or decay. Being stronger and harder, it wears better. This particularly applies if the roof timbers have been infected by beetle. The insects will eat their way through the lead, and if the bore-holes become numerous, water will percolate and in time rot the wood. Through copper no beetle can penetrate.

But there are drawbacks too. Except under very sooty conditions, copper turns bright green in ten or fifteen years on exposure to the atmosphere, and this patina eventually becomes a protection to it. It can also be a great nuisance. Copper, in fact, should not be used for ridges, lanterns or cupolas above a tiled or stone-slated roof because of the virtual certainty of streaks and stains. The verdigris is poisonous, so mosses and lichens will not grow near it. Nor is the texture of copper, seen close to, as attractive as that of cast lead.

Any aesthetic estimate of the comparative virtues of copper and lead in England must depend primarily on the question of the desirability or not of copper's very positive and, in relation to the English countryside decidedly exotic, green. All the houses on which it seems to me to look best are buildings that make a dramatic impact: Sezincote, alone on its Cotswold hillside, where not only the unexpected onion dome but the chimney-pots are of copper; Audley End, bursting splendidly into view from the main road to Cambridge, where the twin groups of turrets with their singing green 'tips' are not original and probably replace leaded roofs of sober grey; and above all Ashdown House on a lonely crest of the Berkshire Downs, where the verdigris-covered domelet of the central lantern, bearing aloft a great gilded ball, offers an experience of rare excitement and delight. In an urban setting too, provided that the air is comparatively clean, copper, employed not over a whole roof as at York, or Chichester, but to give a small vivid accent of colour, can be delightful, as on the conspicuously placed spirelet of St. Peter's church at Sudbury in Suffolk, where it dates from 1810.[1] At South Harting in Sussex, on the other hand, where copper sheathes a spire which was formerly shingled, the change has certainly been for the worse. There are indeed many settings in which a bright green roof does not look well, and many materials—red brick is surely one of them—with which it may be felt that silver-hued lead is always preferable.

---

1 It is the tower of St. Peter's which appears in the left background of Gainsborough's 'Mr. and Mrs. Andrews' in the National Gallery. At that time (1750) there was no hint of a spirelet.

Iron

In the story of English building iron has always played a part, but until the last quarter of the eighteenth century its function was either ancillary or decorative, or both. Under the former heading comes the smallest but probably the most important item of all: nails. Other such utilitarian employments for iron ranged from cramps and tie-bars and the frames of casement windows to the great hoops which Wren devised to help him in the construction of the dome of St. Paul's. A very early use of iron was for strapping together the planks of oak doors; an unique Anglo-Saxon example in the church at Hadstock, Essex, was referred to on page 295. Iron for cramping—that is, for tying pieces of stone to one another and to their backing—was used sparingly before about 1700, and generally for features such as copings and cornices, finials and pinnacles, and the tops of spires and chimney-stacks, all much exposed to the wind; only metal of high quality was employed, and the mediaeval builders often used to coat the iron with lead. Good seventeenth-century and earlier masonry always had massive weight-bearing facings which were virtually self-supporting, and which were bonded into the backing with blocks of stone. In the eighteenth and nineteenth centuries, on the other hand, it became customary for reasons of economy to have much thinner facing stones. Henry Holland, for instance, is known to have built with facings which were no more than 4 ins. thick, without masonry bonds. Slabs of ashlar as thin as these needed to be secured much more carefully to the backings of rough stone or brick, and accordingly the use of iron cramps, not always of such good quality now, became very general. In some districts (but not in the Stamford area) every block of stone in an ashlared wall was fastened back with a cramp. This has given a great deal of trouble, as in time the cramps have become corroded and swollen, staining and cracking the stonework. We now know that they should be of some non-expansive, non-ferrous metal which does not rust, preferably stainless steel or phosphor bronze.

Many of the items of ancillary ironwork, such as locks, hinges, knockers, door-handles and fasteners for casement windows, were given decorative forms. On a larger scale there were the iron armatures of the early stained glass windows, best seen in the Trinity Chapel at Canterbury; they perform an essential function in providing the principal support for the glass, but there is decorative beauty also in their varied geometrical designs. Ironwork of considerable ornamental elaboration survives from the thirteenth century on wooden church doors at Wells, Windsor, York, Lichfield and elsewhere, but this is also functional in so far as it helps to hold together and strengthen the door's planks.

Even the open grilles of this period, of which the most celebrated is that surrounding the tomb of Queen Eleanor in Westminster Abbey, served to protect as well as to enrich.

Before the Industrial Revolution the best iron ore used in England was mostly imported from Spain; some came from Germany. We were not a major iron-producing country, but we were by no means without our native supplies. In mediaeval times most English iron came either from the Weald of Sussex or from the Forest of Dean, with small quantities in Weardale and in Furness to supply the local needs. The Wealden and Dean ores, at least, were known to and worked by the Romans. Both these areas were well-wooded, with adequate water-power; furnaces and forges were sited beside streams that were dammed to produce the 'hammer ponds', of which many still survive in these parts of the country. The smelting of the ore was done with charcoal. This is the reason for its extraordinary durability by comparison with coke and coal iron, which has a high sulphur content. 'Charcoal iron does not readily rust; as can be seen on ancient decorative ironwork almost everywhere, it corrodes in a way that leaves a black coating of magnetic oxide which protects it indefinitely.'[1] In time, however, the demands of the charcoal-burners denuded the countryside of woodlands; in 1611 we find John Speed recording that the woods of Gloucestershire were 'much lessened by making of Iron, the only bane of Oake, Elme and Beech'. Unfortunately oaks served the charcoal-burners' purpose best, and a public outcry arose which forced Parliament to act. Neither in the Weald nor in the Forest of Dean were ironworks prohibited, but from the time of Elizabeth I no new ones were permitted. The Weald still has plenty of ore, but after the Industrial Revolution the industry moved away from this region to tap sources closer to the coal-fields, where smelting was cheaper. The last furnace in the Weald closed down in 1828.

Apart from the Weald, almost all our iron ores occur in the rocks of the Jurassic and Carboniferous systems. The former are principally to be found in Oxfordshire, Northamptonshire, Leicestershire, Lincolnshire and the Cleveland district of Yorkshire. They long remained unexploited on account of their high phosphorus content; only in 1879 was a method of smelting discovered which enabled this impurity to be satisfactorily extracted. So they play no part in England's building history before the present century. After the Forest of Dean and Weardale, the earliest iron workings from the Carboniferous rocks were in Shropshire, where a number of charcoal-fuelled forges were set up in Tudor times. Later, when the use of timber was restricted, it was at Coalbrookdale that, in the reign of Queen Anne, Abraham Darby was the first to develop the use of coke-fuel for smelting. In the early part of the nineteenth century other Carboniferous areas, South

1 Maxwell Ayrton and Arnold Silcock, *Wrought Iron and its Decorative Use* (1929), p. 14.

Staffordshire, Derbyshire, South Yorkshire, Furness and West Cumberland, first saw the iron industry growing to really massive proportions.

Until then this metal was so expensive that, even where it could be obtained locally, it was hardly used in the majority of homes. Before the eighteenth century it was all hand-wrought. It could either be worked red hot or beaten into shape when cold, at the bench. If heat were used the metal had great plasticity, but the smith, having decided what he intended to do, had to work quickly: had, in fact, 'to strike while the iron was hot'. To keep it free from rust it was either whitened with tin, blackened with pitch, painted or varnished. Some of the smiths must have greatly enjoyed themselves forging magnificent supports for inn signs. Between about 1690 and 1750 there was a great vogue for wrought iron for staircase and balcony balustrades and particularly for gates and railings, as in Church Row, Hampstead (*381*d). In the grander examples there would usually be a splendid overthrow, as at Pallant House, Chichester (*262*b). Delightful as it is in towns, it was the formal garden which provided the perfect setting for wrought ironwork. This is an essentially linear art-form, unconcerned with mass; and these years yielded some creations of marvellous beauty, of which almost every English county has at least a few examples. Some splendid work can be seen at Oxford and especially at Cambridge, where the gates at Clare, Trinity and St. John's Colleges, all perhaps by a smith or family of smiths named Warren, are of outstanding distinction. Often the name of the smith is unknown; the beautiful gates and screen at Scraptoft Hall (*123*b) have been attributed to William Edney of Bristol, another master of the craft. In view of their situation in gardens, it is ironical that it should have been the landscape gardeners who dealt wrought ironwork its most serious blow, both by destroying part of what already existed and by removing most of the demand for more. Many of the best preserved specimens from this period are now to be found in churches, among which Tijou's ironwork in St. Paul's Cathedral, Robert Bakewell's screen and gates in Derby Cathedral and Edney's former chancel gates at St. Mary Red-cliffe, Bristol, are outstanding. Tijou's park gates at Hampton Court are also very fine, but his screen in the Fountain Garden, although more spectacular, is, with its profusion of solid repoussé pieces, almost oppressively magnificent.

Meanwhile cast iron was slowly beginning to be brought into the service of architecture. Its first important use in England, about the middle of the sixteenth century, was for gun-founding. At that time bronze and brass were superseded as the usual metals for heavy weapons; the ships which sailed to meet the Armada were armed with cast iron cannon, made in the Weald. From the time of Elizabeth I (and in a single instance, at Burwash in Sussex, from a couple of centuries earlier) this material was also used for tomb slabs set into church floors. Most cast iron ledgers (as they are called) date from the seventeenth century, and are in Sussex: Wadhurst church alone has more than thirty. Others are in Shropshire, and there are a few in Herefordshire. Railings in cast iron did not appear before the time of Queen Anne. Among the earliest, all of excellent quality, are those surrounding St. Paul's (1710–14),[1] St. Martin-in-the-Fields (c. 1726) and the Senate House at Cambridge (c. 1730). At the two latter the uprights comprise balusters of massive cast iron and rods of slender wrought iron in alternation. Cast iron was also used in 1719 by the Welsh smith, Robert Davies, for the capitals, bases and some other details of his extraordinary wrought iron entrance gates at Chirk Castle. Georgian builders adopted the charming practice of placing curved fanlights over their front doors. At first these were of wrought iron, lead or wood; Robert Adam used wrought iron with delicate enrichments in copper or brass. But soon he and his brothers James and John were all devising fanlights intended for mass production, so that it was not long before cast iron captured this market; some of the designs were now very light and elegant (246b). In 1772, more unexpectedly, James Wyatt adopted cast iron externally for capitals at Heaton Hall on the edge of Manchester, in place of the unaccommodating local sandstone. Not long afterwards came a momentous development: the employment of cast iron for the first time in an important structural capacity. This was at Ironbridge (as it is now called), a mile below Coalbrookdale, where in 1777–81 was erected the famous and still surviving bridge over the Severn, with an arched span of just over 100 ft. Before 1800 another and more ambitious bridge, with a span of 206 ft., had been built across the Wear at Sunderland, and cast iron had been used structurally in at least four factory buildings, three in Derbyshire and one at Shrewsbury. From these stemmed a vast development, the study of which falls outside the compass of this book.[2]

It was to the buildings of the Regency period that iron made its most considerable decorative contribution, in balconies, verandahs, stair-balustrades, fanlights and much besides. Wherever Regency architecture flourished, from London to Leamington, from Brighton to Bristol, and scattered here and there over every English county but especially in the residential quarters of towns, delicate ironwork added, and often still adds, grace and distinction to house-fronts in stone, brick and especially stucco—for the black-painted ironwork always 'tells' best against a light ground, upon which the sun may throw a

---

[1] Cast near Lamberhurst, on the Kent-Sussex border, and no longer complete. Wren wanted only a low railing of hammered iron, and objected to cast iron; but the latter was held by the commissioners to be 'at least ten times as durable', and the architect was overruled.

[2] The subject of structural cast iron may be pursued in several books, among which are *Cast Iron in Architecture*, by John Gloag and Derek Bridgewater (1948), and *Cast Iron in Building*, by Richard Sheppard (1945). A useful up-to-date summary is presented in Chapter 5 of the fourth (Pelican) edition of Sir Nikolaus Pevsner's *Pioneers of Modern Design* (1962).

counterpoint of intricate shadow (*382c*, d and e). It is in Cheltenham, the most complete and unspoiled creation of the Regency style, that this ironwork is to be found at its most profuse, particularly on first-floor balconies, of which that delightful town possesses many hundreds. Although the designs were now usually taken from pattern-books, with certain favourites like the anthemion (the honeysuckle or palmette of Greek and Roman architecture), the six Cheltenham balconies illustrated (*382a–f*), all hand-wrought, may suffice to indicate that there was no lack of variety. Cast iron designs, common elsewhere, look lighter and more mechanical, yet are nearly always graceful. Some of this Regency ironwork may seem a little too thin and spindly, but it is often very attractive.

After about 1830 there was a rapid deterioration in the artistic quality of decorative architectural ironwork. A florid insensitivity is indeed already apparent in most of the designs in L. N. Cottingham's *Ornamental Metal Worker's Directory*, published in 1824. This degeneration coincided, it is true, with the final triumph of cast iron: the opportunity which casting offered for mass production proved economically irresistible, and the advent of factory-made ornament which could be ordered by the yard, so that taste was no longer fed by local traditions and customs but only by what the nearest iron foundry was placing on the market, was certainly no change for the better. Yet there was technically no reason why a high aesthetic standard should not have been maintained in cast iron, which is a material in its own right, not just a cheap substitute for wrought iron. It was probably the very ease of working that proved its undoing; designers, with this new mechanical power in their hands, did not know where to stop. The dangers were aptly if unwittingly summed up by J. B. Papworth when he wrote, in a spirit of triumph, that 'as iron itself is now at a very reduced price, it may be expected that richly embossed works will come into frequent use, particularly as this metal is now so generally substituted for several other materials, that the century may not improperly be called another "iron age"'. A generation later, this prediction was to prove almost embarrassingly true. The example illustrated (*399a*), also from Cheltenham, is an unusually good one of its type: a comparison with the balcony railings of the Regency period is therefore instructive.

During the Victorian age iron wrought by the smith was almost universally superseded by iron cast into moulds. This favoured not only mass production but the making of solid pieces of metal which could be as elaborately ornamental as the mouldmaker could contrive. Thus the delicacy of Regency ironwork found no echo in the period that followed. Even without ornamentation, Victorian cast ironwork usually looks heavy and clumsy, as can be seen in railings throughout the country. The removal of railings for scrap metal during the second world war was not always carried out with discrimination, and in some places was a disaster, but in others it proved to be a blessing in disguise.

16

GLASS

If one examines the drawings of Inigo Jones or Webb or any of the numerous elevations included in the three volumes of *Vitruvius Britannicus*, one cannot fail to notice that the window openings are merely dark voids, with no articulation. This always surprises me, because the appearance of a building can be transformed by an alteration in the design of the windows; in fact, even a coat of paint can work wonders, as could be seen a few years ago at Blenheim, when the wooden glazing bars, formerly a tedious red, were repainted 'Cotswold grey' (ivory white with a touch of grey in it) with the happiest results. It should not be assumed, however, that all our classical architects were as indifferent to this aspect as some of them appeared to be; in his notes for Coleshill,[1] Roger Pratt provided a careful specification, with exact measurements, for the iron casements glazed with leaded panes and set in wooden frames such as can still be seen at Wolvesey Palace, Winchester. That these windows were afterwards altered at Coleshill was due to the gradual adoption in England, from the sixteen-eighties onwards, of the sliding sash window, visually one of the most momentous innovations in the whole history of our architecture. But whether in sashes or casements, the fact is that as soon as glass was used at all in windows, it became one of the walling materials of our buildings, and aesthetically a very important one because of its highly reflecting surface. In this it differs from virtually all the other materials discussed in this book. Hence, although the remarkable developments of the present century may predispose us to think of glass as predominantly a material of modern architecture, no study of traditional materials which omitted it would be complete.

The glass-maker needs soda and lime, but his principal requirement is pure silica sand. Even sand that appears pure will often be found on analysis to contain iron oxide. This discolours the glass, changing it from white to a dirty greyish or greenish brown. The presence of exceptionally pure sand in Northern France, notably at Fontainebleau, may have been partly responsible for the prodigious development of the art of stained glass there between 1150 and 1250. Throughout the whole of the Middle Ages, all the coloured glass (or almost all: the subject is controversial) and all the best white glass used in England

1 R. T. Gunther (ed.), *The Architecture of Sir Roger Pratt . . . from his Note-Books* (1928), p. 95. This splendid house was gutted by fire in September 1952, and shortly afterwards most reprehensibly demolished.

was imported, either from France, Flanders, the Rhineland or Hesse. The glass made in Hesse, Lorraine and Burgundy reached England via the Rhine and was known generically as 'Rhenish'; that produced in the Seine and upper Loire districts, which was a little more expensive, was known as 'Normandy'. Glass was made at certain places in England, notably from the thirteenth century at Chiddingfold in Surrey, where both the sand and the wood and furze used for fuel were abundantly available. Fragments of this early un-coloured glass can still be seen in the church at Shere. Excavations at Glastonbury and (in 1962) at Monkwearmouth in County Durham have revealed that, in these two monasteries at least, window glass of a sort was being made in this country even in the Saxon period. Glass at Monkwearmouth, and also at Jarrow, is mentioned by Bede. Other early centres of English manufacture, all operating on a most modest scale and producing glass of very indifferent quality, were in Staffordshire, Shropshire and Cheshire. We have ample supplies of good field sand in south-west Lancashire between Southport and St. Helens, where great quantities are now dug[1] and the reserves appear to be inexhaustible—yet no one began seriously to exploit them until after 1615, when James I wisely forbade the use of wood fuel in glass manufacture, and the glassmakers had to move north to where there was also plenty of coal for their furnaces. For stained glass Fontainebleau sand is still considered by English glassmakers to be the best. In Britain it is now known that the purest sand (although variable) comes from Loch Aline on the coast of Morven in Argyllshire, opposite Mull; but exploitation here has so far proved difficult.

There is ample evidence that well-to-do Romans in Britain had glass in their windows, although only small, much tarnished fragments have survived; and in recent years a few fragments of Saxon domestic glass, apparently made in England, have also been found, notably on the site of the Saxon royal palace at Kingsbury, Old Windsor.[2] Yet, despite the exigencies of our climate, glazed windows long remained a luxury in this country which few could afford. By the middle of the thirteenth century, most churches had managed to fill some if not all their windows with stained glass, but before the fifteenth century only the King and his most opulent subjects had glazing in their houses.[3]

Among the various substitutes for glass, one was horn, obtained by peeling or shaving thin slices from the horns of cattle. These were flattened and otherwise prepared for use,

1 The procedure is to remove the topsoil and take out the sand to a depth of 3–5 ft; new drainage is then installed, before the land is returned to the farmer.

2 See D. B. Harden, 'Domestic Window Glass: Roman, Saxon and Mediaeval', in *Studies in Building History*, edited by E. M. Jope (1961), pp. 44–54. Cf. also L. F. Salzman, *op. cit.*, pp. 173–186.

3 Margaret Wood (*op. cit.*, p. 351) cites Eynsford Castle, Kent as having possessed, in the south-east window of its hall, 'one of the earliest known examples of the glazed window in houses'. This was *grisaille* glass with a linear design in black, inserted soon after a fire *c.* 1250.

particularly in 'lanthorns'. No horn windows are likely to have survived, but not long ago, at a cottage in North Wales built about 1580, tiny slivers of horn could still be seen sticking to the sides of the windows.[1] Several pieces would have been needed to fill even a small window. Other alternatives included framed blinds of oiled cloth, preferably linen; parchment dipped in gum arabic, honey and white of egg, which was stretched wet on a frame and varnished when dry; oiled paper;[2] thin slabs of a semi-translucent stone such as mica or alabaster; plain wooden shutters, secured internally with bolts or bars (these were much the commonest of all, and in some countries serve as substitutes for window glass even to-day); and open grilles or lattices of stone, wood, metal, wickerwork or even reeds. An example of a reed grille can still be seen, although no longer *in situ*, at Tewes, Little Sampford, Essex. The reeds, arranged horizontally with $\frac{1}{4}$ in. between each, are held together by vertical plaiting about every 5 ins. Some of these substitutes for glass must have been very ineffective in keeping out the cold, and all carried in varying degrees the disadvantage, serious in an age when lighting arrangements were also primitive, of obscuring or totally excluding the daylight. It was in order to admit a little light that some traceried windows in the thirteenth century had horn in their upper part, when there was a transom, or, if not, in the quatrefoil only, with shutters below.

Towards the end of the fifteenth century and throughout the Tudor period, window-glass gradually became more general, although by the standards of to-day the glass used might still be very indifferent. A rare and interesting survival can be seen in the parlour (now known as the private dining room) at Haddon Hall. The eight windows here contain a good deal of the original glazing put in about 1545; it is far from white and by no means wholly transparent. Yet domestic glass was still so precious that, as late as 1567, the windows at Alnwick Castle were always lifted out and stored away when the owner was not in residence, to save them from being damaged by the weather. Elsewhere wooden lattices were sometimes fitted outside the windows as a protection for the glass. Even the Elizabethan passion for bigger and ever bigger glazed windows was still a rich man's (or, remembering Bess of Hardwick, woman's) game, and it is largely because of their more discreetly proportioned windows that the smaller houses of this age are often much more satisfying. It was not until the time of James I that the ordinary smallholder or artisan expected to have glass in his windows, whilst the labourer in his cottage, especially in the

1 For this information I am indebted to Mr. D. E. Hogan, Curator of the Pilkington Glass Museum at St. Helens.

2 It seems difficult to believe that this would have been sufficiently durable. Yet documentary evidence exists to show that one of the Pilgrim Fathers, Edward Winslow, wrote to England in 1621 from Plymouth, Massachusetts, saying 'Bring paper and linseed oil for your windows'.

West of England, often had to wait until after the Restoration, and in some cases until the early years of the eighteenth century. And even then, to save the cost of iron casements he might get nothing better than leaded lights fixed with wire to iron bars; windows, that is, which could not be opened. Apart altogether from amenity, the absence of glazing in these buildings must have had a very adverse effect on their appearance.

All the earliest glass was blown, as some still is, in cylinders or muffs, which were split along their length and, as they cooled, gradually opened out and flattened. But as far back as the fourteenth century Normandy glass was sometimes being blown in big circular discs, quite a different method about which there will be more to say shortly. The next step was to cut up the glass into small diamonds or rectangles which, as mentioned earlier (p. 379), were held together by means of grooved bars of lead known as cames. Until the advent of the sliding sash, the usual domestic window, if it opened at all, was of the side-hung casement type. At first this was fitted between masonry mullions (363b), an inheritance from Gothic architecture, and later, already framed, into a single wide opening. Where money was plentiful, as at Sparrowe's House, Ipswich (356b), the windows might swell out on the upper storey into handsome oriels, with paired casements under central arched frames flanked by fixed (that is, non-opening) lights of boldly curved form.

The frames might be of iron or of wood; but it was from the lead cames that the windows took their principal character. In the sixteenth century the leading was arranged diagonally, to form a lattice pattern, as at Hardwick Hall (400) or at Montacute (89: renewed), and the diamond-shaped pane of glass might measure no more than 5×3 ins. In the seventeenth century rectangular panes were generally preferred: these were usually a little larger, but not above $8 \times 5\frac{1}{2}$ ins. (239b, 278d, 342a). Roger Pratt gives, for the panes of the principal rooms, a height of $7\frac{1}{4}$ ins. and a breadth of $5\frac{1}{10}$ ins.[1] Their size was not governed by the dimensions of the sheets of glass, which were considerably larger than this, but the pliant character of the lead, which could not be relied upon to support larger pieces against the force of wind. Hence the close mesh of these early windows— often too close, it may be felt, for complete internal comfort.

> ' The glaziers' work before substantial was
> I must confess, thrice as much lead as glass,
> Which in the sun's meridian cast a light
> As it had been within an hour of night',

[1] At this time (the middle of the seventeenth century) the best English glass came from Newcastle, but Normandy glass, two and a half times the price, was still 'much more beautiful'. Pratt advised that the worst glass should be picked out and reserved for the garrets. (R. T. Gunther (ed.), *op. cit.*, p. 72.)

wrote Cotton in 1681 of the early Elizabethan windows of the original Chatsworth.[1] Externally we may be grateful for the neutral colouring of the cames, while they can, as noted earlier, add distinct charm of texture. The panes of glass in an old leaded window, often seen at slightly different angles owing to the action of the wind, may set up a complex of reflections not bright enough to be disturbing yet varied enough to be interesting (*255a, 400*).

* This is not the place to enter into the complicated question of the origin of the sliding sash window. It will be sufficient to say that such windows, whether invented in England or, as is often said, in Holland, appear to have been first used in quantity at Chatsworth in 1676–80—that is to say, before the rebuilding of the house was begun in 1687.[2] These did not long survive, nor did the next set, inserted into Whitehall Palace in 1685 and destroyed in the fire of 1698. In 1686, however, glass for sash windows was already being advertised for sale in the *London Gazette*, and the next five years were to see the introduction of windows of this kind at Windsor Castle (Accounts, 1686–88), Kensington Palace and Hampton Court.[3] After royal patronage on such a scale as this, it is not surprising to find that before the death of William III they had already won a sweeping fashionable success, and in the Home Counties were becoming the standard window-type for all new houses. Into other parts of the country they spread more slowly. Celia Fiennes, on a visit to Bretby Park in Derbyshire in 1698, recorded that 'none of the windows are sashes, which in my opinion is the only thing it wants to render it a complete building.' Ultimately, however, their popularity became so universal that most of the more prosperous owners of Stuart houses had their casements taken out and replaced by sashes, a proceeding which presented little practical difficulty since it so happened that the sizes and shapes of the apertures required for these two very different types of window design often closely corresponded. That partly explains why so comparatively few seventeenth-century casements survive; and although Georgian windows do alter considerably the appearance of a

---

1 Charles Cotton, *The Wonders of the Peake* (1681), quoted in John Buxton's *Elizabethan Taste* (1966), p. 84.

2 Francis Thompson, *A History of Chatsworth* (1949), p. 28. In 1676–80 'large windows of the sash type were inserted on all fronts' in place of the 'original narrow casements' of the Elizabethan house.

3 Churchill House at Alcester in Warwickshire has sash windows with flat glazing bars which are obviously very early, and the date 1688 on the rain-water heads. If these windows were made at the same time, which *prima facie* appears not unlikely, they are perhaps the oldest surviving examples in the country. At Thoresby Hall in Nottinghamshire they appeared probably in 1686–7, but this house, designed by Talman, was burnt in 1745. Dyrham Park preserves a few sash-framed windows dating from *c*.1692 with very small lights: 8 up and 4 across = 32 to each window.

Stuart house, my own view is that, for classical buildings such as Wilton (45c) or Belton, the substitution of sashes for casements was always, aesthetically, an improvement.

The reasons are three. In the first place, whereas the design of the typical Stuart casement window, bisected down its centre, is a duality, the great majority of sash windows are three lights wide. Secondly, as soon as a casement window is opened, the harmony of the elevation is broken; an array of open casements is formally only a little less disturbing to the eye than a house hung with flags. And thirdly, the painted wooden glazing bars of a Queen Anne or Georgian window, enclosing panes of glass considerably larger than the earlier leaded lights, are bold enough, especially when painted white or off-white (as they almost always should be, and usually are), to make a positive contribution to any elevation in which they occur (123b). This was quickly realized, and the grace and dignity of Georgian houses throughout the country derive in no small measure from the beauty of their windows. Except to some extent in Holland, the sash window found very little acceptance in European countries outside the British Isles. Here we had the good fortune, or the good sense, to hold on to it for close on two hundred years, and it became beyond any other single feature the particular hall-mark of Queen Anne and Georgian domestic building. The high regard for houses of this type in the United States—reflected in their own 'Colonial' style—no doubt explains why wooden glazing bars are now more usual in that country than in any other; and how right they are.

Most of the glass used in Georgian windows was not blown in muffs but in large circular discs, a method introduced into Normandy probably from the Near East, early in the fourteenth century. The red-hot 'metal' on the end of the blowing-iron was spun round and round; in his other hand the glass-blower held a wooden bat with which, by flattening out the bubble, he was able to produce a disc of anything between 3 ft. 3 ins. and 4 ft. 6 ins. in diameter, and occasionally as much as 5 ft. The disc in this 'crown' glass (as it is called) was always thicker towards the centre. The 'bull's eye' in the middle (also known as the 'bullion' or knob), the lumpy piece bearing the mark of the blowing iron, was rightly discarded in the eighteenth century. Much of the charm of Georgian windows derives from the glinting and often slightly wavy surface of their spun crown glass, as at Middlethorpe Hall near York (399b) and at Chichester (262b). The region which specialized in this type of glass was Tyneside, but small works were established in various parts of the country. Crown glass owed its lustre to not coming into contact with any other surfaces during manufacture, thus preserving a natural fire-finish. It was always more expensive than cylinder glass, partly because its circular form involved more waste; but so superior was it in brilliancy that by the middle of the eighteenth century it had largely displaced the other.

In contrast to the leaded casement, the sash window with its wooden glazing bars is admirably articulate. The panes, in grand houses occasionally bevelled, are large enough to avoid fussiness; in a very lofty sash window, say 7 ft. × 2 ft. 6 ins. between the glass lines, there would only be eighteen of them, as compared with seventy-two leaded lights of the average size. Every window, therefore, makes a positive statement, clearly visible from a considerable distance so long as the bars are painted white, or nearly so. In many Georgian elevations, particularly of the less pretentious kind, it is hardly too much to say that the whole design is constructed around the orderly tiers of windows (239d, 267d). In other types of house, the windows are often only an incidental, not a vital, feature. They may be large, even very large, but their size and shape may depend on little more than the whim of the designer (147c). The scale and proportions of the building as a whole do not depend upon the windows. In Georgian architecture, on the other hand, the character of an elevation may be mainly determined by its designer's sense of proportion as displayed in the shape and glazing of the windows themselves and in the spatial relationship between windows and walls. Fortunate indeed is a town such as Blandford, in which many of the Georgian houses have retained not only the glazing bars of their sash windows but also their original crown glass.

The bars themselves, which in Scotland are known as astragals and in the United States as muntins (a term confined in England to the framing of panelling), were sometimes as much as 2 ins. broad in Queen Anne houses, but gradually they became narrower, until by 1820 they might measure no more than $\frac{1}{2}$ in. These $\frac{1}{2}$-in. glazing bars might be as much as $1\frac{1}{2}$ ins. deep, however, and that looks distinguished. The early bars are unmoulded on the inside and may look rather clumsy. In the latter half of the eighteenth century the bars were always moulded, and contribute a note of graciousness and refinement to every house built during the reign of George III in which they have been allowed to survive, even though, by 1800, they were already in danger of becoming too slender, sometimes, for the character of the architecture (148a). About this time metal was occasionally used in place of wood: at Grimsthorpe Castle some large mahogany sashes have bars of brass only $\frac{3}{8}$ in. wide, and at Dodington Park, where the very thin bars are also of brass, the huge panes of glass measure 29× 18$\frac{1}{2}$ ins. The date of both these is c.1800. Ultimately, in the second quarter of the nineteenth century, the bars became even thinner when iron was employed instead of wood, as at Storrs Hall, Windermere. The iron bars were carefully cast to look like moulded wood, and when painted it may be impossible to tell the difference by looking at them. Touch them, however, and one knows at once: iron is so much colder! These extremely slender glazing bars were in harmony, certainly, with the delicate wrought-iron balustrades referred to in the last chapter, but they are often too thin to 'tell' as one would wish, too thin also to counterbalance the heaviness of some of the period's elevations.

The triumphs of Georgian window design are all the more remarkable for having been achieved under the incubus of the window tax and, from 1746 onwards, of a heavy excise duty on glass. The window tax was first imposed in 1696 in an attempt to recoup the Exchequer, on the issue of a new silver coinage, for the losses on the clipped and defaced old coins which were then called in. It was really a rough and a most unwise form of property tax, levied according to the number of openings on all inhabited houses worth over £5 a year, with more than six windows.[1] (Business premises were exempt.) In 1747, by which time the incidence of the tax had been gradually mounting, it was observed in the House of Commons, on a motion to repeal what was described as a system of collecting taxes on air and light, that the practice of blocking up windows was becoming dangerously prevalent. Readers of *Tom Jones* (which appeared in 1748) may recall the outburst of the innkeeper's wife, at the inn to which the eponymous hero was taken after his adventure with the ensign. 'It is a dreadful thing', she exclaimed, 'to pay as we do. Why now, there is above forty shillings for window lights, and yet we have stopt up all we could; we have almost blinded the house, I am sure.' Blocked windows, sometimes with simulated painting (*245c*), are still to be seen on Georgian houses throughout the country; and although it would be a mistake to attribute all these to the window tax, the large majority are certainly due to it. Yet this wretched imposition was further augmented on six separate occasions between 1747 and 1808, notably by Pitt in 1784 and again in 1802. After the close of the Napoleonic war its unpopularity was so great as to cause something of a scandal, so that it was at last reduced in 1825, and finally repealed in 1851. The equally frustrating excise duty on glass, and all the obstructive regulations which that impost involved, had been abolished six years before.

By this time glazing bars were fast disappearing from English windows. Plate glass, a French invention, was made in this country for the first time, under French supervision, at Ravenhead, St. Helens, Lancashire in 1773.[2] The essential characteristic of this glass, which could be blown in cylinders but which was best made by casting, was its thickness. The object was to produce glass of such strength and of such even consistency that it could be ground and polished, thereby removing all flaws and irregularities. The cost of this technically very fine glass was so high that more than half a century was to elapse before its production became commercially feasible. The crucial date was 1838, when it was

1 An early example of the deplorable aesthetic effect of this tax is illustrated by the three pairs of blocked up casement windows at The Crown House, Newport, Essex (*356a*). A pattern of lead lines, painted thickly on to the wooden boards, is still just visible under layers of paint.

2 The old casting hall, with its great brick arches, sharply pointed, still survives. It is known locally as 'the Cathedral'.

discovered how to make sheet glass, the much thinner and cheaper glass produced by the cylinder method. This enjoyed considerable success in the eighteen-forties, and it was sheet glass—a million square feet of it—of only 16 oz. per sq. ft. thickness which was used by Chance Brothers in 1851 for the Crystal Palace: an incomparable advertisement for it. Small wonder that every villa now had to have its conservatory! In their houses people became entranced with the notion of an 'unhampered' view of the street or garden; new buildings were provided with windows of plate or sheet glass as a matter of course, and owners of Georgian houses tore out their glazing bars with fervour. Later came the manufacture of sheet glass by different and still less expensive processes, which served only to increase the determination to be rid of the allegedly obstructive bars. The makers of crown glass, which is never wholly free from optical distortion, could not compete; of the nineteen firms working in 1843, only five were still in operation fifteen years later.[1] The Tyne area alone in the 1830s was producing over 7,000,000 sq. ft. of crown window glass annually; by 1863 every one of the six glass works had closed.

This romantic delight in large undivided areas of window-glass is quite understandable, especially while the invention was still new. Yet aesthetically, in relation to buildings of traditional post-Renaissance form, it was catastrophic. Even when viewed from inside, a barred window adds substantially to the character of a room. From the external aspect, as two otherwise identical houses in Pavilion Parade, Brighton, effectively demonstrate (191a), the removal of glazing bars converted the window openings into no more than a series of dark, cavernous holes in the wall. Such windows wear a vacant look, devoid of expression, like a drawing of a head on which the face has been left out. If in the end glazing bars became excessively attenuated, at least it can be said that bars which are too thin are still very much better for this type of house than none at all. The only variant which is no better is the window bisected by a single bar down its centre, a favourite Victorian alternative to the unbarred window. The immeasurable inferiority of this design to the Georgian can be well appreciated by comparing the windows at Rye (245b) with those at Chichester illustrated on the same page (245c).

In recent years, it is good to record that the aesthetic value of glazing bars has become more generally realized, so that the tendency nowadays is to put them back into windows too long deprived of them, rather than the reverse. The improvement to the south front of Chatsworth, when this was done some years ago, was remarkable. Any owner of a house of classical derivation who restores missing glazing bars to his windows is performing a service both to himself and to his fellows.

1 Quoted by Marian Bowley, *Innovations in Building Materials: an Economic Study* (1960), p. 100, from *A History of the Firm of Chance Brothers*, by J. F. Chance, Chapter XIV.

VICTORIAN CAST IRONWORK
a. *Royal Parade, Cheltenham*

GEORGIAN CROWN GLASS
b. *Middlethorpe Hall, near York*

The revolutionary character of contemporary architecture has rendered it necessary to think on radically new lines about the part played by glass. The possibility of spanning wide areas with skeletons of steel or reinforced concrete, and of using non-weight-bearing materials like glass to fill the intervening spaces, has seized the imagination of every architect of note, and some enchanting effects have been obtained. One side of many a modern room is nearly all glass; 'picture windows' are particularly agreeable in conjunction with lawns, trees and water. In streets composed of buildings with the gentler, light-absorbing qualities of the traditional materials, 'walls of glass', because of their brightly reflecting surfaces, are admittedly less happy. It is obviously important that every site should be considered both for itself and in relation to surrounding buildings.

Science has fortunately made available to us new materials which have enabled us to rescue the art of building from the stagnation of stylistic revivals. In the field of glass Britain now leads the world, owing to the inspired conception, by Sir Alistair Pilkington, of float glass. This is a method of producing glass of the utmost brilliance and clarity by floating the molten mix across a 'bath' of liquid tin. The irksome labour and high cost of grinding and polishing to achieve plate glass have been rendered obsolete by this new process, which went into production for the first time in 1959. Tens of millions of square feet of this glass are now manufactured at St. Helens annually, and glass is no longer one of the more expensive building materials. So much so, in fact, that architects are now in danger of using it to excess. A recent survey of two hundred new office blocks revealed that nearly half their occupants complained of discomfort in summer through an excess of radiant heat from the sun. Nor does it follow that modern buildings are always 'good mixers'. There are places where excellent effects have been obtained through contrast, and others where the existing buildings are patently not good enough to merit any special consideration. There are also certain places where even the most distinguished building needs to be very carefully sited, and where a high building might well be a disaster.

This book has been devoted to types of material which, it is only sensible to recognize, have now lost some of their former paramountcy, not only for economic reasons but also because many of the needs of to-day cannot be satisfied by adhering to them. We have entered a new, exciting, and in some respects bewildering era of architecture that presents problems with which some of the traditional materials have little concern. Yet because our country, unlike most of her continental neighbours, has had the immense good fortune never to have been wrecked by an invading army, and because we still have many buildings in good preservation which go back three, four, five hundred years, and some still longer, a special responsibility falls upon us in England to show consideration for the

SANDSTONE, LEAD AND GLASS
Hardwick Hall, Derbyshire

past. We return, in fact, to the concept upon which continual emphasis has been laid throughout this book: the *genius loci*. Let us by all means exploit the wonderful opportunities which new materials and new techniques have placed in our hands; but let us also be vigilant for our inheritance. There are plenty of sites, both in towns and in the countryside, where modern architecture, handled by an artist, is obviously right. There are others, mainly in old towns or villages, where a building in steel or concrete and glass, particularly when it is allowed to play havoc with the scale of the surrounding buildings by rising too high, is patently not the proper answer. There are, in a word, more ways than one of being a good neighbour.

GLOSSARY

ADIT: A gallery driven more or less horizontally into a hillside for the purpose of mining (in this book, stone).

APRON: A rectangular panel of shallow projection below a window-sill.

ARCHITRAVE: (1) The lowest of the three divisions of the Classical entablature. (2) The moulded frame surrounding a door or window.

ARRIS: The sharp edge or line made by the junction of two surfaces, forming an external angle.

ASHLAR: Masonry of hewn or sawn stone, in blocks which are usually large but often quite thin, carefully squared and finely jointed in level courses.

BARGE: The overhanging edge of a roof up the slope of a gable. (Said to be a corruption of Verge).

BARGE-BOARD: A wooden board, usually with decorative carving, fixed to the lower edge of a barge (q.v.) in order to mask the ends of the horizontal roof timbers.

BATTEN: A strip of wood, normally sawn, used for attaching slates, tiles, etc., horizontally to a roof or wall, also internally for attaching panelling and for fixing generally.

BED: (1) A plane of stratification in a sedimentary rock. (2) The term is also applied to horizontal layers of mortar, cement, sand, earth, etc., upon which blocks of stone, bricks, paving slabs, etc., are laid.

BEVEL: A surface cut at an oblique angle to a plane surface.

BOND: An arrangement of stones or bricks whereby the vertical joints in one course do not coincide with those in the courses above or below. See also ENGLISH BOND, FLEMISH BOND.

BRACE: An inclined timber, either straight or curved, introduced, usually across an angle, to strengthen others.

BRESSUMMER, BREASTSUMMER: See page 319.

CAMES: Grooved bars of lead for framing glass in casement windows.

CANTILEVER: A structural member which projects beyond the line of the support.

CASEMENT: A window hinged on one side, so as to open outwards or inwards.

CHAMFER: A bevel (q.v.) from one plane surface to another at right angles to it.

CLADDING: Thin slabs of stone or other material used externally as a non-load-bearing covering to the structure of a building.

COPING: The capping or covering to a wall, often of a gable.

CORBEL: A block of stone or piece of brickwork projecting from a wall to support a floor, roof, vault, parapet or other feature.

CORE: A filling of undressed stone used in the interior of a wall.

COURSE: A continuous layer of stones or bricks of uniform height.

COVE: A concave surface, usually of plaster: externally below the projecting portion of any structure, or internally between a wall and a ceiling.

CRAMP: A short length of metal or slate suitably bedded into sinkings cut in stones; used to tie stones to one another or to their backing.

CROW-STEPS: Projections in the form of steps on the sloping sides of a gable.

CROWN GLASS: Glass made in large circular discs by blowing and spinning round.

CRUCK: A section of a tree, usually with a natural curve, so that two sections from the same tree, one placed in reverse, formed a rough arch.

CYLINDER (or MUFF) GLASS: Glass blown in cylinders or muffs, which were split along their length and, as they cooled, opened out and flattened.

DAMP-PROOF COURSE: A layer of material impervious to moisture, e.g. slate, interposed between other materials to prevent the passage of water by capillary action or otherwise.

DAUB: Clay or mud.

DENTILS: Small rectangular blocks, resembling a row of teeth, under a cornice.

DIAPER: An all-over pattern usually composed of diamond, square or lozenge shapes.

DORMER: A window projecting vertically from a sloping roof.

DOUBLE-LAP TILE: A tile which overlaps not only the next course but the next but one below it.

DRESSINGS: See page 48.

DRIPSTONE: A projecting moulding over the heads of doorways, windows and archways, to throw off rain. Also known as a 'hood-mould' and, when rectangular, as a 'label'.

DRY WALLING, DRY-STONE WALLS: Walls in which the stones are laid without mortar.

DUTCH GABLE: A gable of curved form, sometimes crowned by a pediment.

EAVES: The horizontal overhang of a roof projecting beyond the face of a wall.

ENGLISH BOND: The method of laying bricks in alternate courses of all headers and all stretchers.

ENTABLATURE: In Classical architecture, the upper part of an Order, comprising architrave, frieze and cornice.

FASCIA BOARD: See page 319.

FEATHERED: Sloped off to a very thin edge.

FENESTRATION: The arrangement of windows in a building.

FINIAL: The topmost feature, generally ornamental, of a gable, roof, pinnacle, canopy, etc.

FLAG, FLAGSTONE: A heavy slab, suitable for paving or roofing, of any fissile, fine-grained rock: in practice almost always of sandstone.

FLARED BRICKS: Bricks burnt to a darker shade through direct contact with the flames inside the kiln; sometimes also vitrified or semi-vitrified.

FLEMISH BOND: The method of laying bricks with every course consisting of alternating headers and stretchers.

FLUSHWORK: The decorative use of flint in conjunction with dressed stone to form patterns, monograms, inscriptions, etc.

FORMWORK: See 'SHUTTERING'.

FREESTONE: See page 47.

FROST-WORK: Dressing the surface of a block of stone to suggest stalactites or icicles.

GALLETING: Inserting into mortar courses, while still soft, tiny pieces of stone, chips of flint, etc., sometimes for structural but usually for decorative reasons.

GAUGE: Of a roofing slate or tile, that portion of it which is exposed to view.

HEADER: A brick or stone so laid that only its end is visible on the face of the wall.

HERRING-BONE: The setting of stones, bricks or tiles obliquely in alternate rows so as to form a zig-zag pattern.

HIP: The sloping intersection of two inclined roof surfaces meeting at a salient angle: the converse of 'valley' (q.v.).

HIPPED ROOF: A pitched roof with sloped ends instead of vertical gables.

HOOD-MOULD: See 'DRIPSTONE'.

JAMB: The vertical side of an archway, doorway or window.

JETTY: The overhang of an upper floor on a timber-framed house.

KEEP: The loftiest and strongest part of a mediaeval castle.

KEYSTONE: The central stone of an arch or ribbed vault.

KNAPPED FLINT: Flint cobbles or nodules split and used in walls with the split face showing.

LABEL: See 'DRIPSTONE'.

LACED VALLEY: A valley (q.v.) in which each pair of horizontal courses turns upwards as it approaches the point of junction, to meet in a specially large slate or tile laid aslant on a wide board in the valley.

LAMINATED: Stone separated or split into layers.

LANTERN: A small circular or polygonal turret with windows all round, crowning a roof or dome.

LATH: A thin, narrow, flat strip of wood, riven or (as to-day) sawn, used to provide a backing and to form a key for plaster.

LEDGER: (1) A flat stone covering a grave, and often forming part of a church floor. (2) A rod of split hazel or willow pegged on to the surface of a thatched roof: also known as a 'ligger'.

LOUVRE, LOUVER: A turret-like erection on a mediaeval roof with lateral openings for the passage of smoke or light.

MANSARD ROOF: A roof with two pitches on each side of the ridge, the lower one steeper than the upper.

MODILLIONS: Small projecting brackets, often placed in series below a Classical cornice.

MORTISE AND TENON JOINT: A mortise is a cavity cut into a piece of wood in order to receive a tenon, a projection at the end of another piece, shaped to fit it.

MUFF GLASS: See 'CYLINDER GLASS'.

MULLION: A vertical structural member subdividing a window.

NOGGING: Brickwork employed as infilling for half-timbered buildings.

OFFSET: See 'SET-OFF'.

ORIEL WINDOW: A window projecting from an upper storey, supported upon corbels.

OVER-AND-UNDER TILES: Rounded tiles laid in each course with the convex and concave surfaces facing upwards in alternation.

OVERTHROW: The fixed panel or arch, often elaborately decorated, above a wrought-iron gate.

PARGETING, PARGETTING: External plasterwork treated ornamentally, either in relief or incised.

PEDIMENT: In Classical, Renaissance and Neo-Classical buildings, a gable of low pitch, straight-sided or curved segmentally, above a door, window, portico, etc.

PIANO NOBILE: The principal storey of a house containing the state rooms; usually the first floor.

PILASTER: In Classical buildings, a flat pier of shallow projection attached to a wall, and having a base and a capital.

PLAT BAND: In Classical buildings, a rectangular moulding of shallow projection usually denoting externally the horizontal division between the storeys.

PLINTH: The projecting base of a wall or column, generally moulded or at least chamfered (q.v.) at the top.

POINTING: Filling in the joint-lines of brickwork, stonework, etc., with mortar or cement, smoothed with the point of a trowel.

PURLIN: In timber-framed construction, a longitudinal horizontal beam or pole supporting the common rafters of a roof and, in post-and-truss structures, framed into the trusses.

PUTLOG HOLES: See page 254.

QUARRY SAP: Natural moisture in quarried rock.

QUOIN: A dressed stone at the external angle of a wall. Quoins are often alternately large and small.

RAG: A hard rubbly or coarse shelly stone. Cf. page 65.

RANDOM: Not laid in courses.

REBATE: A groove cut along the edge of a board to receive that of another board.

RENDERING: Covering an outer wall with plaster, etc.

REPOUSSÉ: Ornamental metalwork raised into relief by hammering from the back.

REVEAL: The side-wall of an opening or recess which is at right angles to the face of the main wall; especially the vertical side of a window-opening or doorway. Known as a 'splay' (q.v.) if cut diagonally.

ROCK-FACED: The natural face of the rock or a dressing resembling it.

RUBBLE, RUBBLESTONE: Unsquared and undressed stone, not laid in regular courses.

RUSTICATION: The practice of surrounding blocks of stone by sunk joints in order to produce shadows. When only the horizontal joints are sunk, the device is known as 'banded rustication'.

SASH: A glazed wooden frame which slides up and down by means of pulleys.

SCAGLIOLA: See page 190 n.

SET-OFF (pl.: SET-OFFS): A sloped horizontal break on the surface of a wall, buttress, etc., formed where the portion above is reduced in thickness. Also 'Offset'.

SHINGLES: Thin pieces of wood having parallel sides but one end thicker than the other, used for covering roofs and walls.

SHUTTERING, SHUTTER-BOARDS: Boards between which semi-liquid material can be poured for building a wall. With concrete, shuttering is used for roofs and floors as well as for walls and may be of steel: here 'formwork' is a common alternative term.

SILICEOUS: Containing or consisting of silica, an important mineral substance which in the form of quartz enters into the composition of many rocks. Sand is mainly siliceous.

SINGLE-LAP TILE: A tile which overlaps only the next course below it.

SPALL: To split, splinter or chip off.

SPANDREL: The space, approximately triangular, between the outer curve of an arch and the rectangle formed by the mouldings enclosing it; or the space between the shoulders of two contiguous arches and the moulding or string-course above them. Also any vertical infilling between a horizontal surface and a sloping plane, such as a stair spandrel.

SPLAY: Any surface inclined to a main surface: for example, an inclined window reveal.

SPROCKET, SPROCKET-PIECE: A short length of timber attached to the face of a rafter a little above the eaves in order to give the lowest part of a roof a flatter pitch.

STRAIGHT JOINT: In masonry or brickwork, a vertical joint exactly over a vertical joint in the course below.

STRAPWORK: Flat interlaced decoration seemingly derived from bands of cut leather, popular in the later sixteenth and early seventeenth centuries.

STRETCHER: A brick or stone so laid that only its long side is visible on the face of the wall.

STRING COURSE: A moulding or narrow projecting course running horizontally along the face of a building.

STUD: A vertical timber in the wall of a half-timbered building.

SUMMER: A horizontal beam supporting the joists of a floor. When on the face of a building it is properly called a bressummer: see page 319.

SWAG: An ornamental wreath or festoon of flowers, foliage or fruit fastened up at both ends and hanging down in the centre.

SWEPT VALLEY: A valley (q.v.) in which each course is carried round horizontally by means of specially cut wedge-shaped slates or tiles.

TENON: See MORTISE.

TERRACOTTA: Clay of fine consistency mixed with sand and fired to a hardness and compactness seldom reached by brick.

TONE: The prevailing colour effect of a material, building, painting, etc., seen only in terms of comparative lightness and darkness, without colour.

TORCHING: Filling in with lime and hair mortar the uneven spaces between the undersides of tiles or slates on an unboarded or unfelted roof.

TRANSOM: A horizontal structural member subdividing a window.

TRUSS: See pages 306 and 310: Fig. 7.

TUCK POINTING: See page 244.

TUFFS: Beds of volcanic ash, now compacted and hardened. Some of the finer tuffs have become slate.

TUMBLING: See page 251 and Fig. 4.

VALLEY: The sloping junction of two inclined roof surfaces, usually at right angles to each other.

VEIN: An irregular intrusion of rock or minerals differing from the surrounding rock.

VENETIAN WINDOW: A window with three openings, the middle one arched and wider than the others.

VERMICULATION: Dressing the surface of a block of stone so that it appears to be covered with worm-tracks.

VOUSSOIR: A wedge-shaped stone for an arch.

WALL-PLATE: A timber running horizontally along a wall-top to receive and distribute the load from the roof-rafters.

WATTLE: Interwoven sticks, twigs, etc., frequently employed as infilling in timber-framed buildings, and as a backing for 'daub'.

WEATHER-BOARDING: Boards providing an external covering for a wall-surface, usually fixed horizontally and generally overlapping.

WEB: Used of a vault, the web is the infilling.

BIBLIOGRAPHY

Of the very large number of books, booklets and articles which have contributed to the writing of this book, it has only been possible, for reasons of space, to list the most valuable. Others, including a number of important articles published in the journals, proceedings, transactions, etc., of various learned societies, are cited in footnotes throughout the book.

This short bibliography is divided into three parts: (1) general works concerned with traditional building materials or in which they occupy an important place; (2) books on specified materials; (3) topographical works—i.e., books concerned with particular regions. Inevitably there is some overlapping.

GENERAL WORKS

SALZMAN, L. F.: *Building in England down to 1540: A Documentary History.* Oxford, 1967.

SALZMAN, L. F.: *English Industries of the Middle Ages.* Oxford, 1923.

INNOCENT, C. F.: *The Development of English Building Construction.* Cambridge, 1916.

DAVEY, NORMAN: *A History of Building Materials.* Phoenix House, 1961.

BRIGGS, MARTIN S.: *A Short History of the Building Crafts.* Oxford, 1925.

Preservation of Historic Buildings: Detailed handbook of an Exhibition of specialist techniques developed by the Ancient Monuments Branch of the Ministry of Works, at the Royal Institute of British Architects, London, Dec. 1955.

The Architectural Use of Building Materials: A Study by a Committee convened by the Royal Institute of British Architects. H.M. Stationery Office, 1946.

BOWLEY, MARIAN: *Innovations in Building Materials.* Duckworth, 1960.

BRUNSKILL, R. W.: *Illustrated Handbook of Vernacular Architecture.* Faber, 1970.

ATKINSON, T. D.: *Local Style in English Architecture.* Batsford, 1947.

LLOYD, NATHANIEL: *Building Craftsmanship in Brick and Tile and in Stone Slates.* Cambridge, 1929.

DOBSON, C. G.: *Slating and Tiling.* Langley London Ltd., revised edition, 1957.

Official Architecture and Planning, Vol. 23, No. 9: Slating and Tiling Number. Anstey Press, London, Sept. 1960.

Church Roof Coverings: A Survey of alternative materials by a Committee set up by the Central Council for the Care of Churches in conjunction with the Society for the Protection of Ancient Buildings. The Builder, London, Oct. 1952.

ADDY, S. O. and SUMMERSON, JOHN: *The Evolution of the English House.* Allen and Unwin, 1933 (revised and enlarged edition).

LLOYD, NATHANIEL: *A History of the English House.* Architectural Press, third edition, 1951.

COOK, OLIVE and SMITH, EDWIN: *The English House Through Seven Centuries.* Nelson, 1968.

WOOD, MARGARET: *The English Mediaeval House.* Phoenix House, 1965.

TURNOR, REGINALD: *The Smaller English House, 1500 to 1939.* Batsford, 1952.

OLIVER, BASIL: *The Cottages of England: A Review of their Types and Features from the 16th to the 18th Centuries.* Batsford, 1929.

COOK, OLIVE and SMITH, EDWIN: *English Cottages and Farmhouses.* Thames and Hudson, 1954.

BARLEY, M. W.: *The English Farmhouse and Cottage.* Routledge and Kegan Paul, 1961.

OSWALD, ARTHUR (editor): *Old Towns Revisited.* Country Life, 1952.

WICKHAM, A. K.: *The Villages of England.* Batsford, 1932.

BOOKS, ETC., ON SPECIFIED MATERIALS

Supplementary to the treatment of materials in the general works listed above.

STONE

WARNES, ARTHUR R.: *Building Stones: Their Properties, Decay and Preservation.* Benn, 1926.

WATSON, J.: *British and Foreign Building Stones.* Cambridge, 1911.

HOWE, J. A.: *Geology of Building Stones.* Edward Arnold, 1910.

SHORE, B. C. G.: *Stones of Britain.* Leonard Hill, London, 1957.

CLIFTON-TAYLOR, ALEC and IRESON, A. S.: *English Stone Building.* Gollancz (in association with Peter Crawley), 1983.

ELSDEN, J. V. and HOWE, J. A.: *The Stones of London.* Colliery Guardian Co., London, 1923.

Reports on The Selection of Stone for Building the new Houses of Parliament, 1839 and on *The Decay of the Stone of the New Palace of Westminster, 1861.* Printed by order of the House of Commons, August 1839 and August 1861.

ARKELL, W. J.: *Oxford Stone*. Faber, 1947.

ARKELL, W. J.: *Rutland Stone*. Article in *The Leicestershire and Rutland Magazine, No. 1.* Edgar Backus, Leicester, Dec. 1948.

OSWALD, ARTHUR: *The White Stone of Yorkshire*. Article in *Country Life Annual*, 1959.

NORTH, F. J.: *Limestones: Their Origins, Distribution and Uses*. T. Murby, London, 1930.

Various Authors: *Memoirs of the Geological Survey of the United Kingdom*: especially *The Jurassic Rocks* and *The Cretaceous Rocks*. H. M. Stationery Office: mainly 1892–1904.

BAGGALLAY, F. T.: *The Use of Flint in Building, especially in the County of Suffolk.* R.I.B.A. Transactions, New Series I, 1885: pages 105–124.

SCHAFFER, R. J.: *The Weathering of Natural Building Stones:* Building Research Special Report No. 18. H.M. Stationery Office, 1932: reprinted 1949.

NIELD, D.: *Walls and Wall Facings*. E. and F. N. Spon, 1949.

KNOOP, DOUGLAS and JONES, J. P.: *The Mediaeval Mason: an economic history of English stone building in the Later Middle Ages and early modern times*. Manchester University Press, 1949.

BRICKS AND TILES

LLOYD, NATHANIEL: *A History of English Brickwork from Mediaeval Times to the End of the Georgian Period*. H. G. Montgomery, London, 1925: second edition, abridged, 1934.

WRIGHT, JANE A.: *Brick Building in England from the Middle Ages to 1550*. John Baker, London, 1972.

BRUNSKILL, RONALD and CLIFTON-TAYLOR, ALEC: *English Brickwork*. Ward Lock, 1977.

MCKAY, W. B.: *Brickwork*. Longmans, second edition, 1968.

HANDISYDE, C. C. and HASELTINE, B. A.: *Bricks and Brickwork*. Brick Development Association, London, 1975.

WOODFORDE, JOHN: *Bricks to Build a House*. Routledge, 1976.

First, Second and Third Reports of the Committee on the Brick Industry. H.M. Stationery Office, 1942–43.

ZAIMAN A. and MACINTYRE, W. A.: *Economic and Manufacturing Aspects of the Building Brick Industries:* Building Research Special Report No. 20. H.M. Stationery Office, 1933.

THE UNBAKED EARTHS

WILLIAMS-ELLIS, CLOUGH and EASTWICK-FIELD, J. and E.: *Building in Cob, Pisé and Stabilized Earth*. Country Life, revised edition, 1947.

WOOD

SMITH, J. T.: *Timber-Framed Building in England: Its Development and Regional Differences.* The Archaeological Journal, Vol. CXXII (for 1965), pp. 133–158. Royal Archaeological Institute, 1966.

CROSSLEY, F. H.: *Timber Building in England from Early Times to the end of the Seventeenth Century.* Batsford, 1951.

WEST, T.: *The Timber-framed House in England.* David and Charles, 1971.

BRUNSKILL, R. W.: *Timber Building in Britain.* Gollancz (in association with Peter Crawley), 1985.

HEWETT, C. A.: *English Historical Carpentry.* Pergamon, Oxford, 1980.

CHARLES, F. W. B.: *Mediaeval Cruck-Building and its Derivatives.* Society for Mediaeval Archaeology Monograph, 1967.

FORRESTER, HARRY: *The Timber-Framed Houses of Essex: A Short Review of their Types and Details, 14th to 18th Centuries.* Tindal Press, Chelmsford, 1959.

THATCH

The Thatcher's Craft. Rural Industries Bureau, 1961.

PLASTER, ETC.

EELES, F. C.: *Wall Surfaces: Ancient Usage and Modern Care;* ANON.: *Limewash.* Two pamphlets. Central Council for the Care of Churches, 1946 and *c.* 1952.

THE METALS

WEAVER, LAWRENCE: *English Leadwork: Its Art and History.* Batsford, 1909.

AYRTON, MAXWELL and SILCOCK, ARNOLD: *Wrought Iron and its Decorative Use.* Country Life, 1929.

HOLLISTER-SHORT, G. J.: *Discovering Wrought Iron.* Shire Publications, Tring, 1970.

LISTER, RAYMOND: *Decorative Wrought Ironwork in Great Britain.* Bell, 1957.

LISTER, RAYMOND: *Decorative Cast Ironwork in Great Britain.* Bell, 1960.

TOPOGRAPHICAL WORKS

Books concerned with specific regions and places have been very widely consulted during the writing of this book. In addition to innumerable short guides devoted to particular houses and churches, these include all the volumes so far published in the ten series listed below. Of these, at present only two, the *Little Guides* and the *County Books*, cover the whole country, but a much more ambitious undertaking than either, *The Buildings of England*, in 46 volumes, was completed in 1974.

Royal Commission on Historical Monuments: Inventories. H.M. Stationery Office.

Victoria County Histories. H.M. Stationery Office.

The Buildings of England. By Nikolaus Pevsner and others. Penguin Books.

The Little Guides. Methuen and Batsford.

The Shell Guides. Architectural Press and Faber.

Murray's Architectural Guides. John Murray.

The Making of the English Landscape. Hodder and Stoughton.

The Face of Britain. Batsford. (Complete except for North-Eastern England.)

The County Books. Robert Hale.

The Regional Books. Robert Hale.

Among many other works from which help has been derived are several of major importance which do not belong to any series and which are not all primarily topographical, although best classified thus in the present list:

SUMMERSON, JOHN: *Georgian London.* Pleiades Books, 1945.

ARCHIBALD, JOHN: *Kentish Architecture as Influenced by Geology.* The Monastery Press, Ramsgate, 1934.

OSWALD, ARTHUR: *Country Houses of Kent.* Country Life, 1933.

MORSHEAD, OWEN: *Windsor Castle.* Phaidon Press, second edition 1957.

OSWALD, ARTHUR: *Country Houses of Dorset.* Country Life, 1935.

HOSKINS, W. G.: *Devon.* Collins, 1954.

DEAS, JOHN H.: *Building in Norfolk.* Unprinted thesis at R.I.B.A., 1939.

East Anglian Buildings: Catalogue of an Exhibition at the Castle Museum, Norwich, 1956.

HOSKINS, W. G.: *The Heritage of Leicestershire.* Edgar Backus, Leicester, 1946.

ABERCROMBIE, PATRICK and KELLY, S. A.: *Cumbrian Regional Report.* Liverpool University Press and Hodder and Stoughton, 1932.

BOUCH, C. M. L. and JONES, G. P.: *The Lake Counties, 1500–1830: A Social and Economic History* (Manchester University Press, 1961). Included in chapters 1 and 4 are short sections on Lake District houses by R. W. Brunskill.

ACKNOWLEDGMENTS
FOR ILLUSTRATIONS

Just because the range of possible choice is limitless, the task of selecting the right photographs to illustrate this book has been formidable, and would have been still more so but for the generous help of a number of friends, Edwin Smith above all, and unfailing coöperation from the National Monuments Record. A certain number of photographs had to be taken specially, and for this kindness the Author and Publishers are particularly grateful to Peter Bartlett (40a, 191a and b, 192d and 267d), Mervyn Blatch (84d, 239c and 240b), Joan Cheer, A.R.P.S. (334d), Myles Cooper (246c), E. G. Eves (381c), Joan Feisenberger (307a), Athol Murray (168a) and Richard Rieu (40b, 181e and 333c).

Thanks are due to the following for their kind permission to reproduce photographs of which they own the copyright: Hallam Ashley, F.R.P.S., for 114b, 221c, 256b, 284d and 314d; F. L. Attenborough, for 350b; J. C. Bamford, for 123a; B. T. Batsford, Ltd, for 45a, 74a–c, 221b, 256a, 261a and c, 307c, 308a–c, 328a and c, 341a, 355a, c and d, 356a and b, 381a, 382a–f and 399a; the British Council, for 113; Mary Burkett, for 167a and b and 168c; the Central Office of Information, for 197a; Country Life, Ltd, for 246a and 255c; the Courtauld Institute of Art, for 73b and c; Eric de Maré, for 245a, 246b, 334a, 350c and 381d; H. W. Fincham, for 240c; Leonard and Marjorie Gayton, for 147a and 363a; F. Jewell-Harrison, for 239d; Judges, Ltd, for 333d; A. F. Kersting, F.R.P.S., for 84b, 90a, 129c, 283a and b, 284a, 314a and 364c; Leicester Museums, for 147c; the National Monuments Record, for 39a and b, 40c and d, 107c, 108a and b, 114a, 123b, 124a, 129a, 147b, 181a, 197b, 222a–c, 239a, 255a and d, 261e, 277a, 278b, 314b and c, 327a and b, 333a and b, 334e, 342b, 364a, 381b and 399b; G. M. Oates, for 84a; Photo Precision, Ltd, for 221a; the Royal Commission on Historical Monuments (Crown Copyright), for 45d (from R.C.H.M.'s Inventory: *The City of Cambridge*, Part II), for 198b (from R.C.H.M.'s Inventory: *Dorset*, Vol. 1), for 363b (from R.C.H.M.'s Inventory: *Westmorland*), and for 278e (all reproduced by permission of the Controller of Her Majesty's Stationery Office); Jack Scheerboom, for 267a; Walter Scott, for 73a; Malcolm Seaborne, for 284b and c; Edwin Smith, for 45b and c, 46b and c, 73d, 83b, 84c, 89, 107b, 124b and c, 130a and c, 148b, 167c and d, 168b, 181c and d, 182, 191c, 192a–c, 197c, 239b, 245c, 246d, 255b, 261d, 262b, 268, 277b–d, 278c and d, 307b, 313a, 327c, 334c, 341b, 342a, 349a–c, 350a, 355b,

364b and 400; Peter Smith, for 308d and e; Frank Smyth, for 313b; C. Stringer, for 107a; Sir John Summerson, for 245b; Michael Trinick, for 148a; Reece Winstone, for 74d, 83a, 90b, 130b and 278a; and G. Bernard Wood, for 46a and 129b.

Plates 262a and 328b are from photographs by the late G. Granville Buckley; 114c by the late Marquess of Cholmondeley; 267b and c by the late C. G. Dobson; 198a, 240a, 261b and 328d by the late Nathaniel Lloyd; 181b by the late Rev. F. Sumner; 307d by the late Stanley E. Taylor; and 334b by the late Will F. Taylor. Fig. 9 is based on a photograph by Judith Scott.

LIST OF ILLUSTRATIONS

APPENDIX

Corrections and additions to the main text, referred to by asterisks (*) in the margin.

Page

37 This can indeed be seen late in the seventeenth century at Boughton in Northampton-shire, which was begun for Lord Montagu, soon to be a duke, about 1690. Externally it appears to be wholly of stone, but the parts not seen by visitors were mostly brick.

41.1 A sure indicator—seen in 40d—of wood serving as a cheap substitute for stone is the thinness of the walls, with 'window-frames close to the surface and little inner reveal': R. W. Brunskill, *Vernacular Architecture of the Lake Counties* (1974), p. 93.

41.2 Craythorne House, Tenterden, is a timber-framed building (with no more than a few courses of bricks at the bases of its walls), which has been faced with boards, with chamfered grooves at intervals.

41.3 Amended description: This house is entirely faced with wooden planks, grooved vertically at intervals (of 11 ins.) to suggest blocks. The quoins, with recessed joints, are plaster.

52 Still more remarkable is the masonry at Haigh Hall, near Wigan, built of Coal Measures (Parbold) sandstone in 1827–40. The cutting of the blocks (which are large) was so perfect that they could be laid without mortar, because every block is tipped slightly outwards. There are, moreover, on the main (south) front, no angle joints, because each block is cut like this: ⌐
In the adjacent courses the blocks are reversed.

64 Burwell clunch had been used as early as 1236 to vault the crypt-like calefactorium of Anglesey Abbey in Cambridgeshire: James Lees-Milne, *Ancestral Voices* (1975), p. 239.

77 Mr. Brian Furniss, County Planning Officer, Gloucestershire County Council, states that two quarries within two miles of Temple Guiting (Huntsmans Quarry and Guiting Quarry) are still producing building stone (1986).

85 For some time Ancaster freestone (the Freebed) has been in short supply, but in Mr. A. S. Ireson's opinion the other two kinds, which are available, are both better.

87 Corallian oolite is also found in north Yorkshire and was quarried for building stone at Wath, near Hovingham.

88 In July 1986 there were two current and valid planning permissions for the extraction of hamstone at Ham Hill (information from South Somerset District Council).

100.1 The Gloucestershire church of Slimbridge furnishes another good example of grey tufa.

100.2 Tufa from the Polden Hills was also used at Wells for the vault infillings of the chapter-house, retro-choir and lady chapel; but for those vaults alone.

103 In renewing a roof of stone slates, the customary practice is to trim the worn edges of the existing slates and re-use them at a higher level, introducing new slates for the lower ranges. (Information from Sir Michael Culme-Seymour, writing of Collyweston.)

105.1 They were coarser and heavier than oolitic slates but very durable, and were widely used in Oxfordshire, Gloucestershire and Wiltshire (e.g. at Bradford-on-Avon, for the great Tithe Barn, etc.). The Bradford slates came from Atworth, about four miles to the north-east.

105.2 The western half of Dorset has comparatively few limestone roofs (at Beaminster, for example, they are almost all Welsh slate, presumably superseding thatch), but between Dorchester and Swanage many old houses have kept their slates of Purbeck stone.

115.1 It is in fact a mixture: some lumps of brown sarsen (which are shiny in places and look not so unlike chert) are interspersed with unsquared bits of chalk-stone rubble.

115.2 When the rendering was removed from the house in 1977, it was seen to be all built of sarsens.

127 The grey-buff Keuper sandstone of Tixall was also important in the centre of the county. See *Buildings of England: Staffordshire*, p. 45.

155 Mr. Michael Trinick, in a letter of September 22, 1978, agrees that Trewithen and Antony House are built of Pentewan stone, but says that this is not an elvan or any relation of it: 'it is a completely different article, easy to work and dress'. He adds that no part of Cotehele is of Pentewan stone and that Trerice is built of a local stone very similar in character to Pentewan and known as Growan.

169 Here too traditional names were used to distinguish differences of size and thickness. The old classification was into Londons (the best), Countrys, Peggys and Jerry-Toms: C. M. Jopling, *Sketch of Furness and Cartmel* (1843), p. 86.

172 The green beds are now exploited in only two mines in the district: Penrhyn Quarry, Bethesda, and Twll y Coed, Nantlle. This slate is produced for decorative purposes; it is not suitable for roofing.

179 It was also used as a building stone, as may be seen at the Sussex churches of

Warminghurst, East Chillington and Ashurst. It was laid in courses and perhaps always originally plastered over. At Warminghurst, on the west wall, the rendering was removed during a restoration in the 1950s.

187 Note in 1979: 'But in these marbles, although some shells are present, the most obvious fossils are corals; and while on close examination they show lace-like, starry and cobweb patterns of great delicacy and charm, the general impression is of whitish splodges in a dark grey matrix which is not really very pleasing.'

189 The differences between polyphant and granite are very well seen at Launcells, for the north arcade is granite, grey with a touch of pink, whereas the south arcade is polyphant, and grey blue.

190 Another notable example of the use of Derbyshire alabaster is in the reredos of the Chapel at Chatsworth.

194.1 In 1735 the Corporation of Beverley bought 204 tons of them, at 6d. a ton, to lay down in the streets (K. A. MacMahon, *Beverley* (1973), pp. 55–6).

194.2 Cobbles were also widely used on the Solway Plain, wherever stone of better quality was scarce. They could be split so as to give a fair face to the wall, but they could not be worked in any other way. Cobble walls were usually thick and distinctly battered, and required dressings of slatestone, sandstone or limestone. Often such walls were rendered or whitewashed for improved appearance and better weather resistance. (R. W. Brunskill, *Vernacular Architecture of the Lake Counties* (1974), p. 113.)

201.1 It is also found in north Yorkshire, at Richmond and at Fremington, near Reeth.

201.2 It appears also in the churches of Feniton and Kentisbeare in Devon and of Whitchurch Canonicorum in Dorset.

203 Revisiting the Hall at Southwick on June 25, 1973, A. C.-T. found the porch 'spoilt': 'the caps, frieze and details of cornice have all been removed'.

217 So also, a few years earlier, at Norwich, where the spire of the cathedral was rebuilt in brick about 1480. Few people are aware of this, as the facing material is all stone.

220 One good way of dealing with it is to apply a weak solution of acetic acid (vinegar) to the surface; another is to add barium carbonate during the process of manufacture.

234.1 In 1974 they were still being produced at Arborfield, south-east of Reading. A 'middling' house might require 40,000 bricks, which would then have cost £2,000.

234.2 An important place for the making of white Gault bricks was formerly Arlesey in Bedfordshire, four miles north-west of Letchworth.

271.1 The camber is a British Standards requirement, to enable air to circulate underneath each tile.

271.2 A subsidiary determinant of colour is the position in the kiln. The darker tiles are always those at the top of the kiln. Those at the bottom sometimes emerge pale and underburnt.

276 Except at Sandwich, where many Netherlanders lived from the later sixteenth century onwards.

282.1 Brick-tiles continued to be made at Keymer in Sussex until about 1967.

282.2 Dr. Brunskill has seen a mathematical tile at The Malthouse, Westcott, Surrey, dated 1724. Mr. T. P. Smith and Mr. E. W. O'Shea (of Lewes) persuaded A. C.-T. that brick tiles were a good deal more common before 1784 than he stated here. He summed up: 'My impression is that *the vogue* for brick tiles lasted for about a hundred years—from *c.* 1750 to *c.* 1850. What is now certain is that many examples ante-date the brick tax first imposed in 1784.' See Mr. Smith's article, 'Refacing with Brick Tiles', *Vernacular Architecture*, no. 10, 1979.

282.3 The earliest use of the term 'mathematical tiles' so far recorded is of 1799, found by Miss Dorothy Stroud in a note by Soane on a list of prices by William Wood of Exbury, near Southampton.

285.1 At Althorp the tiles, which were made at Ipswich, were attached to wooden laths. By the early 1960s these were much decayed, so the tiles were taken off and re-hung, with some necessary replacements.

285.2 Brick-tiles are also to be found, in addition to the towns named, at Bridgwater and Newport (Isle of Wight); also at Norwich and elsewhere in East Anglia.

298 Pine is more beetle-proof than oak. According to William Weir, beetle never attacks pitch-pine, where there is resin. See James Lees-Milne, *Ancestral Voices* (1975), p. 66.

304.1 This barn also attains the width of 33 ft. 6 ins. (external), the widest known.

304.2 There are crucks, still existing, that date almost certainly from the thirteenth century; some may be older still. (N. W. Alcock and M. W. Barley in *Antiquaries Journal*, LII (1972), p. 143.)

305 Author's note: 'I have now been proved wrong in saying that crucks are so rare in the South-West. Considerable numbers have been found in Dorset, Devon and especially Somerset, and some in Wiltshire.'

316 A platform resting on twenty-six big wheels was also used for moving a much larger building, the three-storied Ballingdon Hall at Sudbury in Suffolk, in 1972. After having dismantled the chimneys, tractors hauled it to a new site five-eighths of a mile away and sixty feet higher than the old one. This was a considerable feat. A striking photograph of the operation appeared in *The Times* of March 24, 1972.

317 To these two some others may now be added: at Chalfont St. Giles (Buckingham-shire), for instance, St. Fagans (Glamorgan) and Beamish (Co. Durham).

322 The barn close to the church at Frampton-on-Severn (Gloucestershire) has them too, but here none of them is more than $3\frac{1}{2}$ ins. wide.

324 Mr. John Harvey points out that pitch has always been available, and as it was used for water-proofing in other contexts it is possible that it was also used on timbering at quite an early date. John Byng described Bramall Hall, Cheshire, as black-and-white in 1790: *The Torrington Diaries* (1934–38), vol. ii, p. 202.

332 Examples of weather-boarding in houses at Cambridge in 1532 and in London four years later are cited by Salzman (p. 244). Shiploads of clapboards were leaving New England for Old England in the 1620s. (Information from Mr. Abbott Cummings, 1975.)

340 The ridge was covered with true heather, packed tightly, or perhaps more often with sods, bent over and held in place with long pegs of hazel wood.

352 Other notable buildings that have plaster floors are Hardwick Hall and the keep of Bolsover Castle.

357 And the application of a coat of plaster can sometimes be a boon aesthetically in masking ugly flints or bricks, especially Victorian polychrome brickwork.

361 A new rendering, applied about 1972, was both yellower and much more cementy.

377 William Weir held that lead will always perish if laid on oak, owing to some form of acid in the oak, but not if it is laid on pine: James Lees-Milne, *Ancestral Voices* (1975), p. 66.

394 It seems that the first man in Britain to insist on sash windows (though they slid sideways, not vertically) was the Duke of Lauderdale. Accounts for repairs to his lodgings in Whitehall carried out between February 1672 and June 1673 include payments for making 'a shass window' 7 ft. high and 5 ft. wide. A Dutch joiner, Mathias Jansen, installed them at Lethington, East Lothian (now called Lennoxlove), in the winter of 1673–74: J. G. Dunbar, 'Dutch Craftsmen in Restoration Scotland', *Country Life*, August 8, 1974, and letter September 12, 1974.

397 The two blocked-up windows nearest the camera have now been opened up again, with excellent effect.

PLACE INDEX

The arrangement in this index is alphabetical within four successive sections: (1) ENGLISH COUNTIES, (2) BRITAIN OUTSIDE ENGLAND, (3) THE CONTINENT OF EUROPE, (4) NORTH AMERICA. References to illustrations are in *italic type*.

Since this book first appeared there have been a number of changes affecting English counties. In 1965 the boundaries of London were extended at the expense of Surrey, Kent, Essex and Hertfordshire, while Middlesex was swallowed up completely: most of this county has been absorbed in Greater London, but small portions have gone to Surrey and to Hertfordshire. Farther north, the Soke of Peterborough was transferred in 1965 from Northamptonshire to the new county of Huntingdon and Peterborough. Finally Monmouthshire, included among English counties since 1535, was in 1970 returned to Wales. So in this index Middlesex and Monmouthshire no longer find a place.

Editor's note. The names of the counties of Great Britain remain here as they were given in the previous edition, published in 1972. That is not merely a matter of economy: it is what the author would himself have preferred, for he was angered by the changes in the structure of local government made under the legislation of 1972–73 and spoke bitterly of them to the end of his life.

English Counties

BEDFORDSHIRE

Ampthill, *341a*, 345
Dunstable Priory, 64
Eaton Bray, 336 n.
    Ch., 64
Egginton House, near Leighton Buzzard, 241 n.
Husborne Crawley Ch., 120
Keysoe, 234
Quarries: Pavenham, 23; Silsoe, 120; Totternhoe, 64, 65, 72 n.
Brick-fields: Arlesey, 425; Bedford, 229; Luton, 235

Milton Ernest, 23
Northill Ch., 120
Pertenhall, 224, *239d*
Southill, 64, 336 n. 2
Woburn Abbey, 64, 292
Woburn Sands, 116

BERKSHIRE

Abingdon, 226
Arborfield, 425
Ashbury, 115
Ashdown House, 63, 64 n., 384
Coleshill (dem.), 390 and n.
Donnington Grove, Newbury, 235
Faringdon, 87, 219
Folly Farm, Sulhamstead, 235, 272 n.
Harwell, 236

Hungerford, 235
Idstone, 115
Kingsbury, Old Windsor, 391
Lambourn, 115
Lowbury Camp, 195
Newbury, 226
Ockwells Manor, Bray, 319, 325, *333a*
Swallowfield Park, 238
Uffington, 64, *73b and c*, 115

CUMBERLAND

DERBYSHIRE

DEVON

ESSEX

GLOUCESTERSHIRE

HERTFORDSHIRE

HUNTINGDON AND PETERBOROUGH

KENT

SOMERSET

STAFFORDSHIRE

SUFFOLK

WARWICKSHIRE

WESTMORLAND

WILTSHIRE

WORCESTERSHIRE

YORKSHIRE
EAST RIDING

NORTH RIDING

Britain Outside England

The Continent of Europe

BELGIUM

FRANCE

GERMANY

GREECE

ITALY

PORTUGAL

RUSSIA

SWITZERLAND

North America

CANADA

UNITED STATES

GENERAL INDEX

Places figure in this index only when their county is not always mentioned in the text and where there might be some reasonable doubt about it. All will be found in the Place Index.

The most important references are indicated in **heavy type;** *illustrations are in italic type.*

ABBEYS, 44. The following (some now country houses) will be found in the Place Index: Beaulieu, Hants.; Beeleigh, Essex; Bury St. Edmunds; Byland, Yorkshire, N.R.; Colchester; Crowland, Lincs.; Forde, Dorset; Fountains, Yorkshire, W.R.; Furness, Lancs.; Glastonbury, Somerset; Kirkstall, Yorkshire, W.R.; Lacock, Wiltshire; Little Coggeshall, Essex; Monkwearmouth, Co. Durham; Muchelney, Somerset; Netley, Hants.; Pershore, Worcs.; Ramsey, Hunts.; Rievaulx, Yorkshire, N.R.; Romsey, Hants.; Selby, Yorkshire, W.R.; Thorney, Cambs.; Westminster; Whitby, Yorkshire, N.R.; Woburn, Beds.; Wroxton, Oxfordshire

'Accrington bloods', 233

Acts of Parliament, 224, 269, 275, 373

Adamantine clinkers, 235

Adam Bede, 361

Adam, James and John, 171, 367, 388

Adam, Robert, 37, 38, 171, *182*, 185, 367, 388

Addy, S. O., 289, 304, 354 n. 2

Adits, 72 n., 403

Adobe, 210, 292

Aislaby sandstone, 121

'Akenfield', Suffolk, 338 and n., 347 n.

Alabaster, 37, 72 n., *182*, **189–90**, 352, 392, 425

Alcester: Warwickshire

Allen, Ralph, 75

Alluvial clay, 60, 193, 194, 219 n.

Almshouses, *90a and b*, 103, *148b*, 149, 184 n. 3, 214, 217, *246d*, 249, 329, 377

Altar slabs, 186 n.

Althorp: Northamptonshire

Alveley sandstone, *124c*, 128

Alwalton marble, 184 and n. 2, 186 n.

America: see UNITED STATES, Canada

Ammonites, 184 n. 3

Ancaster limestone, 67, 68, 79, 81, **82** and n., **85**, 214; marble, 186 n.

Anderson, F. W., 61 n. 1

Anglo-Saxon: see SAXON PERIOD

Anston limestone, 94, 95

Appley Bridge sandstone, 134

Arbor vitae, 330

Argentina, 210

Arkell, W. J., 50 n., 57 n., 82, 87, 88 n.

Armatures, for stained glass windows, 385

Arschavir, A., 285 n. 2

Asbestos for roofs, 25, 103, 171, 343

Ashburton marble, 187, 188

Ashlar: see STONE

Ash twigs, 320

Aspatria sandstone, 126

Aspdin, Joseph, 368

Aspinall-Oglander, C., 281 n.

Astragals, 396

Atkinson, T. D., 27

Atmospheric pollution: see SMOKE AND SOOT

Audley End: Essex

Austen, Jane, 347

Avebury: Wiltshire

Avoncroft Museum of Buildings, Stoke Prior, Worcs., 317

Ayrton, Maxwell, 386 n.

Babylonia, 210

Bakewell, Robert, 387

Balconies, Regency, *382 a–f*, 388, 389; Victorian, 389, *399a*

Baltic countries, 23, 212, 296, 329

Banbury marble, 185 n.

Banding in flint and brick, *192a*, 195, 211, 216; in flint and stone, *198b*, 204